RETROSPECTIONS OF AMERICA

JOHN BERNARD AS JACK MEGGOT.

RETROSPECTIONS OF AMERICA

1797–1811

By JOHN BERNARD

EDITED FROM THE MANUSCRIPT BY

MRS. BAYLE BERNARD

WITH

AN INTRODUCTION, NOTES, AND INDEX BY

LAURENCE HUTTON AND BRANDER MATTHEWS

ILLUSTRATED

BENJAMIN BLOM   New York/London

First Published 1887
Reissued 1969 by
Benjamin Blom, Inc., Bronx, New York 10452
and 56 Doughty Street, London, W.C. 1

Library of Congress Catalog Card Number 72-83401

Printed in the United States of America

INTRODUCTION.

JOHN BERNARD, one of the brightest of English comedians, and one of the earliest of American managers, was an important figure on the stage of the United States in the beginning of this century. He was born in Portsmouth, England, in 1756. His father was a naval officer, and a relative of Sir Francis Bernard, a British governor of Massachusetts, who was so unpopular in that colony that when he was recalled, in 1769, Boston celebrated his departure by salvos of artillery and general demonstrations of public joy. John Bernard was educated at Chichester, where he acted Hamlet in a school performance of the tragedy before he was sixteen. He shortly after appeared on the professional stage at the village of Farnham, near Portsmouth, in the character of George Barnwell. His father's return from sea at this time put a stop to the young actor's brief experience, and led to his being articled to a solicitor, with whom, however, he could not have remained long, as in 1773 he began a professional career destined to last with honor, if not with profit, for half a century.

He was a member of a strolling troupe for a short time, but soon gained admittance into the regular company which served the Norwich circuit. Here he met Mrs. Cooper, an actress of great versatility, whom he described as "a kind of Garrick in petticoats," and whom he married in 1774. In the winter of 1777–8 Mr. and Mrs. Bernard joined the company at the Bath Theatre, then the most important in England outside of the metropolis. There they made their first appearance as Gratiano and Portia, to the Shylock of Henderson. There they played Sir Benjamin Backbite and Mrs. Candor, in the first performance of the "School for Scandal" out of London, the rehearsals of which were superintended by Sheridan himself. From 1780 until 1784 Bernard acted in Ireland, where he was associated with such stage giants as Miss O'Neill and John Kemble. On Oct. 19, 1787, Bernard made his first appearance in London and at the Covent Garden Theatre, playing Archer in the "Beaux' Stratagem," Mrs. Bernard taking the part of Mrs. Sullen. In London Bernard made many friends; his associates were Sheridan, Selwyn, Fox, and the leading wits and men about town; and in 1789 he was elected secretary of the famous Beefsteak Club, an honor of which he was always very proud.

His first wife having died, he married, in 1795, a Miss Fisher, who had a short and unimportant career on the stage, dying ten years later in America, to which country she accompanied him in the summer of 1797. His engagement was with Wignell, the Philadelphia manager, at a salary of a thousand pounds a twelvemonth, at that time an unusually large amount; and he made his first American appearance on Aug. 25, 1797, at the Greenwich Street Theatre, New York, as Goldfinch in the "Road to Ruin," the elder Warren playing Old Dornton. During the six years Bernard spent in Philadelphia he played, besides the comedy parts for which he was engaged, Shylock, Falconbridge, Hotspur, and others, in the absence of a leading tragedian in the company. He went to Boston in 1803, where, in 1806, he became joint manager, with Powers, of the Federal Street Theatre, and sailed for England in search of new attractions for his company. With a third wife, a Miss Wright, whom he married in St.

James's Church, Piccadilly, he returned to Boston the same year, and remained there at the head of affairs in the Federal Street house until 1810. After professional tours in Canada, he acted in the Thespian Hall at Albany, N. Y., and opened on Jan. 18, 1813, the first regular theatre—that on Green Street—which Albany possessed. In 1816 he went upon a tour through the United States, being one of the earliest moving stars in the American theatrical firmament. In the autumn of 1817 he returned to the stock company of the theatre in Boston, and took his farewell of the American stage in the "Soldier's Daughter," April 19, 1819, delivering a farewell address—and going home to England as heartily liked and as sincerely regretted as his colonial relative of half a century before was hooted and despised. He died in London, Nov. 29, 1828.

John Bernard was much more than a comedian of remarkable brilliancy; he was a shrewd social observer, quick to see, and acute in noting the value of what he saw. He came to America admirably equipped as a student of men and manners ; and he brought with him what is not often to be found in the personal baggage of the British tourist in the United States—an extraordinary openness of mind. There is in his record of his life here in America scarcely a trace of what Mr. Lowell calls that certain condescension of the foreigner. His bias, in so far as he had any, was in favor of the new country and the young nation. This bias, perhaps, may have been due to his intimate association with Fox and Sheridan and the other Whigs of the Beefsteak Club. He had unusual opportunities for the study of American habits in town and in country, and of these he availed himself to the utmost. He was brought into contact with many of the distinguished sons of the Republic in his day—Washington, Jefferson, Charles Carroll of Carrollton—on terms of friendship if not of intimacy, and his record of the impressions they made upon him is vivid and valuable. He was as ready a writer as he was a keen observer. He told an anecdote lightly and brightly, and with a charm peculiar to the men of his profession. He had caught from the Eighteenth-Century comedies, in which he so often acted, a certain sparkle and an easy wit, which play pleasantly along his page.

On his retirement from the stage and return to England, Bernard began the preparation of his biography; and about a year before his death he completed the work, "but," as his son tells us, "in too voluminous a state for publication." His son was the late W. Bayle Bernard, who was born in Boston, Mass., in 1808, and died in London, England, in 1875. He began life as an actor, but soon turned critic and dramatist, and was the author of the "Nervous Man," the "Dumb Belle," and "His Lost Legs." For Hackett he wrote the earliest drama of "Rip Van Winkle," and for Yankee Hill, Silsbee, and other American character actors, he wrote many other plays which entitle him to be considered one of the inventors of the Stage Yankee.

After John Bernard's death, in 1828, Bayle Bernard selected and condensed from his father's autobiography the interesting "Retrospections of the Stage, by the Late John Bernard, Manager of the American Theatres, and formerly Secretary of the Beefsteak Club. 2 vols. London, Henry Colburn and Richard Bentley, 1830." This work met with great and instant success, and is still highly prized by all collectors of theatrical literature on both sides of the Atlantic. It was republished by Carter & Hendee, in Boston, in 1832, but both editions have been long out of print.

The "Retrospections of the Stage" come down only to the date of Bernard's leaving England for America. From those pages of his father's manuscript memoirs which were descriptive of his life and experiences in the United States, Bayle Bernard made at different times three different sets of extracts, all taken literally from the autobiography, and exact, so far as they went, but all incomplete. The first ten chapters of the following book are printed from a manuscript found among her husband's papers by the widow of Bayle Bernard, and by her prepared for .publication.

From the original autobiography of the elder Bernard —now apparently lost or destroyed—the son had previously condensed material for six chapters of " Early Days of the American Stage," published in *Tallis's Dramatic Magazine*, in 1850–51. A few of the more pertinent passages of these six chapters will be found as the eleventh chapter of the present book. The concluding four chapters are from a second manuscript, since discovered by Mrs. Bayle Bernard, three chapters of which were published, in 1884, in the *Manhattan Magazine*, with notes by us.

We have made no effort to correct Bernard's occasional and trivial mistakes in American history and topography, nor have we endeavored to annotate the text generally, but we have appended notes on the early American actors and actresses whose names may not be familiar to the general reader, and of whose careers little is known even by students of the stage. Of course we are not responsible for the abrupt ending of the manuscript.

LAURENCE HUTTON,
BRANDER MATTHEWS.

NEW YORK, 1886.

CONTENTS.

CHAPTER I.

Progress of Society in America..............................Page 1

CHAPTER II.

1797.—Boston and New England.—Reasons for Emigration.—Exercise on Board; Attack by Pirates.—Reception at Boston.—Hodgkinson; an Improvised Tragedy.—Boston's Resemblance to Old England.—Why New England Goes Ahead; its Method of Progress; not Understood by the English.—The New England Stage; its Driver.—Roads.—Mosquitoes Promote Patriotism.—The Yankees; the Swapper; the Jobber; the Pedler.—Anecdotes of Yankee Cuteness.—New England Seamen; a Profitable Cargo.. 23

CHAPTER III.

1797.—New York.—Robert Merry.— My First Appearance and Illness; Rustication and Cure.—Aspect of New York; the Dutch; the Breakfast-table; Merchants' Daily Life; Double Disguises; the Biters Bit; Land Speculators.—Sport.—Anecdotes of the Revolutionary War; Sir W. Howe and Mrs. Loring; Lord Cornwallis and his Friend.—Journey to Philadelphia; a Narrow Escape......................... 49

CHAPTER IV.

1797-8.—Philádelphia; Babylon its Prototype.—Quakers.—Traditions of Penn.—Philadelphian Society.—Street-washing.—Sir John Oldmixon. —Introduction of Quadrille.—Discovery of a Portrait of Quin.—*Cac. scrib.*, the Philadelphian Epidemic.—My Partnership Play.— Merry's Prophetic Pun.—Fennell, his Eccentricities and Career.—Sanguinary Expedient in Macbeth.— Dr. Franklin, his Influence.—Opposition to "Bustles."—An Explanatory Note.—Best Souvenir of a Lady. — A Great Calf.—A Model Foot............................... 63

A*

CHAPTER V.

1798.—Annapolis.—Society in Maryland.—Mr. Carroll.—Adventure with
General Washington; Establishing the Independence of a Chaise;
Washington's Appearance; his Conversation; Observations on New
and Old England, on Slavery, the Abbé Raynal, the Prince of Wales,
and the Drama; his One Jest.—Notices of the Military Heroes of the
Revolution.—The Qualifications most Needed.—Charles Lee, the Second
in Command; his Character and Career; Supposed to be Junius; his
Taking "Five Friends" to the Play; Reply to an Old Maid; Value of
a Sword; his Death.—Green, the "Fighting Quaker."—Colonel Tarleton's Joke.—Gates, the Old English Gentleman; his Repartee.—Arnold,
the "Political Judas;" his Career and End; a Negro Sarcasm; his
Promised Funeral.—Lafayette Compared with Washington; his Reply
to a Royalist.—Baron von Steuben; his Poverty; New Use for a
Sabre. — "Old Israel" Putnam; the Modern Cincinnatus; his Wolf
Adventure; his Daring in War; his Jokes.—Lord Stirling; his Formality; Sayings to his Men; a Private's Retort; Early Rising.—Ethan
Allen, the "Rhode Island Oracle;" his Strange Character; his Simplicity.—Kosciusko's Declaration.......................Page 84

CHAPTER VI.

1798.—Trip to the Delaware.—A Serenade.—A Boat Adrift.—Five Foreign
Ambassadors.—Baltimore.—Madame Jerome Bonaparte and the Mar-
chioness of Wellesley.—Political Discords and Fatal Harmonies.—Elec-
tions.—Merry's Joke; Rival Candidates.—A Petticoaterie.—Negroes as
Humorists; Happiness in Bondage; Theory of the Origin and End of
Evil; Sambotius Quamina; the Burnt Fly; a Planter's Destiny; Fault
in the Solar System; a Pilot's Reply; Significant "Hem"; Sleeping Un-
consciousness; Negro Names; Hen and Egg; Three-fingered Jack.—
Merryland and Merrylanders.—Lord Baltimore: Letter to the Swedes;
Reply to an Indian.—Dr. Franklin on the Origin of Tobacco.—General
Washington and the Dwarf.—Death of Merry; Omens; Epitaph. 116

CHAPTER VII.

1799.—Life in Virginia; a Word for the Planters; the War a Moral Regenerator; Manners, Tastes, and the Ladies.—A Planter's Life before
the War; Stratagems to Obtain Companions; Ordinaries.—Public Diversions: Racing at Williamsburgh; Quarter-racing; Hunting in Virginia; an Adventure.—Native Traditions: Captain Smith; his Discipline; his Replies; Pocahontas in England; an Indian Taking the

Census.—Convicts in Virginia.—Dr. Franklin's Present to Sir Robert Walpole. — A Humorous Criminal; Conviction and Conversion. — A Governor's Speech in 1670.—Lecturing Excursion.—Cooper the Tragedian; his Courage.—Virginia Travelling.—Gallinippers and Mosquitoes.—Patriot Pigs.—Blacksmith's Cure for Insanity.—General Lee and the Quakers. — A Madagascar Monster. — Tradition of "Blackbeard's" Skull.......................................Page 146

CHAPTER VIII.

1800–1. — Tour to the Ohio; Passage of the Potomac; the Alleghany Hills; Three Kinds of Settlers, Squatters, Utopians, and New England Farmers.—Backwoodsmen; Shooting Exploits.—Pittsburgh Smoke.—Indian Wooing-hut and Honeymoon.—The Ohio.—The Aborigines of America. — Indian Antiquities.—Welsh in America. — The Island of Blennerhasset; Art and Nature. — Philadelphia Balls; Travellers' Tales.—American Beefsteak Club.—A Coincidence.—The Quaker and the Irishman.—Desdemona's Revival.—St. George's Society.—Tubbs the Tragedian and his Adventure. — Poetry and Matter-of-fact; the Last Creditor.—A French Bankrupt.— American Advertisements and Literal Mistakes.—Black Nurses and the Yellow Fever; a Colored Lady.—Fennel's Immortality.—My Aversion and Adventure; a Female Falstaff.—Peel's Museum.—Historical Anecdote.............. 176

CHAPTER IX.

1800–1.—The Carolinas.—Journey to Charleston; a Carolina Ordinary.—Social Characteristics.—Deer-killing; a Dead Shot.—A Planters' Ball; the "Caroliny Jig."—Stories of the Swamps; the Spectre Troop, etc.—Legal Latin.—Colonel Tarleton and Major Hanger; Pranks among the Planters.—Baron de Glaubeck's Troop and Title.—Anecdote of the Irish Brigade. — Charleston Society; Varieties of Color. — The Ugly Club; its Rules; Ordeal of a Member.—Carolina Dews.—Fishing and Bites; Scene with a Snake; a Lively Hut. — Alligators; the River Lawyer; a Civilized Specimen.—Samples of Black Humor; the Criminal a Judge.—Byrne's Visit to Jamaica; his Retreat.......... 202

CHAPTER X.

1801–3.—Recollections of President Jefferson; his Observations in France; Neckar and Mirabeau; the Comte de Artois; Marie Antoinette; Jefferson's Compliments; his Rencontre with a Connecticut Farmer; Parallel with John Adams.—Peculiarities of Pennsylvania; Contrast to Virginia.—German Settlers; the Veteran Corps; a Female Recruit; Gas-

tronomic Hessians.—Barbecuing and Bundling.—Marrying in Haste.
—Periodical Whitewashings.—A "Pennsylvany Hurricane."—Recollections of Charles Brockden Brown; his Writings; his Character; his Drama and its Fate..............................Page 232

CHAPTER XI.

Celebrities of the American Stage: Mrs. Whitelock; Miss Fontenelle; Hodgkinson; Wignell.—The Theatres and Yellow Fever.—American Circuits.—Position of the Actor in America.—Mrs. Merry.—Mrs. Malmoth.—Fennell.—Cooper.—"A Histrionic Academy" 256

CHAPTER XII.

Undertaking Management.—Supplies Needed.—Visit to England.—Irish Fishermen. — Proposals and Refusals.—Final Engagements. — Monk Lewis's Irish Friend.—Caulfield.—Transport Arrangements.—A Bath Greeting. — The Theatrical Fund. — Story of a Landlord's Retort.— Whiteley and Macklin. — Bowles's Hoax. — Rolling in Riches. — A Frozen Sheep.—A Russian Tool.—Tragedy of an Actor's Life.—Mr. Williams.—Marriage.—Departure.—A Friendly Foe. —Voyage. —Arrival in Boston.. ... 272

CHAPTER XIII.

1806.—Boston.—Mrs. Stanley; Compared with Mrs. Abingdon and Miss Farren. — Admiration.— Caulfield.— General Humphrey's Authorship. —"Romeo and Juliet" in the Backwoods.—A Long Song.—Mrs. Jones's Death.— Dr. Jeffrey's Youthful Flight.— Caulfield's Singing.—An Actor's Temptation.—New Version of Lord Hasting's Speech.—Powell.— Fennell's Salt-works.—A Sermon on Patience.—Poe and Shaw.—Colored People.—Rival Musicians.—Mr. Williams.—A Lecturing Tour.— Tragedy of Real Life.—Sally Weeks.—Meeting the Devil.—A Military Money-taker.—Curious "Wiscasset" Natives.—1807.—Mr. Cromwell. —A Theatrical Impostor.—Jack Hatton the Great Blackguard.—Snowstorm at Sea.—A Visit to Philadelphia and New York.—Serious Illness.—Acting Under Difficulties.—A Cool Duellist.—Captain Dorgan. —Serious Losses 284

CHAPTER XIV.

Excursion to Vermont.—Concord and Discord.—Monsieur Mallet.—State Characteristics.—Milestones and Finger-posts ; an Irish Finger-post. —Burlington.—A Vermont Farmer; his Dinner and Conversation.—A Musician.—A Medical Innkeeper; his One Story.—Saratoga Springs.

—Sail up the Hudson.—New Engagements.—General Humphreys and Humphreysville.—Connecticut Laws.—A Silent Town.—Profiting by a Fine.—Return to Boston.—1808 Season.—Stirring in a Matter.—"The Pilgrims." — General Theatrical Depression. — The Indian and the African.—Love and Liquor.—The Three Warnings.—The Two John Gilpins.—1809.—Boston.—Failure and Disappointment.—A New Comedy; its Prologue.—Barrett's Last Act.—Graduated Ingenuity.—Yankee Anecdotes. — Borrowing a Horse. — Buying Brandy. — Stars. — "The Forty Thieves."—Contemplated Changes .... Page 317

CHAPTER XV.

Visit to Canada.—Anticipations.—A Retired Actress.—Vermont Travelling.—Wit and Humor.—Mixed Society.—Whitehall Table Fray.—Democrat's Estimate of Titles.—Steamboat Pleasures and Terrors.—A Canadian Vehicle.—Swamp Stories.—Driver's Test of Danger.—View of Montreal.—The Theatre.—Actors' Rivalries.—An Indian Settlement. —Off to Quebec.—A Canadian Cottager.—General Sheaf.—Universal Music.—A Forger's School.—A Bateau Party.—A Lone House and its Mistress; Unexpected Company and Unwelcome Revelry.—Reception at Quebec.—New Theatres Proposed.—Amateurs *vs.* Professionals.—Last Season at Boston.—Native Dramatists.—Tom Moore's Sister-in-law.—"*Femme Propose.*"—George Frederick Cooke.—Heroes and Villians.—Mossop.—Macklin and Cooke compared.—Macklin and his Scotch Schoolmaster.—Cooke's Generosity and Eccentricity.—Kemble's Portrait.—An Intrusive Fiddler and his Punishment 345

INDEX 375

ILLUSTRATIONS.

JOHN BERNARD AS JACK MEGGOT . . . . *Frontispiece.*

JAMES FENNELL . . . . To face page 74

THOMAS ABTHORP COOPER . . . . " " 164

THE HON. MRS. TWISLETON (AFTERWARDS MRS.
    STANLEY). . . . . " " 276

MRS. STANLEY . . . . " " 284

MR. CAULFIELD . . . . " " 286

BOSTON THEATRE, FEDERAL STREET. . . . . " " 292

ROBERT TREAT PAINE, JR. . . . . " " 300

MR. DARLEY AS PERFORMING IN THE ORCHES-
    TRA AT VAUXHALL . . . . " " 332

JOHN HOWARD PAYNE AS YOUNG NORVAL . . " " 340

RETROSPECTIONS OF AMERICA.

CHAPTER I.

PROGRESS OF SOCIETY IN AMERICA.

THE European who has visited America must admit that it gave him an impression perfectly original, however wide had been his intercourse with other countries. It was not that he saw creation on a scale of magnitude—in India he had marvelled at "heaven-propping" hills, and a sea-like rush of rivers—but that the idea of the physical sublime was merged in that of the spiritual. He perceived an enlightened people subduing a giant continent to a giant scheme of civilization. The poising of the powers of mind and matter was the novelty; the bringing into such striking juxtaposition the birth and maturity of creation. This I will not dwell upon. But the visitor must also have remarked the various shades of character which even now mark the limits of the primitive divisions of the United States, though daily growing less distinct in the spread of intelligence. It has often struck me that an inquiry into these decaying records would involve an explanation of many anomalies in the past as well as present aspect of the country, and I therefore beg leave to preface the following chapters of my Retrospections with a brief sketch of the settlement and progress of society in America. At her first colonization she was peopled on the one hand by exiles who fled to worship God in freedom, and on the other by adventurers who only worshipped Mammon. On

the emigration of Lord Baltimore and his friends to Maryland, and under the succeeding period of the Protectorate,
America presented the singular appearance of a refuge for
the three parties which had successively swayed the des-
tinies of England, and overthrown each other. The Puritans were quietly established in New England; the Catholics were safely housed in Maryland; and Virginia, the
depot of commerce, became the refuge of all fugitive royalists and Church people. Meanwhile the Swedes had
lighted upon the Delaware, and the Dutch upon the Hudson. The return of Charles II., the Act of Uniformity, and
the revocation of the Edict of Nantes, sent forth fresh
supplies and settlements. A colony of Huguenots and
miscellaneous English broke ground in Carolina; Swiss
and Palatines poured into New York and New Jersey;
while the truly Christian institutions of Pennsylvania
proved a magnet yearly to the Lutherans of Germany.
The colonial governments had by this time settled into
three kinds: Charter, Royal, and Proprietory; the first,
in New England, where the right of making laws and of
electing officers was ceded to the people; the second, in
New York and Virginia, where the crown had the appointment of the governor and council, and also a veto on the
acts of the assembly; and the third, in all the rest, where
the powers of the king were transferred to the proprietors.
It was thus that in sixty years from its settlement we
see spread together on the continent, Puritans, Quakers,
Catholics, and Church-people, English, French, Swedes,
Swiss, Dutch, and Germans, under the antagonistic influences of monarchic and democratic rule. The question
now is, how were these diversities affected by their institutions?

The first population of Virginia was perhaps the most
miscellaneous. Their allurement had been gold. Sir
Walter Raleigh was not a solitary dreamer with regard

to the hidden riches of the northern continent, for his expeditions to Virginia, his writings, and his waste of wealth to prove that the soil of the country concealed a power which might raise England to a rivalry with Spain, inoculated no small number of believers; and a frenzied eagerness to realize his wonders hurried out some few honest-minded upon the same frail plank with the many reckless and debauched, the spendthrift and the gambler, who thought to repair their broken fortunes by one stroke of their heavy-heeled boots upon the earth, which could thus be made to disclose their yellow idol, like a burst of sunshine through a broken shutter. The dreams of these first treasure-seekers were soon dispelled, and such of them as did not die of disappointment, or the unexpected toils and evils of a swampy country, turned their attention to extracting gold from rice and tobacco. For such men it is obvious that some strict discipline was needed to correct their greed of mammon and their laxity of morals. How far was this afforded them?

James I. in enrolling the Established Church among the provisions of the Virginia Charter, with so marked a silence on the subject of established education, was but extending the intolerance he was so liberally dealing out at home. Pedantic and shallow as he was, it cannot be conceived he was ignorant of the necessity for education in a wild, warm, and luxurious country which offered every temptation to disorder and immorality. We must suppose that he held the church to be in itself a sufficient means of instruction, or the best organizer of any supplementary one. But a school is as important to a country as a church. Upon points of doctrine sects will differ, but there can be no dispute with regard to practical morals, and to expect that grown people who have never been instructed in these when young, will either obey the laws or attend places of worship, is as reasonable as to suppose

that a human being will walk because he has attained the
age of twenty-one, if his legs have been kept manacled
from childhood.   Besides, the due maintenance of the
church itself depended upon a local circumstance—the existence of towns or social communities.   Now it so happened that the planters, distributing themselves along the
banks of the various rivers in this colony, in order that
ships might load direct from their warehouses, found it
their interest to scatter rather than to gather into communities; so that the first settlement, Jamestown, was deserted; and for many years Williamsburgh was a mere
court-house for the legislature.   The church, being thus
unable to support itself, could certainly not organize dependent schools; and for nearly a hundred years from its
settlement Virginia may be said to have had neither
moral nor religious instruction, except such as came privately from the hands of Dissenters.   And here was the
blessing of an establishment.   Not only were the New
England preachers driven out by a church which was unable itself to discharge its functions, but when these men
petitioned for leave to establish schools, it was refused on
the ground of their non-conformity.   Thus while the
seekers of religious freedom in the North were branded
as a set of ignorant fanatics, the settlers of the South,
wealth-seekers at best, were left wholly untaught to cor-
rupt still more, till "the colonies" became, at home, another word for all that was contemptible.   The sovereign
who had coerced the one and patronized the other despised them both.   It was enough for James that in the
one quarter they disliked bishops, and in the other grew
tobacco.

As time went on the growth of the settlements failed
to recommend them any more to the mother country.   A favorite image with Cotton Mather and the old
divines was to style America "the ark of the religious

world in the rising of the flood of persecution." Unfortunately the comparison held good in more respects than one. The ark contained not merely many excellent creatures, but a specimen of every beast, clean and unclean, on the face of the earth. In like manner the colonies, by the time of Charles II., became the receptacle of all the rogues and runagates who had outraged the laws of Europe, a basin into which England, when apoplectic, relieved herself by pouring all her black blood. Every gentleman who was unfortunate in business, or took peculiar views of the laws of property, forthwith crossed the Atlantic. The congenial climate drew the majority southward, and there, under the sanction of the English government, these gentry began that practice which became the plague-spot of America, polluting her constitution to this hour—the importation of slaves. With this capital as their resource the Southern States became commercial, and soon rich; but the devil's system thrived only to entail its curse. The social poison first relaxed the settler's energies and then their never-too-strict morals; African oppression led to European indulgence; libertinism and laziness ushered in gaming and drinking, till this region became a mere bower of Bacchus and Cytherea, relieved in the background by a lively representation of the infernal regions. Nor was this all. Though people went there for a living, they died there so marvellously fast that "the New World" seemed almost synonymous with "the next world," though with more resemblance to its lower than its happier division. The planters seemed to raise equal crops of cotton and of fever, and the term applied to their territory—a swamp—was as dismal as it was indefinite. Nor was the aspect of New England much more enticing. The majority of Englishmen had a horror of solemn faces and psalm-singing, and New England appeared to be a mass of meeting-houses. Yet worse, the conflict with the Indians was still raging, and not a ship came home without bringing news of some bloody work among the savages. These horrors formed the staple of many a winter-night's talk at home, till the poorest wretch who had a roof to shelter him, as he raked up the embers of his hearth, thanked God that he was not condemned to exile in "the colonies." Thus, for a century, America was looked on in England as a land of fevers and fanatics, of swamps and scamps, of self-called saints and savages. It is a question whether it was popular with any one except the Bristol merchants who lived by its exports, expectant bankrupts, and afflicted fathers who had good-for-nothing sons to get rid of.

Nor were the feelings the different sections of the country entertained for each other much more congenial. The lordly South turned with disdain from the plodding North, while the moral New-Englander looked with angry disapproval upon the idle, dissolute Virginian. New England, however, was slowly but surely succeeding in her struggle with the savages, and while some of the ferment of fanaticism worked off, the strength of religious principle remained. Hers was still an agricultural district and a hardworking, well-conducted community; the freedom of the body her strongest rivet in the fetters of the passions; the purity of her life the best title-deeds to the charter of her fathers. Thus she became a reservoir of honest blood; the animating spirit, both as regarded intellect and principle, to the gross flesh of other parts of the country, and the effect of her nourishing this flame of freedom was her kindling the fire of the Revolution. Once lighted, however, it spread readily in the South, for the planters had at least never lost this one purifying influence—a love of liberty. Every one is aware that the champions of the people in England were the friends of the Plymouth settlers, but it is perhaps not so well known that the managers of the

Virginia Company, the first governors of that colony—
established with monarchic institutions and the favorite
asylum of fugitive Cavaliers—were among the boldest op-
ponents of prerogative in both houses of Parliament; to
wit—Southampton, Oxford, and Essex, Selden, Sandys,
Rich, Perrot, and Sir Dudley Digges. Virginia, in the out-
set, was thus thrown into the same ranks with New England as a land of disaffection. The planters had always
held their own prerogatives to be superior to the king's,
and, in the colonial assembly, all the activity they had displayed itself in opposition. At its first meeting, in 1624,
they published a declaration of their rights as a basis of
future legislation. Soon after, they seized and sent prisoner to England Sir John Harvey, a transcript of Charles
I., who tried to play his master's game among them. With
all their loyalty they were the first to oppose the Navigation Act, originating as a mark of hatred in Cromwell, but
confirmed as a piece of gratitude by Charles II. Their whole
history, with that of Carolina, is a series of struggles with
arbitrary governors, who would persist in vetoing their
enactments. The planters were the feudal barons of
America; and even slavery, while relaxing their morals,
served only to stiffen them into more rigid upholders of
freedom. It is one of the original remarks of Burke that
"slavery has always been a cherisher of freedom, since, to
the planter," he observes, "liberty is not merely an enjoyment, but a distinction." And as, with increased wealth, a
desire for instruction arose, as there were no means of
gratifying it in their native land, the rising generation had
to be sent to the mother country, to mix with English
youth, and share with them the influences of liberal education. The rulers of that country forgot how the manli-
ness of the colonists had been fostered by free institutions,
and that the region of "criminals and slaves" had been
sending its sons to learn in England's universities the

spirit of her government, and the landmarks of right in
her courts of justice, when the supporters of prerogative
scrupled not, in 1764, to deny the fundamental principles
of liberty.   When the arm that should have enfolded and
embraced the colonists was thus stretched out to oppress
them, the blow that was meant to crush served only to
animate, and America, despised as a dependence, became
a nation.

The Revolution, in the heat of an all-combining sympathy, fused the great mass of prejudice and repulsion,
and so long as the pressure from without lasted, the
Americans were consolidated in heart and mind as one
man.   It gave an impulse to native migration, which, like
native manufactures, had so long been checked by royal
policy.   The states as colonies were needed only on the
shore; the enterprising, now safe wherever their possessions might be, were tempted to a wider range.   It also
held out fresh inducements to immigration from the most
diverse sources.   Commerce was no longer confined to the
South, for the superior local resources of the Middle States
(New York, Pennsylvania, etc.) rendered them an attractive arena for the skill and capital of Europe, so that in a
short time this new circle rose as superior to the others in
wealth, enterprise, and population as it was distinct in
its diversities of character.   To promote immigration,
which had been thus beneficial, every encouragement was
offered (in Delaware, for instance, a man could hold lands
without becoming a citizen); consequently, for many years
after the great convulsion, the Middle States presented a
sort of sample of the whole civilized world.

Another great and good effect of the Revolutionary
War was the bringing in of a taste for refinement,
through the influence of the gallant French, who had lent
their aid to the patriots in their struggle with England.
This made indeed an era in the progress of society in

America; and however it afforded ground for temporary debate, proved eventually of much benefit. French manners, abstractly considered, are doubtless worthy of becoming universal, the only question is, Can they be allied with sound morality? Many consider the perfect union of the two only a possibility of the millennium; that Morality and Refinement are a couple so repugnant in their natures that no form of government could pronounce their banns, and that the one can only cling to the hut of a republic, the other haunt solely the halls of monarchies. It is curious to observe how America has been the general battle-field of principles, an epitome in her progress of so much that is interesting in the history of man; how, after her freedom was established, the question of her manners was mooted by the Southern and Northern States with all the prejudices of royal and republican communities. As the discussion throws a light upon the times and explains the nature of much provincial feeling, it may not be amiss to give an outline of it. In the South a relish for refinement was readily imparted, and was fostered by local causes. There were so many constitutional resemblances between Frenchmen and the planters, that the habits of the one fitted the other as though they had been made to measure. But the impulse failed to go northward. The New-Englanders, looking back to their ancestry, who, like cocoanuts, had the roughest of rinds with the sweetest of cores, were fully persuaded that purity within was always in proportion to simplicity of exterior, and were unwilling to come out of the security of their antique entrenchments, however offensive these might be to modern eyes. But the Southern epicureans were so full of sociability, they resolved to pour a little into the honest stoics of the North, willy-nilly. Their ideas of patriotism would not suffer them to approve of manners which had an English affinity. "Why," they exclaimed, in mingled wonder and indignation, " do you display to England such a slavish spirit of imitation? when you have thrown off her political shackles, why wear those of her cold, dull, burdensome formalities? What is the impression you convey to Europe of America? If a stranger come among you at an evening party he is not introduced to the company generally, that he may be amalgamated with it immediately, but is led by the host or hostess like a lamb to every chair in the room (their occupants eying as if they would eat him), and at last provided with one in a corner, where he is abandoned to the mercy of Providence, for nothing under a miracle can procure him the least attention. The women sit huddled together in another corner, whispering and winking, evidently in dissection of his personal appearance. When dinner brings them together each person seems to be an independent government that must provide for itself. The wine, he fondly imagines, will be the dawn of sociability, poor fellow! the ice melts to drench him with a springflood. Each person is so punctilious that his own health is ruined in drinking other people's. The cloth removed, he assures himself of some enjoyment in discovering the tastes and characters of the females, when lo! up they start like a covey of pheasants and fly into the next room. He is then condemned to brandy-and-water and the society of men whom by this time he has begun heartily to hate. When he rejoins the women, if the host and hostess are not scrupulous in regard to cards or dancing, their indulgence is limited to eleven o'clock, so that, at the very hour he has carried all the outworks of his new friends' confidence, estimable propriety turns him out, on a nipping winter's night, to go home and keep himself warm—by uttering imprecations." To this the stoics of the North replied: " True, we treat a stranger with reserve, because we are not certain it would be safe to be free with him. Civilized men must be regarded as wild men till you discover they won't harm you. Should a visitor prove worthy of becoming a friend, we make amends for our early fears by endeavoring to detain him. You, on the contrary, in the frenzy of your benevolence, open your arms to every one that comes with a plausible tongue, a genteel exterior, and convivial habits. You stop to make no inquiries or observations; you give him welcome to your house at once, and put it in his power to make himself welcome to all that's in it. Such being French manners, we cleave to those of our forefathers, not because they were English, but because they were good, prudent men, who, knowing that evil was on its travels (the devil is a great walker), as well as good, cared only to make the acquaintance of the latter."

The South tried to escape this rebuff by placing the point in another position. "You may exercise all your present caution," said they, "and still relax a little of your old-fashioned rigidity. Your error consists in keeping your females so much in the background. Women are the great refiners of society; make your wives and daughters eschew the kitchen and the nursery for the drawing-room, and you will easily rise to our level."

The sturdy North saw in this the gist of the argument. "Women," they replied, "may be the refiners of society, but they are also its preservers, wives and mothers being the depositaries of its morals. We are taught by the example of all countries that, with the sex which has the least judgment, morals principally depend on manners; the fruit is guarded by a shell which we won't hazard the experiment of cracking. In this point we are proud of a resemblance to England. There a woman lives for her husband. She is the luminary that irradiates and keeps his world together; and if he secludes her, it is because he compares her in her exceeding preciousness to a vase— a thing which, trusted to other hands, might fall, and in its ruin include his. But you prefer France, where a woman lives for the world and gets a husband as the means; where she is artificial, ornamental, anything but useful; like the watch she carries, made for show, not for service; where her life is an actress's, to play Venus and the Graces before elegant assemblies; and where a husband who thus generously gives up his spouse to others' admiration, thinks it no harm to admire his neighbor's. Every one to his taste; we have fought for our liberties, let us enjoy them. You like the refiners of society, we the preservers. We are willing to admit that our liking is an imitation of England, but are not you imitating England also in attempting to control our liking?"

Many years have elapsed since this social sharp shot was exchanged, and I cannot refrain from observing that among the many changes America has seen, that of the union of these "warring elements" is not the least remarkable. Thanks to the spread of intelligence the rigidity of the North has relaxed, the laxity of the South has been corrected; and now, in every respectable city, French manners may be seen in loving alliance with sound and wholesome English morality—a beautiful superficies to a solid substratum—a pint of Burgundy supported by a pound of beef!

Meanwhile how was the independent young country regarded by the parent whose authority she had successfully defied and cast off? A panic seized the baffled coercers lest this example should prove infectious. It became necessary to show the incompatibility of American institutions with the maintenance of morality and order. Not only was this new equality of rights and comforts a mere hectic on the cheek of premature decay, but the profanation that had been offered to the great Juggernaut of legitimacy could result in nothing less than an absolute cancer. America's claim to protection from the British

constitution had been impertinent; her resistance to an
outrage on that constitution, unnatural; and the success
of that resistance but the mode Divine vengeance had
adopted to bring down upon her head a heavier retribution. She had hurled a stone into the air which, by the
law of nature, must descend to crush her; she had not
"honored her father and her mother," and her days were
not to be "long in the land." These prophecies from
"high places" would, however, probably have had little
effect upon the English people had not America touched
England on her most sensitive point by exhibiting so decided a sympathy with France, and by challenging, in self-
defence, a second war when it was a popular impression
that England was fighting the cause of liberty in Europe.
Such a state of things suspended all generous communication between the two countries. Enlightened travellers
preferred nearer and safer shores, and even men of science
were not tempted to exploration by the riches of America's
natural productions. It is true emigration did not cease.
Not a year elapsed without sending over some of those
brisk fellows who carry the favors of Dame Fortune by
the boldness of their addresses. They found the land re-
freshed and stirring after the calm that had succeeded the
revolutionary struggle. Intercourse was general, money
abundant, and a spirit of enterprise animating all things.
Intelligence of their success soon travelled home, which,
while it failed to disclose its method, magnified its amount.
Each man, it was said, owned his cave of jewels, though
he did not choose to explain the nature of his wonderful
lamp; and a few such cases sufficed to invest the country
with a golden haze of poetic indistinctness, till America,
to English ears, now became the synonym of independence, pecuniary as well as political, and glittered in the
day-dreams of the husbandman as the true region, after
all, where the guineas grew like berries on a bush, and the

wild-fowl fell into the fingers of the hungry, ready cooked
by a sympathizing sun. Still, it must be confessed, these
illusions had their counter-charm, and it was America's unhappy fate to combine the two extremes of being as much
underrated in moral as overrated in physical respects.
People had read strange accounts of the state of manners
in the Union. A deep gloom of savagery overhung the
prospect and rendered it a stalking-place for legions of
chimeras. It was a repeat of fairy-land not merely in its
treasure-caves, but its hippogriffs and ogres, against which
numerous patriotic visitors had put their quills in rest.

The first writers on the subject were chiefly immigrants
who, settling on a certain patch of acres, regarded its horizon as the outline of the continent; flitting visitors who,
like swallows, reviewed a region while on the wing; or
a set of miscellaneous adventurers who, failing in their
speculations, devised the scheme of paying their expenses
home by writing books in dispraise of the country, knowing that England's irritation at American sympathy with
France would readily welcome their perversions. Returned emigrants and bookmakers had the republic entirely to themselves; nor can it be wondered at, when we
consider their positions and their minds, that they should
have taken advantage of a temporary excitement to make
the ink which traced her character a deeper black by the
gall of party spirit.

But what, it may be asked, was the sum of their labors?
Unable to provide their friends with a palatable solution
of her startling political phenomena, finding that her
principles of government were like a block of ice, too mas-
sive to be broken and too pure to defile, they turned to
the more pliant material of manners, in order to show the
impossibility of a people learning how to behave themselves without that expensive governess — an aristocracy. And here, when Error dropped the scourge, Injustice

picked it up. In the spirit of Herod they made war upon childhood. Disdaining history, which teaches that a nation, like a man, has its stages of progression, they required a whole country to be in bloom in less time than an aloe. Ere she had caught the first notes of music they expected her to dance; before she had cleared away her forests they called for palaces.

The New-Englanders, for instance, all stood convicted of that offence to minds polite—poverty. Yet, strange to say, the ardor of their endeavors to overcome this deficiency was regarded as anything but a virtue. Unblest with wealth, they exhibited a distaste for leisure which was perfectly barbarous. Their possessions were few, but their appetite for gain very sordid. It was true they had a variety of vulgar virtues, such as temperance, industry, and honesty, but what were these to compensate for the 'absence of institutions which encourage poetical tastes and a chivalric deportment. In Virginia the case was worse. The land of wealth and leisure, the generous, aristocratic, money-spending Virginia displayed its civilization in horse-racing, cock-fighting, and dram-drinking; indulgences which could only be traced to the change in the government, since these writers were not aware that they had existed a century previous under an established church and state. Clear as were their statements upon these points, they were occasionally eccentric upon the New World's geography and social arrangements, transporting the backwoods to the seashore, linking New England to the slave states, and peopling this sea-bounded forest indiscriminately with Yankees, blacks, and savages. Some people were so stupid as to doubt, from their description, whether places like New York and Philadelphia were really towns or wigwams; whether "local legislatures" were not hunting-parties, which decided cases on a stump, by rule of rifle; and " civil institutions " a handsome mode

of designating whipping-posts. On one point they could
not be mistaken. There was no religion in the country,
because there was no establishment. But, from their am-
biguous remarks upon plantations and slave labor, the fact
that there were plantations in New England led many
worthy persons to believe that the Puritans were, after all,
mere traffickers in black flesh. Local phenomena were a
maze of wonders. What classification, for instance, could
be given to the animal called Yankee? He was a decided
Sphinx. No two persons in England, who had read accounts of him, could agree upon his conformation. Some
imagined him to be a native magician who could conjure
the money out of your pocket by muttering six words of
a peculiar cabala; others that he was an ourang-outang,
or the American satyr, with the brains of a man and the
claws of a brute; while the greater portion set him down
for a crocodile with a large development of jaw, prowling
about the shores and wharves to pounce on the unwary
stranger. However they might differ upon the point of
form, all were agreed that it was his nature to rob, and
moreover to strip. The experience of all travellers had
gone to prove that Puritan New England had set up anew
the office of the Inquisition, where strangers were treated
as heretics and put, without distinction, to the " question."
The Yankee then was the American " Familiar," who not
merely plundered but tortured you.

The red men, too, were a popular bugbear. They were
supposed to infest your house like rats, and their whoop-
ings to be a nightly serenade. Not a bush in your garden
but glittered with their dark eyes, and even your wood-
cellars might be packed with them, so that, in attempting
to throw on the fire what seemed a log of hickory, you
would suddenly see it animate and brandish a tomahawk.

Again, there was much misconception upon the point of
slavery. The Southern States were supposed to be a huge

prison or a fetter manufactory, where not only black but white men might be made to take the place of cattle in the fields, if caught alone by certain Afghans of the West called planters; for kidnapping and the slave trade were their principal sources of wealth; and the devil, like the Deity, was no respecter of persons. Slavery was but an extension of the apprenticeship system, by which the land had been first cultivated, and it was believed that where labor could be enforced the color of the laborer was but of little consequence. It was even suspected that there was a peculiarly deteriorating and barbarizing influence in the atmosphere, which speedily converted white people, native or exotic, into something like savages, even though they had enjoyed the best of educations. This was the change which most people understood by the American term of "naturalizing a foreigner." Gouging was thought to be fashionable fun among the American gentry; and some old ladies even had misgivings whether they were not cannibals, for stories *had* been heard of certain planters smacking their lips over "black-baby broth." As to their domestic feelings, it was well known that, in winter-time, a man would not scruple to thrash his grandfather, simply to promote his own circulation.

Does it seem strange that such absurdities should ever have been credited in enlightened England? The credulity may be traced, not only to a special and temporary influence, but partly to a general and more permanent one. Manners and customs depending, as they do, so much on difference of climate and government, every country has felt itself entitled to set up its own standard, a sort of papacy in taste, a rule by which all other peoples' usages have been judged heathen or heretic. Each land is Athens in its own judgment, and all foreign soils barbaric. The English have always been practical and active rather than ideal, and the security of their possessions has made a

High Church of their hearth—it cannot tolerate a non-conformist. This deficiency in the ideal and contempt for others' social usages may be detected in England's treatment of travellers' tales. While her calm, clear sense has rarely failed to penetrate the fictions of those far-wandering wonder-seekers whom Europe yearly radiates through the circumference of the globe, she has displayed a singular credulity in listening to exaggerations which have tended to exalt her own standard of the proper and convenient. On this point she has strained at gnats and swallowed camels. While she has heard with due allowance of the enormities of savages, with whom there could be no possibility of comparison, she has not always been so just towards the reported barbarisms of a kinsman or a neighbor, who might claim equal authority with herself on questions of taste. Of a mammoth at the North Pole she has required the bones in evidence, but mammoths in the drawing-room have been taken on assertion. Bruce she nobly laughed at, because he seemed ungenerously to belie the simple African. There have been many less truthful than Bruce in America, and few have been discredited.

Of course, refinement can only be attained in a settled state of society where wealth is diffused, and, for this, time is required. To expect, therefore, that America, with resources so vast, population so incomplete, and their diversity so great, should, on the day she took her stand among nations, rival them in other points than bravery and virtue, was to demand no less a miracle than that of Minerva stepping fully armed from the head of Jove. But, waiving this concession, the charge of barbarism, as directed against a large portion of Americans, is shamefully unfounded. What does it involve? The very height of an American's domestic iniquity is that he smokes and spits. Yet who ever saw this at a decent party; or, after

dinner, till the females had retired. Every country must
have its peculiarities, and cards and dice would certainly
be a more elegant stimulus; yet the cigar does but usurp
the honors of the pipe. But then expectoration is unfor-
givable. Certainly there may be much offence to European rule in salivating by tobacco instead of mercury, but,
after all, why is the poor American to be stigmatized for
doing what a polished Frenchman may indulge in with
impunity?

But further, says the bookmaker, the American is very
vain and arrogant, is ridiculously sensitive, prefers his
own country to the world, talks perpetually of the two
wars, and distinguishes himself by being either meanly
inquisitive or brutally blunt. Who is so? The wealthy
and hospitable merchant, the man of science and public
fame, or the jovial and generous planter? No; the shop-
keeper, the tavern-keeper, the driver of the coach, or the
captain of the ship; these are the criteria by which the
bookmaker estimates the heads and hearts of the community. And why? Because, it is most probable, from
some defect in his own character these are the only persons he has been doomed to encounter; and thus, either
from ignorance or envy, he revenges his exclusion by
bringing down his superiors to his own level. But, admitting that the American is vain and sensitive, and likes to
talk of his country and its wars, are these peculiarities of
a nature, I would ask, to excite either wonder or ridicule?
Every young country whose achievements are yet to come
is like a new aspirant in art, who thinks that the eyes of
his elders are bent on him with jealousy, and that the
sneer of the meanest will find a general echo. Such is
American sensitiveness. John Bull, a veteran, surrounded
by glories like Saturn by his belt, disdains to reply to an
antagonist, but silently pointing to a long line of triumphs
smiles the snarler into silence. But is the national vanity

of the American so ludicrous when it is a fact that he
wrested his liberties from the grasp of the mightiest empire of the earth, and beat from his soil, in the last war,
the heroes of the Peninsula, the conquerors of Europe's
conqueror ?   As to the point of preferring his own country to all the rest of the world, he makes but one reply—
that for many years past a large part of the population of
England has concurred in his prejudice.

With little liberality the officers of the American army
have been instanced as mere Goths.   Now conceding that
the historical connection between a soldier and a gentleman (in its European sense) is indissoluble, the Americans
never pretended to be soldiers—they merely called themselves *Patriots*.   They possessed neither colleges nor courts
to mould them into old-world refinement.   Their ambition was to defend their soil; their glory to secure their
rights; they never dreamed of rivalling the fame of professional throatcutters.   Or, if some did so aspire, how
was a general to collect a sufficient number of such when
the blast of an enemy's trumpet was stunning him, or the
blaze, perhaps, of his own beloved dwelling blinding his
eyes ?   Was that a time to hold Chesterfield in one hand and
a mirror in the other, and to determine the strength, edge,
and handiness of a weapon by the brilliance of its polish ?

Descending then to the underlings, the tradesmen, that
class whose savage horrors, duly held up to English consternation, have libelled the characters of American gentlemen—it strikes me that England and Europe have
been the parents of the abomination—that the curiosity
or bluntness of the middle classes are but the forms of
the caution or contempt into which they have been driven
by European imposition—by the deluge that has been
poured upon them of " rascals, runagates, that their o'er-
cloyed countries vomit forth, to desperate adventure and
destruction."

But admitting this were not the case, and taking the porcupine with all his quills erect, which is the least offensive animal, the gruff and blunt Independent, who treats you honestly, or the fawning and obsequious Mr. Smirk, of England, who, pressed to the earth by taxation, can only raise his head by a system which renders him a robber as well as a slave? Government, it is true, models not only the morals and manners, but the tastes of a people, and the aristocrat who has been fed on the homage of his inferiors will pay any sum rather than dispense with it, and despises a country where he finds the standard of excellence not to consist in the perfection of a code of deportment. But even this man (far above the rank of the mass of bookmakers), would be unusually hollow-headed did he expect to find in a young and vigorous republic one of the results of a decrepit despotism.

As the nineteenth century progressed England renewed her intercourse with America and began to laugh at the absurdity of the tales to which she had given credence. Under the affinities of blood, laws, and language, this intercourse must keep increasing, to the expulsion of all error and the establishment of mutual good-will. True that a party fire has been kept up of various leaden volumes to prevent this consummation, but the efforts must be futile.

I am an Englishman: after twenty-three years absence, and nearly fifty years wandering in a profession which has made me appear the veriest citizen of the world, I have returned to die in my native land with unaltered feelings. I love my country, its people, and its institutions, modified so as to augment the people's happiness, and for these very reasons, as each suggests a resemblance, I love America! My experience has conducted me from the presence of my king to mingle with the humblest subjects of a republican government; and the sum of my convictions is this: that in all the higher and nobler elements of the human character there are identities between the Americans and the Britons which should place the former in the relation of brothers, now they have ceased to be sons. This union is pointed out by every principle of policy, and ought to be sanctified by the deepest throbs of affection; and this my prayer that the time may be at hand when every one who attempts to foment instead of to subdue their prejudices will become an object of equal scorn to both countries.

CHAPTER II.

1797.—Boston and New England.—Reasons for Emigration.—Exercise on Board; Attack by Pirates.—Reception at Boston.—Hodgkinson; an Improvised Tragedy.—Boston's Resemblance to Old England.—Why New England Goes Ahead; its Method of Progress; not Understood by the English.—The New England Stage; its Driver.—Roads.—Mosquitoes Promote Patriotism.—The Yankees; the Swapper; the Jobber; the Pedler.—Anecdotes of Yankee Cuteness.—New England Seamen; a Profitable Cargo.

THE causes which led me to make one of the band who were bold enough to face the perils of swamps, snakes, tomahawks, and Yankees in far-off America can be told in very few words. They were the failure of two or three managerial speculations (to one of which I had been advised by my gracious friend the late king) and the patronage of an extensive circle of fashionable acquaintances. In London I was indeed being "killed with kindness." Enjoying the fatal honor of being secretary to the famous Beefsteak Club, of which the prince regent was a member, and treasurer or secretary to half a dozen others, in that most convivial of eras when the cry of "Clubs" was raised in every street in London, though in a far different spirit from that which sounded it in the days of James I., it became a matter of official necessity that I should keep open house, and for those, too, for whom only the best was ever good enough. Better judges than my brother members of port-wine, mock-turtle, coats, guns, dogs, or horses did not exist. The consequences were inevitable. I had to retreat while I could do so with honor.

The habits of an active life prompted me perhaps to

something like restlessness on board the vessel in which
I made the voyage, drawing forth a very characteristic
observation from an Irish fellow-passenger. He was a
sort of sociable Quietist, who would stretch himself on a
bench to the leeward all day, with a cigar in his mouth,
and fix his eyes on a particular spot on the mast, as though
it had been a book of memoranda. " 'Pon my conscience,
Mr. Bernard," he exclaimed one day, "I wonder you don't
wear out your legs." "Why," replied I, "when a man
has but a space of twenty feet by four to turn in, he can
scarcely take too much exercise." "But where's the need
of exercise?" "The need?" "Yes; doesn't the captain
say the ship is carrying us two hundred miles a day?
Surely that's exercise enough."

It would have been out of keeping with the adventur-
ous tenor of my life if this voyage had passed over without some unusual source of excitement; and, accordingly,
all fear of monotony was dissipated one morning, after we
had cleared the Azores, by the sun suddenly drawing up
a veil of mist and disclosing a vessel not far off. Her
features were unmistakably those of a pirate—long, low,
and roomy, with a row of teeth, to use the sea-phrase—
which gave ample assurance that she never barked without biting. The breeze being faint, she lay and looked at
us for half an hour, as a cat does at a canary, and then a
shot came skipping and dipping before our bows to bring
us to, and a large square sail was hoisted to lay her alongside. We could now perceive that her deck was crowded
with an ugly assortment of walking armories, with bushy
black hair on their crowns and under their chins, looking
indeed complete "Kydds," and by no means lambkins.
To describe the confusion on board our packet would be
impossible. We stared, with sinking hearts, in each other's
faces, and then all glances converged upon the captain;
but he proved to be suffering under a sudden and severe

attack of paralysis. Seeing him utterly at a loss how to act, I advised him to crowd all the sail he could and make as expeditious a retreat as possible, while a Virginian merchant, who had property on board, called upon him, if flight were impracticable, to attest his character as a true-born Englishman and at once prepare to fight. But the crew, including the cook, numbered only twelve, and as to the others on board, setting aside the tailor, who was a Methodist and disliked drawing any one's blood but his own; the comedian, who was a philanthropist and hated fighting for "Nipperkin's" reason, "because it's so plaguey quarrelsome," and the captain, who, being a coward, was no doubt a philosopher and believed in "Necessity," there were only fourteen individuals to guard our deck against at least a hundred.

But emergencies are the opportunities of heroes. The Irishman who had been so supine all the voyage no sooner heard the captain's tremulous remark that he should be compelled to surrender, than he jumped three feet from the deck, whirled his cap in the air, and shouted, "Surrender be ———; we'll sink first, and then let him take us. If the captain won't fight the ship, *I* will." The crew, who did not want for pluck, whatever might be the case with their commander, welcomed the proposition with a cheer, and forthwith proceeded to cast off the lashings of four small guns which represented our ordnance. What all our heroism could have done for us beyond irritating the enemy it is difficult to say, but happily at this decisive moment the wind, suddenly freshening, gave our vessel a start which enabled us, before dusk, to run the wretch out of sight.

On reaching Boston I met many London acquaintances at the theatre there, who varied in the reception they gave me. One said I "had come too late by five years;" another that I was "a great fool to come at all;" a third that, as I "looked a florid habit, there was every chance of my being packed in a black box before the spring." The better tempered cheered me in the way an army agent does a cadet in war time. "The yellow fever," said they, "thins the Green Room of at least twenty every summer, so that in a short time the field will be your own!"

Boston possessed two theatres, one of which, under the management of Hodgkinson, an actor from Bath, was now open. Its smaller size as compared with the London ones was a great advantage to the actors. It was not necessary to take the ear by storm, and whereas, in London, the players were so far from the audience that I often thought the old Greek custom of wearing masks might well have been revived, here the naked eye could thoroughly discern the play of countenance, and the face—that living, burning comment on voice and gesture, that flash to their detonation—had its full effect. Especially was this a gain to the ruling favorite of the States, Hodgkinson,[*] whose well-defined features showed every minutest change of thought or throe of feeling; while his voice could be compared to nothing but a many-stringed instrument which his passion played upon at pleasure. While such were his endowments, his method was to work himself up to a certain pitch of excitement which rendered everything he said or did the direct prompting of impulse. I can give a curious instance of this.

Though so great a favorite, Hodgkinson was not overfond

---

[*] JOHN HODGKINSON. Born in Manchester, England, 1767. He first appeared in America at the John Street Theatre, New York, as Vapid in the "Dramatist," in 1793. The next year he became manager of that theatre, and held the position until 1798. He left New York in 1803, played in Charleston, S. C., and elsewhere in the South until his death in Washington, D. C., from yellow fever in 1805. He was good in everything, and played a large range of characters, excelling in low comedy, but appearing with success in pantomime, opera, and tragedy.

of acting, but like Quin, Foote, and others, indulged a gentlemanly appetite for the pleasures of the table and the field. For a day's shooting I think he would have given up six nights of Shakespeare. When he became manager (at New York) his social propensities obtained greater scope. He played but three nights a week, and being well-studied in every character of the "Stock Drama," new pieces, which were not more than two in a season, were the only chances that dragged him to a rehearsal.

In admiration of his talents a native of the city had written him an "original character," which was a sort of backbone to a lumbering frame of five tragic acts. Perceiving that the studying of this affair would absorb many days, if not weeks, which might otherwise be devoted to jovial society, Hodgkinson made up his mind that the piece was too heavy for representation. The author, however, begged he would read it and give him his opinion. This he consented to, and put the manuscript into his pocket as he was jumping into a boat with his dog and gun to enjoy a day's shooting at Brooklyn. In the hurry of his departure he had forgotten to supply himself with wadding, and after two or three successful shots, feel where he would, nothing could his hand discover but the tragedy, which offered neither fly-leaf nor cover to satisfy his wants. Never was sportsman so villainously baffled. The day was beautiful, his gun infallible, and his dog was rousing the birds at the rate of a score a minute. He had now no resource but to return to the city, or sit down and read his friend's play; a more intellectual amusement certainly, but, like all our pure enjoyments, wanting the edge of a forbidden one. The first scene was in a cavern—"Enter Antonio and a Conspirator." Turning over the leaves, he exclaimed, "Six pages in a cavern! what can they possibly have to talk about?

that *must* be tedious." At this moment his dog was setting up his tenth covey. His eye rolled round upon the
sport, then returned to the book. A tempting demon was
tugging at his heart; * [the conspiracy could surely go on
just as well without all that dull talk in a cavern, and it
would make so much more sensation in a gun than on the
stage. Human nature—sporting human nature—could resist no longer, and Antonio's cavern plot was brought
to light in an explosion which resulted in a heavy flutter
of feathers to the ground. The work of destruction once
begun it was easier to proceed. The hour was still early,
the game still plentiful, and more and more wadding was
required. "I'll just leave the other fellows, and take my
own part; there can be nothing unfair in that," muttered
Hodgkinson, and as Antonio had been plentifully supplied with soliloquies and long speeches, every one of
which in turn became a " wad," by the evening the game-
bag was very fairly filled and the tragedy considerably
attenuated. But how was he to meet his friend the
dramatist ? To return the manuscript in its present muti-
lated condition was evidently out of the question, utterly
impossible. The only alternative, therefore, was to accept
it, and trust to his own powers of improvisation to supply
all deficiencies when it had to be performed. " It's odd
indeed," said he, " if I can't speak the part at least as
well as he'd written it, and, anyhow, the audience must be
gainers, for I'm sure to make it shorter."

When the night of representation arrived, although
every word uttered by Antonio came fresh from his
brain, the actor was so] effective as to draw upon each

---

* It is only right to state that a page of Mr. Bernard's manuscript was
here missing : perhaps some one else had been in want of wadding. As I
thought the story too good to be lost, and the beginning and end made it
so obvious what the middle must have been, I have ventured to supply
the part between brackets.—E. G. B–B.

scene a thunder of applause, and when he died, at the end, to create an uproar that threatened to entomb him with the roof. Incredible as the fact may appear, I learned from a person who *was not in the secret*, that there never was more approbation elicited by a performance in the New York Theatre than on this occasion. Hands, heels, and tongues were going continually, the words "Fine!" "Great!" "Very considerable spirit!" "'nation sight of feeling!" "Genuine genius!" flew from lip to lip, and the next day the whole affair was elaborately analyzed and eulogized in the papers.

But what said the author? He sat and listened to the end in a state of petrifaction. The fall of the curtain restored his faculties and roused his indignation at a triumph in which he had had so little share. Jumping over the orchestra, he made his way to Hodgkinson's dressing-room with the bound and glare of a tiger. He found the manager surrounded by his satellites, who were "larding" him on his performance. "Mr. Hodgkinson!" he shouted; "good heavens, sir! what have you been talking?" "Well, sir! what?" asked the hero, with his usual invincible smile. "Nothing but nonsense, sir, d—d nonsense!" "Have I?" he replied, "*then what have they been clapping?*"

In the genteel society of Boston I could perceive no distinctions from that of my own country. They wore the same clothes, spoke the same language, and seemed to glow with the same affable and hospitable feelings. In walking along their mall I could scarcely believe I had not been whisked over to St. James's Park; and in their houses the last modes of London were observable in nearly every article of ornament or utility. Other parts of the state were, however, very different.

America is identified with progress; whether in invention or adaptation, in expansion or celerity, the Western we admit to be the special field of movement. We English rush along ourselves, but our pace as compared with Jonathan's is that of a fast coach to the rail. We gallop, but he flies. Nor is this unaccountable. If mind can act on matter, matter also acts on mind, and the face of a country stamps its character upon a people. If mountainous they are rugged; if flat and fertile they are peaceful. Now America is not only vast, and thus is the source of grand conceptions; has her stupendous lakes and mountains which expand the soul proportionately; but America is also rapid, her streams are torrents and her winds hurricanes ; her lightnings sweep whole territories and her cataracts leap from heaven. It is Nature herself that goes ahead there, the very elements are at high pressure, so it can scarcely be wonderful that the people should catch her tendency. But progress must have its vehicle, a people rightly organized to carry on its changes, and among the various groups of the Western world which has most evidenced this fitness ? Why, evidently the New-Englanders.

The settlement of New England marks an era in the history of nations. Not planted to enlarge an empire or to raise a revenue; not won by fraud or moated round with blood, she alone can boast a philosophic origin. She was the first state founded in the great cause of humanity. Many colonies have sprung from persecution, most have struggled up to intelligence through cheerless shades of selfishness and error; but she, like Adam, was formed in innocence and formed full-grown. From the beginning, too, she was in spirit, if not in name, republican; not only so constituted by the covenant of her first settlers, but unintentionally confirmed as such by the charters granted her by Charles, which, with the view of forming trading-companies, not states, conferred on her the power of electing all her officers, and framing her own laws.

In the brief sketch of the progress of society attempted in the first chapter of these records, the exclusively English origin of this colony, in contradistinction to the motley population of the South, has been pointed out as a fundamental difference, which to this day produces a general agreement or nationality in many social particulars that is nowhere else to be observed, unless it be in the newly formed Western States, the offspring of New England, and reared under peculiar local circumstances. Now this general agreement appeared to me to be productive of one great benefit, since, as in England, it permitted no changes but by the gradual progress of opinion, while, as its precision of ideas was perpetually at work sifting the merely ornamental from the really excellent, it presented a school in which all the materials were collecting for the formation of a substantial public character that would be equal to the demands of the growing interests of the country. Under the influence of this general agreement the fathers of the Revolution had arisen in New England, and the names of John and Samuel Adams, Hancock, Quincy, Warren, Otis, and a train of others are no trifling guarantee that the palladium of American rights will be found in the breasts of their descendants. Were I to give expression to all I felt at a later period, when admitted to a closer knowledge of their excellences, my language might be thought too highly colored, but recurring to my first impressions as a stranger, I could not but perceive that New England contained the stamina of American character. Yet it is useless to disguise the fact that English feeling towards this special group has often been anything but cordial. Most interested of all men in the problem America was solving, the Englishman was yet of all men, perhaps, the least able, a few years ago, to sympathize with the means adopted by New England as her share of the solution. He could not dispossess himself of those ideas of comfort dependent on a settled state of things, which here he found at variance with a hundred novelties struck out by the rough spirit of expediency. Nor was he prepared in all cases to make due allowance for the local causes which had modified the people's character. The hard, hilly, broken soil of the country, more adapted for pasturage than for tillage, together with its plenteous woods and waters, had early turned the attention of the settlers to that "agriculture of the main," the fisheries of Massachusetts Bay, and to building and navigating boats for the transport business of the Union. As a surplus population arose, instead of occupying themselves with increasing domestic comforts, like the dogged and tenacious Germans on the kindred soil of Pennsylvania, a love of change and the alluring accounts of Western fertility drained off the New-Englanders to break fresh ground and become the pioneers of civilization in the backwoods; while another portion began to apply their mechanical talents and natural ingenuity to manufactures. Thus fishing, migrating, and fabricating the country, though with a population doubling in its ratio that of any other of the states, yet very slowly assumed that look of settled permanence which so markedly distinguishes an English prospect. Everything was run up a hurry or struck out at a blow.

My destination had been Mr. Wignell's * theatre at

---

* THOMAS WIGNELL was the son of a member of Garrick's Company. He came to America at the outbreak of the Revolutionary War, but, without appearing on the stage, went to Jamaica, and remained in the West Indian circuit for ten years. In 1785 he made his professional *début* here as Lewson and Squire Groom at "The Theatre" (John Street), New York, where he remained until 1791. A few years later he opened the Chestnut Street Theatre in Philadelphia, then the finest building of its kind on the continent. In January, 1803, he married the celebrated Mrs. Merry, dying suddenly a month later, aged about fifty years. He was considered without a rival in such characters as Faulkland, Joseph Surface,

Philadelphia, but the yellow fever having broken out in
that city drove the manager to New York, where he fitted
up a lately vacated circus, and desired I would meet him
at Newport, a town about half-way. Thither I accordingly started in one of those longitudinal inventions termed
a " New England stage," built without springs on the plan
of an English covered wagon, to contain " a full company,"
eighteen, inclusive of the driver. This, with a ton of luggage at its tail, was capable of being pulled up-hill with
the speed of a whirlwind by four shaggy, scrambling,
equine devils that required neither whip nor rein, but
seemed to enjoy the joke. The structure of this machine,
placing all upon a level, exhibited a republican principle
which as yet was not at variance with a state of means by
which a certain class require distinct accommodation.
The differences between it and the English stage-coach
were not always in the latter's favor. True, it had no outlet but its mouth, at which it gorged and disgorged like
some great Leviathan, and the seats being transverse and
supplied with backs, the last-comers, men or women, had
to stride over the shoulders of the earlier ones to reach a
seat, for each being desirous of keeping as near as possible
to the driver, the law of gravity was suspended in this
vehicle, and very few of the passengers who came in first
found their way to the bottom. When Mrs. Bernard and
myself were at last established in the extreme seat (not
unlike the back of the Covent Garden gallery), we discovered that the floor was lumbered with a mail-bag and a
valuable assortment of earthen and hardware jugs, kettles,
fire-irons, and other articles consigned to a "store" in the
interior, which had the effect, before the vehicle had been

and Darby. Mr. Wood describes him as a handsome man of fine deportment, whose maxim, that "good manners were more nearly allied to good
morals than people generally conceived," was perfectly illustrated in his
own character and conduct.

ten minutes in motion, of dyeing our shins all the colors of the rainbow. The irritation was perhaps augmented by fifteen tongues going, at the rate of ten words a second, upon politics, commerce, and agriculture, broken by the coughing and hawking of those who were further exciting themselves by cigars and pigtail. But above all this storm, like the deep-toned notes of a powerful bassoon, rose the oracular responses of the "driver." As American roads have not yet produced any specimens of the Old Bailey chivalry called highwaymen, the luggage needed not that extortionate good genius the English "guard," the indefatigable driver combining the offices and being the ministry in one. Like the French monarch he could say, "*L'état c'est moi,*" and it was indeed his character that gave the great novelty and interest to the vehicle.

Every man who has travelled in England must acknowledge the stage-coachman to have been a very formidable personage; mysteriously muffled in innumerable yards of cloth, his back tiled with capes, his red face struggling up from the suffocating clasp of woollens and bandannas, and but just visible under a projection which seemed to unite the uses of a hat and an umbrella, he ascended his box by a kind of divine right. He was the autocrat of whips; the Sublime Porte might have copied his manner, his cattle being as the people of Turkey. True, as a proof of England's freedom, you were permitted to sit beside him, but this tended to breed awe rather than intimacy. Every one must have felt the difficulty of drawing that august being into conversation; even the profound responses of the oracle as to whether we should have rain, or if the summer would be fine, being broken by low, mystically worded objurgations to his horses, proving how he was absorbed in the science of government, ready at any moment to resort to coercion, always maintaining a sufficient check.

The very opposite of all this was the New England "driver." He was usually a thin, wiry, long-backed, leather-skinned fellow, sharing the front seat with the company, and flying in and out of the vehicle with the crack of a harlequin. No one more abhorred a superfluity of clothes. A straw hat was his creed, and he would often wear nankeens and shoes in frosty weather. I can remember one—a tall Vermonter, in a village where I resided some time—who, when winter was whistling his sharpest airs, would stand up amid a well-clad undergrowth of travellers, lank as a leafless elm. Placed upon their level, he sympathized with all his company, yet not intrusively. He was a general book of reference, almanac, market-list, and farmers' journal; a daily paper published every morning, a focus which, by some peculiar centripetality, drew all things towards it.

I see nothing of a joke in the assertion of a New England driver being a major in the army. Europeans forget that, in its European sense, the army in America is not a highly respectable separate profession. Butchers there are *sui generis.* Men became soldiers during the war because they had something to lose. The driver was frequently the owner of a farm or inn, and of a share in his conveyance. As he took no fees (the brand of slavery in England) he was never regarded as a servant. As a rivet to his influence very often the driver was a wag, who had a joke for his passengers, perhaps as old as his stage, and as little likely to stop running. He had rambled in his youth half over the Union, and could tell you strange stories of Indians and rifles, and planters and panthers, of deer-killing and horse-racing, and the art and mystery of making mint-sling. The reserve of an English conveyance is proverbial, the animation of the one in which we found ourselves offered the greatest possible contrast.

The road necessarily engages the traveller's attention.

Though far better than in any other quarter of the Union, the frequent jolts and plunges of the vehicle brought it into sad comparison with the bowling-greens of England. Very often we surprised a family of pigs taking a bath in a gully of sufficient compass to admit the coach. As often, such chasms were filled by piles of stones that, at a distance, looked like Indian tumuli. The driver's skill in steering between these dangers was eminent. I found there were two evils to be dreaded in New England travelling—a clayey soil in wet weather, which, unqualified with gravel, made the road a canal; and a sandy one in summer, which might emphatically be called an enormous insect preserve. Here, as around the swamps, reigns and revels the mosquito—lord of the lance—that Arab of the air whose weapon is against every man, or at least every stranger, for there is a superstition that he has the patriotic instinct to spare natives. At any rate, it is certain no native is before him in his attentions to foreigners. America has often been termed by travellers a land of magnitudes, but I question whether it had ever occurred to them to compare the relative power of the mosquito, and that mild torment of Europe, the flea, though thousands who have had experience of both hemispheres would be feelingly alive to the proof; and if refinement curled its lip at the idea, candor would compel a confirmatory shrug. Of the political influence of this insect I had an illustration in a fellow-traveller, but lately arrived from England, and professing to be greatly disgusted with his country. During the former part of the journey he had been continually railing against it, but under the influence of the mosquitoes this rancor gradually softened, and at last the persistency of their stabs forced even this thoroughly disaffected wanderer to exclaim, "England, with all thy faults, I love thee still."

This is, perhaps, the most appropriate place for some ob-

servations on him who plays the "title-rôle" in this part
of the States; though the prevalent absurdity in England
of calling an American of whatever state by the general
title of Yankee is not greater than the misapplication of
the title in America to all classes of New-Englanders. The
origin of the name, indeed, as stated by Heck Welder, is
the Indian pronunciation of "English"—"Yengeese"—
by which appellation they distinguished the New-Englanders from the Virginians, or Southern people, whom they
called the "Long-knives." Yankee, however, is really now
a term denoting character rather than locality, and repre-
sents a certain set of qualities in a particular grade of society. The Yankee is a man of the lower orders, sometimes a farmer, more often a mechanic (the very spirit of
mechanism embodied), and yet more usually a travelling
trader. The Yankee is the Yorkshireman of America; the
same cunning, calculating, persevering personage, with an
infusion of Scotch hardiness and love of wandering. Like
him, he goes upon the principle that all men are rogues,
and like him he is instanced by his customers as the best
illustration of the doctrine. He has the same talent for
expedients; the same keen eye to character and to expedite
a sale; the same want of nicety in regard to means, so
long as they are not legally offensive (going to jail he
considers not so much a disgrace as a waste of time), so
that it would be just as appropriate to call the refined
gentry and enlightened manufacturers of the County of
York "regular Yorkshiremen," as to cite any man who
moves in the respectable circle of Boston as "a regular
Yankee."

This curious class of mammalia, the "Down-Easter" as
it is often called, is divisible into three species—the swapper, the jobber, and the pedler, all agreeing in one grand
characteristic—love of prey—but varying in many striking particulars. The swapper claims precedence in point

of antiquity, his character and name being a direct importation from Yorkshire. The word to "swap," meaning to exchange, is still current there and possesses a high
historic interest, some local historians having proved, I
believe, that it was this peculiarity in the Northern Saxons
which for so many years drove the hordes of invaders to
the South. The swapper is the only division of the tribe
that may be called stationary, though he is not more peculiar in this respect than in the mode he adopts to make
a fortune. He thinks neither of buying, nor selling, nor
growing, nor manufacturing; the key to his El Dorado is
—exchange. With most this practice is a passion, with
many a disease; some are inoculated with the virus, but
the majority have it in the natural way, and it has then
all the precocity of genius, with the tenacity of faith. It
shows itself in childhood, when the infant swaps its milk
for marbles; and at school, when the boy swaps everything but floggings. As his possessions increase he puts
all he owns into a state of transition; house, land, and
cattle are drawn into the whirlpool; even coat, hat, and
boots. He soon loves swapping for its own sake; the
means becomes the end; the mere act and business of exchanging seems essential to his existence. If now analyzed the feeling would be found pure; if it is no love
of lucre, it is much less envy of his fellow-creatures' possessions; it is neither desire of profit nor of accumulation;
it is simply the love of novelty.

The swapper is, of all men, the least affected by relics,
the least concerned about memorials. Turning his back
upon his father's wisdom, he has full faith in the instruction and resources of the future. With him everything old is useless, he keeps nothing long enough to prove
its value by experience, but puts all his trust in the excellences of new inventions. The swapper is a fine moral
symbol, no man illustrating more directly the vanity of

human wishes, or the evanescence of all things. Again, he
is a moral warning, no man displaying more of the spirit
of a gambler, or more often meeting the fate of one.
Yet his is a kind of madness which ought to be harmless
from its singularity, for there is nothing even analogous
to it, except that domestic evil in England—a buyer of
bargains. Thus he spends his days as everybody's agent
or anybody's market. If poor, he exchanges to become
rich; if rich, to become poor; till, having swapped wealth
for want, ease for anxiety, and youth for age, he at last
swaps this world for the next.

I made these discoveries principally during my residence
at a country-box near Boston, where my nearest neighbor
was a specimen of this class, in the last stage of the disorder. Every morning that he heard I was at home he
was sure to pay me a visit in order, as he termed it, to
"make a trade." Whatever object his eye rolled upon it
roused "that one dear thought"—to barter; my plough
for his cart, my horse for his cow, or my dog for his cat.
If I proved obdurate to the advantages proposed on one
point, he attacked me on another. Not an inch of my
property but suggested some article of exchange on his
own premises. Would I swap my peaches for plums ? my
carrots for cabbages ? I verily believe, had I not agreed
to gratify him on some occasions, he would have proposed
to swap the rats in our barns, or the snails in our orchards.
At times I endeavored to soften my refusal by inviting
him to dinner, but the mania still clung to him as his real
hunger and thirst. On pouring out some brandy he remembered that he had a keg at home, he should like to
trade away; and the sight of my mutton suggested the idea
of a score of sheep which he would make over to me for
two oxen.

The appearance of my friend was in strict keeping with
his ruling propensity. His dress was constantly under-

going mutations in which the variety of colors and text-
ures precluded the monotonous impression of a suit. He
was half nankeen one day, half leather the next. Every
market morning furnished some novelty, particularly in
his hats, which were enthroned and deposed with all the
despatch of Grand Turks. A pair of homespun trousers
seemed to stick to him the longest, though their history,
I've little doubt, resembled that which the Virginians (to
whom a swapper was a perpetual source of satire) were in
the habit of relating. They said that a farmer who had
not had a "trade" for some time, feeling rather dull one
Sunday, resolved to "go to meeting." On his way there
he saw a young man hoeing in a field, so he stopped and
began to lecture him on the immorality of his conduct.
Finding that he would not attend to him, the farmer at
last bawled out, "I say, young man, you won't listen to
religion, but you've got on an awful strong pair of trousers,
will you swap?"

I remember a pendant to this from the same source. A
Connecticut dealer who was "down" with a fever, in a
very dangerous state, had had a particular medicine sent
to him, to be taken four times a day. A friend, calling
in, smelt the mixture and pronounced it to be excellent; it
had cured his grandmother. "It is worth a dollar a
bottle," said he. At these electrifying words the dying
man opened his eyes, raised himself an inch, and faltered
out, "A dollar a bottle, Enoch! there are three bottles of
it, and, if you've no objection, I'll swap the whole lot for
your black terrier."

The second species of "Down-Easter," a jobber, is a
man of genius, mechanical it may be, but still a genius.
He has probably been taught a trade, shoemaking for instance, which, being conducive to reflection, leads him into
a view of the varied wants of man from the foot upwards,
from the bed he requires to rest upon, to the roof that

must cover him. All arts agree in requiring certain qualities, such as solidity, convenience, proportion, and dura-
bility, whence it is obvious if a man thoroughly under-
stands the craft of shoemaking (to say nothing of its
philosophy, the giving neatness to an ugly foot, which
will restore enjoyment to a sensitive mind), he has a guide
and handmaid to the sister arts, a pass-key to the cells of
mechanism, in whose works practice will give proficiency.
Thus he superadds to his original vocation carpentry,
cabinet and coffin making, bricklaying, and farriery; and
as soon as his mind is sufficiently stored he collects his
tools (for knowledge, with him, is action), crams them
into a basket, and strides off to the Western States, where
in every new-formed settlement he proves a welcome
visitor, supplying to each house that slight assistance
which their comfort may require. Joking apart, there is
not a doubt that this class of men are among the most
useful in the Union. They unite to a rough expertness, in
all they undertake, the temperance and industry demanded
by the state of things about them, and virtue, in this case,
meets with its reward. The man that can turn his hand
to anything, generally turns everything into his hand;
his leather pouch soon exhibits the appearance of a tumor,
till he is at length enabled to eschew vagrancy, buy a plot
of ground, and build a shop in some fast-rising settlement,
which he opens in "the general line;" when, as the increasing wants of the community call for the introduction
of regular trades, they also introduce customers to con-
sume his cheese and bacon.

A jobber is generally a red-faced, yellow-haired man,
with light-blue eyes and a capacious mouth, dressed in a
nankeen suit which was made for him when a lad, and
from whose expressive restrictions his republican frame is
now freeing itself at back, elbows, and waistband.

But the grand division of the tribe is the New England

pedler, who, unlike the last described, has no inventive ingenuity, save in the art of puffing, and still less like the
first, not the slightest taste for swapping. He considers
his own goods so much superior to his customers' that
nothing but hard cash can represent their value. To buy
cheap and sell high comprehends for him the whole cycle
of human knowledge; the supreme excellence of north-
country stuffs is his religion; and science has taught him
to believe that the world itself would not go round but to
the tick of a New England clock. The same spirit which
carried his ancestors into the backwoods with their train
of teams and children sends him every spring on a voyage
of discovery to the South. This visit is regarded by the
Southern trader in the light of a visitation; he may be
truly said to have Yankee-phobia, and to look upon a
"Connecticut chap" as a commercial Scythian, a Tartar
of the North whose sole business in life is to make inroads
on his peace and profit. He ranks him in the list of plagues
next to the yellow fever, and before locusts, taxation, and
a wet spring; indeed, some go so far as to suppose that a
shower of Yankees was the crowning pestilence which
made Pharoah give up the Israelites.

The panic they occasion is not more from a terror of
their cleverness than of their singularly indomitable spirit.
There is no getting rid of them. None of the usual similes
of a burr, or sticking-plaster, give any idea of a pedler's
tenacity; he has the gripe of a crab with the suction of a
mosquito; you can't deny, you can't insult, you can't
fatigue him; you can only dismiss him by a purchase.
Such a character must be particularly obnoxious to an
indolent and relaxed community. A tornado could not
create greater havoc in the ease and enjoyment of a Carolinian evening than the buzzing and humming of such a
wasp. In some places his mere appearance is the sound-
ing of a tocsin to bar doors and windows, while many even

double lock drawers, to prevent a conjuration over the counter by which the money seems to leap out of the till into the pedler's pocket. It may be amusing to pause for an instant on such a scene.

Suppose a village in one of the rich Virginian or Carolinian valleys, clustering round a road that climbs up a hill so almost perpendicular that it seems to realize the idea of Jacob's ladder. From the gate of the planter's lawn run, or, rather, stagger off, the sheds of the butcher, the baker, and the blacksmith, terminated by that arena for cock-fighting and politics, a tavern. About sunset labor has ceased and the inhabitants are leaning or lying out of their doors, the cows are wandering home, the children are playing about, and the "niggers" are laughing loud in the distant sugar-houses. In this sweet hour of calm all hearts are disposed to indulge in Christian emotions. Look at the group and you'd take them for a colony of Moravians, with all enemies pardoned and all cares forgotten; when suddenly a pedestrian is seen wending down the hill, his legs, in the slanting sunbeams, sending their shadows half a mile before him. By his length of staff he might be taken for a pilgrim, but the sprawl of his walk awakens anything but sacred associations. Gradually his hull looms into distinctness, they perceive he is a long-backed man, with a crouching head and loaded shoulders; suspicions are excited; and at length one who may have suffered more than the rest, perhaps, from the endemic, recognizes its symptoms and exclaims, "I'll be shot if it aint a Yankee!" At these words if there is not a general rout, or springing up, and banging-to of doors, it must be because their faculties are prostrated by the surprise, and they lie spell-bound, as cattle are said to do on the approach of the anaconda. As the enemy advances at a swinging pace among them, his keen gray eye rolling round in selection of a victim, they remember the strange

man who first found out their quiet hiding-place, and the
wonder and contempt this curious species of fellow-creature at first excited—a fellow who would neither drink, bet,
nor talk politics, but kept prying into holes and corners
to prove the extent of their needs, and who ultimately
walked away with all the silver of the settlement. Whatever may have been their former experiences, one of the
number is a doomed man. If he doesn't want a clock
which ticks loud enough to scare away the rats, or a razor
so keen that if you but strop it overnight and put it under your pillow you'll wake up clean shaved in the morning, yet—"Sure alive, missis wants a new cap," and he's
got a small stock, "jest such as the squires' wives wear at
the camp-meetin's;" or, "The young gals need some gowns,"
and he has "all kinds of cotton that are all the better for
bein' turned—for the inside gets fresh as t'other's wearin'
out."

The "Down-Easter's" system of attacking a stubborn
antagonist displays great generalship. He begins by resting his pack upon the half-hatch of the door; its numerous contents presently require a field of display; nowhere
so fitting as on the counter within, if it be a shop; he begs
leave but to show them; "Look at them, mister, they won't
sting you." The outworks once carried, his shot (caps
and combs, "hankychers," etc.) fly about in all directions
and take deadly effect on some of the family. By a
singular fatality everything that is tried on seems to be
made expressly for the wearer; she never looked so well
in anything before. And equally strange is the discovery
that, up-to that moment, they had been living without a
solitary convenience. Every one but the father perceives
the necessity of Sally having a pair of shoes, Enoch a
jack-knife, and the parlor a timepiece. From the shop
Jonathan fights his way into the backroom, and there his
victim, driven into a corner, is beaten into an acknowledg-

ment of his wants and deficiencies, and the capitulation that ensues is a discussion of their number and the expense of supplying them. When the campaign is over in one house he proceeds to another, and so on to all in succession, till he arrives at the tavern, where he usually succeeds in trading the landlord out of bed and breakfast.

Smarting under this infliction, it can be no wonder that the Virginians indulge in occasional vituperations, insist that the Yankee cheats them in every transaction, and that, however he may vary his commodities from the traditionary wooden nutmegs and red-flannel sausages, swindling is still his talent, his stimulus, and local distinction. In proof of this they point to the fact that there are no Jews in New England, the competition being too great for them to exist.

I was told a story of a "Down-Easter" mode of creating a demand for a supply which, amid all the ingenuities of modern commerce, may fairly claim originality. One of the class called a "hickory dealer," or seller of wooden ware, came down to the South in summer-time with a well-laden wagon, but was destined to encounter a sweeping opposition in the yellow fever, which had commenced business about a week previous in such a wholesale way that the only wooden ware in requisition was a coffin. The ravages of the plague were at this time so dreadful that it will be supposed there was a general tendency to try the most desperate and absurd expedients to avert it, though many such proved but pioneers to its progress. This the pedler was aware of, so resolved, as regarded his own fortunes, to extract good from evil. Dressing himself as respectably as possible, he mounted his horse and rode up to a printing-office in Williamsburgh, where, under an assumed name, he had a hundred bills struck off to this effect:

"WANTED IMMEDIATELY,

"Wooden ware in any quantity for the fever hospital at Philadelphia, such being found not to convey the infection.

"By order of the Board of Health, Seth Adams.

"N.B.—All persons are cautioned how they use crockery, which is the cause of plague to thousands."

Fifty of these placards he sent his boy to stick round the streets of a village lying in his road, where the fever had begun to show itself. A discovery so important, so simple, and apparently in such close connection with a remedy, created an instant sensation. The doom of crockery was pronounced. Jugs, bowls, basins, teapots, and other utensils most esteemed or necessary were hurled out of the windows in showers. No grandmother's gift, no ancestor's relic, survived this fall of China; the streets soon exhibited a series of domestic tumuli, and looked like a pottery after an earthquake. About noon, when the work of destruction was at its height, a wagon made its way into the village, with a man vociferating with all the power of his lungs, "Wooden ware!" His arrival was hailed as a God-send; a crowd collected round him as to a magician who brought talismans; and in less than two hours his plague-averting platters were all disposed of at exorbitant prices.

A more defensible piece of cleverness was that of a Passamaquoddy captain who, arriving in the port of London soon after the peace, was inveigled into a low tavern by some sharpers, with the intention of plundering him at cards. Failing, however, in every endeavor to draw him into play, they drank three bottles of wine with him and then went out. The landlord, coming in, expressed his surprise. "Are your friends gone?" he asked. "My friends?" replied the captain; "they brought me here, but I don't know them." "Ah," said the landlord, "I see you are not much acquainted with our London blades." "No, I ain't."

"Well, you'll grow wiser in time; you must pay the reckoning." "What, for all four?" "Certainly, for all four." "Well, if that's the case," rejoined Jonathan, drawing out a handful of silver, "I may as well have another bottle." The landlord stepped out eagerly to get it from the cellar, when the captain, taking a piece of chalk from the mantelpiece, wrote on the table, "I leave you a Yankee handle for your London blades," and quickly walked off also.

Whatever may have been the delinquencies of the land traders of New England, the local character appears to have been redeemed by their maritime brethren, who were among the most exemplary productions of the Union. To skill, activity, and temperance they joined the strictest sense of rectitude, and as rapidly became the carriers of the states as they are now advancing to fulfil that office for the world at large. To this cause must be attributed the slow progress of New England in manufactures. The facilities offered for ship-building by its wood and water, and the nautical taste of its inhabitants, rendered the carrying-trade a more profitable pursuit than the experiment of creating goods for exchange or exportation, in the hitherto imperfect state of their machinery and the high price of labor.

Georgia and the Carolinas, the most inveterate against New England, could not but allow the merits of her seamen, even when they saw them in such numbers taking possession of the Southern harbors. The reason was obvious. In the old times a Carolinian owned a schooner worked by negroes, who finding slavery perhaps somewhat lighter or more diversified at sea, made no exertions to expedite a trip, but would sleep away whole tides that had been in their favor, and take so little care of their vessel that the first heavy gale blew it into harbor to refit. The Northern coasters, on the contrary, were principally

manned by their owners, usually a company who, with a
truly Northern spirit, carried the principles of a common-
wealth even into their speculations. This trait, distin-
guishing, perhaps, no other seamen in history, fully accounts for the vigor and success of their exertions. As
an instance of the way in which they distanced competition,
it was no unusual thing for a New-Englander to send to
Philadelphia for flour, carry it to the West Indies, bring
back molasses to New England, take the same to Philadelphia, and then undersell those who traded directly between that city and the islands.

The ingenuity of these traders fully equalled their enterprise, and the constant good-fortune of some of them,
whatever the nature of their speculations, almost established
the idea of fatalism. I knew a merchant of Boston who
was so buoyed up with his successes that he laid a wager,
at a party one evening, that no one present could propose
a speculation which he would not turn to account. This
being considered a piece of gasconade meriting ridicule,
one of his hearers named a cargo of warming-pans to be
sent to the West Indies. A laugh, of course, followed
the announcement, but he seemed in no way disconcerted
at the selection, and pledged himself to fulfil the engagement within six months. The difficulty of obtaining the
warming-pans was not trifling. One half of the order he
was obliged to send to the English manufacturers; the rest
he set about collecting from bankrupt stocks in the Union;
but, sure enough, in less than six months the freight was
prepared, and the schooner set sail for Barbadoes and St.
Thomas. There, such had been the negotiations of the
consigner, the warming-pans were all disposed of at a
profit, as substitutes for shovels in scooping up sugar!

CHAPTER III.

1797.—New York.—Robert Merry.—My First Appearance and Illness; Rustication and Cure.—Aspect of New York; the Dutch; the Breakfast-table; Merchants' Daily Life; Double Disguises; the Biters Bit; Land Speculators.—Sport.—Anecdotes of the Revolutionary War; Sir W. Howe and Mrs. Loring; Lord Cornwallis and his Friend.—Journey to Philadelphia; a Narrow Escape.

THE first person to shake my hand in New York was my old club and Green Room associate, Robert Merry.* When I met him on landing he exclaimed, " Ah, John, have you come to make your fortune like the rest of us? I'm afraid," shrugging his shoulders, " you'll be bit." " I plead guilty," said I; " but what in the name of Mammon tempted you—you, that I've heard so often say you could never live in America?" " Nonsense, John," he replied, " you know that I always liked to be in A-merry-key." Poor fellow! here was the ruling passion strong in exile: he had given up home, friends, fame, poetry, pleasure, politics—everything but punning.

My commencement was hardly encouraging. On the 25th of August I made my first bow to an American au-

---

* Mr. ROBERT MERRY was one of the founders of the Della Cruscan school of poetry—a sort of anticipation in the last quarter of the last century of the affectations of the Æsthetic School in the last quarter of this century. It arose among certain English residents in Florence in 1785; it spread to England, where, by a curious anticipation, its organ was a paper called *The World;* it was crushed by Gifford's slashing "Baviad," published in 1794. Merry married Miss Brunton in 1792, and withdrew her from the stage; but when his means failed, a tempting offer from an American manager brought them to America in 1796, and he died here in 1798.

dience, in the character of Goldfinch, and my reception was everything I could wish; but on the second night of my performance (Lord Ogleby) I was seized with the cholera - morbus, so that half of the apparently affected pains of the character were the spontaneous effects of my disorder. After the first treatment the doctor ordered me to go immediately into the country and to take brandy-and-water. This was no disagreeable prescription; I fixed on the little Dutch village of Haerlem for my retreat, and Robert Merry's joy at having met with me was so great that he insisted on sharing my rustication, remarking, in his old way, "it was not the first time he had found it a pleasure to cheer me." When thus together we had so much to remember, discuss, reply to, propose, and project, that we sat up night after night, administering plentifully the doctor's elixir, till in a few days I found myself completely restored, having experienced, perhaps, the pleasantest cure upon record.

I have termed the Middle States an epitome of Europe. New York was an index to the Middle States. The one great market to the enterprising foreigner, it was also a sort of Mecca to the hungry backwoodsman, who was sure to make a pilgrimage once in his life to yield his homage on its counters to the gods, Mercury and Mammon. It resembled a large fair or a cluster of inns rather than an abiding city, all its inhabitants looking like birds of passage, with the exception of the few aboriginal Dutch who had not been swept away by the European flood to their yellow brick dwellings on the banks of the Hudson. But these kept themselves distinct even from the other natives, regarding the entire body as a variety of Arabs who had been expelled from Europe for their robberies. They maintained their houses like fortifications, their doors and windows ever closed and barred, their garden walls armed with glass bottles in a bed of mortar, and they sitting on their " stoops " (the porches of their door-steps), so dilated as not to leave room for a cat to pass, and rolling waves of smoke from their melancholy pipes to warn the stranger off. The Dutch have never borne the character of an inhospitable people, but certainly in this case they seemed to interpret every glance a stranger cast at their peaked roofs and comfortable orchards as the possible preliminaries of some burglarious attempt. Their cumbrous, ox-like frames, and drowsy, ruminating faces, as they crouched in the stalls of their " stoops," are before me at this moment, a marked contrast to the spare, but muscular proportions of the other residents, the eternal restlessness of the foreigners, or the slashing, sprawling progress of the Yankees. The world seemed to be standing still with the one; the others seemed to be carrying all the world before them.

The house I stopped at gave me a tolerable specimen of the varieties of society now converging at this great exchange, and enabled me thereby to solve a mystery which had puzzled the heads of numerous travellers—the multi-fariousness of an American breakfast-table. Here was a French gentleman of *l'ancien régime* looking melancholy and mysterious, in a bag-wig and point-lace ruffles, who had two cards of address, the one styling him " Marquis," the other " Dancing-master." Here was an English agriculturist just arrived, a firm believer in the doctrine of ready-roasted pigs squeaking " Come, eat me." Here was a Kentucky landowner, proving London to be the Babylon of the Apocalypse, and predicting England's downfall, in order to heighten the value of his disposable property. Here were major-generals from Vermont, walking encyclopedias of the war, and planters from " Caroliny," who were alternately explaining the free principles of their " Constitution " and reading the description of runaway slaves.

Here were Italians who had brought over Fantoccini to refine the taste of the infant country; Germans who had come to hunt out some distant relatives ; lean and voracious Scotchmen looking as if they could swallow the continent ; and Irish " jintlemen " of slender figures and fortunes, who having come to America to live cheaply, had spent a year's income in crossing the ocean. To meet such a variety of tastes it was necessary that the board should do something more than merely gratify the impulses of an American stomach. Each must be pleased, and we were accordingly provided with fish, ham, beef, boiled fowls, eggs, pigeons, pumpkin pies, lobsters, vegetables, tea, coffee, cider, sangaree, and cherry-brandy!

The habits of the New York merchants reminded me of my friends at Guernsey. They breakfasted at eight or half past, and by nine were in their counting-houses, laying out the business of the day; at ten they were on their wharves, with aprons round their waists, rolling hogsheads of rum and molasses; at twelve, at market, flying about as dirty and as diligent as porters; at two, back again to the rolling, heaving, hallooing, and scribbling. At four they went home to dress for dinner; at seven, to the play; at eleven, to supper, with a crew of lusty Bacchanals who would smoke cigars, gulp down brandy, and sing, roar, and shout in the thickening clouds they created, like so many merry devils, till three in the morning. At eight, up again, to scribble, run, and roll hogsheads. What a day's work this would have been for a Carolinian! Thus the New-Yorker enjoyed his span of being to the full stretch of the tether, his violent exertions during the day counteracting the effects of his nocturnal relaxations, besides giving him a relish to return to them. Certainly few men throughout the Union worked harder for enjoyment.

I could so little credit their daily public metamorphosis,

at first, that I was guilty of many unintentional insults, particularly to two or three gentlemen who had taken a great liking to me at a friend's table. Happening one day to penetrate the mysterious sphere of their avocations, in order to see a ship get under way, I heard a group of porters, as they appeared to me, shout my name and beckon to me. This familiarity I set down to the account of their nationality, and walked on, consoling myself in the manner of Edgar, that " Every one knows poor Tom." A day or two afterwards, at a dinner-party, I observed that I thought I was likely to become a favorite, for the gallery people had patronized me already. "Indeed," said one of the company, " they must see more of you than we do, then. Why, yesterday, when you were passing the wharf, we called to you till we were hoarse; you looked round, but you wouldn't return." " Oh, you must be mistaken," I replied. "The only persons I can remember hailing me were a crew of blackguards—fellows rolling hogsheads." The roar this declaration elicited defies description. "They were we," shouted my respondent. I was petrified. The laughter went round the table in peals, each seeming to grow louder as I attempted to stammer an apology or explain away my words. The position was not pleasant either for myself or the persons alluded to, till one of them, with prompt good-humor, filling a glass of wine, said, " Well, well; Mr. Bernard was not obliged to know us in our stage-clothes!" I was glad, however, to change the subject, by gratifying the first person who asked me for a song, and as this had the happy effect of making the merriment general, I had no doubt that, at our breaking-up, which was some hours afterwards, my infernal Malapropism was forgotten.

The next morning I received a note from one of the party, requesting me to call at his counting-house on the quay, to taste some very superior port-wine. I, having been secretary to the Beefsteak Club, the fame of whose port had reached even to America, enjoyed a reputation, which I believe I deserved, for a critical acumen of palate. Delighted with the summons, I set off as pleasantly as if a bottle of the aforesaid were already harmonizing all things in my interior. On my way, however, I met another of the party, who, learning my destination, burst into a laugh and said he could not refrain from letting me into a secret. "You have mortified our friends so much," he continued, "by that unlucky mistake last night, that they swear you can only tell a gentleman by his clothes, so they have resolved to prove their charge by playing you a trick. They have dressed up some carmen in their own clothes, and mean to introduce them to you as merchants and great proprietors, not doubting but that you will pay them every attention. Then they mean to take you home to dinner, where all their friends are invited, to hear the *exposé*." For a minute or two the news overcame me. I had entirely forgotten the provocation, and dreamed not of such malice. Feeling, however, that this was meeting me too much on my own ground, a plan presented itself which promised, by effectually turning the tables on my antagonists, to bring the affair to a speedier and different conclusion. I disclosed it to my friend, who, tendering his assistance, I ran home for a black wig and whiskers, a smock frock, hat, stockings, and other constituents of a working man's dress; then, returning to his house upon the quay, I speedily assumed them, accomplishing so complete a transformation that he with difficulty recognized me. I then wrote a note to my trap-setting friend for myself to deliver, stating that business at the theatre would detain me half an hour or so, but that I should join him without fail the instant of my liberation.

I found the conspirators assembled in high glee and expectation; the laborers, clean-shaved and tricked out with profuse finery, seated at a table with the decoy-duck port; my friends standing about in the costume which had caused all this mistake, chagrin, and stratagem. Tendering the note, I said, in the best brogue I could assume, that "I was told by Mr. Burr-nard to wait at the quay till he came." Viewed on all sides by the party, no suspicion was excited, but my words suggesting an apprehension that I might interfere with their hoax, I was invited to a stool in one corner, and some brandy handed to me. Now came my enjoyment. Pulling my hat over my eyes, I soon remarked all the details of the scene and its points of contrast. The carmen at the table, who certainly had the best of the joke, filled and sipped their glasses in fine burlesque of gentlemanly nonchalance; the principal actors stood in a group near the door, talking in an undertone, winking, rubbing their hands, and digging each other's sides, till the fulness of their anticipations would ever and anon overflow in bursts of electrical laughter, which rattled the window-panes. Then one of the outposts would shout, "He's coming!" at which all was hushed and every man stood to his gun. The next instant the news was contradicted; then came another tornado of risibility and another pause. In this manner the half-hour elapsed, and no Bernard. Then I began to observe the quicksilver go gradually down, and signs of uneasiness master their complacency. They sat down, whistled, jumped up, walked to the door, muttered, "D—n it! he must be rehearsing all Shakespeare, I hope he *is* coming." In a few more minutes there was a dead pause; the laughs were all flown, and they stared in each other's faces with a sheepish vacuity. A man was sent in search of me, and one or two ventured to suspect that I had " smoked " them. At this moment my friend and accomplice arrived, and with a well-feigned anxiety inquired for me. An hour had now elapsed, and their impatience could no longer be controlled. All was uproar as, stamping about, they commented on my want of punctuality (as the result of professional habits), with the aid of all those emphatic words by which the lower orders have so materially strengthened the English language, and which they could not refrain from pressing into their service. The men were then told to leave off emptying the bottles and doff their borrowed plumes; upon which I, rising up and divesting myself of wig and whiskers, begged also to resume my real character.

The scene that ensued I must leave to my reader's imagination. Suffice it that all my anticipations were realized; the good-humor of the biters thus bit returned, and the port, a bottle of which I had been invited to taste, was not left till at least half a dozen had set their generous seal to our articles of confederation then and there immutably established.

The most amusing species of scum on the surface of New York society were the land speculators, who prowled about the wharves and hurried, like so many alligators, to pounce on the unwary emigrant. Everybody arriving with a ruddy, round, moneyed-looking aspect they conceived must necessarily want to buy land, and they forthwith produced a list of soils, like a tailor's pattern book, which they had to sell cheap; land possessed of such wonderful properties as would turn all the poetry of the Fortunate Islands into poor prose, all the golden coloring of Oriental fertility into mere barrenness. It was capable not merely of growing everything, from a gooseberry to a grape, from a pumpkin to a buffalo, but it emitted various kinds of effluvia which contributed to skill in all kinds of trade, the atmosphere being impregnated with an indescribable something which made a man cleverer there than in any other part of the Union. One of their rogueries was to plant hickory-trees, which will only grow in the best soil, about the edges of the worst; the fact of their production being considered a sufficient guarantee. What a world of new ideas would a Hogarth have received from half an hour's lounge through the scene of their vocation, to observe the backwoodsman grasping his victim by the collar, and pouring into his ears a torrent of talismanic sounds; and the good, easy, innocent English farmer rumbling the money in his pockets, and gloating with his half-unsocketed eyes on the vision of fairy-land set before him.

These worthies were in the habit of selling the same land to two and three different customers, and emigrating before the parties could make a discovery of the fraud. But it was not to be supposed they could have all this fun to themselves. Europe was perpetually pouring over professors of the dark sciences, whose talents ably supported the credit of their birthplaces, and "When Greek meets Greek," etc. I heard an amusing story of a Frenchman who had assumed the title and forged the deeds of a marquisate in Normandy. Meeting a Kentucky man with ground to sell, which had already passed into the hands of more than one gull, they effected an exchange. Which received a balance I don't know, but the one took a voyage to France and the other a pilgrimage to the lakes, to discover the identity of their schemes.

During our short but very pleasant and successful season at New York, Merry was the constant companion of my fishing and shooting excursions, and he still proved that his spirit was a true echo to his name. And here were no game laws to tax the pocket and principles of an Englishman; you could take your rod or gun, jump over a gate, and wing or hook your victims before the door of a mansion, without the trouble of inquiring whom it belonged to. Here were no eternal " Trespassers be-

ware!" or "Spring guns!" to warn the reader that a rab-
bit's legs were of more value than a man's. The benevolent Americans forgave every man his trespasses, and
pointed their guns only at the enemies of their country.

In our rambles we gathered many laughable anecdotes
of the war. At a farmhouse where we dined we learned
that the owner had formerly lived in West Chester, where,
on one occasion, he had been compelled, at the point of
the sword, to give assistance to the Royalists. The Provincials, who were numerous in that quarter, came upon
him the next day, cudgelled him soundly, and carried off
his cattle and all they could lay hands on, except some
winter provisions in his barn, because he was "a d——d
Tory and had given assistance to the king." The day
following down galloped a corps of cavalry with capacious bags, and pillaged all that was left—his beef, pork,
and gammons—on the plea that he was "a d——d rebel,
and had supplied the king's enemies." There were some
humorous peculiarities about these West Chester boys,
who, from their Jack-o'-lantern movements and nightly
annoyances were called "General Howe's Mosquitoes."
The general at one time being short of provisions, sent a
party overnight to drive off some cattle from Long Island.
The watchword for the guard in that quarter was "Cambridge," and the password, "Swamp." The foragers
luckily stumbled on an outpost who piqued himself on his
superior caution; a "fellow that would sleep with one
eye shut and both ears open," especially on a foggy night.
Hearing them approach, this vigilant sentinel exclaimed,
in a shrill snuffle, "Cambridge!" Receiving no response
he repeated, "Cambridge, I say! If you don't say Swamp
I'll shoot!" The English, subduing their laughter, shouted the word, and, passing on, before morning drove off a
magnificent herd.

On another occasion, when the levies were being raised,

and a commanding officer was hearing the pleas of exemption (all men beyond a certain age, with so many children, or disabled by infirmity), a hale, well-built, active-looking fellow petitioned to be excused on the ground of an impediment in his speech. "I—I—I stut-ter, sir." The officer stared at him, and replied, with some emphasis, "What the —— does that signify? we want you to fight, not to talk." "Y-y-yes, Captain, y-es, but—but sup-po-pose we—we happen to be beat, I should g-g-get cut in halves before I could cry out qu-qu-quarter!"

At New York I met with several veteran survivors of the Revolution, who, among the anecdotes with which they enlivened our eventual intimacy, favored me with one disclosure which I confess amused as much as it startled me. It was a proof of how ignorant is the world of the little causes of many great events. American independence, for instance, every one supposes was owing to George Washington, with some support from his countrymen, and a little assistance from the French. Nothing can be more erroneous, according to these worthies, by whom it was attributed to a female patriot, the beautiful and fascinating Mrs. Loring. Seeing the affairs of the Provincialists veering, like an unruddered vessel, into the suction of a whirlpool, she conceived the noble enterprise of their rescue, by exerting all her arts and charms to entrap the affections and influence the counsels of that modern Antony—Sir William Howe.

The crisis of affairs in 1776 is well known. England had landed an army in Canada under Burgoyne, and another at New York under Howe, with one grand plan of action; the junction of the two on the banks of the Potomac, with the consequent pitching of Washington, Lee, Gates, Green, *cum multis aliis*, into that stream; and then, the stately march of this force to the South, to brush the rest of the insurgents from the face of the earth like so many mosquitoes. Everything seemed to favor this project. The Independents were beaten in all quarters, and Washington, their last stay, was permitted to stay nowhere. Dislodged from White Plains, he had retreated to Bound Brook on the Delaware. Then what was the course General Howe, with his thirty thousand regularly fed veterans, was expected to pursue? Every corporal exclaimed, "Drive the enemy from their entrenchments on the river, to keep open the water communication with Burgoyne" (no alarming task, considering that the American force was under ten thousand), "and then march direct to Philadelphia." This was the pivot on which the fortunes of the struggle turned. But what did Mark Antony? He ordered his men to get on board ship and proceed to Philadelphia *via* the Delaware. This was transporting them indeed, but with fury! The consequences were foreseen. The Hudson remaining closed, Burgoyne, after kicking Arnold out of Canada, was obliged to surrender for want of supplies; Howe was driven back to his old position; and Cornwallis was eventually surprised into the same predicament as Burgoyne. What could have led the general to the above perverse and fatal preference has been a matter of much speculation to statesmen and soldiers. It need be so no longer, when they learn that Mrs. Loring, being at this time in as critical a condition as the country, required the benefit of sea-air, and her wish was law!

Cornwallis, the ablest officer of the war, was certainly much hampered by local circumstances, but he wasted his time in attempting to conciliate the planters and stimulate their negroes, the latter being as unconscious of the value of their liberty as the former were alive to it. An anecdote was related of him which attests the true English nobleman. He had a friend in Virginia, a Colonel Vanhorn, who, throughout the struggle, had appeared to favor the

royal cause. This gentleman was yet a personal friend
of General Lincoln, who had been sent to the South to
keep Cornwallis at bay. Lincoln, unable to restrain early
feelings, was rash enough to pay the Virginian a visit in-
cognito; but the secret, by some means, reaching the
camp, which was not very distant, the earl ordered out a
party of dragoons and surrounded the house just as the
American general was sitting down to his coffee. He had
scarce time to spring up-stairs before Cornwallis entered
the breakfast-room, and, by the dismay on every countenance, perceived the truth of the report. With great
mildness, taking Colonel Vanhorn's hand, which shook as
if palsy-struck, "My good friend," said he, "what would
you say if, after our intimate acquaintance, I should bring
a bear here some morning to break your glasses and chairs,
to tear your carpet, and root up your garden? You would
execrate my barbarity. Is it kind, then, of you to harbor
a man who has come to thwart my designs, and bring the
cause I am engaged in to confusion and ruin? I see where
he has sat, but your house is sacred, I will not interrupt
his breakfast; let him make a hearty one, but I trust he
will have finished it before two o'clock, because I intend
then to return and do myself the pleasure of dining with
you." He then paid his respects to the family, mounted
his horse, and rode off with his party. It is hardly necessary to add that Lincoln's breakfast terminated his visit,
and that, on the earl's return, no allusion was made to
him.

The yellow fever having vacated Philadelphia at the
setting-in of winter, Wignell made preparations for our
approach, and Merry, Morris,* and myself, with our re-

* OWEN MORRIS. Was the earliest performer of comic old men in
America. Mr. Ireland believes him to have played at Cruger's Wharf
Theatre, New York, as early as 1759. He remained upon the stage for

spective spouses, engaged a small four-horse coach to convey us to the Western Athens. Our enjoyment of this
ride was interrupted by an event which had nearly proved
a very awful coincidence. On crossing the ferry at Trenton, in one of those flat-bottomed, low-sided, Dutch boats
called scows, Morris began to relate the circumstance of
having lost his first wife in this river some twenty years
before, through the fore-horses of the stage taking fright,
leaping over, and dragging the coach after them; the rapidity of the tide and the weight of the vehicle sending it
to the bottom with more than half the passengers. He
had scarcely concluded this horrifying narration when the
square sail of the boat, flapping suddenly in the leaders'
faces, like a shot over they instantly sprang, and, but for
the dexterity of the blacks in cutting their traces, there is
not a doubt we should have shared the fate we had just
heard described.

---

many years, and died in New York in 1809, when, according to W. B.
Wood, he was eighty-four, and according to Dunlap ninety years of age.

CHAPTER IV.

1797–8.—Philadelphia; Babylon its Prototype.—Quakers.—Traditions of Penn.—Philadelphian Society.—Street-washing.—Sir John Oldmixon.— Introduction of Quadrille.—Discovery of a Portrait of Quin.—*Cac. scrib.*, the Philadelphian Epidemic.—My Partnership Play.—Merry's Prophetic Pun.—Fennell, his Eccentricities and Career.—Sanguinary Expedient in Macbeth.—Dr. Franklin, his Influence.—Opposition to "Bustles."—An Explanatory Note.—Best Souvenir of a Lady.—A Great Calf.—A Model Foot.

DEAN PRIDEAUX, in his "Scripture Commentaries," says that Penn laid out the city of Philadelphia upon the lines of Babylon, a fact which speaks as much for the good sense of the worthy Quaker as for his love of order. Many would have considered that regal nest of idolatry an inauspicious, and even profane, prototype for a city which was meant to be the shrine of a true faith; but Penn regarded it as a goodly vessel that had been polluted, and perceived the harmony that would subsist between the principles of his brethren and a place of straight ways. A pleasing modification of the plan was his dispensing, in this "temple of peace, not power," with the gates and walls of the original; and blending the city with the forest. Not only do trees, lining the streets of a town, conduce to health by purifying the air and affording shelter from heat, but there is something peculiarly beautiful in thus introducing the works of the Creator amid those of man, and establishing in the abode of traffic the groves sacred to meditation.

The Quakers were to Philadelphia what the Dutch were to New York, but they were a far more interesting race.

As they silently stole along at twilight in their plain garb, under the shade of their ancient trees, casting sad glances at the motley multitude around them, they looked like spirits of their forefathers come to sigh over the dwellings they could no longer defend from the unhallowed tread of the stranger. It is to be regretted that a people so distinguished for many virtues, should exhibit, ordinarily, such a repugnance to cultivate their mental faculties. One would think they believed that because Christianity was first promulgated in times of barbarism, such a state must be essential to its continuance. Penn, Green, and Benezet were, however, brilliant exceptions, and to the general credit of the sect we must place their early abolition of slavery and their treatment of the Indians.

My friend, Judge Kelly, of Annapolis, related to me two or three traditions of Penn which prove that his practical application of religion was the truest policy. Nearly all his fellow-adventurers fell into the most contradictory mistakes respecting the character of the Indian; they gave him credit for peculiar ingenuity in devising stratagems and tortures, but denied him sufficient sense to test the white man's professions by his acts. They would never have thought of breaking up a frozen stream with spade and pickaxe, instead of waiting till spring sunshine should thaw and melt it, yet could not apply the same principle in dealing with their fellow-creatures; or see that retaliation had been the cause of the Indian's ferocity; that blood for blood was *his* creed, and if the white man adopted it, he only confirmed the redskin in a more deadly hatred, by showing the hypocrisy of his own pretensions. To subdue the Indian it was necessary to excite either his love or his fear. The means of conciliation were many; to show respect for his rights, faith in his honor, attention to his comfort; it was but in one way that the brave fellow could be intimidated, viz., by a dexterous use of his religious impressions. In the latter respect Penn was as sagacious as, in the former, he was benevolent. On one occasion the chief of a tribe, who had come to form an alliance with the "Children of the Rising Sun," committed some theft, which being observed by another Indian, he reported it to the governor, and pointed out how ample were his means of retaliation. Penn replied, "I will take from him only what is mine own. When the redskin robs the white, he thinks the white man is his enemy; his mind is in a cloud: the white man cannot rob the red, because Maneto has told him that all men are his brothers." The wondering listener was so impressed with this goodness that, determined Penn should be no loser by it, he pursued the culprit and himself enforced restitution. Another time the offence was more serious; a party from a tribe, not in Penn's alliance, had fallen suddenly on a settlement up the Susquehanna, and nearly reduced it to ashes. One of the assailants having been seized, he was confined for the night in the strong-room, and at daybreak the allies assembled to witness, as they expected, his execution. When Penn took his seat, he thus addressed the prisoner: "Red man, I have been all night inquiring of the Good Spirit how I should deal with you. Maneto said to me, 'Take your choice! he has burned your huts and killed your sons and brothers; if he dies, his blood is but a few drops for a mighty stream; but if he goes back to his tribe Maneto himself will send down the thunder and lightning, and raise the great waters to sweep off his villages.' Red man, go back to your tribe. Maneto's hand shall do justice to the white man!" The Indian departed, but his alarmed people very soon came to offer reparation. Thus Miquon (the good man), as Penn was called, enjoyed a reputation and tranquillity which are the best proofs that Indians are not wanting in either honor or gratitude. In honorable juxtaposition with Penn stand the patriot Green (the only instance of a fighting Quaker upon record), and the philanthropist Benezet (the American Howard), a man whose life was one long series of benefits to the community, while his death earned an epitaph which a monarch might be proud of, that, "He never made the world mourn till it lost him." Such instances only deepen our regret that the sect should, as a rule, suffer their prejudices to hinder the fulfilment of their duties to society. What could be more absurd than their refusing supplies, during the war, to the men who were defending their homes from spoliation!

Certainly Philadelphia laid no claim to the character of the Western Athens until the shackles of Quakerism were broken by the Revolution, in the ferment of which event social prejudices evaporated, and an intelligent liberality was established. Thus the better part of Philadelphian society presented one of the most agreeable admixtures I had ever met with, having all the ease and animation one could desire, with a sufficient tinge of thoughtfulness to give decorum and dignity. A vein of inquiry pervaded conversation, which was enlivened by a perpetual flow of anecdote. The native was as eager to test the excellence of its institutions by a comparison with those of Europe as the stranger was to explore the resources and realize the grandeur of the New World; and so general was the spirit of concession and of *bonhomie* that one never met with an arrogant assumption, or the obtrusion of an offensive prejudice; a wider and higher philanthropy than that which induces love of country seeming to prompt every one to wish for the general good. This might be attributed to the growing taste for literature, establishing on the ruins of bigotry and ignorance that republic of letters whose influence constantly tends to impart to political institutions its own catholicity.

I soon noticed that one of the external characteristics of the Philadelphian was a short-stepping fidgetiness in the streets, which, since his broad pavements, in direct lines, offered every inducement to a firm, easy pace, seemed rather mysterious. The cause was peculiar. It was a custom here to wash the steps and pavement every summer evening, not so much to cleanse as to cool them (for they rivalled the bottoms of bakers' ovens); to perform which, the maidens stood in a line along the passages, handing buckets from a reservoir, while the most athletic undertook the task of discharging the mimic Niagara over her subjacent domain. Now had it been the fate of the President himself to have passed at this moment, he would, to a certainty, have cheated the thirsty stones of their due; and had he made any complaint, doubtless the fair Sabrina would have told him that she considered her office to be, like his government, no respecter of persons, and, as a true patriot, she regarded his health but as dust in the balance, when weighed against that of the city. Thus the inhabitants, accustomed to this visitation, contracted a habit of perpetual suspicion; as they passed along their eyes glanced around, vigilantly as an Indian's in a thicket, and their limbs exhibited an elasticity as if prepared on the shortest notice to "jump the bucket." In this respect all the citizens were *Quakers*, though none wished to become *wet* ones. Never—until after one or two damping hints as to its necessity, I had adopted this fatiguing precaution—did I understand the meaning of the term *flag*-stones. The Philadelphian was said to be recognizable in New York and Boston by his air of apprehension, and thus exposed himself to the sarcasms of his companions; while the residents of those cities, accustomed to tread their own rugged pavements with a happy fearlessness, carried their system with them when visiting Philadelphia, and received the balance at the hands of the

housemaids.   I remember, in particular, one victim to this
evil, a Frenchman, who, having landed from Paris with a
full cargo of independence, vainly endeavored to defy the
custom.   Arrayed in his newest flowered-silk waistcoat
and satin breeches, he was sauntering along, snuff-box in
one hand, and swinging-cane in the other, to pay a visit,
when, at the corner of a street, he received a heavy shower-
bath.   Shocked, saturated, and ensavaged, he *sacréd*,
kicked higher than Vestris, and shook his dripping wig
like a Fury; but neither pity nor apology could he obtain
from the offender.   Deeming it an attack on the liberty
of the subject, he brought an action against the master of
the house to recover the value of his clothes, but, the
court deciding against him, he only lost another *suit* by
this experiment.   He then appealed to the newspapers,
and demanded if America could be called the land of
freedom while servants were permitted to bespatter their
superiors with impunity; which was answered by the following *jeu d'esprit:*

"LIBERTY AND EQUALITY.

" John Tomkins, standing at his door,
  Spit on Jem Dykes, who passed before.
'Sir,' exclaimed Jem, in furious fit,
'When I pass by how dare you spit?'
'Sir,' replied John, with equal brass,
'When I would spit, how dare you pass?'"

It was amusing to notice the different impressions the
city made upon visitors, showing how much habit has to
do with taste.   "How do you like Boston?" said an American to an Englishman, who had just arrived.   "Extremely; it resembles London.   The streets are not very wide,
very straight, or very clean, but I always prefer a careless
irregularity.   If there are any good views or fine build-
ings you are sure to enjoy them more because you come
upon them suddenly."   "How do you like Boston?" said

a resident to a Philadelphian. "Its *society* very much, but really you should do something to improve your thoroughfares. Your streets are so crooked and dirty my mind is perpetually on the rack to find my way and keep my boots clean." The Londoner and the Bostonian walking through Philadelphia alike exclaim, "The town is very clean, very well paved, and very open; no disorder, even after midnight; but what sameness, how fatiguing to the eye! no variety! no surprises! Go up one street, and you have seen the city!"

I made my début at Philadelphia in two of my London characters, at the handsome theatre built on the model of Covent Garden, to contain about £280; and the principal scenery of which had been painted from designs by Loutherbourg, and imported with the wardrobe. I was not more pleased with my success than at the enjoyment opened to me in private circles by the introductions of my London friends, facilitated by some club acquaintances who, luckily happening to be over here on business, did not fail to make known the glories of my convivial career. Among others I encountered my old Bath patron, the stage original, Sir John Oldmixon; but so mournfully changed that, had he not introduced himself, I never should have recognized him. I had left him the most elegant person in the most elegant city of England, the centre of its admiration, revelling in enjoyment. I found him in a distant country, skulking about the streets in a threadbare suit, his hat venerable, his hair unpowdered; he had lost his elasticity and erectness, his teeth were broken, his face wrinkled; ten years had made him an old man as well as a poor one. I lived to see him sunk still lower, driving a little cart into the streets of Philadelphia laden with vegetables, which he sold at the doors of his acquaintance, for his subsistence. " *Sic transit.*"

I made some return for the kindnesses I everywhere re-

ceived, for I became a public benefactor, as the trans-
planter of an elegant recreation and the reviver of a taste
for the fine arts. Noticing in a shop-window the materials
for quadrille, on inquiring the price I discovered that the
owner was ignorant of their use; the fish he sold by the
dozen to accommodate loo players, and the boxes in pairs
to any who would have them. Mentioning this to my
friends, I found that there was not such a thing as a quadrille player in the city! Pitying from the depth of my
soul this Cimmerian darkness, and giving way for the first
time to the belief that these people were but savages in
European clothes, I lost a night's rest in endeavoring to form
some plan for their enlightenment. At a party next evening I disclosed my wishes, and was fortunate enough to
find three individuals who were willing to be rescued from
their ignorance, and devote the next month to my instruc-
tions. Blest with proper tastes, they soon attained proficiency, and before the winter was over my academy had
so enlarged that I beheld, among the other lights of
the closing century, quadrille radiating throughout the
" Western Athens."

My next achievement was yet more important. Having
taken a fancy to an arm-chair at an auctioneer's I walked
into his store to bid for it, when I was struck with an old
portrait lumbered among others in a corner, which seemed
to me a familiar face that only wanted washing. I always
had a fondness for paintings, and having paid pretty dearly for the indulgence, considered I had a right to set up
for a taste. I accordingly extracted the picture, dusted
it, placed it in a proper light, and fell into a reverie.
The broker, delighted to see his most unsalable article
make an impression, exclaimed, "Will 'ee buy that pictur',
sir? I'll sell it cheap. Cover a good bit of wall; it's
Josephus, sir." "Who?" said I. "Josephus, the old
Jewish ginral, or lawyer, or priest, or—summut in the

way of our Mr. Jefferson. Here's his history in folio; you shall have the lot for ten dollars." Forgetting the object of my visit, I ordered them home, and on cleaning the picture found it to be a capital likeness of Quin in Falstaff! so good a painting that it was worth a hundred dollars in America. On disclosing this intelligence, a general rush was made by my acquaintances to the broker, who got more for the rest of his old canvas than if it had been real gobelin tapestry.

I believe it has been denied that that ancient disorder, the disease of writing (*cac. scrib.*—"Mat. Med."), is infectious; though many philosophers have classed it with yawning, bad habits, and the yellow fever; yet on no other ground can I account for *my* becoming a victim. I had had one or two attacks in England, which had passed off harmlessly enough, and left not the slightest evidence by which the world could have detected it. But I had come to a city where it might truly be styled the epidemic. Every one was seized with it, and the literary physicians, who tried to check the inflammation with cold water or wet blankets, were so inefficient that, on the smallest computation, a hundred subjects a day must have yielded to the attack. But my danger was enhanced by my associating with the most infected person in the city, Robert Merry, whose fits were more long and violent than ever. The amount of ink he spilled over paper is incredible; one would have thought he supplied ammunition to all the magazines in Europe. Considering all these circumstances, it can be no wonder that I woke one morning with a confirmed *cac. scrib.* The first symptom I displayed was commencing a novel, after the manner of Smollet (my reader may surmise how far off), when, having brought my hero through the sorrows of childhood, and saved him from imminent peril by sea, I put him in the fire; a mode by which many scribes have, like the Israelites of old,

consecrated their offspring to Moloch. My next attempt
was a history of the stage, but my troubles came on with
King Charles's. I saw all my heroes fighting his battles
instead of Shakespeare's, so stern Oliver Cromwell finished
us together. After these paroxysms my efforts degenerated into mere drivel. I essayed plays and farces out of
number, but my first acts were my last, and my drawers
became filled with skeletons that I never had temper or
talent to put flesh upon. One day I was in fine spirits,
but the sky was cloudy and looked favorable for fishing,
my prevailing weakness; and the next, the sky was fine but
I was cloudy. One moment I was hypercritical, so that
the flame was put out by repeated trimmings of the lamp,
and when I had a tide of thought running with real Mississippi rapidity, Wignell was sure to send an infernal some-
body with a piece just received from London, which I was
to look over and say what I would do in it. Thus time
was lost, till at last I began to impose on myself with the
mock modesty that every field was already sufficiently
cultivated. I'll make no comments on the loss thus inflicted on literature; suffice it that my labors were limited
to a confederacy in a play and a magazine. Of the former,
my old pupil and stagemate, Mrs. Merry,* drew out the
plot, I wrote the lighter parts, and Merry the love-scenes.
It was founded on an anecdote in the life of the benevolent Fénélon. Wignell was so pleased on perusing it,
and expected so much from its production, that he took

---

* MRS. MERRY, known in England as Miss Brunton, was born in 1769, and
first acted at Bath, in 1785. In 1792 she left the stage and married Mr.
Robert Merry. When his means failed, they accepted a tempting offer
from America, and Mrs. Merry made her first appearance in the United
States as Juliet, at Philadelphia, in 1796. Mr. Merry died in 1798, and
in 1803 his widow married Mr. Wignell, who lived but seven weeks after
the wedding. In 1806 she married Mr. Warren, and she died at Alexandria, in 1808.

Fennell* out of jail to play the principal character, but this gentleman's system of living being of a nature which threatened him hourly with a fresh arrest, Merry remarked, "It's Fennell-on to-night; it will be Fennell-off in the morning;" and, much to our chagrin, his pun was a prophecy. Dismissing, therefore, our darling play, which, babe-like, had just opened its eyes, smiled on the world, and died, it may be more amusing to say something of the slaughterer, the said tragedian—a very Herod with dramatic bantlings.

Fennell was one of the most extraordinary specimens of a class it had been my fate so frequently to meet, and my humble endeavor to immortalize—the eccentric. Eccentricity is a sort of orderly disorder; or, if that sound too Irish, a peculiar arrangement by which the greatest contradictions are placed in juxtaposition, as though kitchen utensils were ranged round a drawing-room. Most dazzling schemes for acquiring wealth and fame were, in Fennell's case, the drawing-room furniture; while the kitchen implements were those dramatic talents by which he cut his loaf and cooked his dinner. He was a projector of the most genuine "South-Sea Bubble" species. None of the sages of the flying island, of whom Gulliver makes such honorable mention, could best him in the imaginative faculty which fills a vacuum in a man's head to create an-

---

* JAMES FENNELL, one of the earliest of American tragedians, was born in England, December 11, 1766, not long after his father's return from New York. Fennell first appeared on the stage in 1787, in Edinburgh, where he quarrelled. He then acted in London, at Covent Garden. In 1794 he came to America, and acted first at Philadelphia. He appeared at the Park Theatre in New York in 1800, and again in 1802. He sank into decay before he made his last appearance in 1814. He died in June, 1816, at Philadelphia. He was always erratic and reckless, and these disqualifications kept him from attaining the high position to which his fine histrionic ability entitled him. His rambling and rhapsodic "Apology for the Life of James Fennell" was published at Philadelphia in 1814.

other in his pocket. By a strange perversity, all these
rapid systems of getting riches mostly deposit the project-
or in jail, and Fennell was no exception to this rule. But,
like a tree, his vigor was only increased by clipping. No
man could abound more in faith and resignation, or believe more fully in the resources of the earth and of his
own brain; he was a modern Buckingham, a moral cha-
meleon, perpetually changing—though his clothes were far
from sharing this mutability. That arrant jade, Fancy,
was ever luring him into debt and disgrace, while his
sober spouse, Judgment, would lead him back to the
stage and a subsistence. But, it may be asked, how, without money, did he contrive to put his poetry into practice?
Gentle reader, he had a tongue as oily and as silver-toned
as Cicero's or Romeo's, Sheridan's or John Palmer's; and,
as there are herds of "believers" in all countries, more
willing to speculate for money than to work for it, he became of some use to the community in bringing such to
their senses, and displaying, in the strongest colors, the
loveliness of vulgar industry. He could be an effectual
pump to the deepest mine, and merited Johnson's eulogy
as much as Shakespeare, for he, too, "exhausted worlds
[of capital] and then imagined new."

His career had not been deficient in variety. Educated
at Oxford, and designed for the Church, he decided on the
stage, rode up to town, accosted Mr. Harris in the street,
obtained a début in Othello, was successful, and secured a
three years' engagement. But as anything approaching
to a fixed state of comfort and respectability would be to
an eccentric as water to flame, he visited Edinburgh, incurred debts, was thrown into prison. and set at naught
his obligations to the London manager. The French
Revolution was then breaking out, and every man of
ardent temperament was burning to assist in the great
work of sweeping away old abuses. Accordingly Fennell

JAMES FENNELL.

From the *Polyanthus*, Boston, 1806.

posted to Paris, and opened a school of declamation, in which principles and phrases were equally to be discussed. But this was a field where, however plenteous the harvest, the reapers were too numerous. A rival demagogue denounced him as a spy of William Pitt, and he was obliged to imitate his favorite Cicero in the most unpleasing particular, to decamp at night, and abandon Paris to but one Mirabeau. Returning to London, he commenced his literary career. Finding that Mr. Harris would not renew his engagement, he set up a weekly *Review*, in which, among other evils of the age, he exposed the moral machinery of Mr. Harris's government, with whom it seems the Salic law was not in force. Having considerable talent in clothing truth with the hedgehog garb of satire, the public became interested in the discovery, and the manager was glad to conciliate him with a handsome outfit for America. The Western world opened to him a wider range, and its youthful freshness tempted him like the charms of a first wife. The voyage was a long fit of rumination, but, once landed, his Jack-o'-lantern flittings began. His first project was an academy, in which the boys were to study poetry in bowers, philosophy in groves, and mathematics in Egyptian tombs. Unluckily, the urchins preferred the scenery to the performance; and Fennell was driven to employ his energies for the good of their elders, in devising a system and implements for draining rivers and raising corn in the place of forests. When the result proved that he had only raised expectations and drained his associates, he was ready with an institution that was to become national, a classical Vauxhall, to elevate the tastes of the lower orders. He styled it his Elysian Fields, made the inflexible Minos and Rhadamanthus his money-takers; Ceres, queen of his refectory; the Graces his waiters; the Nine his musicians, with Apollo for their leader; and the heroes of the "Iliad" and "Odyssey," in

towering shapes of pasteboard, dispensers of a lustre unknown to Homer, from variegated lamps. Unfortunately,
not having conciliated the favor of Jupiter Pluvius, a
week's deluge turned this blessed spot into a Tartarus; a
legion of legal Furies rushed in, and Fennell was pitched
into his own Styx (an odorous ditch at the back of his
bowers) without its even rendering him invulnerable, at
least, about the *shoulder*.

Fennell's favorite speculation was salt-works, as he believed he had discovered a process by which any man
possessing twenty yards of sea-beach might stop the
working of the Polish mines, and he tried the experiment
with all the imposing apparatus of vats, pans, and factory,
wherever he could make converts. But the result was invariably the same, and the traveller who was curious
enough to pay his works a visit was pretty sure to find
him sitting on an inverted tub, surveying the general
wreck, like Marius at Carthage. Thus it was a common
joke in the States, when any one remarked that Fennell
was trying another salt scheme, " Yes, yes; he will always be in pickle."

When I state that my second literary enterprise was a
magazine, in which I employed Fennell to write the principal articles, it will be readily surmised that the *Thespian
Mirror* made but very few reflections. Thus was a man,
with talents sufficiently great and various to have enabled
him to shine in any profession, doomed by his evil genius
—an erratic fancy—to exhibit only the fitful, occasional
gleam of the glowworm. Fennell, however, had a gravity
of manner partaking so truly of the humor of Cervantes,
that it seldom failed to extricate him from his troubles,
as was seen in his sermon on patience, addressed to his
creditors. The following affords an instance of his self-
possession. He was playing Macbeth in a summer company, where a native property-man had been engaged,

who became so enamoured of the stage that, forgetting his own duties, he posted himself nightly at the wings to enjoy the performance. Fennell, striding off the stage with due effect to murder Duncan, called for the rose-pink to give his hands and dagger the necessary token. The demand aroused Obadiah to exclaim inquiringly, "Mister?" "Where's the blood, sir?" "Blood, sir? tarnal natur, I ha'n't made none!" "No blood, sir! no blood! when the plot of the play, my very return to the stage, where the audience are expecting me, depends on it!" "Sure alive, sir, I'm mortal sorry, but—I—" here the fellow paused, speechless and motionless, gazing in Fennell's face and Fennell in his. Now I'll venture to say that nine actors out of ten would have felt tempted to knock this man down as dead as Duncan, or have sworn loud enough to have roused any king in Christendom; but Fennell had worked himself up to too sublime a sympathy with Shakespeare to descend to a ridiculous altercation. His genius pointed out the only mode by which the respect due to Macbeth and to the audience could be maintained. Doubling his muscular arm, he planted, with the speed of lightning, a well-directed blow on the nose of the offender. In an instant out gushed a liberal stream of crimson. Fennell, without departing one iota from the dignity of his assumption, caught it in his hands, smeared with it his daggers, then, bending on the stupefied delinquent, who had staggered against the wall, a look of satisfied vengeance, strode back to the stage to exclaim, with more than usual emphasis, "I have done the deed!"

The man whose name a stranger oftenest heard in Philadelphia, and always with interest, was Dr. Franklin, the good genius of the city and the state, the first philosopher, and, with few exceptions, the most serviceable friend America has had. I was now in the daily habit of meeting persons who had been on terms of intimacy with the

Doctor, and who related to me traits of him which I do not think have been published in his "Life," and which may therefore claim a place here. His great principle was that nothing is good or beautiful but in the measure that it is useful; yet that all things have a utility under particular circumstances. Thus poetry, painting, and music (and the stage as their embodiment) are all the necessary and proper gratifications of a refined state of society, but objectionable at an earlier period, since their cultivation would make a taste for enjoyment precede its means. All things have their season, he would say, and with young countries, as with young men, you must curb their fancy to strengthen their judgment. Labor must be their first lot in order to make independence their second. To America, one schoolmaster is worth a dozen poets, and the invention of a machine or the improvement of an implement of more importance than a masterpiece of Raphael. It is by this rule that Franklin's own merits must be judged, and when we consider the fitness of his talents and the measure of his service, who will deny that America could have better spared a dozen Lockes or Shakespeares? He, indeed, deserves, as much as any man, the title of the Father of American Liberty. Many of the early immigrants to Philadelphia had been people of considerable property, who carried over many domestic refinements which raised a restless desire for imitation in the needier inhabitants. Thus envy and discontent on one side, and arrogance and laxity of principle on the other, had, in a short period, rendered this state one of the most factious, dissolute, and indolent in the group, when Franklin, in order to show the people that the true source of happiness was an honest independence, began his "Poor Richard's Almanack," a work which produced an unparalleled effect by the force both of its reasoning and of its humor. His labors may thus be considered one

of the primary causes of the revolution, since, by elevat-
ing the Southern States to a moral equality with New
England, he enabled the tide of liberty to run upon a
level when its flood-gates were pulled up.

In an introduction to his "Almanack," published in 1735,
he tells the story of his stopping his horse at a country
auction, where there was, as usual, a crowd of idle farmers
collected to purchase superfluities. The sale not having
begun, they amused themselves with complaints of the
badness of the times, and appealed to a venerable old man
who was present whether their heavy taxes would not
ruin the country, and ought not government to remit
them ? "It's true," he replied, "that we are taxed heavily on everything we wear and work with, and on much
that we eat and drink; but there are heavier taxes than
these, and which government cannot take off. We are
taxed twice as much by our idleness, three times as much
by our pride, and four times as much by our folly, or we
should be all at our work in the fields instead of loitering
here to buy finery that we can't afford." Surely such doctrine was as applicable in Europe as in America.

One of the Doctor's greatest abhorrences was waste,
not only of time, but also of labor and ingenuity, in the
construction of petty refinements which he called "gim-
cracks." To impress the folly of this he drew up a curious
catalogue of such wasters. One had devoted a whole life
to the copying of the "Iliad" on a piece of vellum which
would go into a nutshell; another (Jerome Faba) presented to Francis I. a coach made from a grain of wheat, yet
containing a lady and gentleman; a third was patronized
by Queen Elizabeth for writing the Liturgy within the
compass of her thumb-nail; while a fourth, mentioned by
Madame Savigny, had constructed a chariot to be drawn
by fleas. When the dauphin asked the Prince of Condé
who had supplied the harness for this equipage, he an-

swered, with much point, "No doubt some spider in the neighborhood."

But of all the evils the Doctor combated, that about which he felt most strongly was the elevation of fashion into a sort of religion. The folly and sin of a man wasting money and time on mint-sling and cock-fighting he could at least understand; but how a woman, with all her weakness, could submit to foreign tastes which, in nine cases out of ten, impaired both her comfort and her beauty, was to him perfectly inexplicable. With what consternation, then, did he view the arrival of a certain adjunct intended to give the outlines of the ladies a more pleasing rotundity. Its effect no sooner struck him than, fearful it might be a new species of tumor, he made inquiries which resulted in discovering that about the year 1783 a certain German duchess had visited Paris, whose Caffrarian distinction fully equalled the magnificence of her other displays. The fair Parisians were paralyzed. They were surpassed in a novelty they had never contemplated. French pride was, however, a sufficient stimulus to French invention, and in a few days an auxiliary was devised which enabled the merest cockboat to sail abroad with the gallery of a three-decker, a projection on which she might have perched one of her livery servants. From Paris the contagion spread to London, and the last ship had brought over, it was supposed, at least six hundred " *Dernier ressorts* " to Philadelphia. The Doctor by some means obtained possession of one, and, finding it was composed of wool, he computed the number of pairs of stockings its material would have afforded to the poor, and stating publicly the amount, along with the origin of the monstrosity, he put the question to the fair sex whether they would not derive more gratification from contributing to the comfort of the indigent, than from applying a muff to that part of their persons which required neither warmth nor ornament.

As a philanthropist, Franklin has had few equals, for while he wrote to prevent misery, by checking error, he lived to afford a practical commentary on his works. His chief pleasure was to encourage the adoption of his principles, yet no man's ear was more open to any plaint of misfortune, though his sympathy was of that highest kind which confers no individual benefit without regarding the collective good.

When riding out one day he passed a farmer sitting listlessly by the roadside, his chin on his hand and his elbow on his knee. Taking this to be a very reprehensible fit of laziness, he drew rein to expostulate, but the first glance at the rustic's face excited his pitying interest. Inquiring into his circumstances, he heard a sad history of failures in regard to land, implements, and live-stock. The details convinced the Doctor of the man's industry, but seemed to throw doubt on his knowledge. "Have you read any of my books, my friend?" said he. "I am Dr. Franklin." At this name the man looked up eagerly, but the next moment relapsed into his former apathy, as if completely heartbroken. "Oh, yes, Doctor," he replied, "I've read your Almanacs—I've worked by 'em, and slept upon 'em—I and my wife and all my boys. But I don't see the good of it; none of your sayings have come true." "No?" exclaimed Franklin; "now which do you mean in particular?" "Why, don't you remember, Doctor, where you say, 'A light hand makes a heavy pocket.' 'He who runs in youth may lie down in age.' 'Industry must prosper,' and all that? Now here have I been sinking deeper and deeper instead of getting on, work as I would." "Humph!" rejoined Franklin; "it strikes me, my friend, that where I say 'Industry must prosper,' there is a note at the bottom to explain." "A note? I don't recollect any notes." "Then it is very likely your copy is an imperfect one; many of my first edi-

tions were; so to-morrow I'll send you a proper one I have
at home, and, if you'll take the trouble to look over it you
will find under the line 'Industry must prosper,' a note
which throws further light on the subject." The Doctor
then bade him good-day and rode on. The next morning
a packet was brought to the farmer's door containing the
Almanac as promised, and after thumbing a few pages he
found the line. Sure enough, beneath it was an explanatory *note*—being one for twenty dollars on the Philadelphia Bank.

Again, what infinite delicacy was mingled with the benevolence of the following : When in Paris, a nightly visitor at a coterie of which Grimm, d'Holbach, and d'Alembert, etc., were the ruling luminaries, Franklin, by his
playful simplicity, captivated a lady of great wealth and
accomplishments, so that they became, in the most English
sense of the phrase, the best of friends. When he was
about to leave the capital she called upon him, and, taking
his hand, her eyes filled with tears, she said, "My dear
friend, you are going home, and I may never see you again.
I shall never forget you so long as I have memory; but I
wish to have some assurance that I shall not be forgotten.
Here is my picture—it is a good likeness; if you will take
it, you will sometimes have me before you." Franklin
looked an instant at the portrait, richly set with diamonds,
and the deeper, better feelings of his nature were stirred.
"Madame," he replied, "permit me to return this picture,
and to propose to you another mode of being kept in my
remembrance. You are very rich. Give me a draft on
your banker for the value of these diamonds, and let me
apply the money, when I reach America, to found a school
for the children of the poor. Such an institution is sure
to prosper; and then, as I grow old, when I go abroad,
I shall see your face in perhaps a hundred miniatures
—the smiles of grateful children, growing up to be hon-

est men." The money was given, and the school was founded.

Franklin's humor had a peculiarly full flavor, it was as direct as his reasoning. One evening he was in company where the conversation turned on the respective merits of the universities at New Haven and Cambridge, each preferring that at which he had been educated. A young prig of a barrister at last interrupted the discussion, by remarking, "For my part, I can't, with fairness, offer an opinion, for I was educated at both." "That puts me in mind," said the Doctor, eying the interlocutor significantly, "of a story, I once heard of a calf that was suckled by two cows." "And what was the result?" asked the prig. "That he was a *very great calf*," was the reply.

He took a very sensible view of female perfection. Walking with a friend in Paris, they were passed by a *degagée* beauty who was celebrated for the symmetry of her nether extremities. "There, Franklin," cried his companion, who was an enthusiast in this particular, "there's a foot! there's perfection! That foot is allowed to be a model for all Europe." "No, it's not," replied he. "No! Why not?" "She has got a hole in her stocking."

CHAPTER V.

1798.—Annapolis.—Society in Maryland.—Mr. Carroll.—Adventure with General Washington; Establishing the Independence of a Chaise; Washington's Appearance; his Conversation; Observations on New and Old England, on Slavery, the Abbé Raynal, the Prince of Wales, and the Drama; his One Jest.—Notices of the Military Heroes of the Revolution. —The Qualifications most Needed.—Charles Lee, the Second in Command; his Character and Career; Supposed to be Junius; his Taking "Five Friends" to the Play; Reply to an Old Maid; Value of a Sword; his Death.—Green, the "Fighting Quaker."—Colonel Tarleton's Joke.— Gates, the Old English Gentleman; his Repartee.—Arnold, the "Political Judas;" his Career and End; a Negro Sarcasm; his Promised Funeral. — Lafayette Compared with Washington; his Reply to a Royalist.—Baron von Steuben; his Poverty; New Use for a Sabre.— "Old Israel" Putnam; the Modern Cincinnatus, his Wolf Adventure; his Daring in War; his Jokes. — Lord Stirling; his Formality; Sayings to his Men; a Private's Retort; Early Rising.—Ethan Allen, the "Rhode Island Oracle;" his Strange Character; his Simplicity.—Kosciusko's Declaration.

OUR season was so prosperous that Wignell delayed his visit to Baltimore till the summer was far advanced, and, as his leave extended but to the middle of June, we opened the house only to close it, and adjourn to the capital of Maryland—which might well be termed the Bath of America—Annapolis.

In this little spot all the best of Philadelphian and Virginian society was concentrated, and here, I am convinced, the most stubborn anti-republican could not but have perceived the absurdity of the common notion that all must be on a level socially because they are so politically. America really contained a true nobility, men of talent, probity, and benevolence, who had been raised by the

public voice to a station which the public feeling bowed
down to—a station not hereditary, or due to one man's
caprice or another's intrigue, but unassailably based on
merit, and open to every one who chose to emulate the
conduct of its possessor. From my Philadelphian friends
I obtained introductions to several occupiers of this position—Mr. Howard, the chancellor, Judge Kelly, Governor
Stone, General Davidson, and last, not least, the excellent
Mr. Carroll, one of the subscribers to the Declaration of
Independence. Perhaps the latter, as much as any man,
was an illustration of my remarks. From the refinement
of his manners, a stranger would have surmised that he
had passed all his days in the *salons* of Paris. He had
all that suavity and softness, in combination with dignity,
which bespeak the perfection of good taste. This attested
the character of his society. Ease may be natural to a
man, but elegance—the union of propriety with ease—
must be acquired; the art of respecting one's company as
well as one's self necessarily implies that one's company is
worth respecting. But Mr. Carroll possessed higher qualities than mere external polish. He had a heart that colored all his thoughts and deeds with the truest hues of
humanity. No man was fonder of doing a good action,
and, certainly, none could do it with a better grace.

A few weeks after my location at Annapolis I met with
a most pleasing adventure, no less than an encounter with
General Washington, under circumstances which most
fully confirmed the impression I had formed of him. I
had been to pay a visit to an acquaintance on the banks
of the Potomac, a few miles below Alexandria, and was
returning on horseback, in the rear of an old-fashioned
chaise, the driver of which was strenuously urging his
steed to an accelerated pace. The beast showed singular
indifference till a lash, directed with more skill than humanity, took the skin from an old wound. The sudden

pang threw the poor animal on his hind-legs, and the wheel swerving upon the bank, over went the chaise, flinging out upon the road a young woman who had been its occupant. The minute before I had perceived a horseman approaching at a gentle trot, who now broke into a gallop, and we reached the scene of the disaster together. The female was our first care. She was insensible, but had sustained no material injury. My companion supported her, while I brought some water in the crown of my hat, from a spring some way off. The driver of the chaise had landed on his legs, and, having ascertained that his spouse was not dead, seemed very well satisfied with the care she was in, and set about extricating his horse. A gush of tears announced the lady's return to sensibility, and then, as her eyes opened, her tongue gradually resumed its office, and assured us that she retained at least one faculty in perfection, as she poured forth a volley of invectives on her mate. The horse was now on his legs, but the vehicle still prostrate, heavy in its frame, and laden with at least half a ton of luggage. My fellow-helper set me an example of activity in relieving it of the external weight; and, when all was clear, we grasped the wheel between us and, to the peril of our spinal columns, righted the conveyance. The horse was then put in, and we lent a hand to help up the luggage. All this helping, hauling, and lifting occupied at least half an hour, under a meridian sun in the middle of July, which fairly boiled the perspiration out of our foreheads. Our unfortunate friend somewhat relieved the task with his narrative. He was a New-Englander who had emigrated to the South when young, there picked up a wife and some money, and was now on his way home, having, he told us, been "made very comfortable" by the death of his father; and when all was right, and we had assisted the lady to resume her seat, he begged us to proceed with him to Alexandria and take a drop of "something sociable." Finding, however, that we were unsociable, he extended his hand (no distant likeness of a seal's fin), gripped ours as he had done the heavy boxes, and, when we had sufficiently *felt* that he was grateful, drove on. My companion, after an exclamation at the heat, offered very courteously to dust my coat, a favor the return of which enabled me to take a deliberate survey of his person. He was a tall, erect, well-made man, evidently advanced in years, but who appeared to have retained all the vigor and elasticity resulting from a life of temperance and exercise. His dress was a blue coat buttoned to his chin, and buckskin breeches. Though, the instant he took off his hat, I could not avoid the recognition of familiar lineaments—which, indeed, I was in the habit of seeing on every sign-post and over every fire-place—still I failed to identify him, and, to my surprise, I found that I was an object of equal speculation in his eyes. A smile at length lighted them up, and he exclaimed, "Mr. Bernard, I believe?" I bowed. "I had the pleasure of seeing you perform last winter in Philadelphia." I bowed again, and he added, "I have heard of you since from several of my friends at Annapolis. You are acquainted with Mr. Carroll?" I replied that that gentleman's society had made amends for much that I had lost in quitting England. He then learned the cause of my presence in the neighborhood, and remarked, "You must be fatigued. If you will ride up to my house, which is not a mile distant, you can prevent any ill-effects from this exertion, by a couple of hours' rest." I looked round for his dwelling, and he pointed to a building which, the day before, I had spent an hour in contemplating. "Mount Vernon!" I exclaimed; and then, drawing back, with a stare of wonder, "have I the honor of addressing General Washington?" With a smile, whose expression of benevolence I have rarely seen equalled, he offered his hand, and replied, "An odd sort of introduction, Mr. Bernard; but I am pleased to find you can play so active a part in private, and without a prompter," and then pointed to our horses (which had stood like statues all this time, as though in sympathy with their fallen brother), and shrugged his shoulders at the inn. I needed no further stimulus to accept his friendly invitation. As we rode up to his house we entered freely into conversation, first, in reference to his friends at Annapolis, then respecting my own success in America and the impressions I had received of the country.

Flattering as such inquiries were from such a source, I must confess my own reflections on what had just passed were more absorbing. Considering that nine ordinary country gentlemen out of ten, who had seen a chaise upset near their estate, would have thought it savored neither of pride nor ill-nature to ride home and send their servants to its assistance, I could not but think that I had witnessed one of the strongest evidences of a great man's claim to his reputation—the prompt, impulsive working of a heart which having made the good of mankind—not conventional forms—its religion, was never so happy as in practically displaying it. On reaching the house (which, in its compact simplicity and commanding elevation, was no bad emblem of its owner's mind), we found that Mrs. Washington was indisposed; but the general ordered refreshments in a parlor whose windows took a noble range of the Potomac, and, after a few minutes' absence, rejoined me.

Though I have ventured to offer some remarks on his less-known contemporaries, I feel it would be an impertinence to say a word on the public merits of a man whose character has been burning as a beacon to Europe till its qualities are as well known as the names and dates of his triumphs. My retrospect of him is purely a social one, and much do I regret, for the interest of these pages, that it is confined to a single interview. The general impression I received from his appearance fully corresponded with the description of him by the Marquis de Chatelluz, who visited America at the close of the war. "The great characteristic of Washington," says he, "is the perfect union which seems to subsist between his moral and physical qualities; so that the selection of one would enable you to judge of all the rest. If you are presented with medals of Trajan or Cæsar, the features will lead you to inquire the proportions of their persons; but if you should discover in a heap of ruins the leg or arm of an antique Apollo, you would not be curious about the other parts, but content yourself with the assurance that they were all conformable to those of a god." Though fourteen years had elapsed since this was written, I could perceive that it was far from being the language of mere enthusiasm. Whether you surveyed his face, open yet well defined, dignified but not arrogant, thoughtful but benign; his frame, towering and muscular, but alert from its good proportion—every feature suggested a resemblance to the spirit it encased, and showed simplicity in alliance with the sublime. The impression, therefore, was that of a most perfect whole; and though the effect of proportion is said to be to reduce the idea of magnitude, you could not but think you looked upon a wonder, and something sacred as well as wonderful—a man fashioned by the hand of Heaven, with every requisite to achieve a great work. Thus a feeling of awe and veneration stole over you.

In conversation his face had not much variety of expression: a look of thoughtfulness was given by the compression of the mouth and the indentation of the brow (suggesting an habitual conflict with and mastery over passion) which did not seem so much to disdain a sympathy with trivialities as to be incapable of denoting them.

Nor had his voice, so far as I could discover in our quiet talk, much change, or richness of intonation, but he always spoke with earnestness, and his eyes (glorious conductors of the light within) burned with a steady fire which no one could mistake for mere affability; they were one grand expression of the well-known line, "I am a man, and interested in all that concerns humanity." In our hour and a half's conversation he touched on every topic that I brought before him with an even current of good sense, if he embellished it with little wit or verbal elegance. He spoke like a man who had felt as much as he had reflected, and reflected more than he had spoken; like one who had looked upon society rather in the mass than in detail; and who regarded the happiness of America but as the first link in a series of universal victories; for his full faith in the power of those results of civil liberty which he saw all around him led him to foresee that it would, ere long, prevail in other countries, and that the social millenium of Europe would usher in the political. When I mentioned to him the difference I perceived between the inhabitants of New England and of the Southern States he remarked, "I esteem those people greatly; they are the stamina of the Union and its greatest benefactors. They are continually spreading themselves too, to settle and enlighten less favored quarters. Dr. Franklin is a New-Englander." When I remarked that his observations were flattering to my country, he replied, with great good-humor, "Yes, yes, Mr. Bernard, but I consider your country the cradle of free principles, not their arm-chair. Liberty in England is a sort of idol; people are bred up in the belief and love of it, but see little of its doings. They walk about freely, but then it is between high walls; and the error of its government was in supposing that after a portion of their subjects had crossed the sea to live upon a common, they would permit their friends at home to build up those walls about them." A black coming in at this moment, with a jug of spring water, I could not repress a smile, which the general at once interpreted. "This may seem a contradiction, he continued, "but I think you must perceive that it is neither a crime nor an absurdity. When we profess, as our fundamental principle, that liberty is the inalienable right of every man, we do not include madmen or idiots; liberty in their hands would become a scourge. Till the mind of the slave has been educated to perceive what are the obligations of a state of freedom, and not confound a man's with a brute's, the gift would insure its abuse. We might as well be asked to pull down our old warehouses before trade has increased to demand enlarged new ones. Both houses and slaves were bequeathed to us by Europeans, and time alone can change them; an event, sir, which, you may believe me, no man desires more heartily than I do. Not only do I pray for it, on the score of human dignity, but I can clearly foresee that nothing but the rooting out of slavery can perpetuate the existence of our union, by consolidating it in a common bond of principle."

I now referred to the pleasant hours I had passed in Philadelphia, and my agreeable surprise at finding there so many men of talent, at which his face lit up vividly. "I am glad to hear you, sir, who are an Englishman, say so, because you must now perceive how ungenerous are the assertions people are always making on your side of the water. One gentleman, of high literary standing—I allude to the Abbé Raynal—has demanded whether America has yet produced one great poet, statesman, or philosopher. The question shows anything but observation, because it is easy to perceive the causes which have combined to render the genius of this country scientific rather than imaginative. And, in this respect, America has surely furnished her quota. Franklin, Rittenhouse, and Rush are no mean names, to which, without shame, I may append those of Jefferson and Adams as politicians; while I am told that the works of President Edwards of Rhode Island are a text-book in polemics in many European colleges."

Of the replies which I made to his inquiries respecting England, he listened to none with so much interest as to those which described the character of my royal patron, the Prince of Wales. "He holds out every promise," remarked the general, "of a brilliant career. He has been well educated by *events*, and I doubt not that, in his time, England will receive the benefit of her child's emancipation. She is at present bent double, and has to walk with crutches; but her offspring may teach her the secret of regaining strength, erectness, and independence." In reference to my own pursuits he repeated the sentiments of Franklin: he feared the country was too poor to be a patron of the drama, and that only arts of a practical nature would for some time be esteemed. The stage he considered to be an indispensable resource for settled society and a chief refiner; not merely interesting as a comment on the history of social happiness by its exhibition of manners, but an agent of good as a school for poetry, in holding up to honor the noblest principles. "I am too-old and too far removed," he added, "to seek for or require this pleasure myself, but the cause is not to droop on my account. There's my friend, Mr. Jefferson, has time and taste; he goes always to the play, and I'll introduce you to him," a promise which he kept, and which proved to me the source of the greatest benefit and pleasure.

As I was engaged to dine at home, I at length rose to take my leave, not without receiving from the general a very flattering request to call on him whenever I rode by.

I had the pleasure of meeting him once after this in Annapolis, and I dined with him on a public occasion at Alexandria, my impressions each time improving into a higher degree of respect and admiration.

I have never heard of but one jest of Washington's, which was related to me by his aide-de-camp, my good friend, Colonel Humphreys. The general, rather priding himself on his riding, the colonel was induced, one day when they were out hunting together, to offer him a bet that he would not follow him over one particular hedge. The challenge was accepted, and Humphreys led the way and took the leap boldly, but, to his consternation, discovered that he had mistaken the spot, and was deposited, up to his horse's girths, in a quagmire. The general either knew the ground better, or had suspected something, for, following at an easy pace, he reined up at the hedge, and, looking over at his engulfed aide, exclaimed, "No, no, colonel, you are too *deep* for me !"

Most of my acquaintances at Annapolis had been spectators of the Revolution, and, as that event was one of our most frequent topics, I gleaned at their tables many anecdotes of its military agents, which were afterwards enlarged upon by my good friends Mr. Jefferson and Colonel Humphreys. It may, therefore, be not unacceptable if I offer my readers a few glimpses of the satellites who surrounded the great luminary, and who, remaining comparatively obscure, yet become interesting in the measure they now appear to have contributed to his radiance.

If the "modern Fabius" possessed a mind so happily constituted that fortune could as little disarm it of caution as adversity of enterprise, it was owing to that sound judgment which, conscious of the military inferiority of his countrymen, saw that his only chance of success lay in either leading his enemies into positions where local circumstances would conquer, or in reducing them in detail. Thus the decisive blow at Trenton turned the tide when it had nearly engulfed every hope; and the events of Saratoga and Yorktown proved the pillars of the Independence. Into only one openly contested fight (Brandywine) did he permit himself to be drawn, and that was in compliance with a general prejudice, its result confirming the soundness of his principle. But, in addition to the adoption of this policy, the success of the struggle depended on certain personal qualities in the leaders rather than on professional ability. Military knowledge was, of course, a great desideratum, and, as the native officers possessed nothing of the kind, when Lee, Gates, Von Steuben, and Montgomery, four experienced disciplinarians, proffered their swords, their value was properly estimated. But to possess this knowledge was one thing; to impart it another. The very spirit which had thrown the Americans together for the defence of their country indisposed them to submit to the regulations which would make their union efficient. They had been so nurtured in the habit of thinking and doing as they pleased that they were not prepared to yield obedience, even for a time, except where their own wills were consulted. Knowing nothing of the good of subordination, they saw only its exactions. Thus the troops of different colonies considered themselves perfectly independent of each other, and would only serve under their own officers; and these disagreements were multiplied in every possible shape when the fever-heat of the first campaign had gone off, and left them to its privation and fatigue. Their leaders were absorbed in the prospective blessings of the struggle; *they* felt more acutely the immediate sacrifice. Thus he proved himself the best commander who was most proficient in the art of reconciling their discordance, and keeping up a spirit of good-will. Unanimity of feeling fed the flame of devotion, steeled them to suffering, and bowed them to discipline. This fact places the personal characters of the officers in a new and interesting light, for the question as to qualification was not here, have you the most courage? are you the best soldier? but, have you the most temper? are you the better man? A knowledge of human nature took precedence of tactics, and to be a great commander was to be no mean philosopher. Thus the mystery is explained how Washington contrived to keep an army about him in all his great straits and reverses; how Lee succeeded in introducing so much organization; and how Montgomery and Arnold were enabled to invade Canada. Nevertheless this popularity was but one step towards success, for only those officers who conformed to their leader's policy throughout the conflict were really instrumental to its grand result.

Green and Gates, it appears, were Washington's favorites. They were men of a similarly cool, considerative character, adherents of his "Fabian system," and by many credited with having shaped his most important plans. Lee and Arnold, on the contrary, were the favorites of the army, and advocates of an opposite principle. To them the delays and manœuvrings of Washington were as wearying as they were to the English, and they averred that the system would weaken the spirit of the pursued more fatally than the resources of the pursuers. The fact was they were both good generals of division, fine fellows for the executive—a pair of fiery, headlong, pell-mell fighters, in the style of the old cavaliers, who thought a victory desirable on any terms. Arnold had more knowledge of localities, and greater talent in collecting resources, and was thus enabled to accomplish his extraordinary march into Canada; but Lee was, in every sense, the better soldier and the cleverer man, and when captured by Colonel Harcourt, six officers of nearly equal rank were offered in exchange for him. Montgomery ("the rebel eulogized in Parliament") well deserved his reputation for bravery, skill, and goodness, though the attempt which cost him his life seems to impugn his judgment. The venerable Putnam, the Nestor of the band, had less military talent than patriotic devotion; and Schuyler, Sullivan, Lincoln, and the rest, if they equalled him in this respect, did not exceed him in activity. To aid the exertions of these single-minded men Germany and France made, in every sense, a noble contribution—witness the Barons Von Steuben, De Glaubeck, and Von Kalb; the Marquis Chastelluz, Count Pulaski, Lafayette, and Kosciusko.

Amid this group stands out Charles Lee, the "second in command," and the first in ability and influence. Lee was a strange compound of good and evil. By nature high-spirited, generous, and jovial, he resembled, in many points, the free and hearty thinkers, livers, and fighters of the Middle Ages, but, unlike them, was free from the love of lucre, and owed all his impulse to an ambition which was patriotic, and, but for its excess, would have been honorable to himself and beneficial to others. But, in his ardor for the general good, he overlooked the necessity for individual example. His temper, naturally impetuous, became soured by long submission to inferior minds, while his convivial habits vulgarized his tastes and relaxed his morals. His disappointments in Europe increased his yearnings for America, and there, when at length his hopes were frustrated, all the energy and dignity he had left fell with them. He had set his heart upon a cast, and loss was moral death.

Those who accused Lee of joining the Provincial standard only out of pique at his treatment at Whitehall knew nothing of his history. He had been a Republican even in childhood, when at school in Switzerland, contrasting the condition of her hardy mountaineers with that of the oppressed peasantry of France; and when in America, serving under Abercrombie, he wrote a pamphlet on the question of ceding Canada to France, which proved his early sympathy with the welfare of the colonies. In Portugal he gained for his exertions the thanks of royalty, but the passing of the Stamp Act, two years afterwards, drew from him a letter which excited general notice by its spirited denunciation of the folly and oppressiveness of that measure; while he also used every effort to increase the spirit of resistance to it in the House of Commons. A soldier whose achievements were of this kind was not likely to bask in sunshine at Whitehall, and he accordingly got leave to enter the Polish service, where he became aide-de-camp to the king, with the rank of major-general. Here he still wielded his pen in behalf of freedom and the colonies; but, when driven home in 1773, by the consequences of a duel, he resolved to throw aside a weapon the time for which seemed past, and to offer America his sword. Thus it appears that, with the exception of Lafayette, not one of the patriots furnished such proofs of devotion to the cause as Lee. By his writings he had sacrificed his interests at home, and, now the hour was come for action, he threw into the scale an income of nearly £1000 a year. His celebrity at this period, both as a soldier and a politician, may be gathered from the enthusiasm with which all classes hailed his advent. Adams, on introducing Paine to him, wrote, "The whole Whig world is blessing your expedition to America, and no one more so than myself;" and, indeed, from the hour that he planted his foot upon the strand, he became a moving firebrand, traversing the States from north to south, to kindle and keep up resistance. It is even very probable that he was the first suggester of the Declaration of Independence, in his letter to Mr. Rutledge, Chairman of the Board of War, in 1775, in which he urges the necessity of the measure, as the only means of giving stability to the government, and obtaining that assistance from France and Holland which would enable the army to continue in the field. Congress eagerly secured his services, and he was appointed to the chief command in the South; but his successes up to the period of his capture by Colonel Harcourt raised a party against him, who averred that, coveting his own distinction rather than the public good, he now aimed at supplanting Washington, by endeavoring to throw doubt on his military judgment. The only circumstance which lent a color to this suspicion was his conduct at the battle of Monmouth, where, being in command, with an opportunity to carry out his favorite plan of attack, Washington, on coming up, found him retreating. An altercation ensued, in which Lee gave way to his usual violence, and was deposed on the spot, Green being appointed in his place. Lee then sent two furious letters to the commander-in-chief, who, to maintain subordination, brought him before a court-martial, which suspended him for a twelvemonth. This ended his career. He retired to a small property, which he had purchased, at the solicitation of his friend Gates, in Pennsylvania, and there, in a wretched hovel, with scarce a window or a door, he passed the remainder of his days, amid a kennel of dogs, whom his philosophy led him to consider preferable companions to men. Of Lee's character, it appears to me, but one opinion can be formed. Whatever were his private failings, his patriotism was really unimpeachable. His conduct at Monmouth was explained by the fact that his orders were discretionary, and that, finding the enemy his superior, both in numbers and position, he looked on a retreat as inevitable, in order to save his men. It is obvious he fell into the error of underrating the stamina of the Provincial troops, who, during the year and a half he had been a prisoner at New York, had greatly improved in discipline, and been fired by one or two successes. Whatever may be thought of the unhappy climax of his career, no American will deny that his zeal had been of the utmost service in encouraging all ranks to the struggle; though it is equally evident he was much more fitted to commence an outbreak than to conduct one to a prosperous conclusion. Had it been the destiny of Washington to fall, and Lee had succeeded him, his impetuosity would very likely have compromised the cause. His abilities, both as a soldier and a writer, are fully evidenced: the former by his campaign in the Carolinas (where from his successes against Clinton he was termed that general's "evil genius"), and the latter by his literary and political publications, and his correspondence with Burke, Franklin, Adams, etc. To his classical attainments he added a wide range of observation, and his writings afford a faithful picture of his mind. With little grace, correctness, or connection, they are marked by an intensity of purpose, a power of sarcasm, and a boldness of deduction which were peculiar to the man. Perhaps the most important tribute to his literary power was the published assertion of Mr. Girdlestone, in 1813, that in General Lee he had discovered that much-disputed, all-engrossing problem of his own time—Junius. With the arguments of this pamphlet I am not acquainted, but I should say they do not rest upon the internal evidence of style. With equal ardor in the cause of freedom, and equal scorn of place-men and abuses, Lee wants the ease and polish, the logical and verbal force, the brevity and apothegm which have rendered Junius, despite of personalities, an English classic.

A happy specimen of Lee's sarcasm is a letter to Hume upon his "History of England," in which he thanks the author for bringing him to a true knowledge of Charles I., whom, in his boyhood, he had conceived to be a tyrant.

His comment upon Lord North, too, is as ludicrous as it is severe. "I do believe," he remarked, "such is his lordship's hatred of the name, that if he knew there was a freeman shivering on the shores of Nova Zembla, and he had his will, he would put his country to the expense of fitting out an army and a fleet to extirpate him."

Most of the anecdotes that were told of Lee had reference to his eccentric love of dogs, and some of them attested that his humor was as strong as his "animal passion." My reader will, perhaps, scarcely credit the following, but it is a fact. After the peace he was a good deal pestered by an actor who begged him to patronize an evening entertainment at a neighboring tavern. Lee for some time demurred, on the ground of his secluded life and changed tastes, but as the applicant went on to lay great stress on his name and connections, he observed, "Oh, then it's not merely me you wish to come, but my friends." "Certainly, general, your friends." "Well, sir, I have but five friends in the world, and those I consent to bring with me on condition that you secure for us the six front chairs, so that we may see and hear without interruption." This proviso was readily agreed to; Lee paid for the tickets, and away hopped the manager, rubbing his hands at his unhoped-for success. When the night came the room overflowed and there was a loud outcry for chairs, but the six in front were sacred to "General Lee and his friends." The candles were lit; the black fiddlers had executed an overture; the time of performance had arrived, but not the general, so its commencement was delayed in deference to the six front chairs. At length, when expectation had reached fever-heat, an altercation with the doorkeeper was heard, and a report arose that the general's friends were refused admittance. Every one rose in consternation, and the gentlemen called out for the manager. Down rushed the affrighted Thes-

pian in time to hear Lee deliver one of those verbal thun-
derbolts which had been said to electrify their objects on
training-days. "Stand back, sir!" shouted the director to
his servant; "don't you know General Lee has a party?
Permit me, general, to apologize." He was advancing to
do so, when the veteran strode in, and, lo! at his heels his
five favorite hounds, each carrying a ticket in its mouth.
The petrified spectator had only breath for an exclamation, as Lee proceeded leisurely to his seat and made each
of the dogs mount a chair and compose himself in the
manner that they usually surrounded his table. My reader may surmise the effect upon the company, the pro-
longed peals of laughter that followed the first simultaneous shout, not a little enhanced by the well-sustained
gravity of the general. At length the person patronized
gave vent to his astonishment in the exclamation, "Good
heavens! general, this is very strange." "Strange, sir!"
he echoed; "you asked me to bring my *friends;* I told
you that I had but five in the world; these are they. I
go nowhere without them. I have paid for their tickets;
you have secured our places; so go on with the performance." These words were decisive; the bell rang; the
singers came forward; but the instant they caught sight
of five such extraordinary critics, each swinging out some
inches of tongue in proof of his powers of discernment
and taste, they, too, found the spectacle irresistible. This
set the audience off again, and the new amusement quite
superseded the announced one. At length the cachinna-
tion reached its climax, for, either by strong sympathy
or Lee's contrivance, the dogs burst suddenly into a loud
and wild howl, which threw the window-panes into an
ague fit, and brought the landlord and his servants rushing up-stairs. Lee now rose, and with infinite gravity
bowing to the bewildered director, observed that his
friends having so loudly expressed their gratification at

the performance, made it incumbent on him to tender their collective thanks, as he most respectfully bade them good-evening. He then bowed to the audience and led his "friends" out. As may be supposed, this expedient quite answered its purpose, and Lee was never again troubled for his patronage.

To balance this one penchant he had a host of antipathies, the strongest of which, perhaps, was to that species of the fair sex who at an age when the sourest crab should lose a little of its acidity, forego their resemblance to angels to delight in the occupation of fleas—back-biting. A slanderous old *cat* seemed to him the true antipodes of a noble *dog*. A lady of this description of whom he had heard much, but who was ignorant of his feelings, met him during a morning's walk surrounded by his usual companions, and lisped, "Good-morning, general. La! how strange; always with these animals about you; you must be very fond of dogs." "Yes, madam," he replied, fixing his eyes most significantly on hers, "dogs, but not ——" the "other animal" was sufficiently understood.

One of the strongest evidences that Lee was a disappointed man was that, much as he loved the inspiration of Bacchus, it seldom had a divine effect. When it failed to lull him to forgetfulness, it roused him to all kinds of splenetic extravagance; yet it was only on these occasions that his sayings kept pace in point of cleverness with his deeds, as cider by particular nursing may be worked up into champagne. When the question was discussed one evening, after dinner, whether the King of France would not be willing to lend assistance to America if the recovery of Canada were held out as an inducement, Lee shook his head. "What," exclaimed a native officer, "do you think America contains no baits for the French king?" "Oh," replied he, "I have no doubt if you asked him he would say we are all *bêtes*."

Let me, however, append to all this a proof that, amid the smoke and soot, the fires of a noble nature would sometimes force their way. It is an anecdote I received from Colonel Humphreys, and which I take great pleasure in repeating.

Lee met one evening, in the streets of Philadelphia, an officer who had served with him in the Peninsula, and then, by a variety of misfortunes, been compelled to emigrate. Finding he was in great distress, he took him home, and, unable himself to relieve him, next day sent his own sword to a wealthy merchant of the city with a note to the effect that Charles Lee, who had drawn this sword for the independence of America, was now without means to take an old friend out of trouble, and therefore offered it in pledge for the loan of a certain sum. The merchant replied by returning the weapon with a check for double the amount. Lee put the money into his friend's hands and observed, with a smile, " Do you remember, Jack, when you used to write me letters abusing me for deserting the king? Now, I hope you'll admit that my sword has done some good in America."

The death of Lee had something in it very touching, as illustrative of the unbroken spirit of the soldier. A friend calling to see him at the inn where he was lying in Philadelphia, found him, attended by a faithful Italian, sitting upright in bed, hands clinched on its frame, and his eyes glaring fiercely. At that moment he imagined himself once more amid the shock and shout of battle, and as the fire of life shot up its latest spark, he uttered his last words: " Stand fast, my brave grenadiers!"

The greatest opposite to Lee in every personal characteristic was Green, one of the most amiable, but also most resolute of men, considering his initiatory triumph in bursting sectarian bonds no less enthralling than those of the mother country. Incongruous as it may seem, there

was, no doubt, much in his education as a Quaker which
fitted him for the duties he afterwards undertook, by forming early habits of temperance, self-command, and endur-
ance.   Green was very aptly compared by Dr. Franklin
to "a pool of clear water suddenly congealed," yet his
manners were marked by a quiet affability so far removed
from Quakerish constraint that friend and enemy found
them equally engaging.   If other testimony than the esteem of Washington were needed to show this man's social
excellence, it might be gathered from his instructive and
conciliatory communications with his sect.   Of his merits
as a soldier his brilliant campaign in the South, which
paved the way for Cornwallis's surrender, after the defeat
at Camden had made the Whig cause almost hopeless, is
a sufficient attestation.   Notable alike for coolness, energy, and forethought, had Washington been called away,
Green was the only man upon whom his mantle could
have fallen.

He was reported to have met an old friend of his father's, when riding out for a survey near Guildford, a
few days previous to the engagement.   The disciple of
Fox knew him in an instant, and with clasped hands and
horrified eyes stood to survey this stray sheep in the obnoxious habilaments of his new calling.   Green drew up
and saluted him.   "So Nathaniel," exclaimed the man in
drab, with a heavy sigh, "it is thou!   I have heard of
thee with sorrow.   Dost thou know thou art the first
man among thy brethren who hath drawn the sword?"
"Yes, friend," replied he, with meek decision, "and, till
our liberties are secured, I shall be the last man among
my brethren to sheathe it."

On his conduct in battle, perhaps Lord Rawdon made
the most amusing comment.   The day after the affair at
Guildford his lordship was breakfasting with Colonel Tarleton, and, talking over the engagement, observed: "Well,

I don't know what this Green may be in a chapel, but curse me if he's a *Quaker* in the field." "And if he's not a Quaker," rejoined Tarleton, as he pointed to the list of killed and wounded, " curse me if he's a *friend.*"

Of such a man Horatio Gates was no unworthy coadjutor, though his success at Saratoga raised expectations which his after-fortunes failed to fulfil. It is a curious circumstance that he should have served with Lee in Portugal under Burgoyne, and, failing to obtain promotion, should have emigrated to America to become the capturer of his old commander. General Gates was an instance of the good old high-principled, well-informed English officer, a class which has presented the world with some of the most favorable specimens of the national character. His manners were so attractive, his mind so well stored, that no man enjoyed a larger measure of personal esteem. Lee, in his eccentric moments, used to say, " The army likes Washington because he's a patriot; me because I'm a soldier, and Gates because he's a gentleman." He was, moreover, a pleasant companion, with a bent for repartee. It was supposed that when he and Lee accepted command, they still held commissions in the English service, and consequently were liable to the penalty of traitors. A friend, hearing this, observed to him, " Good heavens, Gates, is it the fact that if you are taken you are likely to be hanged?" " I believe so," he replied; "but what of that? I have for a long while been suspended."

It was America's boast that the war had produced but one Arnold. Fortunately the world has not produced many. To the credit of humanity such villains are not natural to the events which beget them, and their blackness offends the more from the contrasting brightness around. Arnold was a sort of social wrecker, only thriving upon storms; a foul fungus which still flourished where fruit and flower were crushed. He began life as the keeper of a liquor shop on the wharves of New York; then fitted out a schooner and smuggled slaves from the West Indies; afterwards, as a general agent, brought some scores of people to ruin; and, on the breaking-out of hostilities, took to patriotism, as the only trade left him. But that the service of Liberty surrounds the meanest head with a halo, and is supposed to purify the grossest materials, it would be a wonder how such a man, with all his talent, ever rose to command. It is obvious that while winning the gratitude of his country he was supporting a laborious hypocrisy, anxiously calculating which service would pay him best, till his career at Philadelphia brought him to a decision. There, in emulaticn of General Howe, he kept open house, gambled, intrigued, and plunged into debt, when, finding he could obtain no more supplies, he communicated with Sir Henry Clinton with a view of raising money on his political integrity. To the disgrace of that otherwise exemplary officer, and of the cause he was engaged in, Arnold's plan to betray West Point was entertained, and on its failure his old luck did not desert him. Nicodemus conveyed him safely on board the English sloop, while poor André was seized and condemned to swing alone upon a scarcely merited gibbet. Yet how superior was André's fate, for he died amid the tears of even his enemies, and to this hour his memory evokes sympathy; while the " political Judas," though he lived to possess a pension and to meet, when full of years, an easy death in England, could not escape the retributive execration by which the uncompromising spirit of English honor adjusted the error of public expediency. He lived an exile and an outcast of whom both countries were ashamed.

By Sir Henry Clinton he appears to have been chiefly employed as a Pandour, and it is sickening to observe the activity with which he justified the appointment. A mounted fiend could hardly in less time have spread needless flame and ruin. Yet, however dead he might be to compunction, the general contempt must have rendered his condition anything but enviable. Soon after he landed on the coast of Virginia he saw some horses in a field, and, intent on making an advantageous seizure, called to the negro in charge to inquire their respective merits. Oronoko proved very communicative, and amused Arnold with the appellations by which he distinguished his favorites. "So, then," said the querist, "you call that gray horse, because he carries his head so high, General Washington; and the bay one, because he has a quiet temper, General Green; now, what the devil do you call that black, shaggy fellow, that is looking over the hedge?" "Why, massa, I call him General Arnol', 'cause he so d——d bad; he always run away."

The reply is well known, yet is worthy of repetition, which an American made to Arnold on being asked by him what treatment he might expect from Congress, should he fall into its hands. "Your right leg, which was wounded at Quebec in the cause of freedom," said the patriot, "it would cut off and bury with military honors, but the rest of your body would be consigned to a gibbet."

What a singular contrast to such a character was Lafayette, the most chivalric defender of human rights and freemen's dignity that history bids us honor; one who revived the entire devotion and self-surrender of what has been termed "the most generous era of the world," not for the winning of a woman's smile or a prince's favor, but to promote the welfare of his meanest fellow-creature.

Lafayette was the only man of modern times who has approached the height of Washington. Their difference

was mental and partly due to temperament, for, as regards
moral qualities, their hearts beat pulse for pulse and they
were animated by the same spirit. One were they as
twin children in simplicity and ingenuousness; one as
brothers, in energy and courage. In the profounder at-
tributes of the legislator—calmness, knowledge, and the
power of weighing principles—Washington stood alone;
but on the same level with him of patriotic faith and self-
devotion stood Lafayette. Perhaps in their notions of
liberty the latter was more ideal, Washington the more
philosophic; the one aimed at establishing republics upon
principles only compatible with a large diffusion of intelligence; the other at adapting government to the present
imperfections of mankind, by retaining only just that
measure of restraint with which freedom must necessarily
be limited. Lafayette, however, must be acknowledged
as the high-priest of Cosmopolitanism, or the love of mankind, a loftier kind of virtue surely than patriotism—the
love of man in sections. It has been questioned whether
the defence of one's own home and land is not, after all,
as much a matter of interest as of principle. But what
shall we say of a man who, born to high rank and ample
fortune, placed at court as a captain of the royal guard,
and wedded to the daughter of an influential nobleman,
yet sacrificed every honor and enjoyment to espouse the
interests of a distant country, at a time when its affairs
appeared so hopeless that its agents in Paris were unable
even to provide him with a vessel. His words on that occasion expressed the spirit of his after-life: "Then I will
fit one out myself." Landing at Charleston, in 1777, when
but nineteen years of age, he found the government without resources and the army without food or clothing,
fleeing before the Royalists. He instantly raised and
equipped a body of men at his own expense, then entered
the army as a volunteer. After rendering important ser-

vice in several actions, he resolved, in 1779, to aid America more effectually by inducing France to lend her assistance. Through his exertions this end was accomplished, and he returned to America to command a regiment for whose equipment and support he raised £2000 at Baltimore upon his own credit. His rescue of Richmond, and long trial of generalship with Cornwallis, who boasted that "the boy should not escape him," are among the proofs of his devotion to the cause.

Lafayette's first arrival in America gave such an impulse to the drooping spirits of the patriots that favorable auguries were again entertained of the war, though the royal forces were then everywhere victorious. A gentleman holding a Crown appointment thought it his duty to call privately on the young adventurer and remonstrate with him on his desperate intentions. "Do you not see, sir," said he, "that there is but one fate for the insurgents —a speedy and complete subjugation; and but one reward for their abettors, be they who they may—privation, disappointment, and, most likely, death?" Lafayette, eying him calmly, replied, "I came here to *die,* sir. I could have *lived* in my own country."

A fellow-spirit to this noble man, and an equally important aid to the cause he embarked in, was the Baron Von Steuben, to whom, in conjunction with Lee, the army may be said to have owed all its discipline. The baron had been trained in a good school, for he resigned the dignities of lieutenant-general in the Prussian army, and favorite aide-de-camp of Frederick the Great, for the moral honors of a patriotic struggle. The value of his services was instantly appreciated; Congress appointed him inspector-general of the army; and the result of his efforts fully justified the expectations that had been formed of him. Whatever may be thought of his soldiership, no man surpassed the baron in one of the most popular evidences of Republicanism—poverty; though, in strange alliance with his needs and principles, lived a touch of his baronial dignity, for he was as proud as he was poor. Wishing to give an entertainment to the English officers after the surrender of Yorktown, as other major-generals had done before him, he was compelled to sell his horse, in order to raise the money required. On a previous occasion he had parted with his silver spoons and forks, to gain funds to reciprocate the civilities of his French compatriots; and it was said that when his servant, who had been ordered to dispose of a family relic —a silver-handled carving-knife—asked him how he intended to cut up his beef, he replied, "If I can get nothing better, I'll beg the company's permission to use my sabre."

Most of the native leaders were of the family of Cincinnatus, but no one so strikingly akin to that celebrity as the patriarchal Putnam, whose whole life was such an alternation between fighting and farming that one would suppose he could scarcely have had time to bend his sword into a sickle before he was required to thump it straight again. He led a body of Provincials through the whole of the French war; in 1762 accompanied Lord Albemarle against the Havanna; in 1764 marched a native regiment against the Indians on the Western frontiers; in 1770, joined General Lyman in exploring the Mississippi; and was enjoying his usual relief to all these duties—the act of ploughing—when the news reached him of the outbreak of hostilities with England. Calling to a boy to mind his oxen, and without staying to change his clothes, or even wash his face, he sprang upon his horse, and rode off to the scene of action. "Old Israel," as he was fondly rather than familiarly called, was the beau ideal of a martial Puritan, and, perhaps, the greatest favorite with the country, after Washington, for even

Green did not command so general and deep a regard. Many circumstances combined to cause this result: the useful and exemplary character of his long life; the renown of his wolf adventure; and the singularity of a man, whose days had reached the ordinary limit, rising up, as if endued with new being, to defend the dwellings of his children. But, with all his military spirit, he never had the credit of being a tactician. The fact was he was a soldier upon principle, not upon system. He had full faith in the lawfulness and efficacy of a straightforward plan of exchanging blows, but despised the tricks and artifices which compose the science of what the world calls generalship. Of one warlike essential he had almost a superfluity, for his courage, but for the cause in which it was displayed, might have been termed a madness. He, as an old man, laughed at dangers which blanched the cheeks of the young. With his wolf adventure all, in his day, were familiar. If the reader be not so, I may briefly state that, having pursued the ravager of his fold into a Connecticut cavern, the aperture to which was only large enough to permit his ingress on all fours, he lit a pine branch and crept in, holding the light before him, in order to discover the enemy's position. The bright glare of her eyeballs, shining like two lamps, and a low, significant growl, soon let him know this, and he gave the signal for his friends to drag him out by the legs. He then loaded his gun with a dozen buckshot, and, relighting the pine branch, again entered the aperture—crept near enough to take a certain aim—and, as his victim was on the point of springing, fired. The wolf fell back with a howl, and he, resolutely grasping her by the ears, his friends seized him by the heels, and they were drawn out together.

During the war he coveted all the most dangerous posts and expeditions, and his uniform success created a confi-

dence in him amounting to superstition. What would
have seemed folly in another, with him was a mere matter
of course. When he was encamped with Sullivan and
Stirling, at Flatbush, he undertook to convey despatches
to the Jerseys through Lord Howe's fleet, in an open boat,
and, though overhauled by every other ship, his fearlessness and address insured his safety. He was soon after
pursued by a troop of horse, when retreating through
Rhode Island with a piece of artillery. His party managed to drag the gun to an eminence, which was flanked
by a swamp and thicket, and here he, with a few others,
loaded and fired, keeping the horsemen at bay till nearly
all his men had provided for their safety; then, as the
enemy rode up, he leaped his steed down a declivity
which not one man out of forty dared to risk after him,
and thus escaped.

Old Israel was also the author of a stock of clever sayings, in the style of Franklin, to make the soldiers love
duty and despise danger; and he often indulged a vein of
quiet humor. One day, while at work in his fields, he was
talking over that fruitful topic, the arbitrary conduct of
Parliament, when a laborer asked him what Parliament
was like. "Why, Enoch," he replied, "it's like the Beast
in the Apocalypse—all horns and eyes." More felicitous,
however, was a term which he bestowed on a party of
officers at Weathersfield, when a Scotch regiment was
quartered there, which had imparted a national source of
irritation, elegantly denominated the "Caledonian Violin."
This regiment numbered six noblemen, all of whom partook in the general restlessness; and some baggage of
theirs—containing sundry boxes of ointment—having
fallen into the Provincials' hands, Putnam henceforth
designated them "the Lord's anointed."

The Honorable William Alexander, commonly called
Lord Stirling, though his title was disavowed in England,

was a striking contrast to Putnam. He was as artificial as the other was natural; whether owing to the precise and mathematical nature of his avocations—as king's counsel and surveyor-general of East Jersey—I know not, but all he said and did was methodical, and his life was as much a piece of machinery as his frame. As to his faith in discipline, he believed it was possible to train men to anything; and not men only, for it was said that he offered to undertake raising a creditable regiment of infantry from a forest of ourang-outangs. Yet all his military knowledge was rendered unavailable by his unconciliatory manners, though he was, I believe, the only American officer who made the mistake of putting soldiership above more human qualities. Of so marked a character many stories were current, which must have been exaggerations—such as his seeing a man pull his trigger with the second finger, and, on learning that he had lost the use of the first, exclaiming, "Then why the devil do not you cut it off? Why do you keep a thing you can't use?" or his compelling a recruit, who had walked about forty miles to join him, with a heavy gun, to go back for a ramrod, saying that it was a rule in his regiments "to supply rods only to the refractory." What much disturbed the equanimity of this disciple of the Great Frederick was the men requesting furloughs to go home and see their wives. He could not perceive the most distant connection between military and domestic duty. That a soldier should require the stimulus of grog after a hard day's march, or work in the trenches, he clearly understood, but the effeminate necessity of fondling women and children was perfectly inexplicable. He received, however, some information on conjugal matters from a private, who accosted him one morning, when not in the best of tempers. "You want to go home, sir; what for?" he queried. "To see my wife, general?" "D—n it, sir, aren't you a soldier of Congress? is not duty your wife? isn't your country your wife? "Not exactly, general, for when my country gets licked"—pointing to a scar on his forehead—"I *suffer*, but, sometimes, when my wife gets licked, I *benefit*."

As an instance of the extreme to which he carried system, it was related of him that, in order to correct a lazy habit in a young officer, he appointed him to call him up every morning at five o'clock precisely. Having one night received intelligence which detained him at a council till the day-beam peeped in at the window, he was just stepping into bed, thoroughly worn out, when his pupil gave the summons at his door. Springing up at once, he made a loud clatter with his boots, and exclaimed, "Aye, aye! I was just rising."

Another extraordinary man, who assisted in fanning the flame of the Revolution, was Ethan Allen, the author of a work called "The Oracles of Reason," which exercised so much influence at home that the Southerners termed it "The Rhode Island Bible." Allen was a compound of the most singular extremes; oil and water would not be a more incongruous mixture. He was a graft of the old Cromwellian, psalm-singing, cut-and-thruster upon the free-and-easy, bibacious cavalier; alternately swearing and praying; singing hymns and anacrontics; sending people upwards and downwards. You entered his presence with reverence, and left it with wonder, for he was a Bobadil and Master Stephen combined; a Niagara and its lake—all thunder one moment and placidity the next. He pretended that he alone possessed the secret of enlightening and governing a people, but when stated, this proved to be some absurdity too empty to rebut, yet dangerous to laugh at. Such a man was not likely to be quiet in times of commotion. He put himself at the head of a party of long-sided Vermonters, termed "Green Mountain Boys," and, on being joined by Arnold (who came as his colonel, but whom he made his second), he achieved the surprise of Ticonderoga, the key to the Canadas, which contained much ammunition, but was garrisoned by only a small party. The commander was caught in his bed, and on Allen bidding him surrender, or he'd send his soul to hell like a flash of lightning, he exclaimed, "Surrender? to whom?" "To the Lord Jehovah and the Congress of America," was the reply.

What figure he would have cut in the course of the conflict it is impossible to determine, as his career was unluckily ended in the Canadas by his falling into the hands of Sir Guy Carlton, who sent him a prisoner to England. Notwithstanding his bombast, Allen had much shrewdness, but, unfortunately, the profanity of his clever sayings often neutralized the fun. The extreme simplicity of his tastes made him an object of amusement to the English at New York (where he was released on parole when brought from Halifax). Dining one day with a party at the commander-in-chief's, some olives were on the table, to which he helped himself with the rest, and, seeing they were very small, he put three or four in his mouth at once. This induced a general smile, and his wry faces induced his host to ask how he liked them. "Why, Sir William," said he, "I dare say it's a matter of taste, but I think your green gages are ra-a-ther bitter."

I might refer to others, Montgomery, Wayne, Nash, Lincoln, etc., but, as I fear this string has now been touched until its tone has almost gone, will only try to make its concluding vibration harmonious by repeating the words which I was told the Polish hero, Kosciusko, pronounced on joining the standard, that was here lifted up as much for a set of principles as a race of men: "My name is Kosciusko; I was born in Poland; but I consider myself a citizen of every government which aims at enlarging the happiness of the people!"

CHAPTER VI.

1798.—Trip to the Delaware.—A Serenade.—A Boat Adrift.—Five Foreign Ambassadors.—Baltimore.—Madame Jerome Bonaparte and the Marchioness of Wellesley.—Political Discords and Fatal Harmonies.—Elections.—Merry's Joke; Rival Candidates.—A Petticoaterie.—Negroes as Humorists; Happiness in Bondage; Theory of the Origin and End of Evil; Sambotius Quamina; the Burnt Fly; a Planter's Destiny; Fault in the Solar System; a Pilot's Reply; Significant "Hem;" Sleeping Unconsciousness; Negro Names; Hen and Egg; Three-fingered Jack.— Merryland and Merrylanders.—Lord Baltimore: Letter to the Swedes; Reply to an Indian.—Dr. Franklin on the Origin of Tobacco.—General Washington and the Dwarf.—Death of Merry; Omens; Epitaph.

WIGNELL, having to go to Philadelphia on business, placed me at the helm of his affairs, and as our season had now exceeded its limit, and it was necessary we should fill up our time until the fever should have left Baltimore, I thought it best to divide the company and make lecturing excursions to the smaller towns, an experiment which had been often tried before under similar circumstances. Accordingly, to my friend Warren I committed one division, including Mrs. Merry and Cooper, our tragedians; Mrs. Oldmixon (the wife of Sir Johns, formerly Miss George, the siren of Vauxhall, and, as an actress, heiress to all the honors of Mrs. Mattocks); Blisset, the son and image of a truly original father, and Harwood, a clever transcript of John Bannister. Allotting him the North of Maryland and Virginia, I took the conduct of the remainder—Fox, Francis, Marshall, Bates, and Mr. and Mrs. Gillingham, our operatic force—and resolved upon a trip to the Delaware. For our conveyance I engaged a sloop to Chesterton, a town about forty miles distant, up a river by that

name which runs into the Chesapeake. I found this place
to be so small and so indifferent to the fine arts that,
though I had many letters of recommendation, but two
individuals were inclined to give us countenance, namely,
our worthy landlord, Hodgson, and a Captain McKnight,
who was an actor in everything but name. We delivered
our entertainment of songs and recitations, in the Assembly Room, to about twenty persons (at a dollar each), more
than double that number standing outside and contenting
themselves with reading the bill, catching fragments of
the songs, and imagining the rest. At night, therefore,
some of the company resolved on going round the town
to give all the pretty girls a serenade, flattering themselves that if the women—the most influential part of all
communities—once heard their voices, the next evening
our room would be as packed as the " Black Hole." The
compliment was so novel in the quiet streets of this secluded place that every window flew up and some score
of female faces popped out, which was considered a favorable omen. But the Delaware maidens were better
calculators; the next night we performed to only ten dollars ; and I learned that " they could not think of *paying*
to hear what they had already heard for nothing." This
was a hint, so next day I obtained conveyances and we
visited Dover, Lewiston, and some other places, varying
in size, but agreeing so much in spirit that the pleasure of
the trip soon began to overbalance its profit, and, like
more eminent commanders, I was compelled, with chagrin, to give the signal for retreat. On our way back to
Annapolis we luckily found the packet apparently on the
eve of starting, but also a letter from my wife with the
news of a child's illness, which compelled me to take a
horse from a plough and ride homeward instantly, leaving with the company a sum which I thought sufficient
to defray their expenses. The sloop, however, taking

actually two days longer to disembogue, their pockets had to undergo a similar process, and starting at length with a wind scarcely sufficient to disarrange a lady's hair, it resulted that a boat which, in form, was very like a duck, somewhat resembled that bird in its motion. Captain McKnight had been so fascinated by the party that he resolved to accompany them on their voyage. He was a very pleasant fellow, and though rather too much given to practical joking, proved on this occasion their guardian angel. The way in which he evinced and then atoned for his roguery, as it led to scenes of peculiar eccentricity, I cannot avoid relating.

Gillingham, my singer and musician, was a worthy little fellow whose chief blessing had, from its intensity, become a curse. He possessed a wife who loved him with such ardent devotion that she was perpetually making him miserable by her endeavors to promote his happiness. Her life consisted of a series of endearments; her vital principle seemed to be communicated from his lips, and neither time, place, nor business could be allowed to suspend its operation. Now, as our little fiddler had much more of Apollo in his art than in his person, and Mrs. G. was neither young nor ethereal—being a very matter-of-fact sort of person of about thirteen stone weight—all this Arcadianism was exceedingly ludicrous. Her husband had the good sense to be ashamed of it, and McKnight the impertinence to attempt its correction.

Mrs. G., after a long, long quarter of an hour's absence, coming up to the deck to pursue her poor victim with her usual pretty little spousal slang of "Gilly, my dilly," he was nowhere to be found. Cabin, hold, and forecastle were investigated with the speed of lightning, Mrs. G.'s tones and terms varying from the playful piano of "Gill, my dill, I know where you're hiding!" to the sharp alto of "Gill, you devil, why don't you answer?" but Gill was

not forthcoming. At once the horrible impression became general that he had tumbled overboard. Everything was now in confusion. Mrs. G.'s pipe brought all
hands upon deck, and she flew about like a wild-cat,
charging every one she met with inhuman apathy, yet
preventing any exercise of reflection. Hold, forecastle,
and cabin were again ransacked, Mrs. G. even pulling
the ladies from their berths to see if they had not secreted
her Gill. As the sloop was doing little more than drift
along, the first thought on deck was to jump into the boat
and row back, when it was suddenly discovered that it
had got disengaged and was floating half a mile astern in
the middle of the river. What with Mrs. G.'s screams
and the consternation of the others, the scene had now
reached its climax, when Gillingham, who had all this
while been enjoying a nap in the bottom of the boat,
awoke and perceived his situation. But, as if the alarm
was never to subside, he, instead of seizing the oars and
pulling resolutely after his comrades, began to shout like
a maniac, upon which Mrs. G., who had just sunk into a
fit, reanimated with new vigor, and, darting to the stern,
began a response in tones yet shriller and more sustained.
The little fiddler at length found sense to grasp the oars,
and soon came up with the vessel, when, after his wife
had half-crushed him with her clasp and smothered him
with kisses, they ventured to ask an explanation of the
mystery. He said that, overpowered by his last night's
punch (though the fact was, as they all knew, to escape
his wife's attentions), he had lain down in the boat, but
not before taking the precaution to observe that its rope
was secured by a double knot, consequently it could not
have got loose without human assistance. Crew and company were equally eager in declaring their innocence,
when all eyes, by a simultaneous impulse, settled on those
of McKnight, in which a roguish sparkle, breaking forth

from their affected wonder, betrayed the criminal. They had now some difficulty in restraining Mrs. Gillingham from making the captain undergo the fate she had been led to think was her husband's, but quiet was at length restored by a consideration which, like Aaron's rod, swallowed up all others.

Fully expecting to reach Annapolis that night, the company had expended their last money in laying in a grand but solitary meal; the shades of evening were now falling around them, and they had accomplished but half the distance, so that starvation for that night stared them in the face. A general assembly was therefore held in the cabin to consider the readiest means to adopt for the relief of their wants. As they could not muster tenpence among them, the debate promised to be a long one, when suddenly some peculiar sounds broke upon their ears; they ran up to the deck, and perceived that they were passing a plantation which was the scene of revelry and feasting. The house stood at the end of a lawn that sloped down to the bank, and imbedded a luxurious array of barns, sugar-houses, hencoops, and piggeries. Lights were dancing in its upper windows, shouts were coming from its lower ones; guests were pouring in, in every species of vehicle, and the "niggers" were capering about the green like so many officers of his Satanic majesty's household, come up-stairs on parole. This was a scene which, in their situation, it would have been pleasanter to partake in than to behold, so that on Captain McKnight volunteering to go on shore and procure them a reception, his offer restored him to the good graces even of Mrs. Gillingham. Carrying with him their most heartfelt, or rather stomach-felt, aspirations for his success, he returned in about half an hour to inform them that he had told the planter they were a party of foreign ambassadors proceeding to General Washington's on the Potomac, and being badly accommodated in the sloop, requested the favor of a night's lodging. The planter had expressed himself highly honored to receive them, and proffered the best his house afforded. To hoax him, therefore, it was necessary they should array themselves in some stage habiliments, as fine and as old-fashioned as possible, and play certain extemporaneous characters for the evening. Tempting as was the bait — a Delaware supper, a very encyclopædia of meals — they were at first staggered by the proposition, until a due consideration convincing them that its performance was not too difficult, left them no room to perceive that it was too criminal.   Accordingly Bates took out of his box a kind of Lord Ogleby's dress, for the English ambassador; Marshall selected a sparkling, spangled affair for the Spaniard; Fox spruced himself in the costume of Lord Trinket, as minister of France; while Gillingham and Francis, as Austria and Russia, put on plain brown coats and black-silk breeches; all of them agreeing in certain "properties" which were no doubt mistaken for official insignia — bag-wigs, ruffles, hangers, and snuff-boxes.   None of the ladies would join in this enterprise except Mrs. Gillingham, who, unwilling to trust her treasure from her sight, arrayed herself in black velvet in order to survey the farmers as Queen Catherine did Wolsey.   Captain McKnight, acting as their secretary, with a spirit well worthy of the genius which suggested the hoax, led the planter and his son to the sloop to receive them, the guests following from the house to obtain a view, while the wondering negroes formed an avenue through which they marched with all imaginable dignity. Nothing could have been more *imposing* than their appearance, or more strictly in character; the lights, shining on their buckles and spangles, produced a glitter which quite dazzled the beholders, while they sustained the illusion by their broken-English chatter and grimaces.   In a short time the gayety of the society was quenched, all was awe and observation, the blacks even deserting their gambols on the grass to peep at them through the windows. This gave them confidence; but the supper being the leading cause of this performance, was the grand stimulant to their genius. Whilst that was going down they were winding up. Punch of the very best mixture completed the charm and rendered them quite communicative on the foreign policy of America and the state of Europe. They discussed the resources of Great Britain, the designs of Russia, and the results of the French Revolution (with the frequent iteration of such words as Kamschatka, Seringapatam, and Trincomalee) until every one of the hearers, completely lockjawed, sat round them in a spell-bound circle, fathers, mothers, and children foregoing all the objects of their meeting to glean the least iota of their wonderful intelligence. The captain, perhaps, would state some extraordinary piece of news, which Bates, in English, with a Lord Burleigh accompaniment, contradicted; Fox and Marshall then replied to him in French; Francis attacked them in Low Dutch, and Gillingham rebutted the whole party in Japanese. When they had worked their conversation up to five or six climaxes, and apparently edified their audience to the extent of their capacities, the latter drew off to their vehicles, and they to some exceedingly soft beds. Meanwhile their ladies had been well attended to by the females of the house; and in the morning, after being provided with a sumptuous breakfast, the distinguished party were waited upon with the utmost politeness to the sloop which, before a better wind, speedily conveyed them home.

The planter's guests soon spread the news throughout Delaware of the five foreign ambassadors who had stopped at Squire Polwheel's on their way to General Washington, and in secluded circles, where neither newspapers nor travellers penetrated, I have no doubt they afforded for some time as much speculation as many more important personages.

As soon as our dismal antagonist, the fever, had left the field open at Baltimore, we advanced for our autumn campaign, and, brief as it was, were liberally compensated for our summer losses. The only event which distinguished this visit occurred at the benefit of my friend Byrne, who, having an extensive teaching wherever he went, obtained the singular favor from the principal families of being allowed the assistance of his young pupils in a set of cotillions. Among them he had the honor of numbering Miss Patterson, afterwards Madame Jerome Bonaparte, and Miss Caton, the present Marchioness of Wellesley, both ladies making their *début* in public as dancers on this occasion.

Baltimore was a smaller edition of New York, another market and counting-house, but with one marked distinction. Here society was imbued with a spirit of controversy. Political discussion was as much the staple amusement as literature was in Philadelphia, and whether due to meteorological or constitutional causes I could never discover; but, certes, it amounted to a frenzy. Men, women, and children were alike affected, and all equally argumentative if not equally profound. This gave rise to endless discussions. Brothers and partners, identified in commercial but differing in political speculations, would pass each other in the street without recognition; their wives devotedly took up the cudgels at home; and their little boys pummelled each other into the Adams or Jefferson view of the subject at school. This party spirit was very unpleasant to a stranger, and would have been fatal to the drama (for the men who would not support the same minister would not patronize the same play), had it not been counterbalanced in some degree by a native conviviality which, bringing them together at night, made their discussions flow through a potent stream of port which speedily melted and mingled the most opposite opinions. To the stranger, however, this remedy was more fatal than the evil, for unless a man had gone through a course of Irish seasoning and graduated at a six-bottle college, he found a Baltimore friendly meeting was a danger to be dreaded. In physics we find the source of life to one being is death to another, and the heat which breeds a worm kills a seal. So also in "socialities"—if I may invent such a word—habits are like elements, and the staid liver who daringly rivals the well-trained convivialist is speedily forced into the exclamation of the frogs: "It may be fun to you, but to me it's annihilation."

Elections—in any part of the Union too like volcanic eruptions—here were at their worst. The philosophical traveller who passed through Baltimore at such times consoled himself with the conclusion that all this periodical vomiting forth of fire and dirt was the necessary escape of so much inflammable gas, denied the European vent on a belligerent neighbor. But the temporary resident, exposed to actual collision with the crowd, found the absurdity no joke. Merry was the only man I knew for whom it had a relish. To him it was a substitute for the best Madeira or a fine day's fishing; and though the surprising plasticity of his views, which ever concurred with those of the last speaker, would now and then betray the burlesque, his humor always acted as oil to any irritation. I was walking with him one day in Baltimore, when we met a friend of ours, a Delaware planter, who was conspicuous for provincial patriotism. Merry resolved to attack him, so with consummate gravity remarked : "How is this, Witherspoon ? I hear you have changed your principles." "I !" he exclaimed, in astonishment. "Yes; I heard at Colonel Tomkins's that you are not consistent."

"He doesn't mean to assert that I have given up the necessity of extending the democratic influence? I defy him to say that I am not upright!" "How can that be," replied Bob, "if you are *all on one side?*"

Occasionally these scufflings produced some very good hits. Two gentlemen of my acquaintance, Messrs. A. and B., met after a contest in which B. had been the successful candidate. A., surprised at the announcement, observed, "How was it possible you could beat C.? he had everything in his favor." "On the contrary," replied B., "the chances were mine. In the first place, you see, I had a fluent delivery and self-command; there I had the advantage of him. I had a personal knowledge of most of the electors; there I had the advantage of him. I had nerve, activity, and resolution; there, again, I had the advantage of him. He is a good, honest, straightforward, well-meaning fellow." "And there," replied A., "he had the advantage of you!"

The ladies, as I have before observed, took part in the mania to purify the government, but their deliveries were not always as felicitous as their conceptions, and if literal translations seldom give the meaning of an author, literal blunders are even more to be dreaded. At a tea-table, one evening, where the rival parties were being appropriately discussed in "hot water," two fair Andromaches were blazoning the merits of their respective Hectors. "My husband," observed one, with a deliberate emphasis and look which threw a mountain of contempt on her adversary, "has always stood up for the rights of the people; history will say of him that he was ever a true liberal." "And is not my husband, also?" exclaimed the other, with energetic rapidity, eager to counteract the unfavorable innuendo. "I appeal to you, ladies, I appeal to all the ladies in the room, if my husband isn't known to be the greatest *libertine* in Maryland."

My fingers have been long itching to touch upon a
bright subject — the blacks — the great humorists of the
Union, and, notwithstanding all that has been said of
their debasement and wretchedness, one of the happiest
races of people I have ever seen. The system by which
men are degraded to the level of brutes, or the arguments
which would justify such bondage, every unprejudiced
mind must turn from with horror. It is a stigma on the
age, the people, and the government which permits it, and
the anomaly is more grievously apparent in a Union
which, but for this blot, would present a combination of
the most beneficial principles that the world has yet seen
established. But when this is admitted, if it becomes a
question whether the slave can be happy in his bonds—
if not exposed to actual bodily suffering—the seven years
I had an opportunity of witnessing his constitutional vivacity make me reply in the affirmative. Under a thick skin,
the negro seems to be endued with very sensitive nerves;
climate, music, and kind treatment act upon him like elec-
tricity, and with all the ignorance of the child he possesses its disposition for enjoyment. Toil, in ordinary
cases, is but a dam to his animal spirits, which overflow
with greater violence at the hour of relaxation. A dance,
a song, and a laugh are then his sole desiderata. All this
is, no doubt, merely sensual, and far inferior to the pleasures which an elevation to his just dignity would afford
him; but still, nothing can be more erroneous than the
impression that the negro is not to the full extent as happy
as any of the other unenlightened laborers with whom
Europe abounds. It seems to have been caused partly by
wrong information and partly by reasoning which does
more credit to the heart than the head, and looks on
good and evil as positive rather than relative. Nature
implants equally in all men certain feelings for their
guidance, a sense of honor, gratitude, and affection, a

love of life, liberty, and bodily ease; but education and habit do much to weaken or strengthen these endowments. Thus the Englishman, who has been educated in the love and possession of liberty, cannot see how the slave can be happy without it. But the latter, having no idea of the enlightened man's enjoyments, regards liberty only as a release from labor and an enlarged means of gratifying his senses. He is like a man whose legs have been bound from infancy, and who on reaching manhood, though his bonds are cut, cannot walk. Such. feelings as honor, gratitude, and affection will force themselves out according to the nature of his treatment, but the love of freedom in its higher sense has been paralyzed with his intellect. There is no stronger proof of this than his conduct during the war. When Lords Dunmore and Cornwallis so repeatedly offered the slaves freedom if they would join the royal standard, how few were the instances of compliance. So completely was their natural spirit quenched that the example of their owners fighting for the very right that was theirs also could not fire them. If the slave really felt the loss of his liberty, would he not then have regained it; or indeed, could the Americans at any time have kept it from him? Intelligence made all the difference. The planter, knowing the value of his rights, was willing to die for them; the benighted negro could not weigh them against a whipping. Thus indifferent, were a general manumission to take place, what freedom would be to the black without a preparatory acquaintance with its duties and obligations, let miserable Hayti speak.

But it will be said, if the slave has not mental suffering, look at his bodily oppression. On this point I must confess I have heard much more than I have seen. The outrages which certainly occasionally occur may yet be due rather to individual depravity than to systematic cruelty, for I believe it has been ascertained that the major-

ity of such cases have been chargeable entirely to those
fiends of overseers who, to gratify their own hellish humors, persuaded their masters that rigor with the black
was a necessary economy of time and trouble. However,
the advance of public opinion, which every year becomes
more sensitive to the dignity of human nature, must, ere
long, cleanse out the foul stain altogether. With every
friend to the permanent prosperity of America, I trust
that that day is fast approaching; but to every friend of
humanity who may fret overmuch at its non-arrival, I
think it my duty to tell what I have observed of the
cheering side of the picture.

I have termed the negroes the great humorists of the
Union, and in many respects I have thought them like
the lower Irish; with the same confusion of ideas and
difficulty of clear expression, pouring words out of their
mouths on the high tide of a natural drollery, as broad as
as it is rapid. But this characteristic varied with their
locality and occupation. The black in Maryland, the
most social state in the Union, found more favorable opportunity for its development than in despotic Georgia.
And, again, the liveried and napkined shadow who flitted
behind the chairs at a city festivity, or planted himself as
a background to the snow of his lady's shoulders—like
night in Switzerland—differed materially from his brother
in the fields. The humor of the latter, arising from a
profound simplicity which lowered the most dignified subjects into ludicrous lights and elevated the most trivial
into importance, was Nature's spontaneous product in full
bloom; while he of the city added an observation of all
the petty arts, tricks, and prejudices of the society he
hung upon, so as to reflect his master or mistress in a kind
of hand-mirror; this knowledge of the outside of life in-
vesting him with a comical self-importance. Their manner sufficiently marked their difference. The one was

known by his stooping shoulders, projected head, and eyes half-closed as if in momentary fear that their sparkling fun might be forcibly quenched; with the muscles of his mouth ever quivering to draw up its heavy curtain of flesh and display the grinders of a shark.   The other exhibited all the confidence usually arising from a consciousness of talent, with the jutting breast of a tailor, and the angular hop of a Fantoccini; eyes and mouth ever wide open; legs and arms perpetually whirling; his replies had all the pop and froth of ginger-beer; he was a smart, eternally buzzing, black wasp.   It might be supposed that in every respect the negro would improve in the measure that he departed from his standard hue, and in respect to morals and manners this is the case; but as regards humor I must affirm, geologically, that I never knew a true vein of the precious metal to run through any but a decided "black loam."

I once read the fanciful theory of an old "New England divine," who strove to prove a very awful sympathy between matter and spirit, by connecting the negro's color with the origin of evil.   He asserted that Adam, after the Fall, lost his angel fairness as much in his skin as his soul; that an outward and visible sign of the internal darkness was the means adopted by divine anger to attest the creature's delinquency ; and that the brand of Cain and the hide of Esau were the stages of shade by which human turpitude advanced to the ultimate depths of Ethiopian debasement.   The worthy theorist felt himself thus provided with data to calculate the end of the world, for, taking the extinction of error or sin as the term of its existence, he argued that in the measure in which black began to disappear from the human being externally, the light of truth would progressively dawn through mulatto, quadroon, and octoroon till the universal heart and complexion returned to their primitive purity.

If this theory should seem plausible to my reader, I must, in justice, inform him that it has been controverted by several African philosophers, who have investigated deeply their historical metaphysics, and by one especially whose language, assuming the more inspired form of poetry, has become the creed of his race. The words are these:

> "Adam was a fuss man,
> Eba was anoder."

This little mistake in physiology my reader will overlook when he considers how difficult it is to prove the identity of anything at so remote a period.

> "Cain a was a bad man,
> A cause he kill him broder."

The pure and conclusive strain of this morality forcibly disposes us for the reception of what follows—

> "When Garra Mighty see um dead,
> Massa Cain in such a fright,
> He tremble from him toe to head
> And den he *turn all white!*"
> —SAMBOTIUS QUAMINA, *History and Metaphysics of Negroland.*

This exposition of the phenomenon, while it unsettles our common belief, places the New England divine in a decided quandary; yet if we accept the premises — Cain's trembling — the conclusion seems unavoidable, for the blackest rascals have been known to turn pale with strong emotion. The same learned author—Sambo Quam.—also proves with considerable acuteness that our notions respecting the devil are exceedingly vulgar, and unworthy of an enlightened age. According to his deductions, Sathanas protrudes no distinction of horns, hoofs, and tail, such as might scare babies, but is a tall, thin, well-made person, of a sallow complexion and with rather relaxed muscles and large, bushy whiskers, fond of smoking, swearing, cock-fighting, and mint-sling.

I will now recount some of the grounds of my conviction that humor (as well as, I may add, a vein of melancholy) is specially the attribute of the negro. One of the heartiest specimens of fun I ever heard was the chuckle of a youth who was on duty with a fan to keep the flies from disturbing his master's rest, and who, seeing a persevering blue-bottle light on the planter's flaming promontory and immediately fly off, exclaimed, "Aha, um berry grad o' dat; *oo burn oo foot at last*, massa fly !" A pendant to this, but in a quieter way, was the reply of a domestic who went to communicate the news of his master's sudden death to a near neighbor. The latter, on recovering from the first shock, observed, with a sigh of resignation, "Well, Cicero, there's one thing to console us; your poor master had a d—d bad gout, and he's gone to happiness." "Iss, massa, but um berry sorry he hab'n gone to heb'n." "Not gone to heaven, you black rascal! why?" "Cause, massa, he tell a me he should never be comforbable anywhere where he wasn' berry warm !"

A trait of that simplicity which is usually considered indigenous to Ireland was the remark of the exhilarated fiddler who, going home from a dance one dark night, fell over some rubbish in the road, and with difficulty regaining his legs, exclaimed to his companion, "Now, Cæsar, tell a me iss—why de debil do a sun shine all day when nobody want um, and nebber shine a night, when it's so berry dark gentlum can't see his way ?"

I have heard also of a Charleston pilot who, on being asked by the captain how much water there was within the bar (meaning, of course, how deep), extended his wondering eyes to their fullest periphery and replied, "Why, massa, what a strodnary queshun! do a tink I ebber measure um in a pint pot?"

But this was not the usual characteristic of a Samboism. It was the presence, not the absence, of intelligence which gave it a relish, and lent a more grotesque effect to its mode of expression. Few things have contained more of the essence of meaning than the comment of a Western Cato, invited to take a glass of grog at a tavern by a manumitted friend, who, as first taster, did not withdraw his lips till he had subtracted two thirds of the potation, when, giving a loud "hem!" he said to the landlord, "Massa, I tink iss berry strong; gib a little water." "Top, top, Pompey!" interrupted Cato, with an eloquent wink, "fuss I should like to cry 'hem!'"

One of the stories that amused me most, from the moral justice that gave edge to the retort, I heard during a Southern visit. A Jerseyman, carried by business to Georgia, called on a friend, who accompanied him on a survey of the country. Night coming on when they were some distance from home, they took possession of an overseer's hut which contained a couple of hammocks, leaving a negro, who attended them, to lie upon the floor. This poor fellow it seems had, during the day, offended the Jerseyman, who, nursing a pitiful spite, took advantage of the moment his friend and the black were asleep to reach his hand to his whip and bestow a smart cut on the most exposed portion of the somnolent shadow beneath. Agamemnon bounded up as with a galvanic impulse, and the Jerseyman threw himself back, but not before his motion had betrayed him. The sufferer, fearful of disturbing his master, could only apply friction to the irritation, and lie down again. The next day being passed in the neighborhood, at night they repaired again to the hut, when our hero expressed a strong wish to repose outside. This led to a disclosure, upon which the Jerseyman said, in his defence, "If I struck you, Aggy, it must have been in my sleep; a man may do many things in his sleep which he can't remember next morning." Such an explanation satisfied the planter, and perforce his property, but it conveyed no conviction to the latter, nor was it the unction he required for his skin. It was the Jerseyman's fate this night to go off first and give his victim the pleasure of watching him. Rising softly on his legs, Aggy approached his hammock, and, taking down the brandy-keg suspended by his side, emptied its contents. The loss was discovered the first thing next morning, and Aggy was collared and charged with the offence, when, eying the tyrant significantly, he replied, "Well, massa, if I did drink um, it mus hab been in my sleep; a man may do many ting in his sleep he can't remember next mornin'." This Rowland for an Oliver tickled the planter as much as it dumfounded his guest, and between the two Aggy came off victorious.

Among other American mysteries Europeans have often wondered at the practice of bestowing on slaves the names of all the conquerors, military or moral, in classic history. Cæsar, Pompey, Cato, Cicero, Ulysses, Agamemnon, all constrained to return from the Tartarean regions, but with faces so begrimed by their abode there that it was evident they had not been able to take a dip in the Styx on recrossing it. So singular a fact has given rise to much speculation. Did the planter, intending to teach a political lesson to his child, thus cast down the idols of the old republics whose worship had been taught in academic groves, in order to impress the merits of his country's worthies; or was it that he gratified his own sense of power by exercising mastership over such mighty names? Many commonplace minds, however, refer the cause simply to the natural burlesque importance of the black, and the waggery of his master. My readers will, perhaps, infer that the custom must have added to the name-owner's knowledge of antiquity, which, according to Mr. Jefferson, as a mental stimulant must have proved a political evil. I once asked one of the "high denominations," who looked more than ordinarily inflated, why he was called Cæsar. "Cause, sar," said he, with ineffable dignity, "Cæsar a berry noble name." "Oh, then, you think you have a right to it." "Iss, sar; unqueshonably." "Perhaps you imagine you are the descendant of a Cæsar." "Iss, sar; tu-ba-sure!" "My good fellow," exclaimed I, with a stare, "do you know who Cæsar was?" Here I thought I must have sunk under the reply of his eyes, while his lip, a noble scroll at all times to his Corinthian column, curled into more protuberant majesty as he exclaimed, "Know who um was, sar? Cæsar, Massa Johnny say, was a great *butcher*. So am I!"

But the most conclusive testimony I ever received on the point of natural negro intelligence was from a female, and for force and novelty of application I think it may challenge rivalry with anything recorded of the sages.

An Othello, who had lately married, was plucked from the arms of his devoted wife to attend his master on a journey to the North. His absence extended to many months, but it was oil, not water, to the flame of his affection. The Fates at length consenting to his return homewards, he rushed to enfold his Chloe with a genuine conjugal spasm (by-the-bye, why are all the ladies named from the classic pastorals, Chloe, Phyllis, etc.? Another mystery). As nature is the same under all skins, can the joy of that moment be depicted on paper? Impossible! And equally impossible would it be to describe the consternation with which, the minute after, he perceived a little lump of humanity asleep on the bed, almost white! "Chloe!" he exclaimed, converging, as it seemed, every faculty into that of vision, "what dat?" "Oo child, Cato." "My child?" "Iss, a fuss pledge of my 'fection." "Debbel take a wooman, him quite white!" Cato now stood mute and motionless, gazing at his wife as if his eyes would scorch her up; in another moment his glance, turning to a convenient oak stick, announced that he was about to inculcate a lesson of morality in one of its soundest forms, when intuitive perception threw a flash on Chloe's brain which pointed out a broad passage of escape. Genius acts as it conceives, with vigor. Seizing her husband by the wool she dragged him to the door and pointed to a group of fowls. "Cato," she exclaimed, with equal fervor and decision, "tell a me dis—what dat?" "A hen." "Oo wicked nigger, what color is um hen?" "Black." "And does'n a black hen lay *a white egg?*" Here she paused and scanned him with a smile of triumph; the blow was resistless; it had gone home; had struck him like a wave at sea, capsizing and flooding him. Clasping the clever dear one to his bosom, now wrapped in more than Roman dignity of innocence, suspicion and coolness perished together in the hug.

Of the sensitiveness of the negro to sweet sounds a curious proof was afforded in an anecdote related to me by my friend Morris, who had been with his company in Jamaica when the head and hand of the celebrated "Three-fingered Jack" were brought into Kingston. One of the company, who had a very sweet voice, was of highly respectable parentage, and had quitted England owing to an unfortunate attachment. His melancholy, as is usually the case, led him to take long rambles in the country, in which he was occasionally joined by another of the actors, both duly mindful to avoid certain districts known to be haunted by the terrible outlaw. At the close of one very sultry day he and his friend were skirting the foot of a hill when they came to an umbrageous palm, under which Herbert proposed they should open their wallet and take some refreshment. On doing so they discovered that they had omitted to provide themselves with brandy. The

friend, espying a plantation at a distance, said he would
go there to obtain some, while Herbert threw himself on
the sward to await his return. The loneliness and stillness
of the spot brought back to him the thought of home,
and he gave vent to his oppressed spirit in some vocal
effusion, unconscious that the savage scourge of the island,
driven by hunger from his hiding-place on the hills, had
watched the display of the provisions, and, on his friend's
departure, had crept softly through the brushwood to
despatch him. Jack had drawn sufficiently near for his
purpose, and was on the point of raising his gun, when
Herbert's lips opened, and the breathings of a broken
heart fell upon his ear. They arrested his arm. He listened in mute attention, and, when Herbert ceased, touched
him gently with the butt of his musket and said, "Sing
again, massa!" Herbert started up with a cry of terror
as he beheld the fearful being of whom he had been
warned standing over, and, as he thought, on the point
of destroying him. But there was no violence in the outlaw's eye. He grounded his gun, and, propping his chin
on its muzzle, repeated his request, "Sing again, massa."
The feelings of the singer may be surmised. There are,
perhaps, few men who would not instantly have grown
hoarse through agitation. But it was a matter of more
moment than his ordinary *encores*, and he recommenced
the song as desired, Jack leaning over him and looking
down upon him with a gaze of interest intense enough
for affection. My reader, who must have heard of this
person as one of the most brutal and ferocious of his
class, differing only from the forest prowler in his form,
will scarcely credit that the tears trickled from his eyes
as from those of a young girl, and for many minutes the
whole current of his blood seemed changed. Here was
another mysterious instance of the charm of music—opening, as it seemed to do, some deep and secret spring of

tenderness till that moment unknown, and most likely from that moment closed forever. Before Herbert a second time concluded his friend came in sight, hurrahing and waving a spirit-flask. Jack instantly levelled his gun, but, looking upon the singer beside him, he hesitated, grasped a handful of bread and meat from the wallet, and went over the bushes with the bound of a tiger. In an instant Herbert was upon his legs, and meeting his friend half-way, dragged him back to the plantation before he could speak a word. There, when the alarm was given, a pursuit was at once commenced, and in the space of a few days Herbert again looked, but with very different sensations, upon the head and the hand of " Three-fingered Jack."

I have endeavored to give the leading characteristics of each city I visited; this is not so easy with the States. In the country every man's family is a community in itself. Local circumstances chiefly determined the settler's occupations, and the habits consequent on these his social character. The utmost that can be said is that if New England was the manufacturing, the Middle States the commercial, and the Southern the producing circles, Maryland produced the most original aspect of the group—for it was the independent. It always seemed to me a collection of country-houses where people had either been born with wealth or had retired to spend it; a spot which, from a happy union of influences in its soil and sky, had so moulded its denizens' characters as to become one wide temple of mirth and sociability. Here the grand product was good-humor; the great exchange, hospitality; the one avocation, enjoyment. Here the most restless spirit contentedly folded its wing, and the most inveterate wanderer was tempted to stay his step. The doors seemed to me a useless device; they were made to stand open. And almost equally unnecessary were the roofs, for the sky was always smiling approbation on what was doing below. People of every nation and prejudice met here to subside into brotherhood, and the genius of their hosts exerted itself but in the invention of new spells to support such an influence. To sum up all in a word— this was the Ireland of America! Surely there never was such a permissible corruption of a name as that by which people pronounced this region Merryland. I had but one fault to find with it—Bob Merry should have been its governor!

I feel that my life, as seen in these pages, must seem to have been one long gleam of sunshine. Blessed with a buoyant heart and some good-will for my fellow-creatures, it is true that where I did not find a garden I planted one; but I can truly say that I linger over this retrospect with peculiar fondness. In England I had passed the spring and summer of my days, but here came the *fall* with more than usual plenteousness. It was indeed a season of fruits which fed and fostered every volatile particle of my nature; and, though I passed in a few years to soberer scenes, I cannot trace this reference but that it brightens up in memory's setting ray with the full glow of its departed gladness.

One of the country friends whom I most frequently visited was a Mr. O'Donnell; and at his table I heard some traditionary traits of Lord Baltimore, who brought over the first settlers of Maryland—two hundred Roman Catholic families—under a grant from Charles I. There seem to have been, in this man's character, many pleasing prognostics of the ultimate felicity of his adopted circle. He had fortitude, forethought, and a deep, undefiled spring of benevolence. Thus qualified to head an enterprise which planted the tree of liberty where it was destined to shoot up and spread its grateful shelter over thousands, his spirit seems to have entered into the atmosphere of the country and given to it its happy, harmonizing influence.

Mr. O'Donnell had in his possession a letter from Lord Baltimore to a settlement of Swedes on the Delaware, who had sent to ascertain whether he intended to molest them. As my friend was kind enough to permit my copying it, the reader may not object to my inserting a few lines which, had they been inscribed on every emigrant's banner, might have kept the American woods from the stain of much crimson.

"The oppressed of one country, I cannot become an oppressor in another. To me America is a city of refuge, not strife. The rights which my sovereign may have committed to my keeping I am bound to guard, but these do not include the power of molesting my fellow-creatures. On the soil where I am a stranger our children may become brothers. With God and our consciences for our friends, pride, envy, and dissimulation will be our only enemies."

As an evidence of the intelligence of this nobleman (the emphasis falls properly on the "noble"), my friend related to me an anecdote of the mode in which he received a deputation from an Indian tribe, who sent to him with the same suspicions as the Swedes. The chief speaker, after learning and wondering at the circumstances of the emigrant's origin and advent, remarked: "The pale-face has crossed the great salt lake to fight with the red-skin." His lordship replied that this was not so. "How can the pale-face sit down on the land of the red man and not drive him away?" This conference was being held at night and on the sea-beach, when, through a brilliant dome of stars, the moon was rising from her summer bath. Lord Baltimore pointed to the sky, and (through the interpreter) replied, "Let my brother look at those stars—they are many ; they are bright and glorious. Such are the red men. Will the yellow star which is now coming from the lake displace them or put out their glory? Such is the white man!"

Mr. O'Donnell, whose head was as full of anecdote as his heart was of good-nature, related to me also Doctor Franklin's account of the origin of tobacco, which, it appears, the worthy philosopher was in the habit of repeating whenever he listened to any very marvellous narration, and with a gravity, I understand, well worthy of the credibility of his details. A Swedish minister, he said, having on one occasion convened the chiefs of the Susquehanna Indians to hear an exposition of the truths of his belief, as soon as he had concluded one of them rose and desired he would attend to their tradition. "In the beginning," said he, "we had only the flesh of animals to eat, and if they failed, we starved. Two of our hunters having killed a deer, boiled a part of it, when they saw a young woman walk down from the clouds and seat herself on a hill hard by. Said one to another, 'It is a spirit; she has smelled our venison and wishes to partake of it.' They accordingly offered her the tongue, which she ate with much avidity, and then told them, 'Your kindness shall be rewarded; come here twelve moons hence and receive three presents.' After which she walked up into the clouds again. Our fathers did as she commanded, and found that where she had laid her right hand was a field of maize; where her left, a field of beans; and where she had deposited the most honorable part of her person, a crop of tobacco!"

One of my rambles at this time carried me over to West Jersey, where I was shown the grave of a dwarf who had attracted considerable notice about the time of the commencement of the war. He was scarcely thirty-six inches in height, yet of the most perfect proportions. But it was not his form so much as his spirit that had caused his celebrity. The royal Thumb was not invested with a deeper consciousness of his own importance. This seems another of the curious and loving provisions of Nature, a note in the grand harmony, by which as the frame declines from the ordinary standard its measure of self-esteem increases, so as to keep the object's notions on the point of personal dignity always on a level with those of his companions, even should they be veritable " sons of Anak." To the rest of the world only does this prompting of Nature appear an absurd affectation, because they do not see why, as the bottle grows smaller, the spirit should necessarily become more *essential*. Among the amusing things related of him was his interview with Washington, who, about the time of the Trenton enterprise, passed a night in the house where he was domesticated. The general having discussed a variety of subjects with him, at length inquired his political sentiments. " What do you expect," said he, " will be the result of the war?" " I can hardly at present form an opinion," replied the miniature, " for I have not yet taken an active part."

Our season had sped on with a prosperity commensurate with the enjoyment of our private hours, when both were doomed to close in a shock and gloom which for many months hung over our little circle, defying all attempts to dispel it. This was caused by the death of my dearly esteemed friend, Robert Merry; the amiable, the intelligent, the truly-named Merry; he who from his boyhood had enjoyed the eulogium of never knowing an enemy, and whose life had been one long act of sympathy with others, lighting up smiles on haggard faces, and pouring upon saddened hearts the genial influences of his vivifying spirit. At the meridian hour, which was gathering to him rich returns from all his friends, he descended to the chamber and complexion of his prototype—poor Yorick.

There were some ominous circumstances connected with Merry's death which made a strong impression upon me.

I am not of a superstitious temperament, and in all inexplicable matters have chosen to refer their mystery to some hidden possibility rather than trace trivial effects to divine agency. But so many cases of a like kind have passed before me that they have had at least one good result—they have led me into a more tolerant spirit in regard to points of faith. I have long since felt myself without authority to consider any man's belief a *weakness* because he cannot *account* for it.

Merry had been latterly employed in writing a play, and one morning he called on me to say that he was engaged to dine with a gentleman who was going to London and would take it to Mr. Harris. The same day he requested Mrs. Merry to look over the last act and see if she could suggest any improvement in its catastrophe. He returned in the evening in high spirits from his friend's, where his more than usual effervescence had elicited an observation, to which he had replied, "My dear fellow, what you see me I have been for these forty years, and shall continue for another thirty." Finding his wife earnestly engaged at her task, he would not disturb her, but took a kiss and his candle and went up to bed. Mrs. Merry had dreamed, a few nights before, that her husband had died suddenly and had appeared to her. When she mentioned this to him he rallied her in his usual way; but a night or two after he dreamed himself that his brother had come to him in deep mourning, and when asked the reason had turned away and hid his face; upon which Mrs. M., by some unaccountable impulse, remarked, "It was for you, Robert!"

Not long after Merry had retired, Mrs. Merry heard a groan proceeding, as it appeared, from beneath the table, which she reasoned herself into believing a delusion, until it was repeated. In all that is meant by the term "moral courage" I do not think that this truly lovable and excellent woman was surpassed even by Mrs. Canning, of whose

self-possession I have given so striking an anecdote in a
former volume. Had a robber woke her in the night, with
a pistol at her ear, she would have looked at him calmly
and selected the key of her cabinet with a steady finger;
but her mind was as little proof against the terrors of the
inexplicable as are those who consider them communications from the Deity. She accordingly rang the bell for
her host and hostess, who, imagining it was the trick of
some unfeeling rogue in the street, went out and looked,
but without effect; and in a bleak autumn night, the sleet
falling and freezing fast, they did not think it probable
that any one would purchase amusement so dearly. When
they had returned to the drawing-room, Mrs. Merry, to
get rid of them, assented to their conviction that it was
mere *fancy;* but she read no more that night.

The next morning Merry rose early, apparently quite
well, and in ignorance of the above, and, descending to
the garden, where he usually walked before breakfast, met
the cook, for whom he had his pun prepared as regularly
as she had his coffee. Mrs. Merry came down soon after
to complete her revision of the play, and the servant going out to call her husband when the breakfast was ready,
found him stretched upon the pathway in a fit of apo-
plexy. Here, half-buried in the snow which had fallen
plentifully during the night, it is probable he had remained some time, incapable of rising or calling for assistance. The chill thus received must have hastened the
return of the attack. When the alarm was given, Mrs.
Merry was hurried up-stairs and her husband conveyed
to the drawing-room, where his head was accidentally
placed exactly upon the spot whence she had imagined
the groan had proceeded. The reader may conceive her
feelings when, on entering the room, she perceived this
coincidence.

Merry's name hurried all the skill of Baltimore to his

assistance, but the grasp of mortality was too firm to be unloosed, though he recovered for a brief space the full use of his speech and his mental faculties, and with them the inseparable flow of his vivacity. We were commencing rehearsal when the news reached the theatre, and I flew to his house with Wood,* who had made his *début* a few evenings previous in the comedy of "Secrets Worth Knowing." We found Merry propped in a chair, tapping his snuff-box and smiling a reproof at his wife's emotion, while the physicians were holding a consultation in one corner of the room. When his eye fell upon Wood he could not restrain his ruling propensity, but, taking a pinch of snuff, exclaimed, "Aha! now the consultation will be complete; here's Doctor Plethora come to see me." Three hours after this he breathed his last (and perhaps his only) sigh upon his wife's bosom.

His interment drew forth the strongest expression of private sympathy I have ever witnessed; it appeared to me that half the population of Maryland walked after the

---

* WILLIAM B. WOOD. Wood is only remembered in the present day by his "Personal Recollections of the American Stage," Philadelphia, 1855; a valuable contribution to dramatic history, and a good example of the autobiographic literature in which so many members of his profession in former generations were fond of indulging. Wm. B. Wood was born in Montreal, in 1779, his father, a goldsmith of New York, having gone to the Canadas during the Revolutionary War. In 1798 he made his first appearance as an actor with the Philadelphia Company, under the management of Wignell, at the Annapolis Theatre, and as George Barnwell. He was a member of Mr. Wignell's company in Philadelphia, and treasurer of the theatre for a number of years. In 1804 he married Juliana Westray, an actress of some repute. In 1810, in partnership with William Warren, he became manager of the Chestnut Street Theatre, a position he held for sixteen years. He took formal leave of the stage at the Walnut Street Theatre as Sergeant Austerlitz, in the "Old Guard," Nov. 18, 1846. He died in Philadelphia, in 1861. He was a close student of his profession, and won his way by hard work rather than by inherent talent for the stage. He played many parts and none of them badly.

dismal vehicle which now shrouded the sun of our circle. Many men have passed away who have done more service to their country, and added greater treasures to its literature, and who, let the tide of time sweep at its will, have cast anchor effectually in the public memory; but none have had hearts which beat with a livelier impulse for the well-being of humanity; none have given proofs of a willingness to do more had the ability been greater.

In compliance with Mrs. Merry's wish I wrote his epitaph, which I now insert as a last tribute to his memory:

> Here lies Robert Merry, the generous, the kind,
> Whose name was the truest response to his mind;
> His heart with no burden was destined to heave,
> Save in listening to sorrows he could not relieve.

CHAPTER VII.

1799.—Life in Virginia; a Word for the Planters; the War a Moral Regenerator; Manners, Tastes, and the Ladies.—A Planter's Life before the War; Stratagems to Obtain Companions; Ordinaries.—Public Diversions: Racing at Williamsburgh; Quarter-racing; Hunting in Virginia; an Adventure. — Native Traditions: Captain Smith; his Discipline; his Replies; Pocahontas in England; an Indian Taking the Census.—Convicts in Virginia.—Dr. Franklin's Present to Sir Robert Walpole.— A Humorous Criminal; Conviction and Conversion. — A Governor's Speech in 1670.—Lecturing Excursion.—Cooper the Tragedian; his Courage.—Virginia Travelling.—Gallinippers and Mosquitoes.—Patriot Pigs.—Blacksmith's Cure for Insanity.—General Lee and the Quakers.— A Madagascar Monster.—Tradition of "Blackbeard's" Skull.

THE summer of 1799 I passed in Virginia, my professional visits, alternating between Richmond and Norfolk, being relieved by excursions to various parts of the state, at the invitation of that truly hospitable race—the planters. Among these I met men of high intelligence and even refinement, whose conviviality not making its agent its end, could be, like their own summers, as radiant as it was warm. No class of persons that I know of has been so harshly judged as the planters, the sins of the fathers having been visited upon the tenth generation. Abroad and at home, worthy persons whose hearts throw a mist round their brains have confounded the necessity of the present with the evil of the past, have let the crimes of a few discolor the many, and the iniquity of a system vouch for that of individuals. Herein has lain the error and the wrong. Unless a man has been willing to break up this system at the cost of his own utter ruin he has been pronounced a selfish barbarian, a loathsome maggot complacently fattening on corruption. In nine cases out of ten the supporters of the system have been its greatest victims. I do not hesitate to say they have been among its sincerest detesters. It certainly is no enviable lot when a man, happening to be born on a particular spot which is cursed with an indisposable legacy, can be put in a pillory by every enthusiast who makes feeling, not fact, his rule of reasoning. I do not remember a single instance of a planter defending the origin of his possessions, or one who defended the continuance of slavery by other than this single argument; that human agency is required in the cultivation of the Southern soil, while the extreme heat is not to be supported save by Africans or natives. The negro, if manumitted and paid for his labor, can live upon so little that he would not do half that is required; and, till the country becomes so populated that work shall become scarce, the white will never take his place.

As to the planters, look at their education. Were the many guilty of the atrocities which have been proved against a few, could they be marvelled at when we consider the furnace in which they have been heated and hardened, the mode in which they have been trained into indifference to fellow flesh and blood, a habit of command and unlimited indulgence? Like the old feudal barons, their whole life is a temptation, through absence of restraint. They have had but one check upon their passions —goodness of heart. If all men's forbearance through life could be brought to this test would not the virtue of charity be somewhat more catholic? Again, in the old times it was next to impossible for a man to rear a family without relieving the abrupt contrast of white and black in-doors by certain intermediate shades; while devotion to the mysteries of mint-sling, jockeyship, and cock-fighting arose from his associating only with his own class, or with the worst exportations of Europe. Insensible to the pleasures of refinement, he was unconscious of the necessity of example, and, levelling all below him to a footing with his slaves, felt no obligation to provide for human dignity and comfort by establishing education. In the North the merchants were the leading body, while the farmers and mechanics formed a middle rank. Society in the South consisted but of two classes—high and low. Here the aristocracy were the landowners, to whom the inhabitants of cities were but agents for the export of their produce. In the former, the education of the middle class had led to a general diffusion of knowledge among the poor. In the latter, the parcelling of property into comparative dukedoms annihilated a medium (for the farmers of the slave states were too few to be considered), and there was no public instruction to prevent the poor from falling victims to the worst points of their superiors. It can be no marvel, therefore, that for many years the planters were a race of epicureans, and the lower orders a horde of vagabonds; that the slaves were the only laborers in the state, and that freedom, either in high or low, consisted in a mere despotism of the senses. But the war proved a great moral as well as political regenerator. At the first threat of oppression, Virginia—the effeminate, dissolute Virginia —roused into a masculine energy which fixed the eyes of the colonies. She formed the Southern nucleus of resistance, her proprietors becoming a band of skilful leaders, around whom gathered legions of devoted soldiers. But this was not all—she grasped her less decided neighbors and bound them indissolubly to the Union, for Virginia and New England may be truly said to have "hooped" the confederacy. The contest gave birth to no higher evidences of patriotism than were afforded by the planters, when, in the heart of the English army, they sundered the ties of English patronage, provoking the confiscation of their property, to endure every species of personal privation — some proof that they have not been always the selfish and cold-blooded beings they have so often been termed. In their manners they have ever been austere to their inferiors, and, when abroad, reserved with their equals; but all frost vanished the moment you crossed their threshold. That was a minute but instantaneous division between the frigid and the torrid zone; a warmth —truly Irish—succeeded, and you were welcomed to a land of liberty. In all their domestic arrangements the taste was evidently French, with some local modifications which were not displeasing. Though deficient in architectural beauty or stability, many of their dwellings were internally palaces. Their furniture, pictures, and musical instruments were all imported from Europe. But this did not surprise me so much as the tone of their conversation. Their favorite topics were European, and I found men leading secluded lives in the woods of Virginia perfectly *au fait* as to the literary, dramatic, and personal gossip of London and Paris. But the mystery was soon explained: they had all been educated in France or England (a practice which ceased at the Revolution), had made a tour of the Continent, and maintained a voluminous correspondence ever since. At one house I met with a gentleman who had participated in my revels at the London clubs. His memory was a storehouse of anecdote which he flavored by a peculiarly happy faculty of imitation, the rapturous manner in which the company recognized the originals often making me look round to see if I was not once more snugly ensconced over the piazza at Covent Garden.

Of the planters' ladies I must speak in terms of unqualified praise; they had an easy kindliness of manner, as far removed from rudeness as from reserve, which being natural to them (for they mixed with no society) was the more admirable. In a woman I would always have the

heart to be the chief source of her fascination. The one
thing I did not quite approve of was the juvenile period
at which they bloomed and decayed. A lady here was
in the habit of marrying nearly ten years earlier than a
European, so that at twenty, if she had proved a fruitful
olive, her husband's table was surrounded with tall shoots
sufficient to supply him with shade for the remainder of
his days. At thirty—the glowing summer of an English
dame—she had fallen into "the sere leaf;" and at forty
—the autumn fulness of a royal taste, the *bel age* of St.
James's—the faces of these matrons of the West are cut
up into as many lines as a map of Europe. Nevertheless,
to the influence of their society I chiefly attribute their
husbands' refinement, and, in proof, I cannot, perhaps,
more amuse the reader than by showing the contrast of a
planter's life some twenty years previous, when, marriage
being made a mere mode of conveying property, every
woman was looked on as an animal, and every house was
a harem.

During summer he used to rise about nine, when he
exerted himself to walk as far as his stables to look at
the stud which he kept for the races; at ten he breakfasted on coffee, eggs, and hoe-cake, concluding it with
the commencement of his diurnal potations—a stiff glass
of mint-sling — a taking disorder peculiar to the South.
He then sought the coolest room and stretched himself on
a pallet in his shirt and trousers, with a negress at his
head and another at his feet to keep off the flies and promote reflection. Between twelve and one his throat would
require another emulsion, and he would sip half a pint of
some mystery termed bumbo, apple-toddy, or pumpkin
flip. He then mounted a pony, and, with an umbrella
over his head, rode gently round his estate to converse
with his overseers. At three he dined, and drank everything — brandy, claret, cider, Madeira, punch, and san-

garee, then resumed his pallet, with his negresses, and meditated until tea-time—though he was not particular about tea, unless friends with womenkind dropped in. The inflammation in his throat returned about dusk, and he prescribed for himself cooling washes until bed-time. From this detail the reader will surmise that a planter was a reptile only to be preserved in spirits; but I must guard against the error that he was by choice a solitary toper. On the contrary, he strained every nerve to pick up companions, and it was only when in utter despair of obtaining this pleasure that he gave himself up to bumbo, Dinah, a mattress, and meditation. Many humorous instances were related to me of the plans he adopted to draw guests to his convivial roof in the un-tracked woods of the interior. One of the most striking was the following :

On the morning of "a clear day"—a decided scorcher —he would order a wagon to be packed with a tub con-taining bottles of every compound in his closets—sling, nog, flip, and toddy, together with their elements, spir-its, lemons, sugar, etc. ; a pair of rifles, shot, and powder; a fishing-rod and tackle; soap, towels, clean linen and nan-keens ; and a canvas awning with poles and cords to sup-port it. He then took his seat in the vehicle, and, attended by a train of blacks, was driven slowly to the nearest highway, along which he proceeded till he came to a clear, clay-bottomed pond. The wagon was then backed into the water where the depth was breast-high, the poles were firmly driven into the bottom, the awning stretched over them, and the horses being turned into the woods, the pro-prietor disarrayed himself and descended into this local bath. After amusing himself with a few minutes' splash-ing, a board was slid down from the wagon to support him in a recumbent position, and the tub, like a richly-freighted West-Indiaman, was committed to the deep and moored beside him. Arrangements were now made for the business of the day: while one ebony was placed in charge of the cattle, another carried out a line from his floating fishing-rod, standing ready to give him notice of a bite; a third placed his rifles on the tub, that he might pop at the first bird that offered; and two others were despatched in opposite directions to watch if travellers were approaching. Thus combining the four staple enjoyments of bathing, drinking, shooting, and fishing, this Western Sardanapalus marked the furnace in the skies burn away, but not with a contented heart. He sighed for a victim; his toils were spread and he hungered for his prey. In the deep solitude that reigned around, his ear was triply alive to human sounds; the creak of a cart-wheel had more music for him than the finest notes of a thrush, and the sight of any person, not a negro, more beauty than the loveliest landscape. If at length the form of a stranger appeared, he sprang from his plank and shouted an invitation to alight and take a drop of something sociable. If the traveller refused, up went the rifle to his shoulder, and compliance was demanded in the tone of a European footpad. The stranger now saw that pleasure was policy, however urgent might be his business; but if he were so unguarded as to yield to his next request to "strip and take a swim," he speedily found himself irretrievably in the clutches of this human alligator. The planter fixed in him all the claws of nog, flip, sling, and toddy, until the brain of the victim became so confused that the grinning negroes had no difficulty in stowing him into the wagon, whereupon the poles were struck, the horses buckled in, and the delighted planter returned home with his prize, whom he probably cooped up in a back-room with a *chevaux-de-frise* of bottles, until, by some desperate effort, the captive made his escape.

Another and more civilized plan was to send the negroes round at nightfall to the nearest inns (here very properly termed "ordinaries"), with a note to any lady or gentleman who might be putting up there, stating that if they did not like their accommodation, Mr. —— would be happy to see them at his house close by, to which a black with a lantern would conduct them. This system was often successful; for, in the old times, all you could obtain at these places were eggs and bacon, hoe-cake, and peach brandy; a bed stuffed with shavings, on a frame that rocked like a cradle, and in a room so well ventilated that a traveller had some difficulty in keeping his umbrella erect, if endeavoring, under this convenience, to find shelter from the rain while in bed. But as the planter's hospitality proved such an antagonist to the landlord's interests, the latter always had it made up to him in presents, so that all parties were well content; and, probably, the only sufferer in the end was the cerebellum of the guest. Whether the decline of such a spirit may be deplored or not, it is not to be wondered at. As emigrants began to pour into the woods a planter had seldom occasion to lift his rifle to his shoulder in demanding their society, but, on the contrary, he probably soon obtained those who required some such gesticulation to be got rid of.

I was much amused by a story I once heard of a proprietor sending to an inn one evening, when he was in unusually good spirits, to desire the company of any stray gentleman who would so far favor him; and his sable Mercury returning with a New-England preacher who was journeying on a crusade against slavery, and who immediately commenced tracing a comparison between the planter and Beelzebub, which lasted until daylight.

At the time of which I am writing, racing was still the ruling diversion. To the credit of their taste and feeling, that vulgar brutality, cockfighting, had long fallen into neglect. While of sling, under proper circumstances,

namely, a certain time of life and time of night, I must
declare my unqualified approbation, with their racing,
also, I was highly pleased. I attended their principal
course at Williamsburg, and better order and arrangement I had never seen at Newmarket. Horses of all ages
ran for subscription purses, two out of three four-mile
heats won £100 the first day, and £50 every other, the
races generally lasting a week. The riders were chiefly
their owners; and I was informed that their knowledge
of the science of jockeyship was quite as profound as that
of the English nobility. This is no small praise. To the
eye of an ignoramus like myself everything seemed perfectly fair, nor was my esteem for my acquaintances les-
sened by the position I saw them in, since, when the ride
was over, they did not bring the stable into their houses.
My attention was most attracted by their horses: such a
variety of heights and shapes would have made an English
turf-hunter stare. Imagine, beside the sleek, proud, well-
trained, elegant-limbed English racer, just imported, and
pawing the ground with the conscious dignity of an aristocrat, a low, long-backed, shaggy plebeian, undressed and
dirty, his legs pillars, and his monstrous head set upon a
short, straight neck, poking the earth as if ashamed of his
presumption in venturing into such noble company. Judging with a common eye, I gave the republican no chance;
indeed, I ventured upon a small bet that this four-legged
Caliban, this outrage on all the rules of English stable
lore, would imagine that he had a cart at his tail, and not
achieve the winning-post before sundown. What, then,
was my surprise when, on the signal for starting, away
this fellow went, all fire and spirits, not galloping or
springing *secundem artem*, but scouring the earth like a
demon of pestilence, his nose erect as if he snuffed a distant feed of corn, and his mane and tail floating like a
pirate's pennons. His rider, a tall man in red sleeves,

whose only solicitude was to keep his seat, gave me an idea of Æolus, the god of storms, hurrying over the ocean to engulf a fleet. I need scarcely say that, to the shame of all science and propriety, this animal came in first, and without whip or spur. But he crowned his triumph with a real trait of magnanimity. When the noble Briton arched his neck with his usual air of high-breeding, the victor, heedless of the shouts about him, poked his nose again into the ground, as if only anxious to show that humility which ever ·marks the true hero.

More fun, however, prevailed at another species of this diversion, peculiar to the interior, called "quarter-racing," which was a match between a pair of horses to run a quarter of a mile in a straight direction. This feat usually took place near some tavern, in a field where a path was hedged in, about ten feet wide, for the competitors, the sides of which were generally lined by a motley multitude of negroes, Dutchmen, Yankee pedlers, and backwoodsmen, among whom, with long whips in their hands to clear the ground, moved the proprietors and betters, riding or leading their horses. The cattle for this contest were a peculiar breed, somewhat larger than ponies, shaggy as bears, but frisky as lambs. When the start was given they went off at full speed, so that the affair was over before you imagined it begun. The event was always proclaimed by a tornado of applause from the winner's party, the niggers in particular hallooing, jumping, and clapping their hands in a frenzy of delight, more especially if the horses had happened to jostle and one of the riders been thrown off with a broken leg; whereupon the defeated owner, or some friend for him, always dealt out retribution with his whip, for the purpose, as he termed it, of maintaining order. Sometimes twenty of these whip syllabubs would take place in a day, and then the diversions would be wound up by trials at rifle-shooting, cock-fighting, and boxing; so that, what with the wrangling of the owners, the slang of the grooms, the fun of the niggers, and the diversities of other characters upon the ground— the muscular backwoodsman contrasting in frame and spirit with the lanky New-Yorker, and the quiet calculation of both with the epithetical jabber of the "Connecticut chaps" —a scene of this sort was one of the most animated and primitive I had the fortune to stumble on.

The last and least frequent mode of passing time that I partook of in Virginia was hunting. It is a curious thing that, with few or none of the domestic tastes of the mother-country, the slave states alone were decidedly English in their public amusements. Whether the importation of these had been generally beneficial to so young a country is another question. The planters had wealth and leisure, two incentives to enjoyment, besides a greater than either—a warm climate. Climate, in fact, makes all the difference. It is an easy thing to be a stoic in a cold one, the absence of temptation always leading a man to flatter himself into a belief of his superior goodness. However, hunting, unattended by the Bacchanalian climaxes of Lincolnshire, could not come under the ban of even the "Blue Laws." It was a healthy recreation and served to increase a man's knowledge of topography—perhaps of geology also—for how many specimens of earth does a thorough Nimrod of any country bring home on his garments if, with the true martyr-like perseverance of his tribe, he turns neither to the right nor to the left in pursuit of his object.

But hunting in Virginia, like every other social exotic, was a far different thing from its English original. The meaning of the latter is simple and explicit. A party of horsemen meet at an appointed spot and hour, to turn up or turn out a deer or a fox, and pursue him to a standstill. Here a local peculiarity—the abundance of game—upsets all system. The practice seemed to be for the company to enter the wood, beat up the quarters of anything, from a stag to a snake, and take their chance for a chase. If the game went off well, and it was possible to follow it through the thickets and morasses, ten to one that at every hundred yards up sprung so many rivals that horses and hunters were puzzled which to select, and every buck, if he chose, could have a deer to himself—an arrangement that I was told proved generally satisfactory, since it enabled the worst rider, when all was over, to talk about as many difficulties surmounted as the best.

A friend of mine near Richmond, who had a pack of hounds, invited me to go out with him at the next meeting, proffering the use of a thorough-bred quadruped. I accepted the kindness, but more with a view of discovering what the sport consisted of than from any abstract love of it. My chase through life had been of a different species, and I take the liberty of relating this deviation after other game merely because it gave rise to an adventure and a train of reflection. One cool and cloudy morning I trotted with my friend to the scene of action, where I met a host of acquaintances, all of whom entertained the idea that I was a superior rider, which really means a man who believes his skull to be so thick that there can be no danger of cracking it. Our salutations were soon over, and we proceeded to hostilities by skulking into a dark wood, while I perceived that every eye was fixed upon me in evident expectation of something extraordinary. In a few minutes the hounds opened, a young red-deer went off, and, from the spirit of my horse and the thick array of branches, I was in some danger of following his example. Luckily, however, the game took to a field, and there, with the inspiration of the general yelling, I certainly did master two or three hedges and ditches in a style that surprised myself, and riveted my friends in their delusion.

In a short time I got separated from the rest, and found myself again in that Tartarean wood where, every stump threatening a case for a surgeon, a calculating trot was the utmost I could accomplish. Before long I heard a rustling in the bushes before me, and then saw an animal, which I took for our fugitive, spring away to escape; but, in defiance of all obstacles, I pressed him so close that he took it in dudgeon, and, turning round, displayed a fine set of teeth and uttered a low growl. What this beast was, according to Linnæus, I have never been able to make out. My survey was so concentrated on the con- struction of his jaws that I neglected to note his other features. But I think the most fervid natural philosopher would have concurred in my query—not, Is this beast a wolf or a panther?—but, Has he dined? It was evident I had mistaken the individual, and, as he seemed to con- sider an apology was due to him, I felt that the best would be to desist from further intrusion. Accordingly I turned round, and in a few springs gained once more the open. All sound of the chase had now died away, and I found myself alone in a strange country without the slightest means of obtaining a clew to the track of my com- panions. In this dilemma I threw the reins on my steed's neck (agreeably to the rule of those oft-bewildered gen- tlemen, the knights-errant), and, at an easy canter, he car- ried me some miles across country without my perceiving road, house, or human being. At length, beginning to sus- pect his judgment, I reined up, when the cry of the hounds came suddenly upon us in the direction we were going. My Bucephalus needed neither voice nor spur to renew his best pace—bogs and brakes glided past me with fear- ful rapidity,—and, lo! at a bound he brought me into an area where the deer had been run to bay on the edge of a deep stream, in which all the horses were splashing and snorting. I was actually *the first in at the death!* The compliments and congratulations which I now received on all sides for my extraordinary riding would take pages to enumerate. I must have crossed rocks and swamps which they had been compelled to skirt; in fact, I had done more than any hunter in Virginia had ever achieved before me. As I was not in a humor to quarrel with this reputation, I affected to refer all the merit to my horse; but, as we jogged home to dinner, I could not help settling into the conviction, how much more, after all, a man's fame in this world depends upon accident than on ability!

As I was always interested in local traditions, one of my friends related to me some concerning Captain Smith, the first explorer of Virginia, and his well-known enamoured wild girl—the pure, though passionate, Pocahontas. Of all the early adventurers Smith seems to have possessed the greatest amount of estimable qualities. With considerable skill as a navigator he combined a spirit of enterprise which aimed at honorable ends. Wild as had been his career as a soldier of fortune in nearly all parts of Europe, principles of rectitude and benevolence are seen in his subsequent life, not less in the publication of his discoveries than in his conduct in the government of the colony. One thing is very obvious—his ruling object was not his own aggrandizement; and this is no small praise when we consider the veil which romance has often thrown over the nakedness of robbery; the proverbial ease with which success becomes a cosmetic for the hideousness of crime. Some evidence of his character may be gleaned from the moral discipline which he established in Virginia, apparently so much at variance with the habits of his early life. Leading a party into the woods on one occasion to fell timber, a broken-down prodigal who had been exported by his family as a last resource had handled the axe but a few minutes when his fingers began to blister, whereupon he vented his indignation in a series of emphatic oaths. Smith remonstrated with him on the impropriety of his language, but finding that he persisted, ordered his exclamations to be numbered, and when they returned home compelled the delinquent to have a can of water poured down his sleeve for every offence. This mode of punishment proved a speedy purifier of the language of his followers.

There was much magnanimity in his reply to some old son of Plutus who once proposed to set him up with a ship and stores if he would make a descent upon the South American coasts, where riches were speedily amassed by buccaneering. "I have been told," he replied, "that riches make life pass swiftly and pleasantly, and that 'tis the poor man only who grows really old; but it doth seem to me that could I consent to rob men that never wronged me, the peaceful and well-doing, perchance the widow and the orphan, my days would of a sudden grow to such intolerable length I should pray God to shorten them."

He gave, too, a pleasing proof of ingenuity when Powhattan, the royal father of Pocahontas, inquired the cause of their difference of color, and the white-man's motives in crossing the "Great Salt Lake." "In the beginning," said he, "Manito placed one family on earth, a father and four sons, and they were white. To one son he gave the East, to another the South, and to another the West. He had another portion for the youngest son, but he was wilful, left his home, and wandered by a northern path into the woods of the land beyond the great salt lake, at which Manito was wroth, and the shade of his displeasure fell upon the red-man's face. But the children of the East continued to live in his presence and enjoy his smile, which kept their faces white, until at last Manito bid them go over the great lake and embrace their red brother, and so bring him back to his obedience."

Of Pocahontas, the Indian girl, the fair, fond, and faithful, what can we say but that she is one whom history and tradition alike delight to honor, as an instance of Nature perfecting a work beyond the power of Art to improve. Her heart was stored with so much confidence in others' goodness that it was itself kept pure, and had an oracle of conduct given it in every impulse. In addition to this, when we know that she was the child of a clime where womanhood follows at once on infancy, and where imagination, like an uncaged bird, was ever on the wing, we cannot wonder at the fervor of her passion for the gallant navigator, whose person and pursuits appealed so powerfully to her superstition as well as to her softer feelings. By her intervention the whites were secured from molestation, and their alliance cemented by her subsequent marriage with Mr. Rolfe, a worthy person, who converted her to Christianity and brought her to England. Though she did not herself live to return to Virginia, her child did so, and became the ancestor of my informant.

Among the characteristic traits related of her, none pleased me more than her reply to a lady of the court, shortly after her presentation, who asked her, " What is love ?" The child of the woods paused an instant and replied, " It is life !" Equally happy was her explanation of a storm at sea, which she termed " Manito walking on the water." Her visit to England dazzled much more than it delighted her, for Nature had given her so pure a taste that it kept her senses in subjection. After she had been presented to Queen Anne, and while the full glitter of royalty had just passed before her eyes, she was found sitting alone and in tears. Her husband, imagining this could result but from one cause, said to her, " You are thinking of the many precious stones upon our queen's breast ?" She shook her head. " Why, then, are you sad ?" " Is not the earth sad ?" she replied, " it is now three days that the sun has hid himself." Not all the brilliance of the English court could compensate her for cloudy skies. Tomolomo, her brother-in-law, who accompanied her to England, had been enjoined by Powhatan to take note how many people the country contained, for which purpose he took a short stick, and, on landing at Plymouth, began to cut a notch for every fresh face he met. It may be supposed that this mode of computation did not long suffice. It was night when he landed on returning to his native soil, and the king, bearing in mind the important question, instantly put it to him. Tomolomo replied by a significant gesture. He pointed to the stars.

The least pleasing retrospect in connection with this state is the moral stain which England inflicted upon it in making it a receptacle for convicts. Nothing has proved the source of so much unfounded obloquy, for, to this day, Englishmen entertain the absurd notion that those manacled wretches, on obtaining their liberty, by some hocus-pocus purchased estates and became the fathers of the present gentry. The drunken jest of the comedian Cooke, when he asked for their "family jewels," the "Birmingham bracelets," was but the expression of a very general conviction. It would be awkward, certainly, for most countries to look too deeply into their origin, with a view to prove its perfect purity; but England could not claim to be an exception, since her blood, which has for ages been a pool drained from all Europe, would present to the analyzer some of the most heterogeneous elements.

Dr. Franklin entertained a due sense of the insult offered to his country by the above practice, and expressed it with his usual power of sarcasm, when he sent to Sir Robert Walpole a present of rattlesnakes, to be put in the king's gardens at Kew, "in return for the curious venomous reptiles the minister had been pleased to present to Virginia." But that the subject is repulsive to dwell upon, I might insert some singular particulars respecting these honorable exiles, many of whom, like tigers at play, were amusing to contemplate though dangerous to approach. One especially, of the name of Boroughs, stood out in bold relief. This fellow possessed very superior mental abilities. His reasonings leading him to look on men as, in fact, but a race of plunderers under various names, he inferred his right to make war on all parties—to be, in fact, a social Arab. Such a philosophy, it will be supposed, was accompanied with some humor; indeed, it is a melancholy fact that vagabonds are generally the greatest humorists. Shakespeare thought so, or he would not have favored us with such an illustrious example as Sir John Falstaff. It is related of Boroughs that, conversing one day with the chaplain of the fort, he observed, "Your task, sir, is much easier than that of other ministers." "Easier!" exclaimed the clergyman with a stare—"easier, how?" "Why, you tell me that, in every Christian, conviction must precede repentance. Now we are *convicted* to your hands, you have only got to *convert* us." Another instance was when, for some offence, he was sentenced to mount the "wooden horse," or military stocks. The chaplain, who had entertained hopes of bringing Boroughs to a sense of his transgressions, saw him with mingled sorrow and indignation, and asked what he was doing. "Doing, sir? I am taking your advice." "Mine?" "Yes; I am running the Christian race—'steadfast and immovable.'"

In perfect harmony with the presence of convicts was the mental bondage of the lower orders, which would appear to have been in the first instance the crime of the government. The radical hostility of tyrants to the circulation of thought was never more strongly illustrated than in the reply of Sir William Berkeley, Governor of Virginia, to certain questions respecting the colony, propounded by England in 1670. "I thank God there are

here no free schools nor printing, and I hope we shall not
have them these hundred years; for learning has brought
disobedience and heresy and sects into the world; and
printing has divulged them and libels against the best
governments.   God keep us from both !"

As the autumn advanced I received a summons from
Wignell to prepare for a visit to Baltimore ; but meeting
Cooper at Richmond, I proposed to him to fill up a month's
interim by a lecturing excursion through this state and
the western part of Maryland, which he consented to, as
a more agreeable mode of combining profit with pleasure
than playing in small theatres with the thermometer at
eighty degrees.   Cooper,* whose merits as an actor I have
noticed elsewhere, was one of the most eccentric and yet
engaging of my professional brethren.   I have already
mentioned the large measure of enjoyment which the ease
and freedom of society in the South, combined with the
prosperous state of theatricals, presented to an actor.
Talent, and the manners of a gentleman, were a general
introduction.   To these Cooper added the influence of
native connections, the graces of a handsome person, and
much agreeable information, for his education had been
well attended to in England.   It would be hard to say
whether he were the greatest favorite in public or private,

---

* THOMAS ABTHORPE COOPER was the first great American tragedian.   Born
in 1776 in England, he was educated by William Godwin.   With the aid
and advice of Thomas Holcroft, the author of the "Road to Ruin," and a
close friend of Godwin's, Cooper went on the stage at the age of seventeen,
beginning at Edinburgh without success.   He afterwards acted in London,
and in December, 1796, he made his first appearance in America.   For
nearly forty years he was the foremost figure on the American stage.   In
1806 he became the manager of the Park Theatre in New York.   He made
his last appearance in New York in 1835, and afterwards acted in the
South.   His daughter married a son of President Tyler, who gave Cooper
a place in the New York Custom-House.   He died at Bristol, Penn., April
21, 1849.

THOMAS ABTHORP COOPER.

From the *Polyanthus*, Boston, 1806.

with the men or the women. With the one he would ride, drive, shoot, or bet. For the other he had the eye of Caliph Vathek—"instant annihilation." Such an emptying of Cupid's quiver as on the nights of his performance I suppose had never previously been known in the Union. But all this felicity, strengthening in him a spirit of adventure and a blindness to consequences, was continually throwing him into dilemmas out of which nothing but extraordinary courage could rescue him. In this last particular I have never met with a man who surpassed him. Had he entered the service of Mars instead of Melpomene, death or eminence must have been speedily the result. And his was no Dutch courage, no constitutional apathy or blindness to danger; he had a proud and sensitive spirit, and was always staring the fatal sisters full in the face. Two instances of this occurred during the excursion in question. We were delivering our entertainment one evening at Georgetown, when Cooper, not being prepared with a particular recitation for which he had been announced, apologized and substituted another. A loud hiss, however, was the consequence from a member of Congress named Dawson. Cooper, maintaining his composure, identified the individual, and when his duties were over sent him his card, demanding an apology for the insult or satisfaction. Mr. Dawson, affecting not to consider him his equal, treated the matter with contempt; when Cooper sent a friend to inform him that unless he complied with one or the other of his requisitions, he would follow him to Washington and horsewhip him before the senate-house. This threat had its effect; the member apologized.

But a more striking instance occurred at Fredericks-town on a somewhat similar occasion. We had, as usual, engaged the assembly-room of the tavern, and a short time before the performance commenced had observed a great crowd of the mobility collect under the windows; but, as we were accustomed to this sight in all the small towns, it did not surprise us. Cooper's best recitation was "Alexander's Feast," which he gave with a force and variety that I have never heard equalled. Now it so happened that, in the most energetic passage, where Timotheus wishes to give Alexander a fillip—

> "Now strike the lyre again!
> A louder, yet a louder strain!" etc.—

a crash ensued that was no bad illustration of the desired "rattling peal of thunder:" a brickbat, large enough to have felled an ox, came through the window, flew over the heads of several ladies and gentlemen, and actually brushing a curl on my colleague's temple, concluded its career by scraping an acquaintance with my shins. The room was instantly thrown into confusion: the ladies shrieked; the gentlemen emphasized; I, seizing the missile, limped down-stairs to call an officer, and Cooper— drank a glass of water. Unluckily the only keepers of the peace in this town seemed to be the Quakers, and as the crowd was too great to permit a discovery of the delinquent, I had to return, with my leg and my feelings in an equal state of irritation. To my surprise I found order restored in the room and Cooper continuing his declamation. When he concluded, I had to step forward with some comic interlude, for which I felt little inclined, when he, throwing on a cloak, descended to the bar and asked the landlord for the loan of a small cudgel. Secreting this, he stepped into the crowd and inquired of the nearest person, "Who was the man that threw the brickbat?" "Why should I tell 'ee?" was the reply. "Because," said Cooper, "you'd get five dollars for your trouble." "Five dollars! That be the man—he in the knot of longish chaps there." Cooper was thus directed to a group of about a dozen backwoodsmen in the very heart of the crowd, chuckling over the feat of their companion, and who presented in their tall, muscular frames no contemptible phalanx for a civil disturbance. Towards these he made his way with a firm step and repeated his demand. He was gratified by the object stepping out (in look and length a competent leader of the band), and, surmising his business, asking with a husky laugh, " Well, squire, what if I be he ?" "That's sufficient," said Cooper, grasping him by the throat with the sudden strength of a tiger, and bringing down his cudgel like a stroke of lightning on his head and shoulders. The impetuosity and vigor of the attack deprived the animal, although much superior in brute strength, of all power of resistance, and under a shower of blows that would have indented a wall, he sank upon his knees and begged for mercy, his paralyzed companions offering not the slightest interposition. The fact was that, as regards feelings, Cooper was belaboring the whole group. When his stick at length flew into splinters, he consigned the ruffian to a warm friend below, and—the crowd making ready way for him—returned to the inn. A few minutes after my effusion concluded, and he was at his post with his usual serene and dignified air. Every spark of external evidence quenched which would have given a hint of what had passed, he proceeded to deliver Shakespeare's "Soliloquy on Death" with all the calm abstractedness required, as successfully as he had embodied Dryden's energy after the brickbat, when, according to a gentleman who sat near him, a gulp of water seemed to have washed down all his indignation. The whole circumstances, and especially this power of subduing all appearance of emotion, implied, to my mind, the possession of the highest order of courage—the cool calculation of danger, and its proud defiance.

For our excursion my friend proposed to join me in a

tandem, but I, wishing to give my wife and child an air-
ing, decided on a phaeton.   He would not, however, give
up his whim, so dragged from the recesses of a coach-
maker's yard a tall, rickety affair, like an old-fashioned
coach-box, which a dozen miles of Virginian roads threatened to annihilate.   It reminded me of a palsied octoge-
narian plunging again into the world, to essay once more
the struggles that had already shattered him.   Travelling
at this period was pretty much the same throughout the
Union.   With the exception of the roads between the
principal cities, or immediately adjacent, any thoroughfare might, without a pun, have been termed thorough-
foul.   This was owing to so much of the communication
being carried on by water.   It would be difficult to give
an accurate description of a road in the Slave States after
a slight rain—to portray the lakes which, under the title
of "gullies," slumbering complacently in the midst, compelled you to perform a picturesque tour round their edge;
or the shiny eminences termed hills, whose level it seemed
a presumption to aspire to.   The track of the wheels was
certainly well-defined, in two broad paths full of water;
and where a hollow occurred, some careful hand had usually filled it up with a substantial pile of stones, like an
Indian tumulus.   This rendered the navigation of these
roads no small science, since it was evident if you escaped
the breakers on one side you were pretty sure of founder-
ing in a gulf on the other.   One virtue they certainly had
—consistency.   I never found them deviate but in one
particular, when the path lay through a swamp, when it
was constructed with the trunks of trees laid transversely
together, over which the wheels passed with a distinct
jolt.   A mile's ride was about the most powerful experiment on one's anatomy a man could desire.

But had the roads been as smooth as a bowling-green,
the absence of human nature and the deep, unbroken

gloom of the solitude threw a weight upon my spirits which often made me wish for the highways of England. To a traveller on his first visit "the majesty of the eternal woods" may appeal with poetic effect; also to an ornithologist or a professional sketcher. But it strikes me that all socially disposed persons like myself must heartily wish Nature, in her nakedness, to be confined to romances, and to witness instead her well-clothed beauty in the robes of harvest, with comfortable cottages dimpling her meadows, and a cheering, quick succession of villages upon her roads, clustering round a smooth green, under the wing of some paternal manor-house or church.

One of the local peculiarities of Virginia was an improved breed of mosquitoes, termed gallinippers, in size and sting not much inferior to wasps. The origin of their name I could never precisely discover. This class of natives were, in general, most sedulous in their attentions to foreigners, but the gallinippers, perhaps with a more refined taste, specially preferred Frenchmen; and while the common mosquito appeared capable of adapting himself to every local variation of the country, being found on clayey or marshy soils, rocks or rivers, this species, with more of the air of an hereditary peerage, traced their extraction solely to swamps. Round the brink of these strongholds they lay in wait for their prey like the old robber knights; and, in hot weather, their thirst was not fastidious as to the color of the skin. Imagine the situation of a luckless wight journeying along a road of transverse trees, where expedition would be annihilation, seated, perhaps, on the bottom of a wagon, which bobbed him up like a parched pea—a jolt a second—while the sun streamed fire upon his caput, finding himself suddenly in the grasp of these sanguinary marauders, each of whom, however active the defence, was sure to sheathe his blade in him at the same instant. What was an ancient martyrdom in comparison? What would not Nero have given for such auxiliaries.

I once heard an amusing story of a negro, at an inn, who being blest with an extra thick skin, set an ordinary mosquito at defiance. A traveller who had suffered considerable punctuation, hearing of this, laid a wager with the fellow that he would not lie half an hour on the edge of a swamp close by without moving or expressing pain. Sambo manfully accepted the challenge, and stretched himself at full length on his face, leaving the entire region of his reverse a broad sheet of darkness exposed to the enemy, a party of planters and passengers standing in judgment over him. In a few minutes a thick swarm of settlers alighted on him and commenced experiments in various quarters, but apparently with no effect, for neither in head, body, or limb did the hero wince. Not a muscle quivered. Their number soon increased, and it amounted to a moral certainty that the challengee must speedily cry out, unless indeed he enjoyed the hide of a hedgehog. But the half-hour was elapsing and there he continued to lie, as still and stiff as a column of black marble. At length the traveller, who was now beginning to get the laugh against him, felt so irritated at his miscalculation that he took a cigar from his mouth, and, instead of knocking off its ashes on his boot, pushed its lighted end against the negro's broadest expanse. In an instant, as by an electric impulse, the latter sprang on his legs and shouted, as he rubbed himself, "Cursee, massa, dat a gallinipper."

Virginia was also famous for its hams, which, next to the orthodox Westphalia, are the finest I have ever eaten. By what process the latter attain their excellence I am ignorant, but here the pigs were always turned into the woods, and, listen, O epicure of the East! their chief source of subsistence was the snakes. This strange taste seems to admit of but one explanation—the destruction of

a common enemy, by which they contributed to the public
good as well as served a private end, and which was in accordance with the spirit of the times. The pig proved himself a patriot ! I am unwilling to underrate his motives by
supposing that there was anything particularly tempting in
the flesh of his victim, for the predilection was never heard
of in any other part of the world. The fact stands by
itself, and ought to rescue the swinish character from its
usual degradation. But besides being a philanthropist,
the pig displayed considerable science as a general in his
mode of extirpation. It was an established principle never
to attack a snake but with combined forces, which usually
consisted of a party of three, two vigorous youths in the
capacity of chasseurs, and an experienced manœuvrer as
the main body, who always took up his position in reserve.
The'action was commenced by one of the light corps being
sent forward to dislodge the enemy from his trenches.
The snake, instantly rising, rattled a *reveille* with his tail,
and presented arms with his fang. Drawing himself up
to spring on his foe, the latter watched his eye and grunt-
ed defiance. By this time the other wing had made the
circuit of the bush, and, falling upon the snake in the rear,
began to nibble his tail. Turning indignantly to annihilate this assailant, he left a long line exposed to another,
whose sagacious mind had safely calculated the result.
Down came the main body at a swift trot, and, with determined jaws, seizing the reptile in the middle, crunched
him in halves, upon which, according to the usage of commanders in all ages, he retired with the best part of the
plunder, leaving the obnoxious head still alive to be quieted by his subordinates.

Cooper's tandem, as I had predicted, was speedily shattered by the roads, though they considerably improved
on our getting into Maryland. After patching up the
valetudinarian at various places, it came down with an

ominous crash on our way to Hagerstown, and we were
obliged to stop two hours at a blacksmith's till fresh power
of existence was supplied. Here, however, the delay was
relieved by a curious discovery respecting our son of Vul-
can, who, we found, possessed a reputation for curing
insanity by means of iron rings which he forged and fitted
to the middle finger of the left hand. How to explain the
mystery I know not, unless the imagination was powerfully acted upon by this grim Mulciber, who certainly had
a riveting voice and eye, and who might have practised
some tricks at his forge which appeared like alliance with
powers of darkness. But to this fact I can vouch, that I
knew a Mr. Neith, a merchant in this state, who became
incapable of conducting his business, and that I met him
a twelvemonth after, perfectly restored, with an iron ring
upon his finger, which he seriously acknowledged to have
been the means of his recovery. Cooper, whose hatred
of charlatanism sometimes led him to forget his manners,
burst into a laugh when he heard the disclosure, whereupon this mender of men's heads and horses' feet remarked
with a significance which let out the secret of his system,
"Aye, aye, sir, you may laugh, but it's a strange thing
why men should become mad, and it must be a strange
thing to make them well again."

Near this mysterious farrier's stood a Quakers' chapel,
and Mulciber gave us a standing, or rather circulating,
story of General Lee and this peaceful tenement during
the war. Lee, either from liking or laziness, distinguished
himself by the barbarous peculiarity of a bushy head of
hair and enormous whiskers; his face, like that of the
country, presenting the contrast of masses of shade relieved by deep ridges and deep hollows. Galloping in
this direction one Sunday afternoon, he was overtaken
by a storm, and on reaching the chapel made no ceremony in running his horse under its shed (always, in the

States, attached to country places of worship) ; and, for better protection, himself entering the building, and taking his seat upon the first bench that offered, but which was sufficiently conspicuous to draw on him the gaze of the whole congregation. Men and women waiting patiently for the Spirit were now moved to survey the stranger, so striking was the anomaly of his face and fashion within their simple walls. Even the elder, who had the moment previous risen to exhort, found his inspiration checked by the presence of the Philistine, till at length all the objects of the meeting were at a standstill. The elder alluded to saw the necessity of a decided step. Quitting his seat with a slow and thoughtful pace, he strode up to the general, and eying his hair intently as he laid his hand upon his shoulder, exclaimed, "Friend Esau, thou hast no business here ; thou art a stumbling-block to the meek in heart and simple in attire. Verily thou must return to thy woods," saying which, with a giant's grasp, he conducted the soldier back to the shed, a civility for which Lee thanked him by a string of epithets which, if written down, would burn a hole in the paper.

Mentioning the "Friends," reminds me of a famous negro discovery. It is generally supposed that the first Quaker was a native of England, one George Fox ; but, according to the profound researches of Sambotius Quamina, the honor belongs to Mordecai, the uncle of Queen Esther, for "he would not take his hat off to Haman !"

Our excursion proved an agreeable one both as to making money and acquaintances, until my companion's pleasure was spoiled by the very means he had adopted to secure it—his tandem—which had no sooner escaped the perils of the road to be exhibited with due effect in the streets of a community than it was stopped by a constable, and he was fined for exceeding the pace established

by law. Such a proceeding in a quarter where he had
conceived liberty would be licensed not restrained, wanted
but a slight addition to decide his preference for the better state of things in cities. This was soon forthcoming.
On the second night of our entertainment at Hagerstown
we were opposed by an exhibition which drew at a draught
every spectator engaged to us. This was the first importation of a Bartholomew fair novelty I had met with in
the States, and did not yield to the most extraordinary
in my recollection. It was thus announced :

"This day is introduced to the American public the
far-famed monster of Madagascar called the One-horned
Boukabekabus, whose age, powers, and dimensions have
never been discovered, and must remain a matter of conjecture to the end of time. He will eat, or drink any
given quantity of wine, read or write like any ordinary
gentleman, etc. On Thursday, after performing all these
feats, he will exceed himself, etc. After astonishing the
crowned heads of Europe the proprietor pants to submit
this curiosity to the judges of Hagerstown."

I prevailed on Cooper to accompany me to see a phenomenon which evidently had escaped the notice of Linnæus, when we soon discovered that the extraordinary
monster consisted of an ordinary bull's hide, surmounted
by the canvas head of a unicorn, and distended by wooden
ribs, containing a man in the interior, who roared through
a trumpet and flickered a pair of candles in the glass eyes
to give them a mysterious aspect. We also found that
the ingenious and modest impostor was no other than a
runaway tailor from our wardrobe, who had carried with
him all the materials for his exhibition.

After this appeal to the critical acumen of Hagerstown
(a proper refuge for outcasts), we felt disinclined to continue in the lists, so returned to Alexandria, where, until
our duties called us away, we spent our time in fishing-

excursions to the Potomac, frequently dining at a tavern on its banks. Here a drinking-vessel supposed to give a particular zest to punch was a skull tipped with silver, said to be a relic of the celebrated pirate Teach, or "Blackbeard." The tradition ran as follows :

One evening this scourge of the Southern coast moored his craft at the mouth of the river and went ashore with his crew in two parties, one to obtain provisions, the other to assist in secreting their treasures. He was busy at this work when an English sloop-of-war, which had quietly followed him, suddenly dropped anchor in a position to prevent his escape, and sent a well-manned barge to capture his ship. Teach and his companions sprang into their boat, and by violent exertion reached their ship nearly at the same moment. But the opposing force was too superior to give even more than their usual desperation any hope of success. The commander of the boarders was a brave Scotchman who, desiring the credit of subduing Teach in person, waved his Andrew Ferrara and challenged him to combat. The rover clinched his weapon in defiance, and hostilities were suspended fore-and-aft to witness the result. For some minutes the contest was dubious, but the coolness of the Scot enabled him to plant a severe blow upon the pirate's shoulder which let out a stream of crimson. "Ha!" exclaimed the latter, still firm upon his legs, "well struck, brother seaman!" "Weel," replied the Scot, "gin ye like it ye sall hae more on't," and with the next stroke severed the pirate's black head from his shoulders. He then ordered it to be put in boiling water and thoroughly cleansed, when he took it on shore and made it a present to the progenitor of its present possessor.

CHAPTER VIII.

1800–1.—Tour to the Ohio; Passage of the Potomac; the Alleghany Hills; Three Kinds of Settlers, Squatters, Utopians, and New England Farmers.—Backwoodsmen; Shooting Exploits.—Pittsburgh Smoke.— Indian Wooing-hut and Honeymoon.—The Ohio.—The Aborigines of America —Indian Antiquities.—Welsh in America.—The Island of Blennerhasset; Art and Nature.—Philadelphia Balls; Travellers' Tales.— American Beefsteak Club.—A Coincidence.—The Quaker and the Irishman.—Desdemona's Revival.—St. George's Society.—Tubbs the Tragedian and his Adventure.—Poetry and Matter-of-fact; the Last Creditor. —A French Bankrupt.—American Advertisements and Literal Mistakes.—Black Nurses and the Yellow Fever; a Colored Lady.—Fennel's Immortality.—My Aversion and Adventure; a Female Falstaff.—Peel's Museum.—Historical Anecdote.

At the close of another pleasant season in Philadelphia my good friends, Messrs. Clay and Arnott, proposed, for my summer's pastime, a tour to the Ohio as far as the Island of Blennerhasset, whose romantic loveliness was now an all-absorbing theme both with natives and foreigners. Assured that this excursion would repay my feelings more than any I had yet taken in the Union, I had no hesitation in complying. We accordingly took the fine weather at its flood, and on the backs of three accredited roadsters essayed the path to Pittsburgh in becoming style, making our first important halt at the advanced guard of the Alleghany Mountains, termed the "Blue Ridge," partly, perhaps, from the effect its towering aspect produced on the faces of travellers. Mr. Jefferson, in his "Notes on Virginia," had given such a vivid description of these hills that I could not resist the temptation during the previous summer to visit the "passage of the Potomac," though then residing at a hundred miles' distance. It is unquestionably the sublimest scene in America, after the Falls of Niagara. Let the reader first imagine the " backbone of the States "—as these hills have been happily termed—three ridges of precipitous elevations stretching many hundred miles from north to south, resembling lines of ocean-waves arrested in their swell. Standing on the brow of one of the advanced lines of these, and looking far away into the intermediate valley, he sees on his right the Shenandoah coming up, chafing and foaming like a noble steed, having ranged at the foot of the mountains a hundred miles in quest of an outlet ; and, on the left, rolling on with equal volume and vehemence, the Potomac. He trembles for the thunder of their meeting, but 'needlessly ; rushing with united force upon their prison walls, they rend them asunder, and spring away exultingly towards the sea, while everything around them seems to breathe a welcome; green lands lying in a delightful calm partake their sunshine, and the heavens stoop to print a kiss upon their bosom.

These hills, from the marine exuviæ found embedded in their summits, have given rise to much geological speculation, and Mr. Jefferson, with his usual vivacity, supposes the possibility of their having once formed a barrier to an inland ocean (not the Mosaic Deluge). To the social philosopher they are more interesting from the fact of having long proved a *levée* to a human tide, and thereby exercised an important influence on the national development. Abounding as America does with the wonders of nature, still I think these possess but a secondary claim on our attention if unassociated with the being for whose dwelling-place the world was formed. I have, therefore, abstained from noticing the curiosities which in every day's ride met my eye (even, for instance, the natural bridge of limestone over Cedar Creek in Virginia), because feeling them to rank, in human interest, below the commonplace acclivities of the Alleghany hills.

Rivers and mountains seem to be the two features of the earth which have most influenced the character and happiness of men. The former have led to general inter-course and change; the latter, shutting up communities into inner worlds, have perpetuated their aboriginal rough-ness. The river-valley has been the arena for taste and refinement, but also for oppression. On the mountain-top the flame of liberty has burned brighter in a rarefied air, although the vessel that contained it was unadorned. These opposite conditions, however, both advanced the march of their great equalizer—intelligence—by the les-sons they have given to each other. The hills in question, if they have not, as yet, like those of Spain and Wales, been fled to as a barrier to the step of regal tyrants, have performed the same service against social ones. Rearing their frowning fronts to the great mob of emigrants, they have incited the hardy and industrious to surmount them, but discouraged the lazy and dissolute, who, looking only to immediate ease, assumed their aspect to be a sample of the lands beyond them, and turned away to the more con-genial clime of the South. Thus they secured to the Western region a hardy population, able to cope with the hazards and privations which attended its first settlement, and to promote, by enterprise and principle, its lasting welfare; and at this day they form the line of separation between the two main divisions of character which the Union contains.

There appears to have been three kinds of settlers who penetrated the Western woods, and severally formed eras in their civilization. The first were squatters; men who had outlived their characters and fortunes in other parts of the Union and been goaded by the law into a taste for savage freedom. Accordingly they moved off to the

West, where the rights of property were as yet defined only by the agreeable condition of possession. These necessary pioneers were shaped in frame and spirit to sustain the dangers and difficulties of their undertaking, to defy alike the Indian and the wolf, the tempest and the cold. With a gun and a dog, a wagon and a wife, perhaps with a cow and a pig, they pursued their lonely path through stream and prairie to some inviting spot, there felled trees for a log hut and an outhouse for their cattle, and dug the cleared space to raise a few vegetables; but here their labor ceased. Their gun, snares, and fishing-lines supplied them with abundance of provisions, and they were able to exchange the skins of their victims for rum and ammunition. This was the advanced guard of the whites, which the Indian had to resist or to retire from. If lead or liquor gave them the victory, neighbors collected round by right of purchase, and as the claims of society extended the squatter became again unhappy. Defined right, or the sacrifice of private to the general good, was the fiend that haunted him. His cattle had to be restrained from trespassing, and his traps and lines were discovered within the circle of his neighbor's grant. Turning, at length, indignantly from the grovellers who talked of law, while he professed the older doctrine of discovery, he put his wagon, wife, and cattle once more in motion, and plunged farther into the wood; until, again disturbed by company, he pushed again upon the track of his fellow-savage, with whom he ended his days either in amity or blood. Such was the squatter's illustration of the instability of all things, he being known sometimes to "break ground," as it was termed, three or four times, before the advancing flood of population.

The second class were adventurers, generally with more imagination than courage, and more money than skill—virtuous enthusiasts who had schemed in cities a state of primitive enjoyment to be realized in woods. Their funds were chiefly expended in the purchase of stock and implements which, on reaching the spot, they imagined would, by some intuitive energy or instinct, get to work of their own accord. Instead of a wretched log hut they planned a substantial wood dwelling with appropriate dependencies, but before it was half up, so much more pleasant was it to design than to execute, their cattle had strayed or died, and frosts had come on before their fields were cleared, or their crops under cover; until the Utopian's ideas getting confused, he resigned activity for speculation, and resorted daily to the nearest tavern to consider, over some strong toddy, the best means of recovering his property. This proved such a bellows to his imaginative powers that he invented a hundred schemes before he could adopt one, and the one that at length crowned his term of lucubration was that of turning over the whole affair to some better judge, who would supply him with dollars enough to get back to his old quarters.

On the heels of this class came the third and thoroughly substantial, chiefly New-Englanders, who brought a capital in their heads as well as their purses, a knowledge and decision which swept away all difficulties and lightened all fatigues. By them a frowning wilderness was speedily converted into teeming meadows, and the well-stocked farm into the growing settlement.

On our way to Pittsburgh we met with various specimens of the backwoodsman, and I must say that, when clad in their green hunting-shirts, with deerskin caps and leggings, their muscular altitude fully displayed in the free handling of their long rifles, they presented the most picturesque appearance I had ever seen. I soon perceived in them some decided characteristics, such as a sharp insight into character, a ceaseless suspicion, and a quiet humor. They had a mode of leaning on their guns and

surveying a stranger which struck me as singularly intelligent.   It had nothing of the common vulgar vacuity of
the seashoresman ; it implied conviction, not inquiry ; a
look that said, not " Who are you?" but "I know you."

My good friend, Mr. Clay, had one alloy which, without warranting Dr. Johnson's anathema, certainly depre-
ciated his precious metal—a love of punning.   As a proof,
after we had endured the scrutiny of one of these natives
at the door of an inn for several minutes, I asked, in order
to abash him, " what mountains " the fellow came from.
" Can't you perceive ?" rejoined my friend, " the All-leg-
and-eye !"

With the shooting exploits of these men the world is
generally familiar.   Some of them have been too extraordinary to be credited ; such, for instance, as enlarging the
eye of a tin cock on a church steeple, or sending a bullet
half a mile across a river to perforate a milk-pail on the
head of some Lavinia who, without the slightest intima-
tion of the cause, suddenly perceives the white stream flow-
ing down her shoulders.   Dr. Ramsey, in his " History of
the War," relates, as an authenticated fact, that after the
engagement at King's Mountain riflemen were found dead
on both sides each with one eye shut and a bullet lodged
in his brain, evidently having fired together at each other
and been killed in the act of killing.   I myself witnessed
the feat of splitting a bullet on a razor at a hundred paces,
and cutting the string of a flag at three hundred.   But
their crowning achievement was, perhaps, the most common—" shooting the tin-cup;" when a man had the courage
to place a cup on his bare head and stand at a hundred
paces to have it knocked off, coolly surveying the muzzle
of the rifle as it was levelled at his brow, and guiding the
marksman to raise or lower it until the aim was true.
Had death been even occasionally the result of this amusement, its prohibition by the state must have followed ;

but such a thing was unknown.   Here was William Tell's great feat occurring as a daily diversion, and illustrating how skill creates courage.

On approaching Pittsburgh we were struck with a peculiarity nowhere else to be observed in the States: a cloud of smoke hung over it in an exceedingly clear sky, recalling to me many choking recollections of London. Instead of wood they here use coal, mines of which are plentiful in the neighborhood.   I found the town, which was called the Western Exchange, a reflex of New York, the same earnest bustle in its business, and the same national variety in its thickly thronging strangers.   Here were natives of every state, besides English, Irish, and Scotch, French, German, Dutch, Jews, and Indians. Among this motley group I was destined to make an unlooked-for acquaintance, a Mr. Wools, who had been one of the early actors in America with Morris, but who had quitted the stage about the year 1770, to follow the profession of land-surveying.   This had led him among the Indians near the Mississippi, where he had married a king's daughter, and received for her dowry a tract of land which he soon contrived to convert into a handsome independence.   As he had his time upon his hands, I prevailed on him to accompany me down the Ohio, assured that his knowledge of its Indian customs and antiquities would prove a source of amusement.   Among other things, I asked him to describe the marriage ceremony with his wife, and the nature of a honeymoon among the Southern tribes, which he did as follows:

In every village there was erected what was called a "wooing-hut," containing two rooms, having separate entrances, and a small aperture through which a voice but not a body could pass.   When a pair wished to approximate, if the chiefs made no objection, they were conducted in due form to these rooms and the doors were fastened upon them, when, like Pennsylvanian "bundlers," they passed the night in innocent conversation. If their wishes continued unchanged in the morning, they were appointed their respective tasks as tests of their good condition. The gentleman was ordered to fell a tree, something smaller round than a horse, lop its twigs, and drag it a mile. Other trifling experiments on his spinal column succeeded. The lady was commanded to plunge into a stream and swim against the tide, to display her fortitude; then to pursue and scalp some wild animal, to show her skill in domestic usages; and, lastly, to take a club and defend herself against the attacks of her admirer, to prove her ability to resist a surprise. The zeal with which she demonstrated her affection in this latter trial was very touching: a husband could never press his wife with full rapture to his bosom until she had broken his head. How Wools contrived to elude this ceremony I am not aware. The next day, at sundown, their hands were joined by the parents; a blessing was pronounced by a chief; and rum, love, and harmony were distributed by the bridegroom.

The honeymoon, like a chief's fame, depended upon various contingencies—temper, weather, beauty, leisure, and rum—for to bear the burden of wedlock some Indians required no small stock of spirits. In the first gust of enjoyment they would take long rambles to bring home to their brides a rare skin or plumage; but these walks daily narrowed in their circle, until—unless affection was revived by absence on some military expedition—the redskin fell into the established indifference of European life. The savage actually seized by instinct upon the perfection of a well-educated Parisian husband's deportment—he divided the house with his spouse and took the outside; or, if he remained within, treated her as a part of the furniture. If the lady had noble blood in her veins this was not endured. She smote him in return with a two-edged weapon, her tongue; and perhaps a struggle ensued in which she proved she had sufficient energy when put to the pinch. Too often an Indian wife's happiness depended on this seeming paradox: if her tribe was at peace when she married, war commenced very soon, but if at war, peace was perpetuated.

From Pittsburgh we proceeded about fifty miles by land to Wheeling, a point of junction on the river-bank. Here we were enabled to select a craft with good accommodations, and in a few hours saw ourselves gliding away over the glassy surface of the Ohio.

It is not my intention to give a topographical account of our passage to Blennerhasset. This is not a guide-book, but a record of scenes and circumstances which gave rise to pleasurable feelings. I shall confine myself, therefore, to two things: the general appearance of the river, and the numerous antiquities which line its banks. Well may they call the Ohio "the pride of the Western waters," for it presents the image of the pride of human nature—a young, tranquil, pure-minded female, emerging joyously into life beneath the smile of a benignant sky. Without rock to ruffle, or fall to shatter her calm surface, she glides away to Louisville, where her descent typifies the trial-time of life, till at length she springs into the bosom of a lordly bridegroom, the broad and bounding, the great and glorious Mississippi. A gentle spouse is the Ohio to this master of the North, who rushes from his mountain heights to track three thousand miles in one continued thunder, subjecting the earth on all sides to his sway.

So pellucid is the water of the Ohio that I speak within bounds when I say that I could see clearly to the depth of eighteen or twenty feet, while so magical was the glassiness of its surface that it appeared to me like a broad sheet of crystal, in which the various boats were partially embedded. Nor was this beauty suffered to grow monotonous. Winding perpetually in its course, its banks at every bend present some new feature, from the smoothly sloping savannah to the high and abrupt bluff; a thicket one moment bounding the view on both sides and shading the flood's sweet breast with gloom, but rapidly gliding by to be succeeded by an open range of landscape over which the eye seemed capable of travelling to the blue waves of the Pacific, slumbering on the verge of the horizon, in calm contiguity to heaven.

The banks which riveted our eyes the most were those that bore Indian antiquities — forts or cemeteries — the relics of a nation evidently mighty in intelligence, whatever may have been the amount of its numbers or resources. These relics are the most interesting objects on the surface of the American continent, for they present, perhaps, the only key to the solution of that long-unsettled question, whence came the aboriginal population of the country?

With the generally received opinion set forth by Dr. Robertson, that North America was peopled from the North of Asia, every reader must be familiar. So many resemblances are to be traced between the wandering hordes of both countries, modified solely by local circumstances, that the fact seems undeniable. Admitting this, how is the peopling of South America to be explained, which presents, in almost every point, a decided contrast to its sister land. Whether we take the one broad distinction that the Southern aborigines possessed, when first discovered, a social character, living together in cities, submitting to established laws, and devoting their lives to peaceful agriculture, while the Northern displayed the sternest features of the savage—war their trade, the woods their home, and hunting their sole employment; or whether we go into the particulars of personal formation, language, and domestic arts and usages, we perceive that all are opposite, and that the chief differences are due not to *local*, but *moral* causes. Of these the principal was an established religion which, making the altar of its god the throne of its king, secured general loyalty and order by mental influence; while a mere vague belief in a good spirit prevailing in the North created no law, but left all to individual will. Now, did the political religion of the former grow out of any circumstances of the country, or was it imported? The land had but one peculiarity—an abundance of the precious metals; were these the likely means to build up a faith which should command their actions? Certainly not; they valued gold and silver only for their beauty, not for intrinsic worth. The national character had adapted itself to local circumstances, not been formed by them.

As it is thus evident that the Northern and Southern aborigines were descendants of a widely different stock, the question is, on what nation of Asia might the latter, with some degree of credibility, make out a case of affiliation? Am I too fanciful in discovering numerous affinities between the characteristics, moral and personal, of this race and the Chinese, weakened to their present degree of faintness by time and the distance of their transit, which might have taken place after some rebellion, when a leader and his party were expatriated. The nations have at least these features in common—configuration of countenance, worship of the sun, a love of congregating in cities, and an ingenuity in various arts arising from their social relations.

Some of the principal Indian antiquities—with the general character of which most are acquainted—are to be found at Marietta, where a square area of forty acres is enclosed by a firm wall of peculiarly cemented earth, ten feet high, which has three openings at equal distances on each side. Similar constructions are to be seen on the

banks of the Muskingum, where the ramparts are upwards
of eighteen feet in height, and on a hill near the Tioga
River, where the defences are surrounded by an entrench-
ment and various pits, which had evidently been dug and
covered over to receive assailants—all attesting ingenuity
and the existence of system—besides the sculpture of human and animal heads, helmets, spears, etc., on rocks in
various parts of the country. The surrounding Indians
do not possess a single tradition connected with these
remains, being confident of but one thing, that they were
not the work of their own ancestors, a fact which their
ignorance of system, if not stratagem, in all military matters, fully bears out. It is obvious, therefore, that they
are to be attributed to an earlier people than the supposed
Kamschatkans, who either abandoned them after their
erection, or were killed in them by new-comers. On the
supposition that a band of expatriated Chinese passed
round by the Strait of Behring, once probably an isthmus,
to the Northwest coast, it follows that, in search of a mild-
er climate, they would have pursued their track by the
base of the Rocky Mountains (a direct and natural path,
these being evidently a continuation of the Andes) until,
arriving at the prairies of Louisiana, a diversion was made
to the East for a more fertile country, and afterwards,
either from internal dissensions or the attacks of a strange
race, they erected these works. Then, perhaps, a superiority of numbers induced them to relinquish the struggle
and continue their journey to the South, passing over the
Isthmus of Darien to a country which shut them out
henceforth from communication with their successors.
This conjecture is countenanced by another of Mr. Jefferson's—that the two continents were at one period an
entire body, of which the West India Islands formed the
capes and headlands; that by frequent earthquakes they
were torn asunder; and that the constant operation of the

trade currents from east to west hollowed out the present basin of the Gulf. Thus it is but necessary to suppose that the transit took place before these convulsions, and the flood formed the most effectual medium to wash out the print of their footsteps, and to wall in their character. This is, at least, a somewhat more probable solution of the mystery of the Southern aborigines than the opinion that they were a remnant of the ten tribes of Israel after the first dispersion; or, as asserted by others, that they were visitors from the South Sea Islands who had performed the passage of the Pacific in canoes, a feat which would have required that sea to have well merited its name. The old romance of America's discovery by Prince Madoc has a much stronger claim on our belief, from the fact that Welsh colonies have been found existing in the heart of Indian tribes, and upon the banks of the Ohio we actually stumbled on one, anterior in its date to the earliest historical emigrants, and which had continued so exclusive that it was still scarcely able to exchange ten words of English.

After a slow but delightful passage of twelve days we at length reached the goal of our journey—the fairy creation of Blennerhasset. To describe the effect of its appearance I do not hope; I can only endeavor, by means of a few details, to place the scene before my reader and leave the filling-up to his imagination.

Blennerhasset is an island about a mile in circumference, lying in the bed of the Ohio, which had been made the retreat of a man of equal taste and affluence. The ground rose gradually on all sides to its centre, and on this favorable spot was the house, erected in the style and splendor of a Persian pavilion. It was but sixty feet square, consisting of two stories, connected with wings by a semicircular veranda, luxuriantly covered with myrtle, and commanded an extensive range of one of the loveliest regions in the world. The grounds were laid out with that

better modern taste which superseded the monotonous
straight lines and close-cropped Puritanic borders of old
English gardening.   Everywhere were contrasts and surprises, evidencing an eye that had surveyed the best
effects of Europe; and, to crown the whole, walks, lawns,
and shrubberies were blooming with all the flowers and
fruits, and vocal with all the melody a generous clime so
liberally dispenses to this Italy of the West.   The effect
of this contrast between the perfection of wild and cultivated loveliness, of this discovery of a triumph of Art in
the very stronghold of Nature, was perfectly entrancing.
What changes may have since occurred in it by storm,
caprice, or a conformity to the tastes of a surrounding
population I know not, but until I go to my grave I must
bear with me, as of a dream, the remembrance of the beautiful Blennerhasset.   All that I could learn of the owner
and creator of this Paradise was that he was a European
recluse who had arrived in these regions about the period
of the French Revolution, and, after purchasing the island,
lived on it in seclusion, devoting himself to its adornment.
Mr. Clay computed that the estate could not have cost
less than the building of a town, and that the mere purchase and transport of materials must have involved an
expenditure sufficient to have procured a handsome property in any part of the Union.

Philadelphia, the ensuing winter, proved a scene of unusual gayety.   Balls and quadrilles occupied the inter-
vening nights of the play; not to divide its attraction, but
to make parties for its support; and I attended many,
not from any love of the dancing—for I have always preferred taking exercise in a progressive direction—but to
convince myself of the impudent calumny of a traveller
(an early specimen of a large brood) who had been through
the States, and who seriously assured me that he had been
present at a ball of the first respectability in Philadelphia,

held in a hay-loft, up a ladder, where the musicians were a crew of black fiddlers, and the refreshments were served up in earthen jugs. I was also instrumental in promoting the public convivialty by founding an American Beefsteak Club, round the table of which I was enabled to collect many able supporters in mind and voice. Mr. Jefferson, Mr. Carroll, and C. Brockden Brown were among our visitors. We stocked the cellars with excellent wine; the working of my old regulations spoke a volume on the subject of maintaining order in a free community, and our harmony, in every sense of the word, was perfect. One evening, I remember that it was interrupted by a singular coincidence. We were just singing the glee of "A House on Fire," when a member rushed in to congratulate us on our discernment, since "Rickett's Circus" was at that moment in flames. I instantly dissolved the meeting, and we hurried to the spot to render assistance, but in vain; the destroyer had its prey. The wings had taken fire in the Hell scene of Don Juan, which, getting known, brought a crowd of Quakers to survey what they considered a signal retribution. One of them was so unusually excited that he could not repress his transports, but kept crying out to the unfortunate horse-riders who were endeavoring to rescue all they could, "Yea, yea, struggle with the flames as thou wilt, thou must soon be in them;" at which a worthy Irishman, who was handing the buckets to the engine, replied, "Will they? Then, I tell you what, my darling, it's only right to keep *you* from burning;" and with these words he sluiced the predestinator from head to foot. Mrs. Whitelock,* our tragedian, witnessed this conflagration, and it

---

* Mrs. WHITELOCK was one of Mrs. Siddons's younger sisters, and she is said to have had a full share of the family good looks and acting ability. She was born in 1761; she acted at Drury Lane in 1783, and in 1794 she

so disturbed her nerves that a few evenings afterwards, just as she had been effectually smothered as Desdemona, the front cloudings having dropped a few feet, a boy in the gallery cried out, "Higher! higher!" which similar sounds striking her sensitive ears she started up, thrust aside the curtains, and exclaimed, "Good heavens! fire?" The roar of the audience and the look of Cooper (no mimicry of passion now) threw her back to her recumbency, but the interest of the scene perished with her.

I also became a member of a more important society, the "St. George's," instituted for the relief of distressed English emigrants. The number of instances where unforeseen causes had brought ruin on the truly deserving was so great that a more meritorious fund could not have been established, and I am proud to say, for the honor of my countrymen, that none could have been better supported. It will be supposed that we received many applications which did not come within the scope of our design. Every tourist, in fact, who had quitted England on some sudden emergency, and neglected to calculate his mode of subsistence, made a point of applying to us. In a few months we might have compiled a catalogue of names important to the secretary of state. Cases that showed a lack of prudence rather than principle were met by private subscriptions. One was that of a Mr. Tubbs, who had formerly been a merchant of some standing in London, but who loved a playhouse so much better than his own that his ruin as a trader commenced his career as an actor. Failing to bring the English people to a sense of his merits, he had embarked for Jamaica, where,

---

made her first appearance in America at Philadelphia, in Mrs. Siddons's favorite character, Isabella, in the "Fatal Marriage." She returned to England, and died there in 1835. Mrs. Kemble, in her delightful "Records of a Girlhood," gives a most amusing account of the meetings of her aunts Siddons and Whitelock after both of them had left the stage.

a similar result ensuing, he had expended his last shilling in reaching Philadelphia, to be there told by the manager that there was no opening for his services. Having met this person at the Anacreontic, at a period when he patronized acting, I could not help commiserating the change he had undergone in embracing his vapory Juno, so employed my rhetoric to induce him to give up the pursuit, and my interest to get him appointed supercargo to a West-Indiaman, in both of which endeavors, I am glad to say, I was successful. I was afterwards told of something that had occurred to Tubbs on his way to Jamaica, which struck me as amusing. He had taken his passage with a party of wild Irish emigrants who were going to the West Indies, bent on " picking the guineas from the gooseberry bushes." As he intended during the voyage to "get up" a range of characters, for this purpose he got up every night, when the Hibernians had retired, and traversed the clear deck, muttering " Richard," "Romeo," or others in succession, and imagining he saw around a dense crowd of listening eyes and throbbing bosoms. His illusion was not altogether unfounded. Night after night the watch on the forecastle had been observing him, though hiding themselves by mast and rigging, and on his impassioned gestures and mutterings they could put but one construction. He was blessed with a towering frame measuring about six feet one, with a tendency to distend from a Tubb into a hogshead, which made him seem a very likely person to head the Irishmen in the steerage in an act of piracy. The crew soon made known their suspicions to the captain, who enjoined them to have an eye on him the next night, and, if he gave further cause for alarm, to seize and clap him under hatches. Accordingly, tucking pistols into their belts, the watch crept under the shade of the foremast and took up their usual position. Now it so happened that on this

evening Tubbs had bethought him of an experiment on
the language of Renault in "Venice Preserved," believing that the honeyed villain had more in him than the
public had ever yet seen. Working himself up to a good
acting pitch, he strode towards the sailors and broke into
the speech in which Renault gives directions to the conspirators to seize the city :

> "Durand, you
> Must in the midst keep your battalia fast,
> And, Theodore, be sure to plant the cannon.
> . . . . . But, above all, I charge you,
> Shed blood enough !" etc.

All of which being interpreted as directions to the Hibernians, two of whom happened to steal out at this moment for a breath of clear air, the suspicions of the watch
wanted no further confirmation. Tubbs was seized in a
jiffy, and half a dozen pistols held to his head, as they
opened the hatches and compelled him to descend, assail-
ing him with such Hebrew as, "No, you don't seize the
ship, you pirate ! you big-bellied Picaroon !" etc. Nor
did he regain his liberty until he had explained the fact
to the captain at least half a dozen times : a salutary
lesson to people of poetic animus how they forget that
the world about them is stupidly and substantially matter of fact.

Tubbs rose after this to comfortable circumstances, but
his stomach distended in a greater ratio than his purse, a
keenly imaginative spirit evaporating to leave the sedi-
ment of an animal craving—love for swallowing, rather
than giving forth, good things. This gluttony soon unfitted him for his duties. He ate and ate, and swelled
and swelled, till one captain of a ship objected to taking
him on the score of his bulk adding to the cargo. His
end was, as it deserved to be, a painful one. He fell ill
in Baltimore, got into debt to support his appetite, and

his creditors surrounded his bed in his last moments to
try and get their dues. "Will you pay me for these dinners, Mr. Tubbs?" "Do you know, sir, what you owe me
for oxtail soup?" and so on. They were at length induced to leave him, and the moment after he heard that
particular murmur from the abdominal region which pre-
cedes dissolution; at which, opening his eyes and lips for
the last time, he exclaimed; "What the devil do *you*
grumble for? I owe you nothing."

Of all the stories I heard of emigrants, political or private, during my connection with the St. George's Society,
none touched me more than the account of a worthy
Frenchman who had been ruined by the taking of St.
Eustatius, and who had been required by a public notice,
with all others in the island, to deliver to the admiral an
inventory of his effects. On the day appointed for the reception of these documents he, not having appeared, was
sent for. The officer, entering his house, found him sitting at a table in a poorly furnished room, his head leaning on his hand and his brow deeply graven with the lines
of affliction. On being reminded of the inventory he
took up a pen and wrote simply as follows: "*Point d'ar-
gent; point de biens; point de commerce; point de crédit;
point de réputation; seulement un pauvre cœur rompu*"—
No money; no goods; no trade; no credit; no reputation;
only a poor, broken heart.

It amused us occasionally to read some of the Western
newspapers, whose editors being also the printers, often
composed an article as they set it up. Many provincial-
isms were adopted as the readiest modes of expression,
which, to Europeans, were not very intelligible. For instance, an advertisement to the legal profession would
frequently commence thus: "A gentleman of considerable experience in the law line, wishes a dependency."
Now English people imagining that the "law line" could

only allude to the rope which government gratuitously presents to some of its acquaintance, would naturally conclude that a gentleman of some experience had had sufficient "dependency" already. Again, tracts of land in the Union which connected large towns with small ones were called "necks," as, the Neck of Boston, for instance. It was, therefore, no unusual thing to read, "To be sold, part of Abraham Lawrence's neck." An announcement that might confirm some of the English people in their belief that the Americans were cannibals. These mistakes may be classed with those I have sometimes heard of in houses of business, resulting there, not from language, but penmanship. A merchant I knew in Norfolk once wrote to his London agent to send him thirty thousand black Tacks; the letter T not being distinctly formed, the agent read it black Jacks, and after rummaging Birmingham, Sheffield, etc., could only obtain about a fourth of the number, which he sent on, saying the rest should follow as soon as possible. A more startling surprise was that of a London merchant who in a letter to his agent in Brazil requested that he would remit him one or two monkeys, but inserting figures instead of letters (1 or 2) it had the appearance of a thousand and two. The agent, after scouring the province to collect them, was compelled to engage the entire hold of a ship to convey them. We may imagine the feelings of the sailors with these fidgety passengers during a two months' voyage, but hardly those of the merchant they were consigned to.

The negroes as well as the actors in America were supposed to have profited by the yellow fever. It was believed that, from some physical cause, they were in a degree impregnable to the infection, and they were, consequently, generally employed as nurses. The opportunities thus afforded them of rifling the dead, when the malady had swept off every member of a family, were sometimes too tempting for their ideas of rectitude, so that it became a common remark that you might know where the fever had been raging by the Sunday dress of the black women. But, however confused might be their notions about other people's property, the world could never retaliate by robbing them of what was peculiarly their own—their humor. Various instances of this were given me, even on so grave a subject as the above.

A wealthy female of Philadelphia having been seized with the fever in coming home from a ball, was in a few hours brought apparently to the verge of dissolution. All her relations took flight, fearful of sharing a fate they could not avert, and a black nurse was sent for. While lying in this state a valuable necklace she had been wearing was carefully put away by her attendant, to prevent its getting soiled. It pleased Heaven that this lady should recover, and after a few days, remembering, among other worldly things, her necklace, she asked Hannah about it. The handmaiden replied, she "belieb when missy go to die, she gib neckliss to lady to keep." Naturally concluding that this lady must be one of her friends, she made inquiries when her health was restored, and discovered that no such circumstance had occurred. Her nurse was by this time nowhere to be found; but the lady was fortunate enough to meet with her a short time afterwards in the South, dressed in the highest burlesque of fashion, and with the identical diamond necklace reposing on her bosom, like a line of stars streaking a thundercloud. "Hannah!" exclaimed the owner, with an amazed look; "I thought you told me I gave my necklace to a lady to keep." "Iss, missy," was the cool reply, as the black aristocrat took off the precious ornament and returned it, " oo gib um to *me !*"

Fennel was once taken ill at Baltimore, and on sending for a nurse inquired her terms. " Me ask oo two dollar a day, Massa Fennel." "Two dollars!" he exclaimed; "that's double the ordinary charge." "Iss, why, 'cause oo get well so berry soon." "What do you mean?" inquired the tragedian. "I go to gallery ob a play sometime, and I see oo, massa, always berry bad at night and quite well in a mornin', so I'm tinking I shall nebber get de fibe dollar for lay oo out." Fennel was so cheered by this impression that he got well on the strength of it, and said he never paid an extortion so willingly.

Towards the *fair* sex, in a literal sense, my devotion was never called in question, but I must confess I had always an antipathy to black women. An Englishman, I believe, always associates purity with absence of color, and feels that only whiteness can be angelic. To me the connection has ever appeared so sacred I did not like to have it disturbed by even looking at—" Black scandal and foul-faced reproach." And as to my wife, if I could have consented to her being attended by a negress at a certain period, I should have expected that the result would have come frowning into the world and thrown a shade upon my hearth for the rest of my days. For this prejudice, which was no doubt a ridiculous one, I was now destined to be punished.

On an exceedingly cold though clear night, the snow having fallen to the depth of some feet, I was returning alone from a party; and by the side of a wall in a back street, which was a short cut to my dwelling, but was backward also as regards lamps and watchmen, I had proceeded but a few paces when I heard the pattering of a pair of broad feet behind me; and as I thought it not unlikely these might belong to some necessitous foreigner who wished to make an inquiry respecting my purse, I conceived that I was not compromising my dignity by admitting that "discretion is the better part of valor"—which is to say, less elegantly, that I took to my heels and ran. At this the steps of my pursuer quickened, and a voice summoned me to stop. My fears were now confirmed, and I need scarcely add that my policy was persisted in; but unluckily the hardened snow upon the pathway had become so glassy that it was impossible to plant a step with certainty. Speed was therefore perilous, and in my efforts to maintain mine I at length missed my footing and pitched into a bank which instantly enclosed, in a sort of self-adapting vise, every inch of my body. Feeling that resistance was now out of the question, I endeavored to find my way to my purse, to purchase relief from my prison; and as my pursuer drew nigh turned the one eye I had at liberty to survey him. Him?—oh, horror! it was a *she,* a black woman as large as any two aldermen that were ever distended upon turtle, and whom I concluded at once to be one of those erring daughters of Cytherea, who at nightfall prowled abroad for exhilarated planters. To describe her person I can hardly find terms. She was a latitudinarian of no ordinary dimensions, but her height was equal to her periphery; her head was buried in a mound of fat, with eyes that rolled like moons in an eclipse, half black, half white, divided by a nose as flat as her forehead, and flaming over the abyss of a semicircular mouth. All these bodily enormities were exceeded by her behavior. She looked on all that had passed as so good a joke that her huge frame was convulsed with merriment; peals of echoing laughter came gurgling up her throat, and as she approached, panting, blowing, and roaring, her fat hands tucked into her sides and her pavior's-mallet-like feet shaking the earth at every step, I could think of nothing but an elephant in a tiger-chase. As a climax to the affair it was impossible she could miss me, since it was ordained I should select my bed within four feet of the only lamp in the street. When she reached me, another and another shout succeeded, and then her voice mellifluously framed the exclamation, " Oh, oo naughty man, to run away from pretty ooman !" Fancy the full horror of my situation ! Had it been a footpad, who would have first robbed and then murdered me, I could have submitted with comparative complacency; but to fall into the grasp of such a moral ogre, bound, as it were, hand and foot, with no friend at hand to avert or drop a tear over the catastrophe. I had but one hope —that in attempting to drag me out she might plunge me under the snow, and so consign me to a blissful suffocation.

After calling me alternately "lub" and "naughty man" several times, and finding that neither made me move, she extended a hand, like the wing of a bat, to extricate me. Seizing me by the shoulder, her great eyes distending in triumph, she released me from my position with all the ease of lifting a feather. The moment my feet touched the ground my courage returned, for I heard footsteps approaching, and again I darted off at full speed, this time being luckily able to maintain my footing. To my mingled wonder and delight she did not pursue me, but burst again into a peal of laughter, and as I receded I could hear the ogress still enjoying my fright; nor did the derisive sounds seem to quit my ears till I had fairly passed through and closed my door. On subsequent reflection it struck me that, after all, I was perhaps mistaken as to this person's character. She might have been merely a mad wag in search of excitement — a female Falstaff, a black "Jack;" she was as fat, apparently as funny; and one kind office she had certainly done me, in my extrication. I believe this adventure had its good effect, for I began to look at the color so much more steadfastly after that as to diminish my alarm on all future occasions.

My favorite place of resort in Philadelphia was Peele's

Museum, the first, and for many years the only, public collection of natural curiosities in the Union. Of their extent and preservation it is needless to speak here. No
traveller has entered this city without awarding the pro-
prietor his due meed of praise. The object that attracted
most attention was the skeleton of that wonderful quadruped, the mammoth, which has so sufficiently disproved
the assertions of Buffon about the " belittling influence "
of the climate. Yet this did not interest me so much as a
far less obtrusive feature of the collection: a bow, with
which was connected so striking a history that I shall
take leave to repeat it.

An African prince, defeated in a native battle, gave
himself up on condition that he might retain his bow and
quiver. Bought from his conquerors for some bauble,
and consigned to the Carolinas, he was there again sold as
a slave; but his pleasing face and manners secured for
him in all situations the privilege of keeping his arms,
the only relics of his former power, the sole objects of his
affection. His strength and stateliness recommended him
to Colonel Mottle, a humane master, in whose service he
died, the bow and quiver being gratefully preserved in
the colonel's family as memorials of his fortitude and
fidelity. In the campaign of 1781 the widow of Colonel
Mottle (who had died a patriot) was ejected from her
house on the River Congaree, to make room for a British
garrison. When this garrison was besieged by a small
detachment of Americans, whose approaches were within
gunshot, the widow, who lived in a cottage not far from
her former dwelling, was informed that an unwillingness
to injure her property was the only impediment to its re-
duction. " Regard not me," she replied, " at such a time
as this. I will show you the best means to effect your
purpose." Then producing the bow, " This," said she,
" belonged to a faithful servant, who bent it in the cause

of freedom in Africa. An arrow from it will easily carry a match to the roof." The bow was instantly supplied with the missile, and a blazing roof soon brought capitulation, when the Americans entered the defences, and the Englishmen joined them in extinguishing the flames.

The magnanimity of a prince and the heroism of a woman are nothing uncommon, but the novelty consisted in this primitive weapon, devoted to the cause of freedom in one continent, serving in the same cause, under such different circumstances, long after, in another; escaping all hazards, to be presented, by a struggler in the conflict, to this museum, as a memento equally interesting to traveller and native.

CHAPTER IX.

1800-1.—The Carolinas.—Journey to Charleston; a Carolina Ordinary.—
Social Characteristics.—Deer-killing; a Dead Shot.—A Planters' Ball;
the "Caroliny Jig."—Stories of the Swamps; the Spectre Troop, etc.—
Legal Latin.—Colonel Tarleton and Major Hanger; Pranks among the
Planters.—Baron de Glaubeck's Troop and Title.—Anecdote of the Irish
Brigade.—Charleston Society; Varieties of Color.—The Ugly Club; its
Rules; Ordeal of a Member.— Carolina Dews.— Fishing and Bites;
Scene with a Snake; a Lively Hut.—Alligators; the River Lawyer; a
Civilized Specimen.—Samples of Black Humor; the Criminal a Judge.
—Byrne's Visit to Jamaica; his Retreat.

I HAD been frequently invited by my old friend Placide * to pay a visit to Charleston during the summer
months, but had always objected on account of the climate, which had waged war specially with my unfortunate
brethren. At length good health, curiosity, and the vanity of superior prudence overcame my scruples, and I set
out for Charleston in the summer of 1800, in my usual
conveyance, a light wagon drawn by one horse, and fully
accoutred with fowling-piece, fishing-rod, etc., to take advantage of whatever opportunities the road might afford.
I have mentioned the peculiar state of the roads in Virginia; as they ran southwards they got worse. Houses
were farther apart, intercourse more confined, swamps

---

* ALEXANDER PLACIDE was a native of France, who appeared in Paris
and London as a gymnast and performer on the tight-rope with great success. He came to America towards the close of the last century, and was
for many years manager of the theatres at Charleston, S. C., and Richmond, Va. He died of yellow fever in 1812. His children, Henry, Thomas,
Jane, Caroline (Mrs. Waring—Mrs. W. R. Blake), and Eliza (Mrs. Ashbury
—Mrs. Mann), were important figures upon the American stage.

more abundant, and taverns—their necessary consequence—more wild and provincial. These were the original milestones, for people computed by them all intermediate distances; they were the arena for the chief business of the country—betting, gambling, and dram-drinking; and they were also houses of "entertainment"—that is, to survey, not to inhabit. In order that the nature of a Carolina ordinary (or, as it ought properly to have been termed, extraordinary) may be accurately apprehended, I will venture to depict one, as a sample of some dozen I was doomed to encounter during the journey in question. They were mostly log-huts, or a frame weather-boarded; the better sort consisting of one story and two rooms; the more numerous having no internal divisions, with a truly sociable character placing all upon a level, and forbidding the existence of parties. One corner of the room would be occupied by a "bunk," containing the family bed; another by a pine-wood chest, the family clothes-press and larder; a third would be railed off for a bar, containing a rum-keg and a tumbler. The rest of the furniture consisted of two chairs and a table, all in the last stage of palsy. Their external distinctions were few, but peculiar. You might always know an ordinary, on emerging from the woods, by an earthen jug suspended by the handle from a pole; the pipe of the chimney never rising above the roof; or a score of black hogs luxuriating in the sunshine and mud before the door. On pulling up at one you usually found the landlord gone to market, the landlady cutting wood in the swamp, "Joe" hoeing corn in a field, and only a squalling child upon the floor and a ferocious house-dog to receive you. On some of the family arriving, you were stared at as a Godsend, destined to be made the most of. If hunger and fatigue compelled you to remain, a little Indian corn for your horse, and a blanket on the hearth, with your saddle for a pillow, to represent a bed, were the most you would obtain. In summer a man would sometimes vary his enjoyment by stretching himself outside near the pigs, under the said blanket stretched over four stakes, to keep off the dews and mosquitoes. As to edibles, whether you called for breakfast, dinner, or supper, the reply was one —eggs and bacon; but the meal brought not a gratification, but a task. Here the motto was—ultra independence; every man his own servant. Ten to one you had to cook the meal yourself, while the landlady was searching for a trencher; and, when it was before you, you were sure of only one thing—to pay for it. No sooner were you seated than the house-dog (of the large wolf breed) would arrange himself beside you, and lift his lank, hungry jaws expressively to your face. The young children, never less than a dozen (the women seeming to bear them in a litter in these regions), at the smell and sight of the victuals would set up a yell enough to frighten the wolves, till the hostess quieted them by saying that they should "have some when the gentleman had done," with a significance of look and emphasis which plainly told you, you were not to eat too much. By this time a party of indomitable black cats were clawing at your elbow, to hint their claim to come in for snacks; and, if you were not expeditious in bolting your fare (mastication was impossible), one or the other of these enterprisers would be on the table and unflesh your fork as it was going to your mouth, or clear the dish while you paused in consternation. They had, in fact, a decided system of attack, surrounding you on all sides, and no sooner was one cuffed down than another sprang up, so that your hand, instead of emptying your plate, was kept whirling in defence of it, in the style of the broad-sword exercise. All this was very little recompensed by conversation. If the landlord were present, he talked only of the high price of New England rum (just at the time you were putting yours to your lips), or the market for turpentine and tobacco; so that you were probably driven out-of-doors for amusement, when the best that offered was to see your horse fed; for if you did not stand beside him with your whip, the poultry would hold a consultation round the rim of his meal-tub, and not leave him sufficient to grease his teeth. At a receptacle of this kind I was compelled, on one occasion, to take shelter from a storm, and passed the night in a wooden chair, my legs upon a tub, my head vainly endeavoring to find repose upon the rail; the wind and thunder rocking the hut like a cradle; the lightning blazing in at every window and crevice, till all seemed on fire; and the whole set off, though not relieved, by a chorus of wolves in the woods, who now and then, I thought, were running round the house, as though dislodged from their own tenements, and exceedingly mortified that I did not quit mine. The famished cry of a beast that has no dislike to humanity, and the rapid pattering of his feet round a cabin that was tumbling to pieces, and in the heart of a forest which, from extent alone, deserved its title of "eternal," formed a novelty of which, I confess, I never desired a repetition. Luckily the necessity did not again occur. I was plentifully supplied with letters of introduction to proprietors in North and South Carolina, and at their hospitable residences I made it a point to stop if nightfall was approaching and no town at hand.

I perceived some difference, I must own, in the character of my entertainers and the gentlemen of Virginia. With quite as large a measure of conviviality and frankness, they possessed less intelligence and suavity of manner. Unlike the latter, they appeared to have intentionally narrowed the circle of their intercourse; and here still, as in the old times in Virginia, racing, betting, cock-fighting, and hard drinking formed the staple rather than the auxiliary enjoyments. A planter usually passed his time between his overseers and a tavern, where he called daily to talk politics, play at all-fours, make bets, and "stand treat" for mint-sling, which, as you proceeded southwardly, obtained the medicinal name of an "antifogmatic." Here, if he could light on any companions, like the Virginians he carried them home to dinner : if it proved a wet evening, cards, toddy, and cockfighting formed the sources of stimulus; but if fine, and there was no moonlight, their diversions were varied by an excursion for deer-killing. A party well-armed with guns and brandy sallied into the woods, preceded by a nigger carrying some lighted charcoal in a pan. The victims were so fascinated by the light that they always stared at it transfixed, while its reflection on their eyeballs gave the sportsman an unerring aim. This may seem to a European a very dull amusement, but it was accompanied by so much scratching from briers, sinking in swamps, and dislodging of rattlesnakes, that a man was kept in a perpetual state of excitement. Sometimes, also, very ludicrous mistakes occurred from the multiplying faculty of the shooter's vision, the amount of game being frequently determined by his amount of brandy; so that, after an immense deal of devastation, when the blacks were sent to collect the spoil, they would proclaim, with a convulsion of laughter, the identity of the dead deer with certain stumps and bushes.

I once heard of the joke ending seriously for a host who piqued himself on his superior eye and rifle. He was entertaining a party one evening with a history of his feats, when they expressed a wish to witness a specimen. Stimulated by two kinds of spirit—love of glory and rum—he ordered the necessary preparations, and led the way with his lauded weapon, his friends laying a heavy wager that he would not kill ten deer in twice as many minutes. Now it happened, all unknown to him, that his cattle had been turned into the woods a few hours previously, and he stumbled upon just the spot where they had made a rendezvous. Pitchy darkness, swimming heads, and the order to lie close prevented discoveries till extermination had commenced. The planter, surrounded by blacks who loaded his guns and kept the fire in a bright flame, in less than ten minutes had doubled the required number. At the moment, however, that his triumph and his party's consternation were rising to a climax, a venerable cow, whose back had been grazed by a bullet, felt impelled to get up and send forth a long moan of remonstrance. The mistake was instantaneously revealed; right and left the dead or dying tenants of his meadows were identified. The betters burst into an uproar of laughter; the negroes, fearing that his gun would next be levelled at themselves, threw down the light and scampered. Choked with vexation, but overpowered by drams, the planter raved, swore, and jumped about in the darkness like a demon. Nor did the return home tend to allay his irritation, for a mile's scramble through the woods in the gloom of Erebus usually divested the wanderer of his hat, boots, or skirts, as well as some portion of his beauty.

One of the ruling amusements of the Carolinas was dancing, the French having apparently inoculated all classes with this taste in its most confirmed state. The negroes have always been proverbial for their homage to St. Vitus, being known to walk five or six miles after a hard day's work to enjoy the pleasure of flinging about their hands, heads, and legs to the music of a banjo, in a manner that threatened each limb with dislocation. But their owners, male and female, in these quarters partook of the infatuation. I was present at a wedding-party in North Carolina, which wound up with violent exercise under the title of a ball.   The company, on their arrival, had been shown promiscuously into two rooms, well-lighted and divided by a thin partition, both being laid out with tea, coffee, sling, and toddy.   The sexes, however, soon separated, and, for the space of an hour, the merriment seemed equal on each side of the wainscot.   At length the host gave the signal for clearing decks and preparing for action; the tables and partition-boards (sliding in a grove) were instantly removed by the blacks, to form the requisite arena, and the seats were ranged round the walls.   The musicians (half a dozen operators on catgut, of the same color—Orpheii, born during their father's visit to the Shades) were then introduced at one end, and the diversion commenced by a gentleman leading a lady to the middle of the room, and, after a formal salutation, bursting into an eccentric movement, which to me had a new and peculiar significance.   No regular steps, but a latitude of shuffle was adopted, in a system of alternate pursuit and retreat, now the lady, now her partner gaining the advantage, testing at every turn the respective strength of their sinews.   One moment the lady, pressed closely to a corner, appeared on the verge of a surrender, then suddenly recovered spirit, dashing the besieger back and chasing him into the like peril.   The forces drawn up on all sides were prepared, however, to rescue either party from the shame of a defeat, for at the moment I expected to see a wearied-out maiden sink into her conqueror's arms, or a gentleman make an elegant submission, a friend would start forward to the relief in the full vigor of his or her powers, and enable the exhausted one to make an honorable retreat.   So these tactics were continued through the evening till every Damon and Delia had partaken of them, and some had displayed their abilities three or four times, when the lines were formed for a country-dance, and in this general expression of amity and fellowship the contest concluded. There was evidently much figurative meaning in this performance, as well as a military character, that attested its French origin; for the French have always had the credit of being most expert at fighting and hopping, and history tells us that they have sometimes combined them. I saw plainly, too, that a few such dances must afford good evidence of a lady's tact and bodily condition, and perhaps one of the best criterions by which a man could discover his chance of holding the reins of government in case of their union.

Before concluding my remarks on the mass of planters I should mention that I intend them to apply rather to those in North than in South Carolina, and in Georgia more than in either. The reason I could not discover, but I was most happy to find that the South Carolinians displayed comparative refinement, a love of books and the arts, and a share of polite as well as solid information. Perhaps the secret was that they associated less with their inferiors, and gave their wives and children better educations. Certainly I recognized here a near approach to everything Virginian.

The most marked feature of the Southern country was the swamps, which not only, on account of their fogs, exercised a bibatory influence on the character of those living near them, but supplied endless traditions to the gossips. Some of these related to the war, and required nearly as great a swallow in the listener as was attributed to the swamp. One tale told of the mysterious disappearance of a whole regiment of king's troops, who, late at night, had lost their track over the morasses; and how their spirits were accustomed to come up to the surface on moonlight nights to go through their evolutions, the colonel riding about on a beautiful white horse, and the men marching, presenting, firing, falling into line, and forming solid bodies with the utmost regularity; all of

which the eyes of various travellers had accidentally espied—though I'll take my oath I was not one of them.
The negroes, again, supposed that the devil had apart-
ments in these places, seeing that his powers had such
full play in their neighborhood, and that he lay in wait
for all who incautiously wandered near them, in order to
introduce the intruders by a short cut to his dominions.

A very fair satire by a foreigner upon Southern travelling ran as follows: A gentleman walking near the verge
of a swamp saw a man's hat on the ground. As the beaver
appeared to be in good condition, he stooped to pick it up,
when, to his great surprise, he heard a voice proceed from
beneath, desiring him not to meddle with it. He lifted
it, nevertheless, and perceived a man's head just above the
surface of the earth. Alarmed at his situation, he proposed to call his slaves and have him dug out. "Don't
trouble yourself, friend," replied he of the swamp, "I am
very well mounted." "Mounted? good heavens, sir! is
it possible that you have a horse under you?" "A capital one," was the answer, "for he has carried me some
hundreds of miles." "But permit me," persisted the
planter, "to send for assistance, or you will lose him."
"Lose him?" exclaimed the stranger; "my good sir, he
has travelled fifty miles since daybreak, and this is the
first firm footing he has come to."

But the swamps were not merely useful in growing rice
and entombing travellers; they proved a qualifier to the
rigors of the law, in the manner of the sanctuaries of old;
for to them most of the cockfighters and jockeys who
could not pay their debts fled for refuge. The system
was for the defendant to run in up to his ears, desiring
his pursuer to follow and take him out, which, if the
latter declined (considering his *cloth* suit the more important of the two), it was an understood thing that he forfeited his claim. A constable having once run an old fox

to earth in this manner, and not being able or willing to sit down before the stronghold and starve him out, was puzzled to know how to return the writ, in good legal language, to its issuer.   At length he applied to a gentleman of some humor, who dictated the following line of very passable Latin : "Johannes Dykes—non cumatibus in Swampum."

On my way to Charleston I gleaned many anecdotes of my old friends, Colonel Tarleton and Major Hanger, who, before the commencement of their convivial career in London, essayed the field of glory in this quarter.   Tarleton was formed by nature to be a captain of Cossacks.   In the field or in the street the man was invariably a dasher, having all that reckless, dare-devil, neck-or-nothing enterprise which is always ready for a blow and never counts on a repulse.   In America he deservedly cut a conspicuous figure, for all that was done for the king in the Southern States must be attributed to him and Lord Rawdon.   His pell-mell mode of attack told extremely well on undisciplined troops, since he could cut up the half of a body before it could make use of its arms; while his expedition, in scouring the country, confirmed his successes and retrieved his defeats.   This flying about procured for him a reputation with the old women nearly akin to Lucifer's.   Noises were never heard in the night, no wind could whistle by, but the galloping of "Tarleton's Troop" was distinctly recognized, so that at length his name became the popuar bugbear to scare the babies to bed.

Hanger never came forward in the same manner; partly, I imagine, because he never got the opportunity, and also that he had not a true military animus.   Hanger was a thorough convivialist—a man who loved the whole human race so well that he would have liked to spread the earth like a table and convert the ocean into punch.   He must have hated fighting, since it destroyed good-fellowship, and have despised all manœuvring but that of bringing bodies amicably together. Had he been put in command when a battle was impending, he was the sort of man who would have desired his antagonist to crack a bottle of wine with him, and so settle the matter without the nonsense of cracking sconces.

Tarleton and Hanger, being a good deal together, were in the habit of relieving the fatigues of duty by adventures among the planters, sometimes in assumed characters, though their own were more facetious. It was related of them that learning there was to be some dancing at an adjacent estate, on the occasion of a family festival, they resolved to be present, believing that their mere names would be a sufficient introduction. They accordingly rode thither unattended, knocked at the door of the house, pretended they had lost their way, and desired entertainment for the night. They were respectfully received by the planter, who ordered a room to be prepared for them; but, as this did not meet their wishes, they expressed a desire to join the merrymakers. The gentleman remonstrated, fearing, as the assembly was quite private, that their presence might cast a shade over it. They, however, persisted, and at length their host was compelled to introduce them to the scene of festivity. His fears were verified. In an instant the music seemed to cease, and the lights to go out. The gallants, however, nothing abashed, addressed two of the prettiest girls in the room, and were on the point of leading them back to their diversion (for what Carolinian can resist a dance), when the tramp of horses was heard without, and a servant ran in to inform his master that a party of provincial skirmishers were in the yard, who required to speak with him. The sudden dismay in our heroes' faces, and the triumph which displaced the scowling chagrin of the beaux about them, may be imagined. The host, a superior kind of

man, of mild demeanor, turned to the intruders, and, without any change in his manner, observed, " Now, gentlemen, you perceive that you occupy precisely the same
situation that you placed me in ten minutes ago. I have
no doubt the warning I am about to give you will be
thought very extraordinary." Saying this, he left the room,
and Tarleton and Hanger expected nothing less than the
appearance of a dozen muscular countrymen to escort
them to General Greene's headquarters. In a few minutes
the host returned to them and said, " I have told the officer of the party that this room is full of my friends. In
that character, though you did not come, you can retire.
Two of my slaves have led your horses to the back of the
stable. I trust, gentlemen, that this warning will not be
thrown away." Struck with the spirit of this return, they
warmly acknowledged their offence and his generosity,
assured him the warning should *not* be thrown away,
and, politely bowing to the company, made good their retreat.

From another incident that was told me, it appeared
that they did not long keep their word, for no warning
could subdue their appetite for adventure. Hanger heard
of a jollification to take place among some negroes at another plantation, and, as an observer of life in all its varieties, and a lover of humor under any skin, he resolved to
be present at it, and prevailed on Tarleton to accompany
him. Accordingly they made their appearance at the
scene of action about ten o'clock at night, briefly explained their wish, and produced, as a note of introduction, a gallon of superior rum. Nothing could have been
more decisive. Hanger was voted with acclamation into
the chair, Tarleton became his vice, and in a short time
the scene reached a pitch of exhilaration as novel as it was
vivid. It was like a gala day in the Shades, as the Tartareans laughed, jumped, danced, and sang all their favor

ite ditties—"The Praise of Bumbo," "Virginny Nigger
berry Good," "I Lost my Shoe in an Old Canoe," etc.,
etc.—till the merriment grew so uproarious that an overseer was induced to walk towards the hut; but, hearing
strangers' voices, he paused, opened the door softly, and,
to his great surprise, recognized the visitors. The master
of this person was a patriot in secret communication with
General Greene, and who this evening had a party of
their mutual friends dining with him. The overseer saw
at a glance at once his duty and his interest, and, closing
the door unobserved, ran off to the house and gave the
alarm. The company, though doubting his story, instantly armed themselves and made for the spot; but, as they
approached, perceived a group before the hut as though
drawn up to resist them. The fact was that Hanger had
proposed to the blacks a trial of agility, wagering another gallon of rum that he and his companion would
beat any two present at a race. The two fleetest having
been selected by the general voice, they were now posi-
tioned in due order for starting when a discharge of pistols from the approaching party gave an unexpected signal. In an instant every man became a racer; all was
flight and terror; and so much game presented itself in
the darkness that Hanger and Tarleton were enabled to
gain their horses, in an adjoining wood, before the planters had beaten up the blacks and discovered the right
scent.

I also heard a joke of Hanger's which struck me as
being very characteristic. At the attack on Camden by
Lord Rawdon he pressed every available man into the
service, not even excepting the musicians. When the
prisoners were being brought in, a provincial officer com-
plained of brutal usage from his capturer. "After I had
tendered my sword," said he, "this fellow threw down his
gun and began to pommel me." "Well, sir," said Hang-

er, "that's nothing extraordinary; the man's a *drummer*."

The antagonist that gave Tarleton the most trouble in the South was the Baron de Glaubeck, a German cavalry officer of great skill, and scarcely his inferior in activity. On being given the command of the Carolina cavalry under Greene, he found, at their first review, that a body of three hundred men could not muster ten swords among them. He accordingly ordered them to arm themselves with good hickory sticks, about a yard long, mounted with iron spikes; and when he had trained them by the most effective evolutions in the use of these, he fell upon a body of Hessians, when his party so plied their cudgels that a rout ensued, leaving him master of artillery and baggage. For this exploit he was labelled with a cognomen which has since been applied to a more modern hero, " Old Hickory."

While on the subject of soldierly exploits, I cannot resist mentioning an anecdote of the Irish Brigade—a regiment whose feats and vicissitudes formed so interesting a feature in the military history of the last century. At the siege of Savannah, their commander, Count Dillon, being anxious that they should early signalize themselves, offered a reward of fifty guineas to the first man who should plant a ladder in the fosse which was exposed to the fire of the garrison. Not one of them attempting to advance, the count, in a paroxysm of fury, upbraided them with cowardice. The sergeant - major proudly replied, " No, sir, we are not cowards, and we are not *hirelings*. If your honor had not offered us money for the service we would have gone forward in a body." The count was speechless: he was asked to wave his hand; the men sent up a shout, sprang forward as with one movement, and out of one hundred and ninety-four only ninety of those devoted hearts returned.

On reaching Charleston I found things much more comfortable than I had expected, the day, though intolerably warm, being tempered by breezes in the evening which revived one's spirits and power of enjoyment. Still the theatre, or any amusement which collected a multitude at this hot season, was unacceptable, for either the giving or receiving of "entertainment" was felt to be a labor. Society here appeared to be a curious mixture of all the human complexions which had ever found a place on the earth's broad pattern-book, from the jet-black of the African, through every intermediate stage of creole and quadroon, Spanish olive, Indian red, Mexican brown, and every tint of cream-color, to the clear white of an Englishman. As the proportion was not in favor of the whites, the city had a foreign look, particularly at a time of year when only a dark skin—the favorite of the sun—courted its fervor; and at parties I met always a great number of yellow girls, daughters of creole mothers, who were among the prettiest and most engaging women I had ever seen. They possessed a natural taste for music and singing, while the sparkle of their faces and the fulness of their forms gave great fascination to their dancing and chattering. They seemed like slips of the French engrafted upon a South American stock. Turnbull, an actor, who saw one for the first time at a house in Charleston, was so impressed by the dramatic force of everything she said and did that he could not resist getting up at the end of one of her vivacities, and saying to her, in a tone of great earnestness, "Madam, did you never think of playing Wowski?"

The citizens I found to be of much the same order as the New-Yorkers, entirely divided between business and pleasure. They breathed neither the literary atmosphere of Philadelphia and Boston, nor the political one of Baltimore. They seemed a world in themselves, very leisurely and happily taking things as they went, and twining the locks of old Time as though their hue was not gray but golden. Of course my own reception at these places can afford little criterion. Blessed with good spirits and ample introductions, I was sure of a welcome everywhere. But, as regarded visitors in general, I should say that the chief difference between Northern and Southern hospitality was this—that the one displayed a craving for new faces, the other a desire never to part with any that had once pleased them.

The Charleston people claimed to possess what has formed a primary element in the greatest minds—humor; and a society existed in their city marked by an originality in scope and detail not to be surpassed by the most brilliant records of Europe. It was called "The Ugly Club," and the chain of reasoning upon which it was founded was as follows: "All nature's works are beautiful, though all beauty is not uniform. Social errors only can have created arbitrary tastes. It is man's business, as a reasonable being, to lead back his fellow-creatures to true principles, and to provide for his own comfort and instruction by associating in companies those who are similar." In accordance with this philosophy were the various particulars in the club's constitution. The first law enacted that the meeting was always to be held in the most ill-favored apartment in the ugliest house in Charleston; the windows to overlook either a dock or a dung-heap; the floor to be an inclined plane, the wainscot a rat-bed, and the ceiling a sieve, both colored bright red or yellow; the furniture to consist merely of chairs and tables, rough-hewn out of hickory by a backwoodsman; and a Dutch looking-glass, so full of veins that look who would into it, he should appear a libel on humanity. The second rule explained the ground of admission, which was broad, liberal, and explicit. Any man pronounced by

society ugly—a physiognomical outcast—was entitled to
become a member, making no distinctions as to creed or
country, these being major points with inferior institutions. The third rule enjoined a proselytizing spirit,
which has only to be explained to prove its social service.
It is a well-known phenomenon that all ugly men are vain,
the probable explanation being that in the majority of
cases they are so, as ignorant men are knowing ones: it
is a piece of mere policy to show indifference to the
world's ill-nature. Nevertheless, as the dignified consciousness of merit is more to be desired than the petty
frivolities of display, this third rule enacted that all vanity in the members, whether enrolled or duly qualified to
become so, was to be utterly rooted out; to compass which
the simplest means were found to be sufficient. The
cracked Dutch looking-glass already mentioned, which
hung beside the chairman, was always produced whenever
signs of flightiness displayed themselves, and proved a
never-failing restorer of the delinquent's reason. As vanity, therefore, was known to be the only check to an ample extension of the society's numbers, the social good
was their authority to seek out new members and purify
them of their weakness. Accordingly, whenever the arrival of a qualified candidate was buzzed about the city,
the secretary waited upon him with a polite invitation to
favor the society with his company. As soon as he had
taken his seat at the table, and the rules and objects of
the meeting had been explained to him, the attack was
commenced by one of the members observing, " You appear to have a very long nose, sir." His consternation
probably produced a laugh, but its sting the chairman
qualified by remarking, " Positively long, yet moderate in
comparison; for, if you observe, sir, the tip of mine forms
an acute angle with a line drawn horizontally from my
under lip, and an obtuse one with my chin; though acute

angles, I beg to say, without incurring the charge of vanity, have never been considered ugly, from the days of Euclid." Another member now broke in, "I should say, sir, that your mouth is not deficient in capacity, from its semicircular figure." A second stare, without response from the party, produced a denial from the secretary, who, opening his jaws to show their full extent, challenged the visitor to pack the interior of his orifice with as many square inches of bread and bacon. Another critic would, perhaps, then inform him that his hair was of that peculiar hue which typifies combustion, when a friend was sure to respond that, so far from considering their guest's hair fiery, he, as the owner of a powder-mill, should not entertain the smallest fear of an accident, were the gentleman to walk into his work-rooms.

The chairman would now rise and beg to propose him as a member. If he proved a social, sensible fellow, the utmost hilarity attended his initiation; but if, on the contrary, he took the proposition in dudgeon, the looking-glass was produced in justification. If its reflections did not eradicate his good opinion of himself, and he retreated in a huff, war was formally declared, and plans suggested to drive him into submission. If he walked abroad, he was sure to meet a member, who pointed out how he abused the kindness of Providence by refusing to join a meeting instituted for mutual protection and amusement, of which he might soon attain to the honor of becoming president. If he stayed at home, he received a dozen letters a day from women who had fallen in love with him, and who poured forth their feelings in some such style as the following :

"DEAR SIR,—An epoch has occurred in my hitherto virgin existence. I have seen you, and I am no longer what I was. May I believe the whisperings of my heart that we are destined for each other, from the numerous sympathies of our persons. Your stature, like mine, is ambitious and genteelly thin; your legs form the most graceful curve I have ever seen; your hands have such an amplitude as must give great facility in grasping; and your head appears large enough for two such frames; but it is needed, I suppose, for the quantity of its furniture. I must confess I piqued myself upon the brilliance of my hair, till I saw yours. Now, alas, mine appears but as the sickly flickerings of a lamp; yours the ruddy glow of a furnace. On one point only you have respected my complacency—your eyes. I do not hesitate to say that the obliquity of mine has given me through life a singleness of perception which yours could never surpass, though I admit that in other respects yours, being of the kind termed 'pig's,' are superior to mine, which are named after a poorer character, 'ferret's.' Say, then, dear youth, with all these affinities, are we to remain asunder?

"Yours till death, DINAH PARAGON."

Upon the perusal of this, if the victim lost his composure so far as to deliver a few epithets on ugly clubs, ugly women, and all such conspirators against a man's peace, ten to one the president of the society introduced himself the next moment and repeated his old importunity, "My dear friend, will you go with me to the club? Why do you try to resist the finger of destiny? Do you know what enjoyments you are casting from you, what sympathy you are shutting yourself out from? If you still doubt your qualifications, look once more in this glass." "Heaven's will be done!" at length exclaimed the persecuted being, his vanity thoroughly expunged; "I believe I am an ugly devil, and it *is* the finger of destiny that I should belong to your club!"

That evil ingredient in the Southern climate which proved so destructive to foreigners was, the dews—the condensed exhalations of a marshy coast which nightly descended upon the inhabitants. The term dew, as we understand it in English poetry—a pearly liquid that is in the habit of going to bed in a rosebud — by no means describes "the curse of Carolina." This is an improvement on the Scotch mist, a sort of half-breed between a London fog and a Devonshire shower; which, like the evil one, introduced itself in the most mild, imperceptible manner, and killed before it could be grappled with. Europeans would often leave heated rooms in the summer, with coat and throat open, never deeming that on a clear, starlight night the pestilence was lying in wait for them. Thus exposed a man would walk home, and the next morning find fire and ice playing at bo-peep in all his bones. Actors, of all men, however perfect (occasionally) on the stage, have never affected this peculiarity in their domestic economy; consequently they formed a good proportion of the number who paid the price of inattention. I remember it was my lot, some years after this, when recruiting in London for the Boston Theatre, to engage a person named Hatton, who, for the singular felicity with which he embodied characters of the stamp of "Macheath's Gang," enjoyed the reputation of being "the best blackguard on the stage." Of how he could act this part off the boards he favored me with a proof in his first performance, by embarking, at the bidding of a rival manager, for Charleston instead of Boston. Though warned here of the nature of the night atmosphere, he had the temerity, on going home from a carousal, to take off his coat and waistcoat, and stretch himself on some steps to study the solar system. An hour afterwards he was found by an inhabitant incapable of moving; in the morning the fever was busy with its victim; and by the night, I believe, he was no more.

One of my favorite unsocial amusements—fishing—I felt shut out from while in the Carolinas, where yet the opportunities were ample, owing to two other Southern evils, of which I confess I could never subdue my apprehension—snakes and alligators. These were such insidious enemies, and, like mine Hostess Quickly, being "neither fish, flesh, nor fowl, a man knew not where to have

them." I know not what man, indeed, could complacently look for a bite from the water while expecting one from
the land. If the chances were that you would afford sport
rather than obtain it, there seemed to me an end of the
pleasure. I was even debarred many a pleasant walk
through the woods, where there was cool shade and a soft
breeze, lest I should light upon some dark tail that would
suddenly become voluminous, especially as I was informed
that these reptiles had a foreign taste, *i. e.*, preferred white
flesh to black—in other words meat not so much roasted—
a fact that accounts for the few accidents among the negroes. I may mention that the Southern reptile was not
the rattling inhabitant of bushes, but a burrower in the
earth. My feelings were destined to be confirmed by a
scene that occurred during an excursion to the banks of
the Congaree River, where the entire bank before the
tavern that I dined at was a snake-bed. The ground,
which was a rich, black loam, was thoroughly perforated
with the avenues of these interesting insinuators, and was
supposed to contain a thousand families, which it would
have been impossible to extirpate but by digging away
their territory. Unaware of this, and seeing some negroes
fishing along the bank, I borrowed a rod from the bar, obtained directions as to the sport, and threw in by the side
of a Cæsar who had strewed the ground with his trophies;
but while I was attaching my bait and looking round, I
observed the head of a snake come up one of these aper-
tures and survey the vivacity of the fishes' tails with
evident interest. I instantly mentioned this to my companion, but he, with a grin at my alarm, merely called to
a group of little black Cupids who were running about in
a state of nature, to "look arter de snek," and turned
again to the river. The juveniles not being extra vigilant,
the snake ascended again to his trap-door, coiled out of
the hole, and made a successful dart at a large bass; but

the weight of the fish was so great he was not able to retreat with it before one of his little black-guards observed
him, and with a cry of mixed fright and frolic, grasped
the fish by the gills, and disputed its possession. The
snake, however, contrived to screw his tail into the hole,
and upon this purchase his strength proved a match for
his antagonist's; indeed, for the moment this singular
spectacle lasted, I thought he had the advantage, and that
ultimately he would drag off both boy and fish. But the
little fellow had a noble spirit, and clung on firmly while
he cried out lustily; the fisherman advanced to the rescue,
and the snake, taking a timely hint, retreated. When the
tavern-keeper, who prided himself on being a good shot,
learned the circumstance, he called for his gun and resolved to watch for the snake's return (which was a sure
thing) to see with what neatness he could divest it of its
head. Our eyes were now converged upon the hole, and
some minutes passed in fixed attention, but with no reward. We were not aware of the enemy's generalship.
At length a negro hooked a fish of such weight he was
unable to draw it in, and called out for assistance. The
tavern-keeper laid down his gun and ran to him, when
instantly the snake, who must have been eying him unobserved, made his last and grand sally, darted once more
on his prey, and triumphantly carried it off, amid an uproar of applause.

The fecundity of one of these creatures is truly alarming; two or three females, in the course of a summer, would
stock a plantation. A friend of mine described to me a
very startling scene which occurred to him during a ram-
ble in Georgia, when he was compelled to pass most of
his nights in the overseers' huts. On one occasion their
black had gone to roost on his shelf (no one slept on the
ground) without taking the precaution to fasten the door,
and during the night a pair of these females, who were

seeking a comfortable nook for their *accouchement*, twisted in through the crevice, and made the necessary arrangements. In the morning my friend happened to wake first, and, looking down from his hammock, he beheld the entire floor of the hut a mass of black life, hundreds—as it appeared to him—of little ones were curling round each other and over their parents with the most fond facility. His involuntary cry of terror woke the black, who, leaning over his board, surveyed their pastime with the greatest complacency. A thundering epithet from the overseer (luckily for them at that moment they were all literally *over-seers*), showing that he had detected Sambo's remissness, threw the latter on his resources, when he instantly put his fingers in his mouth and made a noise in imitation of the rattlesnake, which wages war with this other serpent tribe. In an instant the alarmed mothers glided precipitately out of the hut, followed by their broods twining after them. This scene proved such a ludicrous contrast to the first that my friend indulged in a hearty laugh, and saved the black from his superior's anger.

With snakes I coupled another object of aversion—the alligators. These, however, were not so obtrusive or so terrible, supporting the Buffon hypothesis that they are a degenerated edition, both in size and temper, of the Egyptian crocodile. They were only to be found on the banks of particular rivers, leading a lazy, luxurious life, in imitation, as it were, of the planters. Once and once only, through a telescope, I surveyed one who was enjoying himself in a manner truly Oriental, stretched upon a couch of the downiest mud, his scales glittering like precious stones, his jaws extended to receive all chance contributions of flies and insects. He was, in fact, a grand bashaw of one tail, little energy, and ferocious meanness. The amusement, for instance, of extending his jaws until his tongue was spread like a blister with Spanish flies, and then suddenly dropping the gates upon the innocents, was a villainy that nothing could excuse. He must have found larger substances for his subsistence, though cases were, I believe, very few where the blacks kept his digestive organs in order. By happy observers of the analogies which the earth everywhere furnishes between her tribes, the alligator, from the length of his jaw, was termed "the river lawyer."

I once heard a narrative of the successful domestication of an alligator, the singularly civilized result of which may supply my reader with some new ideas. An infant was found in the sedges of the Wateree River, but a few days, it was supposed, after its birth, and conveyed by a negro to his owner, who formed the extraordinary resolution of bringing it up, and observing whether it would develop its destructive propensities under a systematic course of farm-yard regimen. To his great delight the meal-tub won the victory. The taste of blood being the fount of brutality in savages of all kinds, when this animal arrived at maturity he displayed an affability towards his owner, and a propriety of deportment towards the ducks and hens, which amply repaid the planter's care and trouble in his education. Nothing could be more sociable than the mode in which he waddled amidst the group at feeding-time, admitting them, in fact, to the most marked familiarity, even while enjoying his *siesta* in the slush, constituting his back a committee-room for the feathered tribe, and opening his jaws for the little porkers to rub themselves against. His appearance at these times spoke a volume in disproof of his natural ferocity; his whole frame seemed instinct with a spirit of benevolent enjoyment; his eyes emitted a humid sparkle; and his open countenance was arrayed in a broad grin— the heart was liberal though the hide was scaly. But the most extraordinary circumstance of his history, inasmuch as it proved that female influence, with brutes of all kinds, is the highest agent of refinement, was his forming a Platonic attachment to a sow which daily partook with him the tranquillizing pleasures of the tepid slush. Similarity of tastes and habits are known to give rise to esteem and liking in all bosoms. In this case the fact was manifested by the most touching evidences. He regularly *chaperoned* her in her daily walk from the sty to the barn, varied occasionally by a saunter in the swamp adjacent; secured her one of the best places at the trough; and even brought her tid-bits of fried turkey and codfish from the planter's hand.

When it at last pleased the planter to deprive this estimable female of existence, the blow to her friend's peace was instantaneous and decisive. He felt his sweetest tie sundered, and became a solitary being in the world. The boar, like most husbands, bore his loss with patience; but the friend who had reposed with her through so many hours in a congenial element, exchanging grunts, and reciprocating rubbings, was not to be consoled. He ran into an extreme greater even than that of his own head and tail, and, becoming a recluse, he pined away, appeared to grow longer from longing, and at length was found dead in the old scene of their pleasures. On being opened, within him were found the remains of one of the porkers, which, as a last memorial of his love, he had consigned to the seat of his most inward feelings. This well-authenticated memoir opens a new chapter in zoology. Evidently more analogy subsists between the various classes of creation than is commonly supposed. One thing is evident, that if human beings can so often descend to become brutes, it is but fair that the feelings of brutes should now and then ascend to rank with those of human beings.

During my stay in the Carolinas I was favored with extended observations of the humor of my radiant favorites, the blacks, whose spirits, ever lighting up their shade, reminded me of the merry grave-digger in Hamlet. I never could determine whether the happiest display of their faculty was in their power of repartee and apt discovery of anologies, or in a simplicity that contained its own inherent stock of the ludicrous. I must add some specimens of both.

An old negro in Charleston, named Harry, made it a practice to go a-begging, on holidays, among the gentry. Meeting a Mr. Nicholas Brown, a usual patron, but who happened that morning to be out of temper, he accosted him with, "Good-mornin', massa, me wish a melly Clismas; please to gib poor ole nigger suspence dis mornin'." Mr. Nicholas, pretending not to know him, replied, with some sternness, "Who are you?" "Massa no know me?" he exclaimed; "my name Harry; little boy call me ole Harry." "They call the devil old Harry," growled the gentleman. "Iss, massa," was the immediate rejoinder, "sometime ole Harry, sometime ole Nick!"

Another of the tribe was once brought before a magistrate for thieving. The protector of the public morals, sternly eying the delinquent, inquired, "You black rascal, do you know how to read?" "Iss, massa, a little." "Well, sir, do you never make use of a good book?" "Iss, massa; I trop my razor on um sometime!"

The following was an ingenious and only too truthfully stinging defence. A free negro, being strongly suspected of having stolen goods in his possession, was taken before a magistrate and charged with the offence. The fellow was so hardened as to acknowledge the fact and add to his audacity by this speech: "Massa Justiss, me know me got dem ting from Tom dere, and me tink Tom teal um, too; but what a dat? dey be only a pickaninny corkscrew and pickaninny knife; one cost suspence and tudder shillin'; and me pay Tom honestly for um." "A pretty story, truly," said the justice; "you knew they were stolen, yet you allege as an excuse that you honestly paid for them. I'll teach you better law than that, Cæsar. Don't you know that the receiver of stolen goods is as bad as the thief? You must be whipped, you black rascal!" "Berry well, massa, if the black rascal be whip for buying stolen goods, me hope de white rascal be whip, too, for doin' same ting when massa catch him." "To be sure he shall," rejoined the justice; "I myself will see the punishment inflicted." "Well, den, here be Tom's massa; hole him fast, cons'able! he buy Tom as me buy pickaninny knife and corkscrew; he know berry well dat Tom be stole from him poor fader and modder; now knife and corkscrew hab neider!" Whether it was that his worship was a buyer of pickaninny blacks as well as Tom's master I know not, but this home-thrust unsettled the composure of both, and, after a few minutes' deliberation, the charge was dismissed.

An equally direct hint was given, during the war, to a Jamaica planter who became noted for stinting his slaves to the least possible allowance of herrings and meal, on the pretext that all the provision-vessels were taken by the American privateers. This answer to their first complaint sufficed, but on its frequent repetition the slaves saw through it, and he was waited on by a deputation of them, who informed him that, "Since probision taken ebery day by Amerriky pribateer, we mean to take de sloop, massa, to-morrow mornin' and go to Merryky in sarch ob it."

On my return to Philadelphia the first person I met was my Terpsichorean friend Byrne, of Covent Garden, who had filled up his summer by a trip to the West Indies, but had returned with more precipitancy than he departed. As this visit seemed to epitomize a hundred others made during my time by my professional brethren to the land of doubloons, and to convey a useful lesson to adventurers generally, I shall briefly describe it.

Byrne, a most worthy as well as talented little fellow, had been haunted, ever since his arrival in America, by visions of the new Potosi mines to be found in the pockets of the West India planters. Whoever had been to the islands, actors or traders, had painted in brighter and brighter colors the already glowing tints of that glowing clime. To be sure, there were facilities for spending money as fast as you got it, and some men had been so delighted with the society that they made up their minds to die there; but all this was capable of being explained away. Fashionable habits had been in fault, or arid constitutions which, to become genial, required perpetual soakings. A man of prudence, thought Byrne, could contrive to steer clear of these quicksands, and thus speedily allay that pecuniary "yellow fever" which had led him from home. Mrs. B. concurring in his sentiments, and longing as much as himself to get back to England, he had her consent to try his fortune in Jamaica.

All the circumstances of his voyage tended to inspire him with confidence. The weather was delightful, the sky blue, the sea green, the breeze fair, the captain anecdotical, the crew dramatic, the passengers Philadelphic; nothing disordered their minds or their stomachs; and a general theme of praise was the island he was going to. Byrne was, therefore, emboldened to believe this one of the most auspicious steps he had yet taken, and he felt himself about to dance into a sublunary Elysium, surpassing in splendor any that had been got up on London boards. As he sailed into the port of Kingston the calm deepened, the illusion rose; a smile of beauty invested every object, and told of wealth, activity, and enjoyment. Byrne pirouetted upon the deck, cast off his partners gracefully, sprang on the wharf vigorously, and chasseyed up the street. The first vehicle that he met was a hearse. This did not surprise him, as he was aware that death is a peculiarity of every country; but he had scarcely turned the corner leading to the hotel when he met another. That appeared strange, but he was in no humor to investigate grave affairs, so he kept on his pace, and in another twenty yards, lo, a third! He now made a stop and pondered. Devilish odd, he thought, that the only carriages he had yet encountered were the last ones people chose to ride in! Superstitious folks would have fallen to auguring! But a solution of the mystery presented itself : this was the way to the public cemetery, and it was nothing more than a curious coincidence that he had walked up the street at the very moment that, perhaps, the only three coffins in Kingston were coming down. With a laugh which expressed that he had spent too much time in the air to become speedily solid, he skipped into the hotel and called for some refreshment. As no newspaper was lying at hand, he took his stand at the window of the public parlor, to amuse himself with the panorama of the streets. Having passed through the region of business, he was anxious to obtain a view of Kingston fashion—the ladies and gentlemen in their carriages. The first vehicle that passed was another hearse. "Odd!" exclaimed Byrne, "that's the fourth!" but before he had time to arrange his ideas for any further speculation a fifth presented itself, not moving with that decorous slowness which marks its pace in Europe, but at a quick walk ; and this was succeeded by another and another on an improving trot, as though the conveniences for interment in the city were not half sufficient to meet the demand. "Good heavens!" ejaculated Byrne, gazing at them as Macbeth did at the spectres, "is the whole country dying? there must have been a battle or an earthquake!" and, seizing the bell, he rang it till he roused a very corpulent man sleeping in one corner of the room, but whom until this moment he had not perceived. "What's the matter, sir?" inquired the stranger, "are you ill?" "No, sir," said Byrne, "but I've no doubt I soon shall be. I have just arrived in Kingston, and I have seen nothing in the street but hearses." "Oh, sir," replied the other, "if you are surprised at that you must be a stranger. When you have been here as long as I have you will find that if a man can contrive to escape death, the climate makes this a living grave. I am an instance, sir. I was once as slim a figure as yourself, but much more powerful. I lived in London and had a very good income, but I would be so d——d avaricious that I must come to the West Indies to make my fortune; and what's the consequence? In less than two years I have lost my health and every friend I had to welcome me. Look, sir," he continued, his voice breaking into a snivel, "see what a poor, bloated maggot I have swelled to! What good is my money to me now?" Pausing from excess of emotion, he looked Byrne full in the face and exclaimed, "Good heavens! Byrne, is it you? Don't you remember me—Mat Williams, of Drury Lane?" Byrne returned his stare with interest. It was, indeed, his old friend, Mat Williams, the hale and handsome singer of Drury Lane, whom he now beheld transformed into a bag of bile, yellow and big enough for a picture of Plutus in the dropsy. The story and its illustration struck home. Byrne was speechless. The waiter entering next moment, he could just articulate, "What have I to pay?" then, scarcely pressing his old friend's hand, or stopping to bid him farewell, he made one step down-stairs, took three along the street, cut a rapid caper round the corner, and meeting at that point the negro who had charge of his portmanteau, he grasped him by the wool of his head and dragged him back to the wharf. There, seeing a brig hauling off for Baltimore, he hailed her, vaulted on board, and only recovered speech and composure when he saw the woody shore of the island growing dim in the distance.

CHAPTER X.

1801–3. — Recollections of President Jefferson; his Observations in France; Neckar and Mirabeau; the Comte de Artois; Marie Antoinette; Jefferson's Compliments; his Rencontre with a Connecticut Farmer; Parallel with John Adams.—Peculiarities of Pennsylvania; Contrast to Virginia.—German Settlers; the Veteran Corps; a Female Recruit; Gastronomic Hessians.—Barbecuing and Bundling.—Marrying in Haste. —Periodical Whitewashings.—A "Pennsylvany Hurricane." — Recollections of Charles Brockden Brown; his Writings; his Character; his Drama and its Fate.

I HAVE already mentioned that through the kindness of General Washington I was introduced to Mr. Jefferson, who proved one of my sincerest, though not most fortunate, friends. The coupling of his acquaintance with a speculation involving considerable loss and chagrin cannot, however, prevent my recurring to the period with a degree of pleasure which I trust may prove communicable to the reader. In all the chief requisites of the social character Mr. Jefferson appeared to me to possess few equals. His heart was warmed with a love for the whole human race; a *bonhomie* which fixed your attention the instant he spoke. His information was equally polite and profound, and his conversational powers capable of discussing moral questions of deepest seriousness, or the lightest themes of humor and fancy. Nothing could be more simple than his reasonings, nothing more picturesque and pointed than his descriptions. On all abstract subjects he was plainness itself—a veritable Quaker; but when conveying his views of human nature through their most attractive medium — anecdote — he displayed the grace and brilliance of a courtier. His talents may suggest some idea of his manners. Though, like taste and beauty, manners have no general standard, so that refinement in France is frivolity in Holland, and frankness in Holland is boorishness in France, the citizen of the world perceives that an excess of artificiality is as opposed to human happiness as utter barbarity. But if manners be brought to the one test of general consideration for others, my good friend, the President, would certainly not have been judged deficient by any one. To a just balance of qualities his residence in France had no doubt contributed. He had witnessed an extraordinary contrast— the extremes of society under a polished despotism and in a young republic—and tracing their respective effects on the national welfare, the rooting of his convictions had led to the branching out of his sympathies. During the many pleasant evenings I spent in his society at Washington and Philadelphia, I chiefly attempted to draw out his observations upon the period he had passed in France, where his official situation placed him in juxtaposition with the leading characters of the court, as well as most of the agents of the Revolution. Amid this group he was equally intimate with Neckar and Mirabeau, the Duc de Lauzun, and the Abbé Sieyès. Six years a spectator of the gathering of that tornado which began in tears and ended in blood, no man could have written a more animated account of the organization of the Tree of Liberty. Adams, in his boyhood (1755), detected its first shoots in America in the all-engrossing interest of political conversations. Jefferson was destined to witness the effect of its transplantation to Gallic soil. The two great accessories of the French Revolution were the encyclopedists and the patriots, the latter of whom returned from America to make known to their countrymen the enviable condition of a people whose rights were respected. As their verbal accounts must have taken a wider range than literary teachings, it is not too much to assume that these patriots held the match to the explosion, and that Louis, in extending assistance to the Americans, provided for his own dethronement. As Franklin remarked when the outbreak was announced to him, "Ah, they served their apprenticeship in America, and now they mean to set up for themselves." With truer instinct Frederick the Great, when solicited to afford assistance to the Americans, replied, "No, a king I was born, and a king I will remain; it is too much of you to require a man to ruin his own trade."

Mr. Jefferson supported the above supposition by pointing out a chain of sequences among the most striking in modern history. "America," said he, "the child of the Old World, appears destined to become its teacher. Like the heart in the human system, it has received and sent back purified the diseased opinions of England and France. Those countries have fought for its possession in the true spirit of despotism, and have been foiled because the lamb grew up, during the contest, into a lion. We see, in the first instance, English exiles in the cause of freedom settling America and impregnating its moral atmosphere. Then France rearing her standard on the walls of Quebec, and gradually extending her possessions along the margin of the Lakes to the Ohio, and thence onward to the mouth of the Mississippi, with the giant design of spanning the continent from the Arctic Ocean to the Gulf of Mexico; England, rising up at the cry of the colonies, fought through that arduous war which sealed the submission of France with the blood of Wolfe; but after that, inflated with her triumph, we see her next turning round and taxing these very colonists to discharge the burden belonging to other possessions ; the colonies resisting; and France, in the hope of recovering Canada, sending them assistance; the independence following, and the Frenchmen returning home to achieve the liberation of their own country. To conclude, England, placed between the fires of two revolutions, and not less admonished by the lurid excesses of the one than invited by the calm and benign glow of the other, to provide for the general happiness of her people, is working out English freedom on the pattern of American independence."

Mr. Jefferson said he had perceived at an early period that Neckar and Mirabeau were two of the most important persons in France. Of both it was impossible to calculate whether they would save the country from a convulsion or throw it into one. They frequently met, and on the most sociable terms, but their manners in company presented a curious contrast. The financier always began the evening with great spirit, and talked animatedly upon all subjects till about nine o'clock, when a shadow stole over his countenance and he sank into silence, absorbed in public considerations only temporarily put aside. The count always sat down under a cloud and brooded, until the wine dissipated his vapors and warmed him into life. For an hour or two he was then a most agreeable companion. He poured out information, poetry, and anecdote, and flashed his sarcasm right and left with the edge and polish of a true Damascene. But he drank furiously, and, as the wine heated him, his ruling interest regained its sway, and his hilarity rose into a species of madness. His eye dilated, his voice choked, he shook his black hair wildly about his face, burst into political prophecies, and struck the table until the glasses rang by way of emphasis, recalling the image of the Sibyl during the throes of inspiration. In a short time he had reached the pinnacle of his social glory—his antagonists had deserted the table, or he was lying under it.

The popularity of this glittering monster to whom lib-

erty meant license, and power pay, whose life was passed
in a state of moral drunkenness, proves that his talents
must have been very extraordinary, or that the people
were indeed destitute and desperate. In America, where
virtue was its own reward, there had been no Mirabeaus
in principle, save Arnold. The test of patriotism was there
too primitive. And yet the count had the complacency
to hint to Mr. Jefferson that if France was destined to
become another America, the world should see that there
was another Washington, to which the latter replied, with
polite ambiguity, "Pardon me, count, but I consider such
is the striking originality of your character, you would
disdain to imitate any man."

Nor was it with the populace only that Mirabeau had
influence; he was also the idol of the women. Why? Although the ugliest man in Europe, his popularity solves
the mystery. Conquest with one sex led necessarily to
submission from the other. At a convivial party he once
remarked to his companions, "They say abroad 'Mirabeau
must have a great mind, for the women love him though
he is as ugly as the devil.'" As no one answered, he continued, taking a pinch of snuff, "It's very true. I and
the devil have always been their favorites."

Mr. Jefferson did not wonder at the shadow on Baron
Neckar's countenance, destined as he was to resist single-
handed the erection of the court barricades, and to see
the king forwarding by every indirect means the object
of his enemies. A reply attributed to the Comte d'Artois
well exhibits that spirit which at length unsealed the foun-
tains of the deluge. On the baron observing to him the
growing necessity of relieving in some measure the bur-
dens of the people. "My good friend," exclaimed he,
"the people are not the only sufferers; we at court have
a burden much more difficult to get rid of." "What may
that be?" "Our time," was the reply.

My friend quite concurred in the general impression as to the sympathetic weakness of the king and queen, who, in quiet times, would have slid through the world in the fashionable absence of all sense or principle, without exciting praise or blame. The queen, a truly affable creature, was pleased to pay him particular attention, but, as he conceived, more as a curiosity than as a friend. She was always wondering how it was possible the people of America could be happy without a court, and at length said to him, "Surely your great deliverer intends to create nobility?" To which he replied, "Please your majesty, the influence of your own is so powerful that it is the general impression we can do without them."

Mr. Jefferson has put so much evidence upon record, both of his varied talents and his social excellence, that I feel loath to intrude too many recollections; and shall avail myself, therefore, of but a few instances which came within the knowledge of myself and friends.

While he was in Paris a young man waited upon him as a member of a family he knew in Virginia, and by means of a plausible story obtained from him a supply of money. On his return home he mentioned the circumstance to his friends, and discovered it was a gross imposture. But the news did not cost him his composure. "This is the way," said his friend, "in which generosity gets soured; but I wonder, Mr. J., that you gave the money so easily without more inquiry. "Now I think of it, I wonder myself," replied the latter, "but that it is so much pleasanter to *give* than to *refuse*."

When once at a party where the private delinquencies of a well-known individual formed the subject of conversation, every one present opened in full cry upon the unfortunate buck, except Mr. Jefferson, whose silence was at length interpreted as a disbelief of the charges. A friend asked him the question, "Surely you must be as

well aware as ourselves that these are the facts?" "Un-
doubtedly," he replied, "only I can't see how my calling
the man a rascal will help to reclaim him."

He was strikingly happy in illustrations which brought
the fullest amount of argument into the smallest compass.
When a once-applauding public expatriated Dr. Priestley
in his old age, Mr. J. remarked, "His antagonists think
they have quenched his opinions by sending him to America, just as the pope imagined when he shut up Galileo in
prison that he had compelled the world to stand still."

His regard for both science and literature was founded
on this just view of their respective effects. "I consider,"
said he to me, "scientific knowledge to be that food which
alone can enable the mental functions to acquire vigor
and activity; but elegant literature as the wine that should
invariably follow, because without it the mind would never
rise to the full measure of its enjoyment, the power of
sympathizing with itself, after sympathizing with Nature."

In poetry his taste was thoroughly orthodox; Shakespeare and Pope, he said, gave him the perfection of imagination and judgment, both displaying more knowledge of
the human heart—the true province of poetry—than he
could elsewhere find. His prose favorites were Swift and
Bolingbroke. Upon the utility of literature he made another remark that pleased me; "I was bred," said he, "to
the law; that gave me a view of the dark side of humanity. Then I read poetry to qualify it with a gaze upon
its bright side; and between the two extremes I have contrived through life to draw the due medium. And so,"
he continued, "substituting history and biography for law,
I would have every man form his own estimate of human
nature, because it seems to me that precisely the same
directing forces should subsist in the social as in the solar
system; there should be the same attractive or concen-

trating power in our hearts to draw us together qualifying the repelling impulse which we gain from our experience and reading."

With specimens of his humor I could fill pages. Hearing from the profound Dr. Rush that he, in company with a well-known wit of Philadelphia, had nearly been lost while proceeding in a packet from New York to Baltimore, Mr. J. replied, "Well, doctor, such a fate would have suited your genius precisely. You, you know, are always for going to the bottom of things; though it would have been inappropriate for our friend H——, who prefers skimming the surface."

Of a piece with this was a remark upon a captain of Virginia militia, who had once been a waiter at a tavern, and who was so heavy a sleeper that, on training days, the company were compelled to discharge a volley under his window before they could wake him. "Ah," said Jefferson, "it would be a much better plan if you were to ring a hand-bell under his window; then, I'll be bound, he'd at once pop out his head and cry 'Coming! coming.'"

He was deservedly a favorite with the ladies, the elegance of his compliments affording the best proof of his refinement. They had the veritable odor of Versailles. A lady of his acquaintance once congratulated herself upon never feeling cold in the depth of winter. "Go where I will," said she, "I can always fancy it's summer." "And whenever you come under my roof, madam," he replied, "I partake your impression!" On another occasion, a lady at an evening party called his attention to some flowers in her bosom, which were exotics but recently imported. Jefferson, admiring them greatly, inquired their name. She replied by giving their Linnæan designation. "Dear me!" said he, "I thought they were a new species of primrose." "Primrose, Mr. Jefferson?" "Yes, madam, from the snow that's so near them."

Perhaps I cannot conclude these recollections more pleasantly than by relating an anecdote of himself, which he told with great humor as having occurred shortly after his election to the presidency. He was riding one day in the neighborhood of Washington, in his usual plain attire —a black suit verging on brown—when, from a cross-road, a Connecticut farmer trotted up to him, and immediately displayed his provincial spirit of barter by surveying the president's superior steed, and asking him to "swap." Jefferson, however, asked too much money in exchange, so, after a fruitless attempt to draw him into a commercial transaction in respect to the saddle and bridle, the stranger began to favor the president with his history. He had lately quitted "Down East," and was coming South to "explore" a brother, hid away somewhere among the niggers in Virginny. He was anxious, therefore, to obtain all the knowledge he could of the country and the state of politics in parts "contagious" to the seat of government. This wish led directly to the topic of the new president, Thomas Jefferson, who had been elected to that dignity in direct opposition to the said stranger's advice. "I," said he, "support John Adams, a real old New-Englander, after the manner of our forefathers, the Pilgrims of Plymouth Rock. I have smallish faith in these chaps from the nigger states, upon principle. Doesn't it stand to reason, mister, that they must be a largish bit tyrannical?" Jefferson attempted some refutation of the charge, but the farmer scarcely listened to ten words before he rejoined, "Come, come, mister, I guess you don't see the moral sin of niggery; but it ain't only that. This Thomas Jefferson—did you ever see him?" The president nodded. "Well, that's more luck than I've had; but that doesn't matter. Now I hear that this Thomas Jefferson is a very wasteful chap with our hard-earned money" (Jefferson stared), "and you'll allow, mister, that that's unpatriotic upon principle. They tell me he never goes out but he's got clothes on his back that would sell for a plantation, or kiver a wagon-load of immigrants; he's a couple of watches or more, that he never thinks of swapping; rings on all his fingers; and a frill to his shirt big enough to turn a windmill. Now, if you've seen him, mister, you can tell me if that's about right." Jefferson laughed, and replied that, on the contrary, the president was seldom better dressed than himself at that moment. The farmer had his prejudices, and shook his head knowingly as he continued, "Come, come, squire; I see you are a small measure biassed. I guess now this Jefferson's a friend of your'n?" The president confessed it. "I dare say a man you speak to when you please?" Another nod. "Perhaps the smallest eend of a relation?" Nod and laugh. "There, now! I guessed it. I knew you could not speak the truth on principle." At this moment they came in view of the president's house, and the farmer inquired who it belonged to. As soon as he received the intelligence he burst into one of those conventional substitutes for oaths which emphasize the language of the Northern lower orders. "Well, now, may I be 'tarnally starved down for mutton broth, if that sight doesn't come over a man like a suspension of the works of natur'. Now, mister, doesn't that prove my words, awfully strong? There's a house as big as Noah's ark? At the smallest count, there's thirty rooms in it. What can any careful chap, 'pon principle, want with more than *six?* I ha'n't got more than *four.* I say this Jefferson's wasting the people's money, and Congress is winking at it, and I guess it's all naked truth about the frill and watches; and I ain't afraid to affirm that it's my guess the inside of that house shows just as much wastefulness as Jefferson a-horseback." To this charge the president could make but one reply—an offer to introduce the farmer to the mansion, and give him ocular conviction. The latter readily consented, and they rode on, Jefferson planning an elaborate lesson of reproof to his calumniator. But, as they approached the gate, some gentlemen, who were engaged to dine with him, stepped forward and exclaimed, "Good-morning, president; you have had a fine day." At the word "president" the farmer, who was trotting on briskly, drew up so short he was near flying over his steed's ears. He turned and stared at Jefferson with a mixture of curiosity and alarm, which drew from the latter a quiet smile of enjoyment. In another instant he had struck his spurs into his horse and was flying away like a whirlwind, fully convinced that he should in some way pay for his temerity. "Hallo, friend!" shouted Jefferson, "won't you go over the house?" "No, thank ye, president," was the reply; "I'll look in when I come back."

Those who consider that the chief magistracy is a dignity which, to obtain its due respect, should be secluded from the common gaze, must admit that here was a proof of the benefit of its exhibition. This farmer echoed the opinions of many upon the president's character, and, in the only way that could have satisfied him, his suspicions were refuted.

Strikingly singular was the series of coincidences which made the destiny of Jefferson and of John Adams a parallel. Both, bred to the law and skilled in their profession, were early advocates, by speech and pen, of the colonial rights. Both went as delegates to the first Congress; together they voted for independence; were members of the committee to frame the "Declaration," and formed the sub-committee to prepare the draught. Both served their country on foreign embassies; both became vice-presidents and presidents; both lived to see the fiftieth anniversary of the freedom they had accomplished, and both died on that great day within an hour of each other!

Though placed at the head of contending parties, they were firm friends in private, and spent the evening of their days in the exchange of the best sympathies arising from their common patriotism.

I have mentioned that, though Pennsylvania was the asylum of Quakers, it was for many years one of the most factious of the states, owing to the diversity of its subsequent population. It, however, recovered its quietude through the large infusion of German occupants, whose industry, thoughtfulness, and energy grappled successfully with the difficulties of its stubborn soil. Much of the moral difference between two adjoining states, one the most dissipated, the other the most industrious, in the Union, was to be traced solely to their great geological contrast—that whereas in Virginia you had merely to " scratch the earth and it would yield a crop," in Pennsylvania deep digging and manuring were required to effect the same end. Indeed, it was a remark in the early times that the inhabitant of the former, lazily sponging on the blessings of Heaven, resembled Adam in Paradise before the Fall; while his hardworking neighbor seemed to be fulfilling Adam's penalty after it.

Many of these Germans were soldiers, who had done efficient duty in the war; indeed, this state had the honor to contribute a legion whose character it would be difficult to parallel in military records. They were called the " Veteran Corps "—eighty German soldiers, who, after serving under various monarchs of Europe, had retired to America to turn their swords into ploughshares; but, on the first outburst of hostilities, voluntarily formed themselves into a company to defend the land which had received them. Their captain was nearly one hundred years old; he had been a soldier seventy-five years, and fought in above twenty battles. The drummer was ninety-four; and the youngest man in the corps little under seventy.

Such a band might well have been called the Fathers of
the Fight. It is a pleasing fact that nearly all of them
survived the contest, and, their last service having sanctified all former ones, sank peacefully to rest.

Another singular recruit from Pennsylvania was one
Miss Deborah Gannet, who, throwing off all maiden delicacy and timidity, served in the Republican ranks under
the name of Robert Shurtliff, was wounded, yet escaped
discovery of her sex; and at length received her discharge
and arrears of pay, without having incurred a stain on her
honor in public or private.

The Germans mentioned above must not be confused
with the·Hessians who came over in the English service,
to be surprised at Trenton, and to turn the current of the
war.   John Bull has the reputation of never being able to
fight but upon a bellyful ; John Ox, as this race of gas-
tronomes might be called, so far exceeded him that they
could neither fight full nor empty. A corps of London
aldermen would have been equally efficient. All that their
tactics proposed to give a dressing to were — dinners.
True, it might be cited as an amiable feature that they had
not, like most invaders, a savage thirst for human blood,
seeing they preferred drink of any kind whatever, but the
nature of their feats may claim a distinctive niche in the
gallery of Fame.   No troops were ever so signalized for
the arduous routing of hen-roosts, the vigorous beleaguer-
ing of pig-styes, and the successful sweeping of duck-
ponds.   It was evident that they considered the art of
war, which most people regard as a short avenue to death,
a new chapter in the art of living. Had their private
despatches to Germany been intercepted, no doubt the
Americans would have found them to contain, instead of
political hints, valuable recipes. Thus it was but an
appropriate catastrophe that they should be speedily
dished. Washington had but administered a little dex-

terous carving, and a few forced-meat balls, when a succession of removes led to a general desert.

A story was told me of an Irishman in the Independent service who detected a pair of these heroes taking captive a pig near his outpost, and, contriving unobserved to pick up their guns, suddenly headed, and bade them turn about to his own camp. His pointed manner and arms had the desired effect; they released the pig, and proceeded peaceably to the enemy's quarters, doubtless lamenting the loss of their prize as the worst feature of the incident. When the general asked their capturer how he had managed to overpower such unequal forces, he replied, " By the powers, sir, I *surrounded* them."

It must have been a relation of this person, or at least a countryman, who, during an engagement, encountered a man of war among the Quakers, one of the party who, infected by General Greene's example, had taken up arms, and were termed "Resisters." The Irishman, surmising his character from his appearance, shouted as he advanced, " Come on, me darlint; here's the sword that Balaam was going to kill his ass with." The Quaker, troubled at the inaccurate quotation, forgot his own safety to correct him, and exclaimed, "Stay, friend, thou art wrong; Balaam had no sword, he only wished for one." " Well, then," was the rejoinder, "here's the sword he wished for," and a hearty thwack brought the inimical " Friend " upon his knees.

Pennsylvania possessed its own local diversions in addition to many imported ones, the principal being barbecuing and bundling. The first was a feast in the woods, upon roasted pigs, a sort of rough gypsy party, in which the porkers were killed and dressed by the men, while the ladies made a circuit to obtain spirits, milk, and bread; the meal taking place on some favorable clear space of sward, and winding up with singing and dancing, for which a band of black Timotheii were always in attendance. As

the fun of these meetings depended much more on the
spirits of the party than the mode of the diversion, little
can be said of them beyond that the material of the feast—
the pork—supplied some wags with a jest against the children of Israel, who were, at one time, scattered in some
number through the States. Whenever a man owed one
of them a sum which he was not prepared to pay, the
creditor who inquired for him was told, "He was gone to
a barbecue, where he would be happy to give a seat to Mr.
Moses."

The other peculiar institution which, with more liberal
natures, formed a feature in their hospitality—the bundling—I confess I regarded with as much pleasure as surprise. Offensive as it may appear to European delicacy
that a young female should commit herself indiscriminately to the same couch with strangers, merely adopting a
precaution which in any refined country would be thought
ridiculous—confining her petticoat to her ankles—what
did it prove but the highest purity of ideas, and the utmost faith in the honor of the weary wanderer who sought
shelter from storm and darkness beneath the farmer's roof,
that he would not repay the obligation by attempting any
insult to his child. The custom was in the first instance
a matrimonial ordeal, and was most likely imported from
Wales, where, till within a late period, two lovers previous
to their marriage were consigned to the same bed (the
lady in a kind of sack which fastened round the throat),
and thus enabled to discover how their tempers would
agree during darkness as well as daylight. Doubtless
some benefit resulted from this experiment, or a resemblance to it would not have been adopted in the "Tarry-
ing" of the precise New-Englanders, and the "Wooing-
hut" of the Indians.

The expedition with which marriages were knocked up
in this state was surprising, owing perhaps to an overplus

of females or to some domesticating influence in the climate. No sooner did a young man with any means of support think proper to pop the question to a girl, than she, despising all coquetting and affectation as an improper waste of time and feeling, replied with a frank "Yes" or "No." In cases, however, where any want of decision was betrayed by the lady, the lover always displayed a proportionate increase of it, as the following instance may show. A young man who had engaged to marry a girl as soon as his circumstances would permit, through a sudden turn of fortune resolved one Saturday night to fulfil his word instanter. He accordingly set off in a sleigh, for it was in the heart of winter, with two companions, to Weaver Tavern, near the Comestogoe, where he ordered supper, and despatched his friends to fetch the damsel, while he went to procure the minister, having the license in his pocket all prepared. It was now past nine o'clock, and the snow falling heavily. In about an hour he returned and met his friends, who said that they had seen his betrothed, but she had entirely forgotten the engagement, and moreover asserted that she would never marry any man who wouldn't treat her to a "sleighing." The bridegroom, not a whit disconcerted, replied, "Well, she's her own woman, and I'm my own man. I've come out for a wife, and I'm not going to be such a confounded fool, arter I've ordered this supper, as to go back without one. There's Miriam Bush likes me jest as well as she does, is jest as handy, and, I'll bet my harness, would make as good a helpmate. So, now, I'll tell you what, Mr. Peascod"— addressing the minister—"if you'll only be so good as to wait here half an hour, you sha'n't lose your job, I tell ye. So, boys, jest set down, order something strong, and keep supper warm till I get back."

All the parties being agreeable, he jumped into the sleigh, though it was now pitch dark, near midnight, and a storm

coming down that shook the house, laid his whip round
the horses, and went off at full gallop, to the residence of
a maiden whom he hoped to find more complying. He
caught her just retiring to bed, told her his story, showed
her the license, pointed to the sleigh in the yard, and without any unmanly grovelling at her feet, frankly and honestly asked her if she'd go back to the tavern and marry
him. A girl's pride, on being applied to as a last resource,
was not unlikely to have procured an instant refusal. It
appeared, however, that she liked him well enough to consider the match a bargain at any price; a moment's pause
—and consent glittered in her eyes—a genuine, back-coun-
try kiss sealed the compact; her shawl and bonnet were
hastily thrown on, he lifted her into the sleigh, and triumphantly drove back to his companions, defying all the
efforts of the elements to disappoint him. The bride was
then handed to the minister; her name introduced into the
license, their hands were joined, and they all sat down to
the smoking supper, flavored no doubt with double relish
from the obstacles that had delayed it.

One of the local peculiarities of Pennsylvania was the
domestic lustration, or whitewashing, as it was termed,
which the action of the atmosphere on the wooden houses,
generating dirt and insects in abundance, rendered necessary at least once a year, but which, in some parts of the
state, was multiplied to once a quarter, and formed an established recreation of the ladies and purgatory for the
men. The Dutch women had certainly the strongest passion for cleanliness, but that was in a modified way, a mere
scouring of floor and furniture. Here purification implied
totality, requiring superior energy and judgment, and in-
flicting greater disturbance and inconvenience. No well-
brought up wife was known to resign a privilege which
brought so much pleasure, whatever might be the sound
condition of her dwelling or the infirm condition of her

spouse. No plea of asthma, low spirits, or even the presence of friends, could avert the dread decree, when the period had arrived and the word went forth, "We must have a whitewash." Some husbands were enabled to balance the expense of these periodical cleanings by restricting some other amusement, but few succeeded by the most tempting offers in inducing their partners to forego the one in question; while I have heard of some ladies who, to guard against all hazards, stipulated for the full enjoyment of this privilege, with all its rights and appurtenances, as the leading article in the marriage compact.

This whitewashing practice also prevailed in the Jerseys, which were settled in the same mode as Pennsylvania, though presenting a great contrast to each other in their general manners; West Jersey modelled itself upon the quieter though quainter characteristics of Philadelphia, while East Jersey displayed the commercial spirit of New York.

I have endeavored to point out the natural features of each state which had any influence on the habits of the people ; as, for instance, the swamps in the Carolinas, whose exhalations, requiring correctives, led to an excess of ingenuity in the composition of those seducers termed "antifogmatics." In Pennsylvania it struck me that there were some appearances in the country people which might, perhaps, be traced to their most powerful familiar —the hurricane. Not that there was anything boisterous or particularly rapid in their movements, but, on the contrary, a general caution, firmness, and tenacity of purpose, as though they were in hourly expectation of being uprooted from the spot by their envious visitant. Every house, barn, and pig-sty was built with a solid grasp of earth, and every man or woman, on issuing abroad, seemed to fasten coats or caps in due array for a struggle to retain them. With accounts of the gambols of these air-kings

most English readers are familiar, but they have been the
object of as much exaggeration as Kentucky rifle-shooting.
A "Pennsylvany hurricane," like a "Caroliny swamper,"
was, indeed, a common term, nearer home, for a sublime
Munchausenism—vulgarly speaking, a long lie. I certainly myself witnessed the feat of their screwing a tree
out of the earth like a cork from a bottle; but I believe
the story of their carrying a hay-rick to market, and transporting a team of oxen from one farm to another, to be
apocryphal. These were jests invented by the editors of
newspapers whenever they required matter for a corner;
but which, appearing in England, were regarded as evidences of the national veracity. One of the pleasantest
of these inventions was in allusion to the rapidity with
which a settlement was run up in the back states. An
Irish emigrant was described as going to sleep near a few
log huts on the banks of the Ohio, and being seized by a
whirlwind which carried him off and deposited him, while
he slumbered, in the streets of Philadelphia. On opening
his eyes he looked round in amazement, and exclaimed,
"Well, by my sowl! I had heard of your building a
wooden town in a day ; but if you did all this in a night,
the divil himself must have been your bricklayer's laborer!"

One of the most agreeable acquaintances I formed in
Philadelphia was with Charles Brockden Brown, the first,
and for many years the only, novelist America had produced. Few men have united talent and worth in a larger
proportion, or been more marked by a characteristic which
is supposed to be incompatible with the pursuit of letters
—equanimity. In a powerful mind this must be a mental
influence. It bespeaks an active as well as speculative
life, a daily observation of the world's admixture, engen-
dering contentment with its best and respect for its weakest part. It is the fate of writers who seclude themselves,

that, carrying a high standard of character into the world, they are not prepared to put up with the discovery that they have deceived themselves.

Brown, as a writer, has not yet, I apprehend, received his full share of praise. It is true he formed his style upon that of an illustrious modern thinker—Mr. Godwin; but while the latter owed his pervading gloom to German study, with Brown the tinge of sadness took its rise in nature. Mr. Godwin's genius may be likened to a hermit reading the records of his race by a flickering lamp in the solitary ruins of an old abbey or castle; Brown writes as though seated in one of his own primeval forests, with the twilight falling round him and the stars coming out to watch his meditations. Like Mr. Godwin, he is an explorer of the inner world of man, not a painter of its external habits. He is no recorder of the artificial conventionalities which mark the surface of human conduct, but a diver into its depths and a delineator of the sources, not the results, of our ruling thoughts and feelings. In doing this he shows less elegance, less care, less metaphysical minuteness and logical accuracy than his great prototype. He cannot so steadily lay bare the quivering flesh and trace each delicate nerve that shrinks within it, nor can he diversify his pages with the same amount of learning, but the story he writes evolves with more simplicity, flows in swifter sentences, and takes advantage of a sustained interest in the reader's mind to press its moral or its argument with greater force. Both these writers belong to a class addressing but a narrow circle of admirers at present, yet they must rise in estimation as taste and information spread, for the material they work in is permanent, while the ephemeral modes and features of society can interest only those who behold them. "Edgar Huntly" appears to me to be one of his most pleasing productions; the story and character of Cli-

thero rivet the attention from beginning to end. "Arthur
Mervyn" contains the most powerful descriptions (the
ravages of the Plague, etc.), but "Wieland," taken on all
points, must be considered his *chef d'œuvre.*

Brown gave very little idea of an imaginative writer
in his appearance. He was short and dumpy, with light
eyes, and hair inclining to be sandy, while the expression
of his countenance told rather of ill-health than of intellect. The lines on his brow seemed to have been corroded
by consumption, not chiselled by midnight meditations,
and this was partly the case. A weak constitution had
been his parents' legacy to him, and the ebullitions of his
spirit proved too powerful for the vessel that contained
it. Yet vividly in his countenance glowed the light of
benevolence ; that was his nature, and he could no more
have suppressed its expression than he could have kept
his eyes closed.

With all his ill-health and straitened circumstances, for
he supported himself chiefly by his pen, Brown enjoyed
life, and could be a very cheerful if not an entertaining
companion. He said but little, but he had a ready sympathy which drew out clever things in others, so that I
was induced to remark to him upon his difference in society from the sombreness of his writings. His reply struck
me as being curiously illustrative. "I am conscious," said
he, "of a double mental existence. When I am sufficiently excited to write, all my ideas flow naturally and irre-
sistibly through the medium of sympathies which steep
them in shade, though the feelings they bring are so pleasing as to prevent my perceiving it. The tone of my works
being thus the necessary result of the advancement of
those truths or discoveries which lead me to composition,
I am made so happy by it for the time as to be ignorant
of its real effect upon my reader. This I term, therefore,
my imaginative being. My social one has more of light

than darkness upon it, because, unless I could carry into society the excitement which makes me write, I could not fall into its feelings. Perhaps," he concluded, "the difference of the two may be thus summed up: in my literary moods I am aiming at making the world something better than I find it; in my social ones I am content to take it as it is."

The false impressions that we form of the labor of composition from different styles has been often remarked, Johnson's ponderous sentences, for instance, being supposed to be the result of protracted care, and Rousseau's gush of language the pastime of a natural facility, while the very reverse of this was the fact: Johnson was facile, Rousseau laborious. Thus, swiftly as flows the language of Brown, it contains too much thought, feeling, and purpose to appear to have been written as easily as it may be read. Yet such was the case. He told me that when a subject presented itself to him, he walked about fermenting the matter in his mind till it was ready to be drawn off. He then sat down, and all the material came as rapidly as he could write, whether it were argument or description. As a proof, he was occupied but three weeks upon "Arthur Mervyn," and little more in the composition of "Edgar Huntly."

I once remarked to him that I had no doubt his spirits had been soured by the want of literary taste in his countrymen to appreciate his writings as they merited, and to give that stimulus to his ambition which it would have received had he lived in England. He replied that such had been the case in some measure, yet, sensible as he was that a love of fame was the grand impetus to distinction, writing, with him, had been as much a matter of necessity in a mental as a bodily aspect. "As soon," said he, "as I could put two ideas together I felt a craving to invent, which required certain trains of thought to be daily

put in action in order to get rid of a surplus of daily gen-
erated ideas. This employment was just as necessary to
my mind as sustenance to my frame. It was synonymous
with a vital function. Fame I have longed for, certainly;
and sympathy from my friends, much more than from the
world; but, had I been exiled to Kamschatka, I must have
written as a mental necessity, and in it have still found
my highest enjoyment."

It is not known to the countrymen of Brown that he
was once induced to attempt a play. Some one in the
course of a conversation upon the drama had said to him,
"Brown, why don't *you* write a play? you could easily
get it acted." The suggestion threw him upon a new
field of reflection. He went home, considered the subject, as he thought, on all points, fancied that he felt the
power or knew the secret, and, a subject occurring to him,
he set himself to work. A few days after he called on me
with a manuscript. "Bernard," said he, "I am going to
surprise you. I have written two acts of a tragedy, and
I wish to trespass on your kindness to read it and give
me privately your candid opinion." I expressed my great
pleasure in obliging him. "But mind," he added, "I require, as a friend, your *candid* opinion, for I rely entirely
on your judgment to decide whether my own views of a
drama are correct. I have appended to the second act the
plot of the other three, which will enable you to perceive
if the subject is possessed of dramatic effect, and whether
my mode of treating the first portion warrants my completing the remainder. Accordingly I devoted that evening, being a leisure one, to its perusal. The subject was
an imaginary incident of Egyptian history, the interest
turning on the intellectual sway of a magician over a
young Persian, and the attachment of the latter to a Greek
girl, who attempted to combat the magician's influence.
Thus between the powers of love and superstition, the

disciples of Art and of Nature, the magician and the girl, a contest ensued which terminated with the triumph of the sorcerer and the death of the lovers. In this work Brown had gone into all his usual dissection of thoughts and feelings, but without any regard to displaying them by situations, or appeals to the feelings through the eye, the necessary auxiliary in supporting stage interest, which must otherwise be wholly mental, or dependent upon the ear. He was evidently ignorant of the secret that in theatres the most refined minds are in a state of so much higher excitement than at home that they require the story to be told with tenfold rapidity, and therefore to be condensed into its most quintessential elements. At all events his design was only fit for the closet, and even there, I think, would have looked like a metaphysical inquiry hampered with the unnecessary restrictions of being divided into scenes and written in verse. When he called on me again I gave the above as my candid opinion, but begged he would obtain that of other friends, as I made no pretensions, even in stage matters, to infallibility. My reasons, however, sufficed to determine him. He said it was but an experiment, and he should burn the manuscript as soon as he went home. I observed that I doubted his resolution to do that, knowing that the destruction of one's offspring, human or literary, was equally an outrage to the feelings. He smiled, put away the doomed one, shook my hand, and departed. A few days afterwards I invited him to dinner, when, as he was leaning against the mantelpiece, he extended his snuffbox to me. Opening it, I perceived that it was filled with some black dust or tinder. "What's that?" said I. "The remains of my tragedy," he replied, "which I carefully preserved after its combustion in the grate, for you to look at, since you doubted my resolution to destroy it."

CHAPTER XI

Celebrities of the American Stage: Mrs. Whitelock; Miss Fontenelle; Hodgkinson; Wignell.—The Theatres and Yellow Fever.—American Circuits.—Position of the Actor in America.—Mrs. Merry.—Mrs. Malmoth.—Fennell.—Cooper.—"A Histrionic Academy."

THERE were members of this company who must not pass unrecorded. Here I found Mrs. Whitelock, the sister of Mrs. Siddons, and allied to her in genius as well as in blood; the handsome Mr. Williamson, who was famous in the lovers, as well off the stage as on; and that most buoyant and charming of all reckless romps, Miss Fontenelle, the heroine in London of many of O'Keefe's farces, and a sort of miniature Mrs. Jordan, compressed in one act. A girl whose animal spirits led Merry to compare her to brandy above proof! "She takes away my breath," said he. And last, but not least, here I also found Hodgkinson, an actor from Bath, who preferred trying the New World to further toil in the provinces, and, as the brightest of all the lights that have glanced over its boards, well deserving the title he obtained, of its Roscius!

When I associate this actor with Garrick and Henderson (the first of whom I had often seen, and the latter played with) I afford some ground for thinking he possessed no common claims. I do not hesitate to say, that had he enjoyed their good-fortune—the inspiration and discipline of a refined London public—he would have risen to the rank of their undoubted successor. What was his distinction? That which peculiarly stamped them—that union of a sympathetic and an imitative faculty, which, whether of humor or pathos, can draw all the forms and give all the colorings of character. Nature being full of rule, being a law as it were in action, is of course a great classifier, a worker on models, fond of species and types, and thus the old man and the young, the hero and the rogue of tragedy and comedy, being distinct types or models, actors usually come into the world with their own special aptitude; whenever, therefore, nature departs from her scheme, and forms a mind in which merges the most opposite perceptions, as colors that meet, and yet shine in a rainbow, she is evidently in one of her wonder-working moods, fantastical or wearied with her uniform labors.

Hodgkinson was a wonder. In the whole range of the living drama there was no variety of character he could not perceive and embody, from a Richard or a Hamlet down to a Shelty or a Sharp. To the abundant mind of Shakespeare his own turned as a moon that could catch and reflect a large amount of its radiance; and if, like his great precursors, it seemed to have less of the poetic element than of the riches of humor, this was owing to association, which, in the midst of his tragic passions, would intrude other images. An exclusive tragedian will always seem greater by virtue of his specialty, by the singleness of impressions which are simply poetic; while Hodgkinson had one gift that enlarged his variety beyond all competition — he was also a singer, and could charm you in a burletta, after thrilling you in a play; so that through every form of drama he was qualified to pass, and it might be said he "exhausted worlds" if he could not "invent new." I doubt if such a number and such greatness of requisites were ever before united in one mortal man. Nor were his physical powers inferior to his mental; he was tall and well-proportioned, though inclining to be corpulent, with a face of great mobility, that showed the minutest change of feeling, while his voice, full and flexible, could only be likened to an instrument that his passions played upon at pleasure.

Such was this great actor, who, dying in the prime of life of a prevailing epidemic, was prevented from reaching that distinction which must have worthily connected his memory with the drama of his country. It would be gratifying, of course, if I could enlarge as much upon the man; but his early life had been unfortunate; he had never known a due restraint, and, as he rose to fame, he attracted friends who were more willing to share his errors than to pity or condemn them; but it is right I should add that, though wholly self-educated, he had attained to taste and manners, and even evinced some skill in literature, by the production of a comedy.

At Newport I met my manager (Wignell), and received a warm welcome. He was an excellent fellow, whose abundance of heart was unluckily accompanied by a deficiency of head, that kept him always in difficulties. "No one's enemy but his own," we find very often to be every one's friend, and yet such a benevolence but rarely gains praise, and is condemned by a good many, merely because they didn't happen to become its recipients. In a professional light he had but moderate claims. He had variety as an actor, but with limited power. He had enjoyed the good-fortune of being the first general comedian who had crossed the Atlantic; and by the side of the stiff humor of his friends, Henry and Hallam, both of whom belonged to the old school of London, he had certainly shone as a spirited actor; but the term of his partnership proved also that of his fame. When, in 1793, he returned from England, to open the first complete theatre America had witnessed, he brought with him a company containing several comedians who were much his superiors, and who at once obtained a fame that put an end to his efforts. Thenceforward he wisely resigned acting for management—a difference of function that few men have been able to unite with success, the varieties of the one tending sadly to militate against the interests of the other; and I was enabled to see him act but upon special occasions, such as his own benefits, when he reminded me of the accounts I had heard of his father, who was one of Garrick's subordinates.

Established in New York, I was in a position to take a view of the American stage, and as it presented just then some very curious distinctions, I trust their detail will not prove unacceptable.

There were three leading managements at this time in America, conducting three distinct circuits—in the North, South, and centre: that of Hodgkinson and Dunlap, who had succeeded Henry and Hallam, in the direction of what was called the "Old American Company," and whose principal cities were New York and Boston; that of Mons. Solee, whose headquarters was Charleston, but who migrated northward to Newberne and Richmond; and that of Wignell and Reinagle, whose home was Philadelphia, but who also paid visits to Baltimore and Annapolis. Each of these circuits professed to engage actors for ten months of the year, and to employ them in the intervals; but their seasons, owing to the climate, were curiously modified. The English division, of winter and summer seasons, was almost unknown. While the summer was too hot for any acting at Charleston, the winter was too severe, both at New York and Boston, thus dividing the seasons there into autumn and spring. These extremes were the cause of the arrangement I have mentioned, between Charleston and Boston, to exchange forces yearly; and at length, of the system of going to the South in the winter, and to the North in the spring—the heat, at the same time, being so great, even in the North, that nearly all summer schemes were found to be failures. This was novel enough; but, at the period in question, American theatricals had still greater variety. This was owing to the yellow fever — that terrible scourge which, passing from Africa to the West Indies, found its way to America in 1792; and which, though now nearly extinct, then yearly made a tour of two thirds of the Union. So frightful were its ravages that the first news of its approach was sufficient to empty towns of one half of their citizens; and as it came at all periods, though chiefly in summer, it permitted no system to be planned with security. It broke up the legislatures, paralyzed trade, and, of course, put an end to all kinds of amusements. The theatres, need I say, were the earliest to suffer, for, in addition to the panic which the fever created, a crowd was a medium for spreading infection; and though it is true that this scourge rarely entered New England, yet as it was here that theatricals flourished the least, the evils resulting will be readily surmised.

Still I am bound to confess that, if it shut up the theatres it created a thirst for them, which tended greatly to balance the losses sustained. Startling as it may appear, yet the fact is unquestionable that there never was such a disposition to enter our doors as when the fever had departed. The desire for amusement seemed to have increased by suspension. In the very first days of mourning, after thousands had been swept from the bounds of the city, let the theatre but open, and the rush to it from all quarters can be scarcely conceived. All ages and stations partook of an excitement which was usually confined to a particular class. This was scarcely to be viewed as a healthful phenomenon, and yet was as little to be traced to a want of right feeling. It was a startling reaction; in their escape from a terror which had benumbed every faculty, the mere sense of safety provoked an excess—

spread an hysterical feeling, that sought any amusement that would afford it a vent. It was the same in France, after the fall of the Jacobins; and there, as in America, the drama was sought chiefly as the medium of all others that appealed most to the feelings. Such excitements, of course, were opposed to its interests, and certainly supplied no inspiration to actors; one half a population being forced into mourning, my reader may conceive an audience's look in those days, and our satisfaction at finding ourselves linked with the cause of it. The Quakers and others, observing our reappearance on the heels of the calamity, discovered the relation between us of cause and effect, and proclaimed that we moved in a perpetual circle, reproducing each other: the fever, the actors—the actors, the fever!

Of the three circuits I have named I may confidently state that the Philadelphian scheme at this period stood first: not only on account of its superior company, but of its new and improved theatre, which, as I have mentioned elsewhere, was the first complete structure that had been reared in the West. It had been built from plans supplied by Richards, the secretary of the Royal Academy (a relation of Wignell's), and fitted up by the talents of Holland and Milbourne, the first eminent painters that had crossed the Atlantic. All the other cities, Boston only excepted, had either temporary erections in some warehouse or barn, or else some poor wooden building, such as that of New York, which was equally meagre in look and appointment. Which of these circuits, however, was also most prosperous, it would be harder to say. If their evils were in common, so were also their fortunes. In the course of my extended connection with the stage I can remember no period that conduced more to its welfare. The progress of the war had not only freed the Union from England, but from prejudice; and had prepared for a calm which naturally tended to a spirit of enjoyment; while the revival of trade soon made money abundant, and supplied this desirable spirit with means. But there was another favoring circumstance. The enormous emigration, caused by the French Revolution, not only supplied the theatres with excellent orchestras, a most attractive addition, but with a great mass of patrons, who, however shattered in fortune, still continued to find means for their favorite pleasure. The only alloy of this benefit was the fact that among the musicians and patrons of the theatre were numbers of the poor *noblesse*, stripped of even their names.

But, however advantageous to a manager's pockets, this was also a period that respected his pleasures. It gave him little other trouble than to attend to his treasury. Both his system and actors were imported from England, and the one, for some years, worked as well as the other. The modern rage for novelties had as yet to set in. The drama itself was a novelty, which proved quite sufficient. Thus a manager, in those days, was not perplexed for new pieces, or obliged to risk a fortune on those abysses of capital—modern ballet and spectacle. As yet, even a melodrama was unknown to the stage; the nearest approach to it being serious pantomimes, such as "La Perouse" and "Don Juan;" all of which, however, presented a strong human interest, and were as cheaply produced as they were occasionally popular. Shakespeare and O'Keefe were the staple attractions, varied with Farquhar and Cumberland, Goldsmith and Sheridan; and the performances also were only three nights a week, and yet probably averaged as much as our six. Thus he had nothing to do at the opening of a season but to put up a cast of the common stock plays—"Hamlet," "Othello," the "West Indian," and the "Rivals;" with the "Padlock," the "Poor Soldier," and the "Agreeable Surprise." The actors were all studied, hardly a rehearsal was needed, and if the fever kept off, the house filled and closed without one jar to his nerves. And his social existence was hardly less enviable. Hodgkinson, for instance, possessed every luxury; he had his town and country house, drove his curricle or tandem, and gave dinners to all the leading people of the city, which would have made a London manager thoughtful as to his following pantomime.

The actor's position was quite as good as the manager's. As yet the supply of talent was not beyond the demand, and consequently incomes maintained a fair level. There was no salary at this period under four pounds a week, while many reached as high as twelve and fifteen; and as benefits occurred at least twice a year, these ordinarily added one third to the amount. If an actor were unemployed, want and shame were not before him: he had merely to visit some town in the interior where no theatre existed, but "readings" were permitted; and giving a few recitations from Shakespeare and Sterne, his pockets in a night or two were amply replenished. This easy resource, in rendering the actor independent, compelled the manager to be generous, and put both upon a footing which tended not a little to uphold their pursuit. When actors grew abundant this level was broken, and their reputations in consequence began to decline. We seldom think how much morals depend upon means. If the rich struggle to be virtuous, how much more must the poor. When salaries sank, owing to the increased competition, characters sank also (the resource above named becoming quickly exhausted), and thus many who found themselves without food among strangers were forced into misconduct which they would have otherwise scorned.

I shall now review the talent which, at this period, distinguished the American stage; and to do so more clearly, will take it as it stood in the principal companies. To begin then, with Hodgkinson's. His leading supporters were Mr. and Mrs. Hallam, Mr. and Mrs. Johnson, Mr. and Mrs. Tyler, Mr. and Mrs. C. Powell, Messrs. Jefferson, Dickenson, Martin, and Prigmore, Mrs. Melmoth, Mrs. S. Powell, Mrs. Brett, and Miss Hardinge. Solée's force consisted of Mr. and Mrs. Barrett, Mr. and Mrs. Williamson, Mr. and Mrs. Whitelock, Mr. and Mrs. Harper, Mr. and Mrs. Jones, Mr. and Mrs. Placide, Messrs. Chalmers and Mackenzie, and the Misses Broadhurst and Green. While Wignell numbered the following: Messrs. Fennell, Cooper, and Morton; Harwood, Blisset, and Francis; Marshall, Warren, and Hardinge; Warrell and Bernard; Mesdames Merry, Marshal, Oldmixon, Hardinge, and Lestrange.

Of these companies the second was considerably the weakest. It wanted, in the first place, a leading trage-dian. Neither Barrett nor Williamson, who divided that honor, having any pretension to it. With good physical requisites (the latter especially, who was remarkably handsome) and some versatility their deficiency was the more obvious, since, in addition to Mrs. Barrett, who was not without genius, they could boast of Mrs. Whitelock, an admirable actress, who was in no way unworthy of her illustrious sister, and till Mrs. Merry arrived had deserved her distinction of "the American Siddons." Her defects were her person, which was short and undignified, and her heavy, thick voice; but she had the family face, and a genuine passion, which could kindle the sympathies and blind the spectator to every deficiency. Let me add, that this lady was an honor to her profession in every sense, and was happy in a husband who partook all her worth, and some amount of her powers. In the fathers of tragedy he had singular merit; his venerable appearance being worthily sustained by his pathos and dignity.

The force of this corps lay rather in comedy. Chalmers, for instance, was an able comedian, though rather artificial, and more active than humorous. He had been originally a harlequin, but, unlike the great Woodward, had continued his movements to the displacement of character. Lewis was his model, but he had unluckily caught only that great actor's legs. Jones, his associate, had much higher claims: he was true and artistic, and, while founded on Edwin, had original powers. Again, Harper, though old, retained much of his humor; while the charming Mrs. Williamson, *alias* Miss Fontenelle, reigned supreme over all transatlantic soubrettes.

Hodgkinson's company had far greater force. Its leader alone turned the scale in its favor. I have already tried to show how this wonderful actor was indeed a host in himself, and that his variety, combined with his depth of conception, would have bestowed on him the fame of a Garrick and a Henderson, had he enjoyed the good-fortune of an adequate discipline. His history in America was somewhat amusing. He had been imported by Henry and Hallam to annihilate Wignell, who, at the time he deserted them, was the great favorite of the States in all the broad comedy, the other two managers reigning supreme as tragedians; but no sooner had the new actor accomplished their object than he turned his fire on themselves, and tore from them also their long-possessed honors, shooting out into the most opposite fields of art, and assuming Richard and Lear, as easily as Mungo and Shelty. Hallam, who was now on the borders of sixty, presented only the wreck of his former capacity, but still was a various and elegant actor, though formed more on the model of Quin than of Garrick. He enjoyed the distinction of being the first youthful star of the American stage (playing, as a boy, at New York as early as 1752), and had thus the good-fortune of being the first

representative of the heroes of Shakespeare. He had, consequently, a traditional fame that still clung to him, though
he was shorn of his beams, and only allowed to take the
leavings of Hodgkinson's genius. Messrs. Johnson and
Martin were good, useful actors, who stood next to Mr.
Hallam; and Mr. Tyler was a singer, who was put into
tragedy owing to his singular resemblance to General
Washington, which made it good policy to array him in
powder and small - clothes as often as possible. Mr.
Charles Powell, of Boston, was a thoroughly artistic,
though rather hard, actor; and Messrs. Jefferson and
Dickenson already showed signs of being two of the best
ornaments of the American stage. The ladies were Mrs.
Hodgkinson, who was young and agreeable; Mrs. Johnson, who was an elegant and dignified actress; Mrs. S.
Powell, who was maturing as an able tragedian; and my
old friend, Mrs. Melmoth, who still retained powers
which commanded respect. This lady was the wife of
the then famous Pratt, the author of "Gleanings," who,
under the name of Courtenay Melmoth, had eloped with,
and carried her on the stage. They had been parted
for some years; but she had saved sufficient means to
purchase a property on Long Island, where she retired,
and died amid general esteem. Mrs. Melmoth had
taste and judgment, which, combined with her beauty,
had always made her a favorite; but her misfortune, in
latter years, was to expand to a size that no tragedy and
black velvet had power to subdue. In the matrons, of
course it was not so much noticed; but on her performing
the Grecian Daughter, in which she made her _début_, at
her cry to save her father, "Tyrant, strike here!—here
you will find blood enough," a laugh was the result, that
almost ruined the play.

I now come to our own corps, which I think the superior; and yet, whatever its claims, which was scarcely less

marked by individual traits. And foremost stood Fennell. Elsewhere I shall attempt to describe him in full: suffice it now, he was a character of no ordinary occurrence. With a tall, commanding person, a full, fleshy face, and a deep, solemn voice, he united a spirit the most light and mercurial. He was the king of projectors, his whole life having passed in a series of schemes which had emptied their owner of all possessions but faith. Educated for the Church, his first project was acting, which he deserted for politics in Paris, and for literature in London; when America presented a new field for his efforts, he sought it, and successively became saltmaker, bridge-builder, schoolmaster, and lecturer, going back, on the failure of each, to the stage as the only true friend who would give him a dinner. As an actor, he certainly laid small claim to genius, being rather what is known as an excellent reader; but he had great cultivation; and in particular characters, where his coldness and person were equally needed, such as Brutus and Zanga, he could exhibit great force, and tower at moments into positive grandeur.

Cooper, his colleague, who, after Hodgkinson's death, became our ruling tragedian, had also his distinctions. The son of an Irish surgeon, he had been educated chiefly under the care of Mr. Godwin, and so derived that independence which marked him through life. Endowed with great genius, and the highest qualifications in face, voice, and person, he had little or no art, which he never strove to acquire, being content to cover its want by his impulse and freshness. Thus, as he grew older, he failed to improve, while his luxurious habits abated his force, and left but gleams of the fire which, at first, was continuous. His history is significant. Appearing as Hamlet, at Covent-Garden, when scarcely turned twenty, he produced the most signal impression, even in the face of John Kemble. But, instead of remaining, and winning his way upward by study and art, he thought America a field which he could seize without effort, and there found he had to grapple with the successor of Henderson. Thus rendered more careless, he failed in 1803, when he sought a second time to win the verdict of London; though, on returning to America, he became its great favorite, until the arrival of Cooke, whose light, though it was setting, extinguished all others. Still, with all his defects, I look back to his youth as displaying a power which I can only rank second to the greatest I have seen. I still think his Macbeth was only inferior to Garrick's, and his Hamlet to Kemble's; while his Othello, I think, was equal to Barry's itself.

Next to Cooper ranked Morton, a young native actor, of singular promise, who had also the advantage of great personal requisites. He was the ideal of a lover, having a natural elegance, as well as great tenderness, which rendered him the Holman of the American stage. His *forte* lay in sentiment rather than tragedy, rendering his Belcour and Harry Daunton quite marvels of acting. But he could rise above these; and his Romeo and Jaffier were the very best I have seen. He was doomed to die early, and his loss, in my experience, was never replaced. Our comedians were Harwood, a clever transcript of Bannister, but who added, however, various traits of his own; Warren, who displayed much of the vigor of Dowton; and Blisset and Francis, two excellent actors, if somewhat narrow in range. To such a strong list of men, when I add that our ladies were in no way inferior—that Mrs. Oldmixon could have fully replaced Mrs. Mattocks, and Mrs. Marshall deserved the name of the American Jordan, I shall complete it by adding the name of Mrs. Merry, whose triumphs in London would render any eulogy almost a slur on her powers.

Divided into two ranks as are the Shakesperian heroines —the queenly and thoughtful, the loving and passionate—

if Mrs. Siddons, in the one, ascended to a greatness that almost became an identity, Mrs. Merry, on the other, I think, was equally perfect, and equally gifted to enrapture an audience. With a voice that was all music, and a face all emotion, her pathos and tenderness were never exceeded; and if unequal to the grandeur of Katherine and Constance, her Juliet and Imogen were indelible images.

My acquaintance, at this period, with Messrs. Hallam and Morris, two of the earliest members of the "Old American Company," enables me to recount a few particulars of the drama before and after the Revolution, which may, perhaps, be acceptable. During their early campaigns they only played twice a week, and to an average nightly receipt of about £70, their current expenses ranging under £15. The original theatres of New York and Philadelphia were fitted up to contain £150, and, as a proof of their simplicity, at an average cost of about three times that sum; the expense of scenery and wardrobe amounting to as much more—so that the entire outlay, at starting, came under £1200. I have elsewhere referred to the vigorous opposition they had to meet on all sides. This led to peculiar customs. To conciliate their enemies, they always acted one evening in each season for the benefit of the poor; while to obtain even a hearing, they were forced to travel with a "character" from the governors of the respective states—in the manner of the old companies in the time of Queen Elizabeth. My reader is aware that actors, in those days, always carried a passport from some nobleman, to escape being pounced on as vagrants, a fact which explains their turning lacqueys (the duke's servants, etc.), instead of seeking, as in our time, their true patron, the public; their chief object was protection against the fangs of the law. But another resource, in America, was even more characteristic. To

elude the objection to plays, they either opened (as did
Douglas) an "Histrionic Academy, in order to deliver
dissertations on subjects instructive and entertaining,"
and to qualify their visitors "to speak in public with propriety;" or they announced an entertainment which they
called "Moral Dialogues," which were still more expressive; and as Mr. Morris had fortunately preserved a bill
of one of these, which he allowed me to copy, I am happy
in being able to present it to my reader. This singular
document, presenting so clear a method of vindicating
Shakespeare, ran in the following manner:

KING'S ARMS TAVERN, NEWPORT, RHODE ISLAND.

On Monday, June 10, at the Public Room of the above
Inn, will be Delivered a Series of

MORAL DIALOGUES,

IN FIVE PARTS,

DEPICTING THE EVIL EFFECTS OF JEALOUSY AND OTHER BAD PASSIONS,
AND PROVING THAT HAPPINESS CAN ONLY SPRING FROM
THE PURSUIT OF VIRTUE.

"Mr. Douglas will represent a noble and magnanimous Moor named
Othello, who loves a young lady named Desdemona, and after he has married her, harbors (as in too many cases) the dreadful passion of jealousy.

> Of jealousy, our being's bane,
> Mark the small cause, and the most dreadful pain.

"Mr. Allyn will depict the character of a specious villain, in the regiment of Othello, who is so base as to hate his commander on mere suspicion, and to impose on his best friend. Of such characters, it is to be
feared, there are thousands in the world, and the one in question may present to us a salutary warning.

> The man that wrongs his master and his friend,
> What can he come to but a shameful end?

"Mr. Hallam will delineate a young and thoughtless officer, who is
traduced by Mr. Allyn, and, getting drunk, loses his situation and his
general's esteem. All young men whatsoever, take example from Cassio.

> The ill effects of drinking would you see?
> Be warned, and keep from evil company.

"MR. MORRIS will represent an old gentleman, the father of Desdemona, who is not cruel or covetous, but is foolish enough to dislike the noble Moor, his son-in-law, because his face is not white, forgetting that we all spring from one root. Such prejudices are very numerous and very wrong.

> Fathers beware what sense and love ye lack,
> 'Tis crime, not color, makes the being black.

"MR. QUALCH will depict a fool, who wishes to become a knave, and trusting to one, gets killed by him. Such is the friendship of rogues—take heed.

> When fools would knaves become, how often you'll
> Perceive the knave not wiser than the fool.

"MRS. MORRIS will represent a young and virtuous wife, who being wrongfully suspected, gets smothered (in an adjoining room) by her husband.

> Reader, attend; and e'er thou goest hence
> Let fall a tear to hapless innocence.

"MRS. DOUGLAS will be her faithful attendant, who will hold out a good example to all servants, male and female, and to all people in subjection.

> Obedience and gratitude
> Are things as rare as they are good.

"Various other dialogues, too numerous to mention here, will be delivered at night, all adapted to the improvement of the mind and manners. The whole will be repeated on Wednesday and Saturday. Tickets six shillings each, to be had within. Commencement at 7, conclusion at half-past 10, in order that every spectator may go home at a sober hour, and reflect upon what he has seen before he retires to rest

> God save the king,
> And long may he sway
> East, North, and South,
> And fair America."

CHAPTER XII.

Undertaking Management.—Supplies Needed.—Visit to England.—Irish Fishermen.—Proposals and Refusals.—Final Engagements.—Monk Lewis's Irish Friend.—Caulfield.—Transport Arrangements.—A Bath Greeting.—The Theatrical Fund.—Story of a Landlord's Retort.— Whiteley and Macklin.—Bowles's Hoax.—Rolling in Riches.—A Frozen Sheep.—A Russian Tool.—Tragedy of an Actor's Life.—Mr. Williams.—Marriage.—Departure.—A Friendly Foe.—Voyage.—Arrival in Boston.

AFTER nine years' pleasant experience in America as a successful actor I had determined to try my fate as a manager, and agreed to take a third share of the Boston Theatre, in conjunction with Powell & Dickinson. But to lease a theatre was but a small part of the business; we needed actors and actresses, scenery, dresses, etc., such as could not be found on this side of the Atlantic, and it was, therefore, resolved that I should proceed to England to obtain all that was required; a task not without its difficulties, as my narrative will show. I left Boston in April, 1806, and after a three weeks' prosperous voyage found myself once more near the Irish coast. The first sight which impressed me with the fact that I was "home" again was a battered, patched-up fishing-smack, with a solitary sail, consisting of as many pieces and colors as a New England farmer's counterpane, and manned by three tatterdemalions, who might well have served as scarecrows. On hailing this precious craft, she came alongside, and, assuming the best brogue I could, I addressed myself to the helmsman:

"How is it wid you, darlint?"

"Better than it was, and not so well as it may be," was the reply.

"What luck since you left shore?" I continued.

"Bad enough; we've eat all the fish we caught and a dale more—let alone the praties."

"But have you any garden fruit left—any raal apricots, now?"

"Oh, bushels, delight to you! you've only to open your mouth and they'll find their way into it."

As we had exhausted our stock of potatoes some days ago, a supply of this vegetable, and from their favorite soil, proved very acceptable, and I gave the Hibernian a quart of rum in return for a bushel of his "praties."

The man thought himself so liberally paid in this exchange that he warmly expressed his gratitude, and then added:

"But you are an Irishman, dare; where does your family come from?"

"Limerick," replied I.

"Limerick! why, 'tis my own swate birthplace! Oh, I'll spake to you, darlint."

Saying which, he prepared at once to run up the side of the vessel, when one of his companions caught him by the leg, exclaiming:

"Stop, Patrick, stop! how do you know but what they will kidernapper you?"

"Oh, bother," he replied, good-humoredly,"and if they did kidernap me, they wouldn't kidernap the boat, you know."

Our Irish passenger being informed that a fellow-countryman had come on board, came towards him with great eagerness, and a dialogue ensued as to what the fisherman would ask for landing the other on the Irish coast, which he would prefer to proceeding with the ship to Liverpool.

"Will I take you to land?" said the fisherman. "Sure

an' I will. I wouldn't take you to the bottom under double price. There's Phelim, Teddy, and myself—three jinteel lads we're allowed to be—and as for Molly Monaghan, you shall say before you've gone a herrin's length on the water that she's the swatest craythur intirely you ever sailed with in your life."

"And who's Molly Monaghan?" inquired the passenger.

"Why, the smack, sure; we couldn't get ashore without her, you know. I call her Molly Monaghan after my first wife, to remimber me of her vartues."

"And what terms do you want, countryman?"

"Tarms! I'd rather have money."

"Well, money I mane."

"Where did you come from, may I ax, when you was in Ireland? Cork, was it? Well, then, if you had happened to have come from Ballyshannon I'd have taken you all the way to land for nothing; but if it's from Cork you came I couldn't do it for less than thra thirtaners."

This offer being agreed to, the Irishman's trunks were thrown on board the smack, and he began to take leave of his fellow-passengers. One of them, an American, now asked the boatman if he never met with accidents in so shattered a boat.

"Accidints! bless your honor," was the reply, "why, doesn't your honor see that bit of a horseshoe nailed under the bow?"

"Aha; yes, I do."

"Well, and did you ever hear of a fisherman's smack that met with misfortin when he had a never-worn horseshoe nailed to his bows?"

This question, involving more familiarity with the details of nautical disasters than the Yankee possessed, completely puzzled him.

"But," he at length resumed, "I calculate, friend, that your boat is very old."

" Old, sure enough, is she, but that only makes her the more *exparienced*, you know. Molly and I were launched the same summer, and that's thirty-nine year ago, come next May, and we both get the wiser as we grow oulder. What did she or I know about fishing or sailing when we were both youngsters?"

"Nay, but I think you must allow that the older a vessel grows, she grows the more dangerous."

" Well, your honor, and if so?"

" Then, I reckon, you encounter some toughish weather off this foreland sometimes?"

" Ah, and you may say that, honey."

" Well, friend, I should like to know why you think it worth while every day to run such a risk of death?"

" Why, your honor, isn't it for a livin', to be sure."

Two days after this we ran into Liverpool, and after purchasing a variety of articles for the theatre, to be sent off at once to Boston, I made my way to the metropolis. On visiting Drury Lane and the Haymarket, I liked Messrs. Rae and Bartley sufficiently to address them on the subject of a trip to America, which, however, both declined; and I then wrote to Dublin to Miss Walstein, Mrs. Edwin, and Montague Talbot. At Covent Garden Mr. Harris received me very kindly, congratulating me on the success I had met with in America, though he added, as he shook his head significantly, that I had marred my fortunes in quitting England. He even offered me such liberal terms to make my reappearance before the London public that, had I been free, I could hardly have refused; but, as it was, this was out of the question. Disappointed again in my applications to Dublin, owing to the disinclination of one performer and the exorbitant demands of another (he actually wanted twenty pounds a week—modest in the extreme!), I now made overtures to Mr. and Mrs. H. Johnson, and everything was settled except signing the articles, when the lady was persuaded to give up the design and declare off, whereupon her husband came to me in a great passion, very honorably offering to proceed to America directly and keep his own word with me, although his wife had forfeited hers. I could not, however, think of separating man and wife, when, too, they had good prospects in their own country. At last I succeeded in engaging Cipriani, the "Clown," who was recommended to me by my old friend, Macready;* and I also came to an agreement with Mrs. Stanley (otherwise the Honorable Mrs. Twisleton) to support the leading characters of comedy and tragedy. During this time I had daily invitations to go abroad, but, apart from my professional duties, only found leisure to cultivate one acquaintance, that of a young lady named Wright, to whom I had been lately introduced, and whose person and manners so charmed me that I determined to try and induce her to return with me as a governess for my motherless children.

Among other invitations at this period Andrew Cherry asked me to dine with him, and brought together a host of old companions to meet me—Incledon, John Emery, Macready, Johnny Quick, and several others. When the bottle began to circulate we amused each other with indulging in recollections of our early life—"Every Man in his Humor"—some of which recollections may perhaps bear repetition. Quick told us that during his strolling days the company in which he was enrolled had, on one occasion, proceeded to a miserable village which, proving incapable of supporting them, they soon ran up a longer bill inside the landlord's bar than the one they had hung outside his door. As they seemed to have no means of discharging this, since, however there might be a slight

---

* William Macready, the father of William Charles Macready.

THE HON. MRS. TWISLETON (AFTERWARDS MRS. STANLEY).

From the *Monthly Mirror*, London, April, 1796.

vein of brass in their foreheads, there was certainly neither silver nor gold in their pockets, the host came to the conclusion that—as sometimes with man as with the elephant, the trunk may be the most valuable part—he must look to the goods of the company as an indemnification for their evil. At length Quick and his companions gave out, with much literary pomposity,"The Tragedy of Macbeth, with all the Original Music," in hopes of inducing a livelier attendance from the inhabitants of the place. However, when the night arrived, but few people dropped into the room, and they were again disappointed. Still the play proceeded, and without interruption, till they came to the music of "We Fly by Night." No sooner did the words reach the ear of the perturbed landlord, who was sitting at the end of the room ruminating on what must be the end of the matter, than he started up in surprise, listened an instant to the reiterated, "We Fly by Night, We Fly by Night"—then, catching the notes, responded to the same tune with a grim smile of satisfaction, "And I'll stop your trunks! I'll stop your trunks!"

On calling in at one of the theatrical houses to make an inquiry, I accidentally encountered another old acquaintance, Mr. Robert Bowles. Poor Bob was a most original and extraordinary eccentric. Twenty years had passed over since he and I had parted at Dublin, and Bob had somewhat declined into the vale of years, but still retained all the frolicsome and facetious character of his disposition. It happened that I had just received an invitation from Cartwright (of the musical glasses) to dine with him at Richmond, with a request that I would bring a friend with me, and, as among the company I knew that I should meet Mr. Monk Lewis, Kemble, Cherry, Harry Johnston, and some others who would be disposed to be convivial, I conceived that my comic friend, Bob Bowles, would prove an agreeable addition to their number. He was in high spirits, and proved, as I had expected, the chief source of amusement for the evening. Among other of his recollections he related an affair in which I had been a participator. On his first visit to Plymouth Dock (about 1780) he found a very dashing innkeeper there of the name of Rogers, who, from being fond of theatricals himself, induced the actors to make his house their rendezvous. Frank Rogers, as he was familiarly called, though a bustling and conversable man, was extremely weak and credulous, too much so for his own interest, considering the business in which he was engaged. Having taken a great liking to Bowles's company during the season, Frank, on some occasion, promised him a supper, which promise, however, on some pretence or another, he had evaded fulfilling. Bowles, however, did not forget it, and when the comedy of the "Bold Stroke for a Wife" was about to be performed, during rehearsal he took up a letter from the prompter's table which was intended to be delivered to Obadiah Prim, and the chief contents of which ran thus: "Friend, there is a design formed to rob thy house and to cut thy throat this night," etc., etc. This letter Bob secreted, and then sent, duly directed, to Frank Rogers. The latter, unfortunately among other youthful neglects, had paid so little attention to what he called "spelling and scrawling," that, though capable of suggesting a bill with any innkeeper in the county, he was quite unable to draw one out, and found it not very easy even to read handwriting. Bowles, therefore, who took care to follow immediately after the delivery of this letter, found Rogers, as he had expected, puzzling himself mightily to decipher it, and at his request took it from him, and read it out with a distinct voice and a seemingly thunderstruck countenance. "Oh," exclaimed Rogers, "they are coming at last, are they? I've been threatened by the rascals a long time. Friend Bowles, what would you have me do in this situation? had I better get a guard from the garrison, or half a dozen constables to sit up and receive these ruffians?"

"Why," said Bowles, "in my opinion, either of these plans would make the matter public, and then the thieves would perhaps defer their visit. What firearms have you in the house?"

"Why, two fowling-pieces," replied Frank, "besides my duck-gun, which carries fifty buckshot; but then I could borrow a couple of guns from my neighbors without suspicion."

"Well, then," continued Bowles, "the best thing you can do, my dear Frank, will be to invite half a dozen friends to sit up with you on this occasion, and give the rogues a warm reception when they come."

In this plan Rogers coincided heartily, and Bowles undertook to bring the friends, while Frank employed himself in procuring arms and ammunition, and in preparing a good supper. Bowles thus found that he had carried his first point—a supper—but he had now a second in view —the hoax, which, of the two, was to him infinitely the more agreeable. Among the companions he procured for this purpose I was one, and we were all soon put up to his roguery, and resolved upon a piece of good acting throughout the evening. The supper Frank prepared for us was excellent, and wine and punch were abundantly provided in order that our courage, by sufficient libations, should be exalted to its very highest pitch. Bowles, who had the loading of the guns, of course omitted putting in the bullets, and each man being then provided with his piece, examined and placed it beside him with military precision. An hour or two passed over very pleasantly; but when twelve o'clock struck we agreed to remain silent, and only fill our glasses at a nod from the chairman. Every footstep that went by was now felt to be a robber's.

Frank would start up, exclaiming in a whisper: "Stand to your guns, my boys! Here they come." Whereupon all of us would seize our weapons, and hold ourselves in readiness, Bowles catching up the long duck-gun, hammering the flint with his knife, calling in suppressed tones for the powder-flask, till the noise had gone by, when we all returned softly to our seats, and emptied our glasses in silence. Now it happened that on this evening a stranger, who, when he had arrived in Plymouth, had put up at Frank's house, having been out to pay a visit, had delayed his return so long that he did not get back before one in the morning. On reaching the inn he knocked pretty loudly at the front door; but Rogers having sent all the servants to bed with strict injunctions not to stir until morning, the summons, of course, met with no attention. The noise, however, put us on our guard. At length, descrying through the crevices of the window a light in the parlor in which we were sitting, the stranger came and thumped there as loudly as he had done before. In a moment we were all on our legs, with our guns levelled in the direction of the sound.

"What do you want?" demanded the landlord, in the gruffest and most intimidating tone he could assume.

"Want? why, to come in, to be sure!" replied the voice outside.

"I dare say you do," said Frank; "but you'll get a brace of bullets through your skull for your pains, and so I warn you."

"A brace of bullets through my skull! and what for?" was the astonished rejoinder.

"What for! what for?" repeated Rogers, losing all command of his temper, "why, you throat-cutting rascal, because you want to break in and plunder my house, certainly. Don't try to impose upon me! I know all about you and your designs; and now—I warn you—here's myself and a dozen friends, armed with guns and blunder-busses, and if you and your whole gang don't decamp immediately, d—n me (with great emphasis), but we will blow you all into atoms, and cut you into mincemeat."

The stranger, though no doubt somewhat surprised, took the hint thus gently conveyed, and departed.

In this manner we continued our foolery till daybreak, when Rogers announced to the family, in great triumph, that the house had been assaulted during the night by a gang of bold, bloodthirsty thieves, and that we had successfully repulsed them!

Bowles was a great romancer, but the most humorous in his nonsense I ever listened to. When a young man he had accompanied old Fisher, the manager, out to St. Petersburg, with some other performers, to establish an English theatre there under the especial patronage of the Empress Catherine, and under the title of "Russian Recollections" often gave us some extraordinary anecdotes of his stay in that country. "In St. Petersburg," said he, "for the first time in my life I *rolled in riches*. And how do you think that was? Why, on my benefit night I received a blanket full of roubles, which I ordered a couple of porters to carry home and lay on the floor, when I pulled off my coat and tumbled about in them until bedtime."

Speaking of the cold in Russia, he observed that it was so intense that in crossing a field one day in the course of a walk, he espied several sheep frozen to death, and one in particular sitting on its hams in the act of nibbling something from a bush. "This sheep I accidentally struck with my stick, and it flew to pieces like a glass bottle!"

He then gave us a long description of Russian ships, pointing out several niceties of art in their build, but seriously affirming in conclusion that they were constructed entirely with one single tool. Cartwright thereupon inquired what that tool might be. Bowles replied that it was a sort of hatchet. "Ah, then," said Cartwright, with a good-humored shake of the head, "they will never build another ship, Bob." "Why not?" inquired Bowles. "Because you have brought away *the hatchet* with you!"

Meeting one day a Mr. Williams, of Philadelphia, whom I had known there as a gentleman of great talent and respectability, I found he was now in partnership in London with his brother. He told me also that he had a schooner just ready to leave port, in which he meant to embark for America in pursuit of a vessel belonging to the firm, which had been run away with by the captain and crew, and as he should carry out no freight he offered to transport to Boston all the company and the luggage I was returning with free of all expense. Unluckily for me my previous arrangement at Bristol precluded me from availing myself of this generous offer.

I have little more to say of the remainder of my stay in England. I made no further engagements except one with Mr. Hatton, of the Haymarket, whom I saw perform a character in the farce of "The Finger-Post," in a broad style of low comedy, much to my satisfaction. As he was not able to accompany me, he agreed to follow me to Boston at the termination of his present engagement, and he proved to be an extraordinary personage. I now despatched Mrs. Stanley and Cipriani, Messrs. Caulfield, Vining, and Vigers to Bristol, took leave of all my friends (save one), and, having shaken their hands, prevailed on this one—the fair Miss Wright—to bestow hers upon me, at St. James's Church, for I had soon discovered her fitness to be something more than a governess to my children. Until that morning she had never seen me by daylight, since, having no longer the advantage of youth in my endeavors to render myself agreeable, I had never paid my visits to her until after dark and in evening dress.

As, however, exposure to sunlight wrought no change in her sentiments, I thus secured a good mother for my little family, and for myself an amiable and beloved companion for the rest of my days.

Finding everything ready for our departure on arriving at Bristol, we embarked immediately and set forth on one of the longest and most disagreeable voyages I ever experienced. When about fifty miles at sea we were boarded and inspected by a French frigate, but as we were sailing in an American bottom, and as, too, by a lucky chance, the commanding officer, having resided the winter before at Boston, recognized with great friendliness "*le comé-dien*," we were suffered to pass on unmolested. The rest of the voyage was but a disagreeable monotony of bad weather. Owing to contrary winds we ran about fifteen hundred miles farther about the ocean than we intended, and it was not until after a fifty days' voyage, when both ourselves and our provisions were pretty well exhausted, that, on the 25th of September, 1806, we at last reached the harbor of Boston.

CHAPTER XIII.

1806.—Boston.—Mrs. Stanley; Compared with Mrs. Abingdon and Miss Farren.—Admiration.—Caulfield.—General Humphrey's Authorship. —"Romeo and Juliet" in the Backwoods.—A Long Song.—Mrs. Jones's Death.—Dr. Jeffrey's Youthful Flight.—Caulfield's Singing.—An Actor's Temptation.—New Version of Lord Hasting's Speech.—Powell.— Fennell's Salt-works.—A Sermon on Patience.—Poe and Shaw.—Colored People.—Rival Musicians.—Mr.Williams.—A Lecturing Tour.—Tragedy of Real Life.—Sally Weeks.—Meeting the Devil.—A Military Money-taker.—Curious "Wiscasset" Natives.—1807.—Mr. Cromwell.—A Theatrical Impostor.—Jack Hatton the Great Blackguard.—Snow-storm at Sea.—A Visit to Philadelphia and New York.—Serious Illness.—Acting Under Difficulties.—A Cool Duellist.—Captain Dorgan.—Serious Losses.

On our arrival in Boston I found a residence in Pleasant Street (a strange misnomer, for it was one of the dullest I ever inhabited), collected my family about me, and was thus once more "settled" in the States. The theatre had been opened about a fortnight when we arrived, but expectation ran so high with respect to the reinforcements I was bringing that very little had been done. I congratulated myself afterwards that it was not disappointed. Mrs. Stanley* (otherwise the Honorable Mrs. Twisleton) made her *début* in Elvira to the Rolla of Mr.

---

* As the Honorable Mrs. Twisleton, Mrs. STANLEY was, for a number of years, well known, in aristocratic circles in England, as an amateur actress. She appeared on the regular stage, in Boston, Philadelphia, and New York, as Mrs. Stanley. Her success in America was never very great, although she was beautiful in person and charming in manner. She may be considered the mother of the large family of professional beauties who have become professional actresses. She died early in this century.

MRS. STANLEY.

From the *Polyanthus*, Boston, 1806.

Caulfield. To this singularly accomplished and ill-fated actress it is but meet that I should devote a few words as to one who, in her time, excited so much both of pleasure and of regret in the minds of others. Of her merits only, however, shall I speak here—of her fate hereafter.

In the course of my professional career it was my chance to see three elegant actresses, Mrs. Abingdon, Miss Farren, and Mrs. Stanley. The first showed most the tone of high life in her acting, but I have been told by those well competent to judge that this was chiefly due to its case, dash, and animation. The second was perhaps the more fascinating, her chief charm being an easy simplicity, combined with a bewitching playfulness; but the third was more intuitively elegant than either. She had not the *vis comica* of Mrs. Abingdon, nor the fascination of Miss Farren, but then she had the manners—of Mrs. Stanley. In one respect, indeed, she fell far short of her rivals, for her voice had not the flexibility or music of either; but in another point again she surpassed them—yes, even surpassed Miss Farren!—in her person. I know not that her features were as regular as that lady's, but their expression was much more beautiful; and if a form, rather exceeding the medium height, but moulded in the most symmetrical proportions and perfect in every respect most insisted upon by the anatomical *connoisseur*—if this, I say, could merit to be called loveliness, then might Mrs. Stanley claim the term.

Any similarity which might be traced in Mrs. Abingdon and Miss Farren when performing the same characters was owing rather to constitution than to cultivation, nature having cast them both in nearly the same mould, though art had wrought great differences; but between Mrs. Abingdon and Mrs. Stanley there were few if any striking points of resemblance. The first was the more natural, for she faithfully depicted life as it was, while

the other had the exquisite fault of attempting to show
what it ought to be. Her *chef-d'œuvre* was the Widow
Belmour; her rival's, Lady Betty Modish; but a more opposite contrast cannot be selected than the characters of
Lady Townley and Lady Grace, with which, if my reader
will identify Mrs. Abingdon and Mrs. Stanley, he will perceive at once the difference of their styles and the beautiful illustration which Cibber intended of fashionable and
refined life. Both actresses enjoyed intercourse with the
higher orders of society in England, but Mrs. Stanley was
the only one of her profession that was ever admitted to
the Pump Rooms at Bath, a distinction which many of
the sisterhood envied and sought after, but none other attained.

Caulfield* was very well received in America. He was
by no means an original actor, since he plagiarized from
Kemble and others in the same manner that Harwood did
from John Bannister; but as in each instance this was
very cleverly done, and as the Americans had not had the
pleasure of seeing either of the originals, they considered
both actors to be not only very good, but very genuine.
As regards little Vining, the singer, he quite answered my
expectations.

As soon as I became comfortably settled in my new
residence I had visits and invitations from all quarters.
To a friendly summons from General Humphreys—one of
the most sincere and valuable friends I had met with in
the States—I attended the first. This gentleman, in addition to his military and diplomatic abilities, had also distinguished himself in the region of poetry and the drama.
His poems are well known, but I have omitted to mention
that on my proceeding to England I took with me a com-

---

* Mr. CAULFIELD was an actor of general utility, good in everything, but
in nothing great. He appeared at the Park Theatre, New York, during
the season of 1813–14, and died in Cincinnati in the following year.

MR. CAULFIELD.

From Parson's "Minor Theatre," London, 1794.

edy of his writings for the perusal of a London manager, which, but for a trivial localism in the plot, had sufficient merit to have been brought before the public. Many years previously he had produced a clever tragedy entitled "The Widow of Malabar." At his table I met with several agreeable people, and a good deal of original anecdote circulated.

The general (who was an ardent lover of theatricals and in the habit of dropping in to an entertainment wherever he met with one) gave us an amusing account of an exhibition at which he had been present, many years before, in the interior of Virginia.

One day, seeing a play-bill pasted up on a post in some village, announcing that the tragedy of "Romeo and Juliet" would be performed in the evening, at the Tavern Assembly Rooms, interspersed with a variety of music and dancing, the whole to conclude with "the celebrated song of 'Yankee Doodle,'" he could not resist the opportunity of attending and becoming acquainted with the state of theatricals in the back countries. The price of admission was very low, but when he entered he found only about twenty people assembled, sitting on chairs and benches before the dirty green rag which hung across the room at the other end to conceal the dramatic paraphernalia. The band consisted of a man with a drum and a little boy with a "wry-necked fife," who prefaced the entertainment by playing a not very melodious tune. The tragedy then commenced. As the curtain drew up, discovering, for scenery, a very mean chamber, Romeo came forward alone, and began repeating what from its length and character was evidently two or three dozen speeches compounded into one, pretending during the recital to address himself in turn to the different personages who ought to have been with him on the stage. This rather original idea proved not a very satisfactory one to the audience, and at

length finding this to be the case, he very abruptly broke
off his speech and broke into a hornpipe, to which the fife
set up an ear-piercing accompaniment. After getting
himself into a thorough perspiration with this exercise, he
shuffled off, with about as little elegance as it could be
supposed that a Romeo could display.

Juliet now made her appearance at the opposite side,
and went through a scene *solus* in exactly similar style
to that of her lover. The audience were thus, at length,
made fully aware of the singular fact that Romeo and Juliet were not only the principal actors in this tragedy, but
on the present occasion were the only ones. Juliet's conversations with invisible companions being, however, also
too mysterious and imaginative for the spectators, in addition to being slightly prolix, they manifested fresh signs
of impatience. The lady was equal to the occasion, for,
taking the hint at once, and quitting blank verse for
rhyme, she soared into a song, which, though very genteel, was, for the greater relief after previous tediousness,
executed with such rapidity that the drum and fife (ras-
cally attendants on such sweet sounds) followed after at
some distance with what should have been the accompani-
ments, thumping and squeaking with all their might in
vain attempts to overtake the fair singer. On reaching
the end of her own part of this performance she made her
exit, like the swan, in the midst of melody, leaving the
farmers an interval in which they might " calculate " the
degree of merit she had displayed. Thus concluded the
first act. In the second the interest might fairly be said
to double, seeing that the two performers came on the
stage together instead of singly, Romeo leading Juliet forward as though to bear witness of the truth of the story
which he then pithily epitomized for the enlightenment
of the audience, telling how they two had fallen in love
with each other, and so into trouble also, and how that

they were very unfortunate, and had, therefore, made up their minds that as they couldn't live with each other they were resolved to die with each other. This appeal to the sympathies and sensibilities of the audience was not in vain, for eyes began to be rubbed and noses blown to some purpose. Then, at length, monologue became dialogue, and speech rose into action at the parting of the lovers previous to their commission of the dreadful act of self-destruction, which, being found to be affecting in the extreme, was protracted for about half an hour, while they blubbered together like hungry children crying for bread and butter, and uttered with every variety of pathetic emphasis a long catalogue of ohs! ahs! and alases! duly chorused by the pitying spectators.

The " last scene of all " that came to close " this strange, eventful history," was a truly horrifying one, for when the curtain drew up it discovered the unhappy lovers lying dead on the stage locked in each other's arms. Now, it being believed that the performers enacting Romeo and Juliet were *bona fide* man and wife, what would have seemed to them otherwise the indelicacy of such an exhibition did not shock the worthy rustics, but this only left them the more freely and fully under the influence of its intense lachrymoseness. The drum and fife, too, were all the while exciting and keeping up the dismalness of the scene by playing throughout some dead march or shrieking dirge, shrill enough to have buried a wind with, and which quite answered the desired end.

The audience were suffered to gaze on this spectacle— or rather upon this pair of spectacles—for a period of about ten minutes, when the curtain closed down upon the unfortunate bodies, in the imaginations of most present cutting them off henceforth from the world as completely as though it had been a coffin lid. Some in the room, however, either less deeply affected or imbued with truer spirits—rough-coated patriots with sound cores, who felt that let who will die the country survives—began to kick on the floor and call loudly in a fit of enthusiasm for the national song with which it had been announced the whole was to terminate. Obedient to their summons Romeo forthwith ran forward and bowed, to the great surprise and severe disappointment of the damsels, at least, who had given him credit for being really dead, but whose smiling appearance gave proof that his ten minutes' nap on the floor had rather tended to the invigoration of his faculties than their dissolution. The band striking up briskly with the tune, he began his ditty, sang twenty verses through without stopping (repeating every second verse again), then drawing his breath went on for another fifteen, but with rather less spirit; halted again to take in a fresh atmospheric supply, then, but with difficulty, added another ten, making in all forty-five. Here he appeared perfectly exhausted, in memory as well as windpipe, and it was only after making two or three pantomimical gesticulations that he found sufficient air in his bellows (as Voltaire vulgarly calls it) and sufficient words in his cranium to acquaint the audience that that was all he knew of the song, but that if they would like to have any more, his wife (the dead Juliet behind the scenes) would come on with pleasure and favor them with seventy-three verses more.

This information had an electrical effect upon the whole body spectatorial. Love of country and love of song alike fled before it. If a dead lover could get through forty-five verses with so much spirit, thought they, a resuscitated woman with seventy-three more was beyond what mortal patience could endure. Romeo could not have given them a better hint to " *avaunt*," for, hardly staying to say, " No, thank you," they clapped their hats on their heads and their damsels under their arms, and departed from the room with the utmost expedition.

It was with great expectations that I had embarked my capital in the Boston Theatre,* for Powell had cleared during the preceding season upward of ten thousand dollars, and I had most potential friends in the city to support me both as an actor and a manager. The season began prosperously enough, holding out great prospects of success before its close; but ere three months had rolled over our heads it seemed as though misfortune, owing me a grudge perhaps for my previous ten years' successes, had determined to overtake me. The Embargo and Non-importation acts coming into force, Boston, as a great commercial seaport, was at once vitally affected. Trade was checked, the amount of money in circulation diminished, bankruptcies became general, living grew dear, and families of all ranks were obliged to retrench. That superabundance of cash which, when it was plentiful, had been devoted to amusement, forming now but part of a mere sufficiency to pay necessary expenses, was, as it were, drawn out of our treasury. The theatre, dependent as it was upon a state of circumstances similar to those of preceding years, was, of course, importantly affected by the change. For that winter our prospects were entirely ruined; nor was the shock recovered from to any beneficial extent for the four succeeding ones during which I was connected with this theatre.

Since, from the above causes, the public were less ready to support us than they had heretofore been, we were obliged to put forth as much novelty as possible in our performances. " Cinderella "—the scenery and machinery for which, as I have mentioned, I had brought with me at a great expense from London—was a sure card for

---

* The Boston Theatre, on Federal Street, was built in 1794. It was destroyed by fire, and, being rebuilt in 1798, remained the most important theatre in Boston until the opening of the Tremont Theatre in 1827. It was finally demolished in 1852.

the close of the season.   In addition we had some comedies and farces in rehearsal, which, from the strength of
our corps, we could cast very effectively, especially as
we received two or three accessions to our company.
Among these I must mention Mr. and Mrs. Usher, both
clever people, though little known.   The theatre, too, at
this time had an excellent friend in R. T. Paine, Esq.,
whose dramatic critiques were looked upon as the oracles
of the day, and who lent his aid very efficiently in directing public attention to the well-founded claims we put
forth for support.   We were accustomed to say that
" whenever one of our stage pieces went off, the audience
felt the flash, and Paine made the report.

I heard at this time of the death, at New York, of that
clever actress, Mrs. Jones, whom I had engaged to Mr.
Harris at a salary of £10 a week and upward for three
years.   She was a better comedian of the style of Mrs.
Jordan than any I had seen in London.   A letter was
forwarded to me which she had written to me when she
found that her illness was assuming a fatal aspect, tendering me her thanks for my interference in her behalf, now
frustrated by her untimely decease, and begging me not
to forget her children, her husband having died a month
or two previous in that theatrical burial-place, Charleston.
In conjunction with my partners I accordingly gave the
little orphans a benefit, the receipts from which yielded
$760; and, as a proof of the great estimation in which
this fascinating actress was held throughout the States,
benefits were also accorded to her children at New York,
Charleston, and Philadelphia.

Fennell now arrived in Boston on a visit, avowedly to
see some salt-works near Portsmouth, but he hinted to
several friends a wish to perform.   What a whirligig,
weathercock fellow was that Fennell !   I told him that it
was lucky for him he had such a spouse as the profession

BOSTON THEATRE, FEDERAL STREET.

From Snow's "History of Boston."

to furnish him with funds, when he had so many mistress-
es in his speculative fancies to squander them away upon.
I met him at a party at the house of my friend and medical attendant, Dr. Jeffries, the gentleman who years before had crossed from Dover to Calais in a balloon, in
company with a French emigrant. Whenever this circumstance was recalled, the doctor used to shake his head
good - humoredly, and reply: "Ah, of all my youthful
flightinesses, that is the only flight of which I am ashamed
to be reminded."

About Christmas, when the theatres in the States, even
during prosperous seasons, do little more than pay their
expenses, Cooper arrived in town from New York, where
he was now manager, on purpose to engage Mrs. Stanley.
He proposed playing six nights at Boston for a benefit,
and my proceeding to New York to do the like, to which
I agreed, and accordingly he opened in Hamlet at my
house the same night that I did in Lord Ogleby at his
theatre. The exchange, I think, answered the expectations of both parties. On my return to Boston I found
that Caulfield had not played during Cooper's nights, and
on inquiry learned that this was due to two causes—his
love of his profession, which would not suffer him to acknowledge the dramatic superiority of another, and his
love of company, which was beginning to render him re-
gardless of anything else, even of this very profession.
This was very injurious both to himself and his manager,
but it was hardly surprising, for Caulfield was specially
qualified to render himself agreeable at table. He was a
good mimic and a humorist; his memory abounded with
facetious anecdotes both of the stage and of private life,
and he had a pleasant, mellow-toned voice that was heard
to great advantage in a chamber. There was, indeed, a
spirit and an expression in his singing rarely to be met
with, and which rendered his Anacreontic songs, in par-

ticular, very charming. On one occasion I remember he especially surprised and delighted me during our voyage, when we were driven by adverse winds into the Bay of Biscay and there becalmed for several days. One beautiful, still, moonlight evening, when we were all on deck enjoying the scene, watching the shores of France in the distance and the white sails here and there dancing in the moonbeams, Caulfield suddenly sprang forward and began that favorite sea-song which took its title from the place where we lay—" The Bay of Biscay." I had heard Incledon and several other celebrities sing it before, but whether it was from the circumstance of the locality and the train of feelings aroused by the scene, or, as I am inclined to believe, far more from the exquisite expression Caulfield threw into the song, I was never before so affected by a piece of music. When he had finished, Mrs. Stanley turned to me with a smile and observed : " If Mr. Caulfield can speak on the stage as well as he sings here, you have indeed a valuable acquisition."

When we landed in Boston I was induced, for the above reasons, to take Caulfield with me on the first club night, to the "St. Cecilia," a musical society which I had been instrumental in founding, and where he became a great favorite with all the members. Unhappily, however, what was intended for his benefit had an injurious effect. Introduced into better society than he had ever been accustomed to in his own country; finding money, wine, and amusement abundant, his head grew giddy with pleasure and success; and wanting judgment to impose restraint upon indulgence, he, by degrees, grew indifferent to his professional duties and forgetful of the respect he owed both to the public and to himself. I have mentioned this particularly in order that I may remark, from my own experience in America, that the fate of Caulfield is but an instance of that of half the profession besides, who have come over and died in the very prime and vigor of their lives, owing to having given way to pernicious habits. It is wholly unknown and unimagined in England how vast a number of meritorious actors have, within this last twenty years, mingled their dust with the soil of the American States. I do not speak of performers who have appeared in the metropolis and thus become partially known to the British public in general; but I allude solely to those who have poured over from Bristol, Liverpool, and Ireland, young and unknown in the profession, and who, after careering for a limited hour indeed of success, have been gathered untimely into "the tomb of all the Capulets."

But to return to Caulfield. As Mrs. Stanley wished to perform Jane Shore as one of her tragic characters at Boston, I had given him the part of Lord Hastings to study during our passage. Supposing, therefore, that at this late day he must be quite prepared, we, without hesitation, announced that tragedy as soon as I returned from New York. Much to our surprise we found that he knew little or nothing of the character, and came to a distressing standstill in several passages. When left to his soliloquy at Gloster's exit, he remembered but a line here and there of that admirable climax, and began with a deal of solemn, slow pomposity, in order most likely to give himself time to recollect. The scene went on something as follows :

CAULFIELD.—"I—know—the—*Duke*—is (*to the prompter*)—what ?"

PROMPTER.—[*whispering*]: "Noble."

CAULFIELD.—"*Noble ?*—noble (*to the prompter*); well ?"

PROMPTER.—"But he touched me—"

CAULFIELD.—"But he *touched* me (*to the prompter*); where ?"

PROMPTER.—"On the tenderest point—"

CAULFIELD.—"On the tenderest part—no! point."

PROMPTER.—"The master string—"

CAULFIELD.—"The master's string — the string — the master—that makes music—music—master—"

Here the prompter grew bewildered, and Caulfield, in a fit of inspiration continued:

"Music — music has charms to soothe — the Duke — d—n him!—here he comes again."   [*Exit in a hurry.*

Charles Powell, my old Taunton acquaintance, and the original Boston manager, came to me on a visit from Halifax, where he had established a theatre under the patronage of H. R. H. the Duke of Kent, and played a few parts, in which he was well received. When he dined with me we had a pleasant conversation upon past times when we had spouted and strolled together in the reckless but ambitious days of boyhood. As he was dwelling on his present matrimonial felicity I asked him if he remembered the first "bone of his bone" whom he had taken unto himself about thirty years previously, and whose former name had been Mrs. Skin. "Flesh and blood, Jack" (his favorite oath), "to be sure I do," was his appropriate reply.

For a month after Christmas a great deal of domestic amusement was going forward in Boston—parties, balls, and concerts—and the theatre suffered in consequence; but this was inevitable. I, too, had a variety of invitations; among others one to the British consul's, Mr. A. Allen, where I was introduced to General Sheaf (who afterwards rendered me many attentions in Canada) and shook hands with Mrs. Morton, the poetess. When the conversation turned on professional topics Fennell was spoken of, and in a strain which informed me that he was in request, though I knew at the same time that the public were less desirous of supporting him than formerly. A few days after, on receiving a letter from him proposing an engagement, we concluded one with him on safe terms for a limited number of nights. His present application was caused by his complete embarrassment at New London, where his salt works had again failed *in toto*. This was the fourth of his salt speculations that had fallen to the ground, yet he seemed to deny by his conduct the truth of the old saying that "experience teaches." There was, I thought, a species of lunacy in this, for the folly of undertaking such schemes did not appear more obvious than the madness of continuing them; and the ingenious scheme he devised to escape from the difficulties in which they had involved him would hardly perhaps be accepted as a proof of perfect sanity. When I asked him how he had contrived to pacify his creditors at New London, he related to me that on the Sabbath before he quitted the salt works—as they were getting clamorous for their money—he invited them all to assemble there to hear him deliver a discourse, promising that the doctrine therein set forth would be very much to their satisfaction as well as his own. The congregation, though consisting merely of his creditors, proved to be a very large one. He met them at the appointed time, and taking up his station at a point where he was conspicuous to all, he gave forth the text which he was about to expound: "Have patience and I will pay you all." This he divided into two heads—first, and most importantly—the virtue of patience; lastly and referentially—the act of paying. On this no doubt his auditors formed two conclusions: first, that to display the virtue of patience might be the best religion, but, secondly, that the act of paying was the most applicable to trade; and considering themselves primarily men of business they would regard the latter point (with all due deference to Fennell's opinion) as direct instead of referential, and by far the more important of the two. However, he proceeded with his exposi-

tion, placing patience at the head of the cardinal virtues, and giving it the pre-eminence over every quality
which can adorn a man's character, every feeling which
can animate his bosom; after eulogizing and apostrophiz-
ing, commending and recommending it with all the glowing words and most beautiful images his florid fancy and
learned brain could suggest (though from the uneasy manner in which his auditors all listened the doctrine was evidently doing very little for their conversion), he at length
came to the second and far more attractive division of the
text, "I will pay you all." Pronouncing these words with
much emphasis, he looked them all in the face for a few
moments in silence, then deliberately added, "but not
being prepared to treat upon this point at present, I must
defer the opportunity until it shall please Providence and
the Boston managers to afford me another—" saying which
he turned upon his heel and hurried from the spot.

As I expected, his coming to the theatre was of no material benefit either to himself or the management.

During the season we were joined by Miss Arnold,* a
clever little actress and singer who had lately married a
Mr. Poe, whom we also engaged. There were a Mr. and
Mrs. Shaw in the company at the time, and it was a standing jest for these two couples to retort on each other by
the use of their respective names—"Poh-Poh!" "Pshaw-
Pshaw!"

"Bachelors' Hall," the residence of some spirited, sociable young men of that day, in Boston, became this winter the scene of much mirth and conviviality. I attended
two or three of their meetings in celebration of the pleas-

---

* Mrs. Poe was a beautiful English actress, who, as Elizabeth Arnold,
fascinated David Poe, Jr., a law student in Baltimore. Her husband
abandoned his profession for hers. Mr. and Mrs. Poe acted together for
several years. They died young and in poverty at Richmond, leaving three
children, the second of whom was Edgar Allan Poe.

ures of celibacy, and to make merry over the miseries of matrimony, whereupon some of my worthy friends used to remark that I (being a married man, and so happy a one) came there for my *bane* and went home for my *antidote.*

I really think, however, that the greatest amusement I had in Boston was derived from the colored people, as they call the free blacks, who mostly keep shops, or are waiters in gentlemen's houses. What particularly distinguishes them is their ridiculous contempt for those of their own color who happen to be slaves, and their continual imitation in manners and sayings of the white people, with whom they affect to be upon an equality. Delayed in the street one day by some stoppage, I perceived, on turning round, a couple of colored people at my elbow. The elegant pomposity and affectation of breeding which they assumed towards each other pleasantly contrasted with their version of the English language. " Ah, Massa Frederick," said the first speaker, "how a your honor do a-day?" "Mosh obliged, Sharley, berry well," was the reply, "got um catch-cold, dat's all." "How you lady, Massa Frederick?" "Missee Frederick? oh, she'm beautiful, so mosh you never can tink—she berry mosh so." "And how you little shild, Massa Frederick?" "Oh, she charming; I tank you one thousand time—*she'm dead!*"

On another occasion two ladies of this race met under my window and began their usual bombastic greetings with—"Miss Marie Caroline Henrietta, how your honor do dis day?" "I was, tank you, Miss Charlotte Teresa," replied her friend, "I was among de middlin'." "Yes," rejoined the other, "so Long Peter say, you very middlin' indeed." The emphasis with which this was pronounced raised the ire of the dark beauty, who forthwith declared, "Long Peter betta pay him debt afore um 'buse a lady what have been so good to him as me have!" "You good

to my Peter," exclaimed her rival in equal wrath—"den
may devil take un bote !" By this time a mob had drawn
together to hear this scolding-match between the tender
black virgins, which soon rose to a pitch no language but
their own could describe. After the duel had continued
for some time, Miss Teresa gave a decisive blow by uttering a philippic of at least a minute's length, with such
severity and so rapidly that it fairly took away the breath
of Miss Marie and struck her nearly speechless. At length,
recovering a little, she seemed to put away her anger in a
moment, and looking her adversary full in the face, made
her a very low courtesy, said quite quietly, "I dank you,
madam, I owes you won," and walked slowly away.

As the spring advanced I thought that a summer residence a few miles out of Boston would prove agreeable,
so drove my wife out to look at a little seat near Dorchester, which was for sale, and which we so highly ap-
proved of that I at once arranged for its purchase.

The management at this time consented to give a night
to the proprietors for the purpose of commencing a fund
for lunatics. A good deal of pleasantry was excited on
this occasion. Fennell, the greatest madman of whom I
had any knowledge, spoke an ode to madness in very fine
style, which some attributed to sympathy; but Caulfield
was absent, on which Treat Paine* remarked that "he

---

* ROBERT TREAT PAINE, Jr., born in Taunton, Massachusetts, in 1773,
was the second son and namesake of the signer of the Declaration of Independence. After some experiences as a merchant, and later as a lawyer,
he became infatuated with the theatre, and determined to devote himself
entirely to the drama and to dramatic literature. He was appointed
"Master of Ceremonies" to the Boston Theatre, then a salaried position,
and in 1795 married a Miss Boker, an English actress, and a member of
the Boston Theatre Company. By this step he lost his social position,
which had been a high one, and became estranged from his family. He
lived latterly a reckless life, and died in 1811, a comparatively young man.

ROBERT TREAT PAINE, JR.

After an engraving published by Joshua Belcher, Boston, 1812.

was deranged indeed, for this negligence might exclude him from the benefit of the institution."

To my musical friends and the members of the St. Cecilia I gave my concert at the conclusion of the season, which was numerously attended. General Sheaf even honored us by taking up the flute and performing several pieces with great taste and execution. A Mr. Von Hagen, a German of no small musical talent, presided at the piano. He was at this time organist at the Episcopal Church, and held in general estimation; though, soon afterwards falling into irregular habits, he lost both his friends and his situation. Our leader in the orchestra was a Monsieur Mallet, an *artiste*, as he called himself, of not very striking ability, although, as in most such cases, inclined to think the contrary himself. Von Hagen, meeting him one day in the street, held out his hand to him, and observed, with a good-humored smile:

"I vas go to the theatre lasht night, Meister Mallet, to hear your new muzeek."

"*Eh bien*," said the Frenchman, "and how vas you pleased, sare?"

"You was one great composer," continued Von Hagen. "You zet all the beoples ashleep! aha!"

Mr. Mallet, starting from him with some indignation at such a witticism, retorted, as he thought, with this unintentional compliment:

"You vas much vorse, Monsieur Von Hagen, aha! much vorse. I was go to ze shursh ze oder day to hear you play von voluntary, and ven I vanted to go to sleep, aha!—by gar—you—vould not let me!"

He was a brilliant writer, and published most of his best work under his own name, Thomas Paine. But in 1801, to avoid being confounded with, and by, the author of the "Age of Reason," he petitioned the Legislature of Massachusetts to be allowed to call himself Robert Treat Paine, Jr., on the ground that "Tom Paine was not a *Christian* name."

The benefits now commenced, and went off with general success. Mrs. Stanley, by agreement, had two, one nominal and another in the regular course. Caulfield, notwithstanding his truantism, had a very fair one; as did Fox and Dickenson; Mrs. Powell once more drew a bill on the public which they never failed to honor; and I myself netted $1000, some compensation as an actor for the losses which I had sustained throughout the season as a manager. In despite of the various novelties we had brought forward and the very effective condition of the company, " Cinderella " was the only piece which repaid the expense of its production, the public, for reasons already mentioned, finding themselves unable, rather than unwilling, to yield us the support we merited.

As I knew circumstances would not permit me to pass the whole of the summer at " The Lodge," as I called my new residence, I thought of again visiting the north of New England on a lecturing tour, and arranged with Caulfield to accompany me, his style of singing and recitation rendering him a desirable coadjutor. The limit of our journey was to be Wiscasset, the extremest seaport of Maine, a part of the country over which I had travelled before. Our first halt was at Newburg Park, where I made out a bill containing many "provocatives" (to use a theatrical term), and where our expectations were well answered. Passing on to Portsmouth, I stayed with Mrs. Bernard at the residence of my friend, M. Casso, the French consul, who narrated to me some incidents which had lately occurred in the town, and the simple pathos of which deeply impressed me.

Sally Weeks, an amiable and rather personable girl, in humble circumstances, was, a short time before, to have been united to her lover, a young sailor named William Day. This marriage, which had been settled with the concurrence of all their friends, was expected to result in much happiness, as it had been prompted by but one motive, that of pure, mutual affection. Their wedding-day was accordingly fixed, but on its morning, William, with some acquaintances, went on board of his vessel, then lying in the offing, to take leave of his old shipmates, who expected to sail that evening. A breeze springing up, the ship was obliged to weigh anchor and proceed to sea, whereupon Day's companions got into their little skiff to return to shore. The captain, thinking her perhaps overladen, as the sea was becoming very rough, would not allow Day to accompany them, but insisted on his remaining on board until he could be put ashore somewhere down the coast. As had been fearfully anticipated, the skiff containing his unfortunate friends, when half-way to land, met a heavy sea and was swamped. Two of their bodies were picked up soon after on the beach, and from their fate that of William Day was surmised.

With every hope thus apparently blighted when on the very eve of happiness, poor Sally was so affected at the supposed loss of her lover that she fell sick, and, on recovering her strength, it was found that she had lost her reason. Sunk in a state of despondency, she was accustomed to take daily walks on the beach, about the spot where the bodies of the sufferers had been washed ashore, and near which fancy led her to imagine that her William must himself be lying. Every one knew and pitied the amiable maniac, who thus, under general protection, roamed about unmolested.

Meanwhile the ship in which Day had been carried to sea, owing to the continuance of the breeze, kept on her course. He was, therefore, constrained to accompany her abroad, and could only return when she did. At length she arrived once more in port; the boat was manned; he was the first to enter her, the first to spring on shore. In a moment he espied a female in the distance who bore

some resemblance to his Sally, and ran towards her calling her by name. It was she. She looked at him, recognized him, uttered a piercing shriek, and, falling in his arms,
expired. To see once more the beloved form which she
had believed to be lost to her forever had been too great
a shock, and the joy which in an instant restored her to
reason, at the same instant robbed her of life.

There was singularity enough in these circumstances
for a romance, yet it was a tragedy of real and of humble
life. Its simplicity rather augmented its interest, and I
must confess that nothing in my reading or experience
ever touched me more. The poor victim of sensibility
died within a day of completing her nineteenth year; and,
little fitted as so pathetic a story might seem to inspire
anything like pleasantry, this suggested to some one in
the town the following epigrammatic epitaph :

> " Poor Sally Weeks here sleeps and seeks,
> Mould'ring, her kindred clay;
> Some months she sighed—at nineteen died
> Wanting a *single* Day."

After a remunerative stay at Portsmouth we proceeded
to Portland, where we procured for our entertainment the
long room in which the company had formerly played.
An itinerant preacher at this time in the town, who had
arranged to deliver a discourse once a week in this same
room, on hearing with whom he was now to share it, declared that he was glad "for once to meet the devil on
his own ground !" He was somewhat mortified, however,
the night after, to find that we had attracted a much
larger assemblage than he had, and that it also comprised
many of his own congregation.

On reaching Brunswick I was invited to join a fishing-
party up the beautiful river Androscoggin, which takes
its name, I was told, from the English emigrant who first
discovered it—Andrew Scroggin. There had been a great

storm lately in this district, and as we rowed up the river
the curious effect of it became apparent in the form of
quantities of oily sturgeon which had been thrown ashore,
and were now strewn abundantly on both banks, putrefy-
ing in the sunbeams, and forming a regale not very agreeable to either the olfactory or the optical sense.   Learning here that the little town of Bath had never been visited by any amusement whatever of our kind, we drove
there and issued an attractive bill of fare for the ensuing
evening.   The news soon circulated, and from the commotion it excited we were led to expect wonderful support.
Before long a *ci-devant* major in the American army, a
resident in the place and a very military and methodical-
looking person, who impressed me at first sight very favorably, waited upon me at the inn and begged to express to
me in person his high sense of gratification at our visit.
Becoming soon very friendly, he offered, out of pure good-
nature, to stand at the door in *propria persona* and dispose of tickets for us; "for," said he, "that appears to
me, my dear sir, a very important office, and really there
is no knowing the character of people you might obtain
and be deceived by."   Considering this offer to be extremely kind, both Caulfield and I were profuse in our ac-
knowledgments, and gladly accepted so unimpeachable a
money-taker.   When the evening came the room was
crowded to excess, and I distinguished at the lowest computation above one hundred and thirty heads, which, at a
dollar apiece, promised a handsome return.   At the close
our self-elected treasurer presented himself to give in his
account.   "Really, gentlemen," he began, "I sincerely rejoice that you intrusted to me an office in which so much
must depend upon the honor of the person to whom it is
confided."   I have no doubt he did rejoice, and we soon
found what good reason he had for doing so when he continued—"I am now able to pay over to you no less a sum

than eighty-nine dollars!" Perhaps he thought that an
officer was nothing without a "commission," or, it may
be, his extreme good-nature had induced him to admit all
his friends and relations gratis; at any rate, the fact remained that we had to pay at least fifty dollars that evening for the honor of having a military doorkeeper.

At Wiscasset we put up at an inn kept by an Irishman,
and our bills for the ensuing evening being distributed
directly, no sooner did the news become public than the
little town, which I apprehend had never before been visited in a similar manner, became generally disturbed. A
crowd soon collected round the windows of the inn parlor
in which we were taking supper, to discover what kind of
people we were. Several of the more respectable inhabitants took the liberty of stepping into the room, drawing
a chair by the window and listening to our conversation.
Others merely walked in as if to make an inquiry, and
taking a comprehensive view of us from head to foot, at
once withdrew to impart the information they had acquired to their friends; while a still larger class, more dif-
fident than the rest, only opened the door, took a hasty
glance, and then again quickly closed it. We were most
amused by a portly, farmer-looking man, who, by his careless manner and easy speech, seemed to be a person of
some consequence in the town, and who walked into the
room, tilted his chair back by the window, and, throwing
his boots over a bench, set himself deliberately to listen
with great earnestness to our discourse. It happened that
Caulfield was just relating in his humorous manner some
ludicrous circumstances he had taken notice of during the
day, and before long the farmer was so pleased that, clapping his hands to his sides, he threw himself back in his
chair and burst into a loud roar of laughter. We put
down our knives and forks, and looked round at our unin-
vited auditor in some surprise. On getting over his fit of

risibility, he returned our gaze with a highly satisfied expression; then, getting up, put his hand in his pocket, and exclaimed:

"Capital, gentlemen! capital! You are right humorsome, I calculate. What's to pay?"

This produced a responsive roar from us, whereupon the rather puzzled worthy explained that from the humor and eccentricity Caulfield had displayed he had supposed that he was relating one of the stories from our entertainment, and, therefore, in the true spirit of honest trade, he wished to pay for what he had received. On being informed that we would accept no remuneration for what he had heard, he departed with a high opinion of both our talent and our liberality.

Less agreeable was the disappointment, on another ground, of a personage who merely put his head in at the door and withdrew it the next minute, apparently with much dissatisfaction, for we heard him exclaim to a companion outside, "Tarnation, Squire Shaw, they're not so *savage* after all!"

These singular attentions, however, though they only excited our smiles, were to my wife as annoying as they were astonishing; and Caulfield, perceiving this, hit upon a plan of relieving us of our wondering spectators without giving them offence. Taking a hint from the offer of the honest farmer, he called in the landlord and desired him to acquaint the people at the windows (which had neither blinds nor curtains) that our prices were a dollar apiece to hear our entertainment and half a dollar to *see ourselves.* They were too good judges of a bargain for this not to take effect.

The great success of our two nights at Wiscasset would have induced us to remain there a little longer, but that my wife's condition made me anxious to reach Boston without much further delay. We accordingly turned our horses' heads homeward, and lecturing again at Portland, Portsmouth, and Newburyport, as we passed through them, arrived in Boston about five hundred dollars in pocket from our excursion.

My wife soon after presented me with a boy,* and then, removing to our new residence, we passed a delightful autumn in retirement and recreation, having found the first year of life as a manager in America, if not very profitable, at least very pleasant.

The season of 1807–8 commenced early in September with some slight prospect of improving upon its predecessor, and with some new additions to the company. As Caulfield, from the very irregular habits he had fallen into, could no longer be depended upon, we were constrained to look about for some other hero to be ready to supply his place, and just at this time a gentleman arrived from England on a dramatic visit to the States who appeared to be the very man we wanted. Mr. Cromwell, the person in question, was, however, in reality only one of the most ingenious and amusing impostors I ever met with. In his style as an actor, hovering between a bad imitation and a worse originality, he had no qualification for the stage but one—self-confidence—which yet only led to a fuller display of all his other deficiencies. He had been formerly a small tradesman, but being smitten with a passion for the stage, he applied to, and appeared at, the Bath Theatre. Fearing, perhaps, that the editors might not have sufficient discrimination to find out his merits, he wrote a glowing puff upon his own *début*, and forwarded it to the provincial papers. Once in print, he then proceeded to London with these public recommendations, and, procuring an opening at one of the principal houses, managed to secure the insertion of

---

* W. Bayle Bernard.

a similar homemade article on his own performance in the metropolitan journals. His attempts on the stage were, of course, a failure, and his critical remarks a tissue of falsehoods, but, nevertheless, they answered his purpose. Putting the latter in his pocket, he went off to America, landed at Boston, waited on the manager, announced his profession, and, in proof of his talents, showed all the papers containing those striking criticisms written by himself, but of the authorship of which, of course, he gave no hint. Powell, who saw him in my absence, believing he would be attractive and a good substitute for Caulfield, engaged him on the spot for three years at twenty-five dollars a week. We gave him Octavian as an opening character, and from the reports that had been circulated about him public attention was very generally excited. He performed; a worse specimen of histrionic quackery I had never seen, and the spectators would hardly permit the announcement of his name for a second night. The next day I went to consult my solicitor, who briefly told me that an agreement was an agreement, and as we had entered into one with this man, whether injurious or beneficial, we must abide by it. The idea, however, of being burdened with such a fellow for three years was insupportable, and at the end of the season, on payment of $100, he consented to oblige us, in a most unexpected but gratifying manner, by taking himself off.

Notwithstanding the annoyance he had caused, Mr. Cromwell's whimsicality had rendered him sometimes very amusing. Every night he made his appearance the audience distinguished him from all the rest of the performers by a peculiar loud hiss at his entrance and exit, neglecting him entirely while on the stage. Thus, though no "star," he certainly exerted the malign influence once attributed to those bodies by exciting what, in the pit, amounted to a hurricane of displeasure, which, in its collective elements of hisses, abuse, and stampings, it might have been imagined no one could have withstood. He, however, remained always unbending as the oak before the blast which assails it. He continued his speech, he maintained his position, he looked his adversaries in the face—aye, and with a smile. He might have borrowed the language of Richard, "I can smile, and smile, and murder" (as regards his part) "while I smile." One evening, during the performance of the "Mogul Tale," in which I played Johnny Atkinson, the cobbler, Mr. Cromwell, who was playing the Mogul, instead of making his exit at the proper time, and leaving me to take my flight home by myself, persisted in remaining on the stage. Unable to conjecture his reason for this embarrassing conduct, I kept making signs to him to go off, but all in vain; and even when called from behind the scenes, he imperturbably maintained his position until the curtain dropped. On inquiring immediately with some asperity what was the meaning of his paying such disregard to the stage directions and the plot of the piece, he replied at once, "I had an excellent reason, sir." "I should be glad if you would favor me with it, then." "Oh, certainly; you must be aware, Mr. Bernard, what would have been the consequence if I had made my exit at the proper time." "Indeed, I'm not; what would?" "Why, a long and loud hissing that would have lasted, perhaps, for fifteen minutes." "Well, sir!" "Well, that hissing at my going off must, you know, have interrupted your scene; so from no interest of my own so much as to preserve you from annoyance I continued on the stage, knowing they wouldn't hiss until I was gone, and not caring, you know, when once the curtain was down, whether they hissed or not. Don't you see my reason now?" To such an argument I was not prepared to reply.

I had now a communication from Placide, the Charleston manager, informing me of the death of Jack Hatton, the theatrical eccentric, whom I had engaged when in London to come to Boston at the close of the Haymarket season. Instead, however, of keeping his word with me, he accepted an offer to go out to Charleston, where he became a great favorite. He there played a great variety of characters, some of them I should imagine very badly, yet as regards a particular class he was one of the most original actors I ever saw. But few, I am aware, have made pretensions to play the kind of character in which he excelled, but as far as my own observation goes those who have done so have wanted most of the qualifications to do them justice which he possessed. But what was his excellence? Why, something with which neither sentimental nor refined minds would, perhaps, be much pleased, because they could not sympathize with it, but which a judicious critic must, nevertheless, admire as a dramatic singularity. He was the accurate representative of low life, equally happy in the blustering boldness or swaggering gayety of the bully, or in the heartless villainy or savage triumph of the ruffian.

Though clever and original, his reputation in the profession was not very high, which arose from the fact that he rarely played, by his own consent, the characters in which he so greatly excelled, for, through a strange infatuation, which, however, I have known to bewilder some hundreds besides him, he thought himself most happy in others, for which he was in reality totally unfit; and thus he seldom came before the public but in a wrong point of view. It was this which accounted for his breach of agreement with me. I had engaged him to play low comedy; the Charleston manager offered him high tragedy; his inclinations got the mastery over his judgment, and accordingly the actor was condemned while the man was gratified.

Christmas was now approaching, and hitherto the season had proved lamentably bad. The novelties that had been successively produced had failed. To make amends for Mr. Cromwell, Fennell had been engaged for a number of nights; also Webster, the singer, almost as clever as his celebrated namesake of Drury Lane; and Mrs. Warren, late Mrs. Wignell, had concluded an engagement profitable enough for herself ($1400 for nine nights), and had returned to Philadelphia. Twaites, the comedian, who succeeded her, did not attract sufficient faces to the gallery to tell whether he looked best in a brown wig or a black one. Our "stars," in fact, however they might shine upon the stage, by no means threw a golden gleam into the treasury. At this critical period the equestrians came to town, and their novelty carried away, in a great measure, such portion of the public as had hitherto supported us. As we had honorably discharged all our obligations, and the company were continued on full salaries, our loss had been very heavy, and for the first time in my life my spirits began to sink under the depression of ill-success. The profits of my ten years' career in America as an actor had been mainly sunk in the purchase of lands, now of little or no realizable value to me; my domestic expenses were increasing, and I had reached a time of life when a man should be, not merely maintaining himself, but laying by some provision for the future.

My reflections, too, were embittered by a consideration of the certain prospects of success I had quitted in making this speculation and the profitable offers I had refused in England, both from Mr. Wroughton and Mr. Harris on account of it. However, as it was necessary I should exert myself in order to prevent matters from getting still worse, my good friend Mr. F. C. Amory addressed a letter for me to General Sheaf, in Canada, to inquire how far a professional trip to that quarter might be eligible in the summer; and I made an arrangement with Warren and Cooper to visit Philadelphia and New York at once. When we went on board the packet for the latter place, on a fine day and with a fair breeze, we augured a pleasant trip, but the wind changing in the night brought on a severe frost and a snowstorm, and the sailors' hands became so frost-bitten that they could no longer handle anything. Our situation soon grew very dangerous—a heavy sea washed away our boat and smashed the caboose house; and another, striking the vessel on her stern quarters, broke through the windows of the cabin and filled it two feet deep with water. Luckily both Mrs. Bernard and I had upper berths. The storeroom door was also burst open by the shock, and, on looking down, I saw the released turkeys, geese, and loaves dancing about merrily in the little waves; and among them my portmanteau, containing a packet of New York bills to the amount of $2000, which my bankers at Boston had intrusted to me to get changed for them. While contemplating this pleasant scene the captain came down-stairs and told us in a very serious tone that he had done his utmost and we must now take our chance for safety, a disclaimer of responsibility which might be very satisfactory to himself, but which by no means tended to tranquillize the minds of his passengers. In the next berth to me was a young sea-captain, who, having laid up his vessel for the winter, was proceeding to New York with a newly-wedded wife to make merry during Christmas. Springing upon his legs directly, with myself and one or two others after him, this gentleman ran up on deck to ascertain the real amount of our danger.

Never before had I looked on so dreary a scene. The wind was blowing hard, but the frost had glued the sails up about the mast, and stuck all the cordage together so that there was scarcely a running line at liberty. Snow,

mingled with some sleet, was falling heavily, and froze as
it fell, and the miserable blacks who composed the crew
were huddled together, quaking and shivering, and unable
to render any assistance, while all the time we were running unconsciously on the breakers a short distance ahead.
Casting a sweeping glance around, the young captain
espied the Falklands light, ran at once to the helm, put
it aside, and as the sloop veered round we heard her audi-
bly graze upon a rock before she righted. The jib was
then hoisted, and we soon after ran to shore in safety, un-
feignedly thankful for our escape. Our rescuer, on returning to his cabin, begged his lovely spouse not to be
alarmed, and inquired if she would not like some spirits
and water. Drawing a long sigh, she replied, with a droll
quaintness, which, even under such circumstances, provoked a smile:

"Spirits, indeed, I have none; but it seems as if I should
have more water soon than I wished for;" an opinion in
which we all at the time concurred.

Having at length safely reached Philadelphia, among
its hospitable, liberal, and refined inhabitants I found
many friends to remember and welcome me. My reception was a brilliant one, and I had the pleasure of seeing
every night of my performance numerous faces which
awoke the most agreeable recollections. Far more invitations flowed in on me than I could possibly accept, but
they were gratifying, nevertheless, as proofs of the continued kindly feelings which the Philadelphians had ever
shown towards the comedian, and which were fully manifested at my benefit.

At New York I opened in Lord Ogleby, but as Cooper,
Twaits, and Harwood were gone to Boston, and Mrs. Darley was ill, I found it a hard task to struggle through a
performance with so little support as I received. An invitation to my old friend's, Governor Crawford, gave me

the pleasure of being introduced to Mr. Washington Irving, an agreeable, conversable, and unprejudiced man; but in the middle of the evening, finding a peculiar taste in my mouth, I looked into the cigar stand at my feet and found, to my great surprise, that I had been expectorating blood for some time. Much alarmed, I informed my friends of the circumstance, and as they were of opinion that I must have ruptured a blood-vessel, the governor sent me home at once in his coach. As my doctor had unluckily just gone out and could nowhere be found, I lay till morning bleeding profusely from my lungs, till at last, medical assistance arriving, the hemorrhage was temporarily assuaged. Alone with a young wife three thousand miles away from her family and friends, and with my affairs in so deranged a state, our feelings during this terrible night are beyond my powers to describe.

The next day Cooper, Harwood, and the rest were to return from Boston and join me in the comedy of the "School for Scandal," and I actually played Sir Peter that evening, with a physician at the side scenes, in momentary apprehension of being stopped by a return of the hemorrhage. The next night was my benefit; but as by then I was quite unable to leave my bed, Green performed Major O'Flaherty instead of me. The receipts, however, equalled my expectation. Before long I began to recover; but my doctors agreed that I ought to abstain from all professional labors for the rest of that winter, and by good nursing and retirement try to effectually heal up the ruptured vessel and re-establish my health. To this advice I resolved to conform, and prepared at once to return to Boston. The evening before we started, Mr. Coleman, the editor of the *Evening Post*, dropped in to chat for an hour or two in his usual friendly way; but at length, pulling out his watch, rose in haste, saying he had an appointment to which he must attend. I asked him if he would not call on us in the morning before we left.

"Why," he replied, pleasantly, "I don't really know, my good friend. I should like to."

"Well," said I, "we shall not go very early, and if you are awake—"

"Oh," he interrupted, in the same peculiar tone, "depend on it, *if I'm awake*, I'll drop in to see you."

In the morning we saw no Mr. Coleman; but a week after I was informed that he had fought a duel with some gentleman of New York on the very day in question, and that he had in fact sat in my parlor and conversed with us till within half an hour of the appointed time, which pleasantly enough accounted for the ambiguity of his parting expressions.

CHAPTER XIV.

Excursion to Vermont.—Concord and Discord.—Monsieur Mallet.—State Characteristics.—Milestones and Finger-posts; an Irish Finger-post. —Burlington.—A Vermont Farmer; his Dinner and Conversation.—A Musician.—A Medical Innkeeper; his One Story.—Saratoga Springs.— Sail up the Hudson.—New Engagements.—General Humphreys and Humphreysville.—Connecticut Laws.—A Silent Town.—Profiting by a Fine.—Return to Boston.—1808 Season.—Stirring in a Matter.—" The Pilgrims."—General Theatrical Depression.—The Indian and the African.—Love and Liquor.—The Three Warnings.—The Two John Gilpins. —1809.—Boston.—Failure and Disappointment.—A New Comedy; its Prologue.—Barrett's Last Act.—Graduated Ingenuity.—Yankee Anecdotes.—Borrowing a Horse.—Buying Brandy.—Stars.—" The Forty Thieves."—Contemplated Changes.

As the spring advanced my health gradually improved, and my hopes increased of retrieving during the summer some of the time I had lost. My partners, Powell and Dickinson,* now proposed to me an excursion through

---

* SNELLING POWELL, of the firm of Powell & Dickinson, was a native of Wales. He made his American *début* in Boston in 1794, and after a varied career died there in 1821. His wife, Elizabeth Harrison, ranked very high in her profession both in England, where she supported Mrs. Siddons, and in America, where she was very popular. She succeeded her husband in the management of the Boston Theatre, and died in 1843, in the seventieth year of her age. DICKINSON, whose real name was Dickson, made his first appearance on any stage in Boston in 1796. He became joint lessee of the Boston Theatre with Powell and Bernard in 1806, and played an important part in theatrical management in America, introducing George Frederick Cook, the Duffs, and other noted actors to the American stage. He ceased to act in 1817, but continued before the public as a manager for many years, dying greatly respected in 1853. He also married a Miss Harrison, sister of Mrs. Powell, but not her equal in genius.

Vermont, with a small company and a limited wardrobe, to give an entertainment of play and farce. As this promised to be a successful trip I agreed to go, purchased a light little travelling carriage for my wife and self, and left The Lodge, our country residence, in possession of a friend, who promised to get my hay in and send my fruit to market. Our party, consisting of Powell, Dickinson, and their wives, Mallet, Morgan, myself, and Mrs. Graupner, set off from Boston in three travelling-carriages and in the best spirits and expectations. Mallet merely played—his instrument—and Mrs. Graupner was only a singer. The remaining six, therefore, had need to have had each the versatility of a Garrick in order to assume the variety and number of characters our little plays afforded, even cut down, condensed, and adapted as they were, so far as it was possible, to the strength of our miniature corps. Dickinson, for instance, in "The Jew," played Frederick Bertram, Jubal, and a fiddle in the orchestra; but, to his praise be it spoken, he played them all very well. This is a sufficient specimen of the shifts and devices we were put to.

At Concord, which from its name I should have suspected to be a settlement of Quakers, we met with but a poor reception from the genteel inhabitants and a much worse one from the lower order. Before our entertainment commenced a large throng assembled outside of the inn and began abusing and villifying us, in even worse terms than those with which these same worthies had assailed Lord North. Powell was intimidated, and would not go on with his character, but his wife, with a courage I could not but admire, persevered like a heroine. I tried to put a comical face on the matter and laugh off our annoyance, but it still continued, and in consequence little or nothing could be heard of the entertainment. At this critical juncture Monsieur Mallet, who was a better poli-

tician than a fiddle-player, came to the rescue. He had
received the rudiments of his musical education in one of
the revolutionary bands that had stirred up the Jacobin-
ical spirits of the French soldiery in 1793, and perhaps,
therefore, felt rather in his element than otherwise when
surrounded by a mob. Putting down his instrument, he
ran to the window and shouted: "Gentlemens! gentlemens!" A silence immediately prevailed. "I vas speak
one vord to you; vat vas you vant?"

"Tarnation," replied one of the mob, "why, we want
none of your company, I guess; you are reg'lar British
spies and mountebanks."

"Aha! vhat vas dat you say, sare? ve no mount on de
back—no spy. Ve artistes de Théâtre from Boston."

"Are you British, squire?"

"No; I am von Frenchman."

Here a great murmur ran through the crowd.

"A Frenchman! a Frenchman!"

"Yes, I vas von Frenchman, sare, and I glory in the
name of Frenchman, sare; I vas serve vid Napoleon in de
battle of Marengo; and I vas know vat it vas to put one
rascal to death that makes a noise outside of de vindow."

Whether the mere announcement of nationality had
satisfied them, or this latter piece of information, delivered in a very emphatic tone and with appropriate gesticulation, had its effect upon the simple-witted though turbu-
lent Vermonters—at any rate they shrank back as though
in fear, and sank into a submissive silence before the
wrathful and menacing musician. Flushed with success,
Mallet strode back to his fiddle with the air of an Alexander taking his seat among his compeers, and we finished
our performance in peace. In those days Concord certainly contained some very quarrelsome fellows.

The next town we wished to reach was Walpole, but
the roads offered by no means easy travelling. The in-

habitants of Vermont, noted for their industry, their honesty, and their stationary character, are also distinguished for a peculiar turn of humor in their remarks and some oddities of manner, being in the latter respect even more primitive than the Pennsylvanians. Their neighbors of Massachusetts (by some termed the Scotch of North America), in passing continually through this state on their way to and from Canada and the back countries, are frequently exposed to the ridicule of the inhabitants. One of the many stories in circulation bearing on this subject was that of a Bostonian travelling through Vermont, and overtaken by night on a lonely road, who at length saw a youngster some distance ahead, and apprehensive that he had mistaken his way, called out to the lad :

"Jack! Jack! I want to know which is the way to Chesterfield ?"

"How did you know my name was Jack ?" responded the youth.

"Why, I guessed it," replied the traveller.

"Oh, then you may guess your way to Chesterfield !"

Fearful of being nonplussed in a similar way myself, I was very particular each morning before I quitted the tavern to learn all I could of the road we were to pursue throughout the day, as there were few opportunities afterwards of ascertaining anything on the subject. Notwithstanding this caution, I lost my track one day, and was actually retracing my steps to Boston. I learned this in a characteristic manner when I pulled up to inquire of a countryman who was felling a tree by the roadside—

"My good friend," said I, "am I on the right road to Walpole ?"

"Yes," replied the man; "you are on the right road; but I reckon you must turn your horse's head or you'll never get there !"

The two things, however, which at this time proved the greatest annoyances to travellers through Vermont were what are generally intended to produce the very contrary effect — viz., the milestones and the finger-posts. The former were mostly either misleading from their inaccuracy or useless from their indistinctness. A peculiarity that distinguished them from the highway guides of other countries was that they invariably lay on the road with their heads pillowed softly against some knoll or bank, instead of standing upright on the ground, as we are wont to see them in England. One stone, nearly illegible from the obliterating pressure which the finger of Time had laid on its inscription, I was obliged to get out of the carriage to inspect more nearly. Neither words nor figures could I distinguish, and so far my purpose was frustrated; but just below where the information should have been I found that some one had traced two lines in pencil which were very distinct and somewhat funny, though by no means consoling—some tourist, I imagine, whose greatest merit in the matter lay in his not signing his name to them. They ran thus: "Notice to travellers! No reliance to be placed on the milestones all the way to Burlington, for they *lie*, every one of them!" But finger-posts are, of course, of much more consequence on an unknown road, intersected by cross-country lanes in abundance, which every few miles branch out again into others. Very few, however, were supplied, and the utility of these was often negatived by the careless manner in which they were attended to. For instance, you come to a branching-off in the road where either way looks as likely as the other to be the highway to the place you are seeking. You see at the moment neither house nor human being to afford you any information; but luckily, as you think, your eye lights on a board nailed against the bark of a broad-spreading oak-tree, growing just at the separation of the roads—a painted board—which will surely prove a guide. This board, however, has merely the name of the next town and the number of miles thence inscribed upon it, and though commonly called a finger-post, has no representation of either hand or finger pointing one way or the other to signify "go there." Furthermore, it has by some economical blacksmith been rendered an adjunct to the tree by means of a single nail driven through its middle. The wind and the weather shaking the tree have necessarily loosened the nail, and the board, therefore, acting on mathematical principles and the law of gravitation, has turned round on its axis, the nail, and now hangs lengthwise, with its heaviest end to the ground. The consequence is that on riding up to it for information, as I did myself, since the direction of the place can only be judged of by the direction of the letters that form its name, according to this you are led to imagine that the Sammytown or Dickyville—the object of your journey—is either from the infernal suggestion of the board some subterranean settlement in a coal-pit, or an Aladdin's cave to which you perceive no descending avenue, or, from the sublime direction of the letters, that it is situated somewhere in the celestial regions, a fact which the topography of the country, not to say the character of the inhabitants, most likely altogether denies. I must own, however, that I am puzzled to decide whether this evil of a board pointing in the wrong direction is greater or less than that of a board pointing in no direction at all, which was what I found on another occasion, when, on riding up to where four roads met, I perceived the finger - post, instead of maintaining its perpendicular, like an upright preacher, to point the true way, was lying at full length in the road, blown down most likely by some spiteful wind travelling in an opposite direction to that which the post indicated. Anyhow, here was the post entirely at my mercy, so that it was certainly in my power to raise it up again, reinstate the lower end in its abandoned hole, and then gratify my fancy by pointing its board to either of the four roads which I might choose to select.   Now, to a stranger and a traveller what could be more annoying than this, except it were that yet more peculiar highway directory which I remember meeting with in my youthful wanderings in Ireland, and which actually served the twofold purpose of a finger-post and a weather-cock, indicating both the way and the wind.   I will inform my reader how this came to pass.   The post of this truly Hibernian invention was very long, and socketed in a hole dug in very firm clay, wide enough for the post to move round in, and yet too deep for it to fall out.   The board was a long shutter, which had in its youth, I believe, flapped backward and forward at some sheeben-house window, employed only to darken its few inhabitants, but was now set up on high to enlighten the community at large on sundry topographical and aerial matters.   Standing on a heath where four roads met, it had pointed originally in the direction of a principal town attainable by one of these roads, till the wind beating the shutter had gradually loosened the post, and now whirled it round at will.   The few cabins, therefore, that skirted the heath within sight of the finger-post took their weather observations from it accordingly; as, for instance one might hear:

"Teddy, darlint, which way does the finger-post point this morning?"

"To Ballyborough, daddy."

"Oh, by the powers, thin the wind's north."

The next day, perhaps, it would be:

"Shall we have any luck to-day, Judy?"

"As sure as black's the blue of your eye."

"And why, thin, jewel?"

"Bekase the wind's south, and south's always a lucky wind."

"Ah, but where does the finger-post point to ?"

"To Crooskeen, dare."

"Oh, tunder and turf! does it point there, Judy. Sure enough, no luck for us then; for doesn't the steward live in Crooskeen, and who the divil ever heard of luck coming from him ?"

Our performance at Walpole, when at last we reached it, did little more than pay our tavern bill; we therefore pushed on to Burlington, the principal town in Vermont, situated on Lake Champlain, where we expected better success. Meeting here with some friends from Boston on a tour, a fishing-party was proposed, and a worthy Vermont farmer, whom I met with at the inn, undertook to conduct us to a good spot for sport; nor were we disappointed, as Lake Champlain abounds with rare and delicate fish of all kinds. At our guide's pressing request I then rode out to his farm, a few miles from Burlington, to dine with him. Here, having walked me about his grounds two or three hours, in order to give me an appetite, he set me down to pork and beans, with their everlasting accompaniment of molasses, to be washed down by a jug of sparkling cider. Then followed a pumpkin pie, with some peaches and melons as a dessert, the whole winding up with a tumbler apiece of old St. Croix rum. Such was a Vermont dinner, and though it might seem to an English epicure rather an odd assemblage of sweets and sours, I confess that my appetite at the time was too good to find fault with it. The farmer was a good sample of his class, and a very worthy and industrious, though prejudiced and illiterate, sort of body, whose language and ideas were eminently characteristic of the Northern American. As he luckily touched neither upon politics nor agriculture, excusable as the latter would have been in a man of his profession, I was spared the trial of listening to accounts of how many British were thrashed in one place, or how much corn in another. Far different from these was the farmer's favorite theme, which was certainly, for him, rather a singular one, being none other than literature, upon which subject he took every opportunity of discoursing, with some degree of fluency, and in a manner which well brought out his character. Having no objection myself to this topic, he found in me an amused as well as surprised listener; so, sipping a mouthful of his liquor, he locked his toes in the under rail of his chair legs, and hooking his thumbs in the armholes of his waistcoat, threw himself back against the wainscot and enunciated his opinions in that particular tone which I have often observed in such talkers, mingling the pride of simplicity with the authority of indifference. In the first place he informed me that he reckoned himself a tolerable good scholar, having been soundly instructed in the knowledge of those two instruments of literature—reading and writing, besides a branch of geometry, viz., arithmetic. Then he "always 'voted his evenin's to readin' and larnin'," and besides the constant perusal of three books in his own possession, namely, the Bible, the almanac, and the dictionary, he took in a weekly paper and regularly rode over to Burlington once a fortnight to see what there might be new and cleverish in the book-store. "Now," he continued, "I've read Goldsmith's 'History of Rome;' that's rather a cute book, I reckon, and I like it much. And then there's them volumes of Josephus—ha'n't you never read 'em? they're considerably well done, I think. And then there's the Nat'ral History, Buchan's 'Med'cin,' and Lindley Murray's Grammar, and some more of the like I know well. Them are all judgmatical books, I reckon. What do you think on 'em? I never have read no rumances or poetry, but two—'Pilgrim's Progress' and 'Robinson Crusoe;' don't see there's much genius in 'em; them are too 'belittling' as Mr. Jefferson says, for a man to read." With such a stock of information, of course, the farmer considered himself a literary man, and was of opinion that one was able, after all, to get quite a sufficient "lot of larnin'" without going to any extraordinary trouble or expense for it. Classical acquirements he ridiculed altogether, because "what, in all creation, had livin' people to do with dead languages?" while he looked on all colleges and universities as nothing more than aristocratical institutions, expensive without utility, and very unfit for a free country like the "States," since they shut out the poor from instruction only to receive the sons of the highborn and rich to make them acquainted, under the show of study, with the vices of gaming, drinking, and wenching. Thus declaimed my eccentric but worthy entertainer, until, at a very late hour, I bade him farewell, saddled my horse and rode back to Burlington.

Though our performance here was pretty well attended, yet, as it did not equal our expectations, we gave out a second, rather more attractive, but which did little better. At this Powell gave in, thoroughly disappointed with the excursion, which had merely paid our expenses, and resolved to return to Boston instead of proceeding any farther. Dickinson coincided with him, having come to the conclusion that we were too many for any country town to remunerate properly; and the others being of the same opinion, they agreed to form a party and take a circuit northward by themselves. Thus I was left alone to prosecute the intended trip to Albany and the Springs. I did not despair, nevertheless, thinking that perhaps, after all, the arrangement might prove to my advantage.

In order to provide myself with cash I disposed of my horse and carriage, the latter at cost price, the former for one hundred dollars, having only given thirteen for him. Horses have been through life one of the few things in which I have been lucky, either in purchasing or selling.

Fortunately, too, a gentleman whom I had met with at the inn, and who was proceeding to Albany with his newly-married wife in a light pleasure wagon, made me and Mrs. Bernard a friendly offer to bear them company, a proposal to which I agreed with much pleasure.

As the horses, decked each with a row of bells on its collar, were young, spirited animals, the wagon ran lightly on springs, the weather was extremely fine, the roads good, and the country we passed through green and luxuriant, everything seemed to unite to render this ride, a distance of nearly a hundred miles, very agreeable. We slept the first night at an inn on the road, where we not only met with good accommodation, but also with what was rather a curiosity, namely, a private museum. This had been the collection of some unknown *virtuoso*, whose name even I could not learn, and who had found valuable resources for his purpose in the unexplored and hardly-spoken-of regions of the interior of the States. It contained a large gathering of rarities in mineral and vegetable productions, insects and reptiles, which had evidently cost some trouble and expense to obtain, and which, if I could at all rely on the opinion of my friend, who professed to be acquainted with the subject, exhibited much knowledge and taste in their arrangement. America, although the country which of all others presents, from its newness, a fine field of research to the *connoisseur* and of description to the poet, is at present rather exclusively the sphere of scientific and commercial genius. No doubt, therefore, the person who adopted such a pursuit as had been here followed occasioned no little surprise to his neighbors, and met with some ridicule for the unprofitable manner in which he employed his money, not suffering it to accumulate in a bank, or putting it out to the common uses of trade, but actually converting it into odd-looking stones and dead insects, of no intrinsic or exchangeable value whatever. Then, too, the idea of a man's affording so much rubbish the best room in his house, and seeming to derive so much pleasure from inspecting and arranging them! At this gentleman's death he left his house and museum to a relative, who, not possessing similar tastes to himself, very much undervalued his acquisitions, and sold both to the present occupant, who turned the house into an inn and the museum into a public exhibition.

On reaching Salem, a neat little town, somewhat smaller than its namesake in Massachusetts, we put up at an inn kept by Dr. Allen, a physician. Here I met with an agreeable surprise. Some person who had lately been on a lecturing tour in this direction had assumed my name, but being very deficient in talent, suspicion arose, from my known popularity, that he was an impostor. As we drove through the town some one recognized me, and the news getting abroad, before we had been housed half an hour a dozen inquirers dropped in to know if I were the real Simon Pure. This seeming a good hint to me to perform, I sent out my bills for that evening, and was very well received.

Our medical host was a conversable and rather clever man, though noted for one peculiarity which more often raised a laugh against than with him. He had an only story, which, like parents with an only child, he took pleasure in bringing forward on every occasion. The humor of the matter, for one who was aware of his propensity, lay in observing the various modes he would adopt to make an opening for its introduction. A man with one story is not a very unusual character in society, and is generally, I think, an amusing one. I read once, in some old volume of essays, of one who, being a man of property and in the habit of seeing much company, used to keep two or three fowling-pieces ready loaded in his house, which his servants were ordered to discharge several times a day about his grounds, just to supply him with a cue for telling his story, a device which served his purpose very well at first, but in the end ruined him, owing to the expense he was at for gunpowder. The doctor had no such costly, preconcerted signal, his ingenious brain suggesting ever-new pretexts for the repetition of his favorite anecdote. Of its general applicability the reader may judge when I thus retail it. The doctor had a particular friend in the town who had hired a highly-recommended Massachusetts man to take charge of his garden, and was himself very fond of assisting in this work. One day, while pruning a tree in his orchard, with the gardener standing by, his hand which held the knife slipped and inflicted so severe a wound on his leg that the blood gushed from it in a torrent. His helper, looking on quite coolly, merely remarked: "Them stockings, I reckon, squire, are worth three and sixpence a pair; how unfortunate to spoil 'em!"

At Albany we parted with our friends, and set off the next morning by stage for Balston and Saratoga Springs. From the medicinal properties of these waters and their agreeable situation in the midst of a fine country, they are now becoming the summer point of attraction to all the gentry of the States who leave home either for health or pleasure. Powell and I thought, therefore, that they would support the establishment of a theatre for a few weeks in the season, and the object of my present visit was to ascertain how far such a plan might be likely to succeed. This year there was so great an overflow of visitors that I had great difficulty in procuring accommodation for my wife and self, from which fact I augured favorably. I was so fortunate, too, as to meet at the principal hotel with Governor Crawford, Judge Kelly, from Annapolis, and Mr. Pinkney, the member of Congress, who took the matter in hand for me with the most friendly readiness. The result of their inquiries, however, was contrary to what I expected, for they advised me to decline the business altogether, since from the small number of residents, the great uncertainty of the seasons, and the distance between Boston and the Springs, which must inevitably render our travelling expenses very heavy, the chances of success were against us. With thanks for their kindness, we took their advice. I gave a night's entertainment at the Springs, which, owing to the numerous and potential friends I had met with there, was brilliantly attended, and then returned in good spirits to Albany. In this city, which was afterwards to be the scene of my management, I made my *début* as a lecturer, and was well pleased with my reception.

Steamboats were now running on the Hudson between New York and Albany, and from their elegance, certainty, and convenience, no less than their novelty, were eagerly resorted to. I must confess that I felt them to be the most surprising and delightful conveyances I had ever beheld. Unluckily for us, however, so great was the throng of passengers that we found all the berths already taken in the first boat that sailed, so that we had no resource but to go by the sailing-packet. As, however, we met unexpectedly some agreeable companions on board, who seemed, like myself, to have plenty of time on their hands, with proper disposition to enjoy it, we had a most pleasant trip. We were specially favored by the gentle humor of old Æolus, who wafted rather than blew us along, permitting us to sit under an awning on the deck and enjoy the luxuriant and picturesque appearance of the banks; and, when we had reached the Highlands, to take leisurely views of some of the most romantic spots to be witnessed, perhaps, in America. Though, therefore, we were full five days in performing the distance, which the steamboat would have done in thirty-six hours, yet every one but the captain thought our dilatory progress a singular advantage, and to this hour I remember my first sail upon the Hudson as the most delightful of all my voyages, whether on sea or streams.

The object of my visit to New York was to engage Mrs. Woodham, an actress singularly clever, both in comedy and melodrama, Mrs. Stanley having accepted an engagement from the Charleston management on rather higher terms than we could afford. The latter was the superior actress in her special line, but Mrs. Woodham was the more versatile, and played characters of greater novelty and attraction. I renewed the engagement with John Darley, Sr.,* whose English ballad-singing was so delightful and well appreciated. I likewise came to terms with Mr. Mills, since we could no longer depend at all upon

---

* JOHN DARLEY, Sr., was originally a bucket-maker in Birmingham, England. He possessed a remarkably fine voice, and appeared in concert, and afterwards upon the regular stage in his own country. He was not distinguished as an actor; but as a singer of English ballads he is said to have been equalled, in his day, only by Incledon. He was carried to America by Wignell, with his son, John Darley, Jr., in 1793, and first appeared in Annapolis, Md. In 1796 he was in New York, but at the end of ten or twelve years he returned to England, where he died in 1819.

The younger Darley, after singing in concert with his father, saw some service in the United States Navy, married the beautiful and brilliant Ellen Westray and returned to the stage in 1804, sustaining the leading parts in English opera without a rival in America for many years. He retired with a competency in 1840, and died in 1853.

John Darley, Sr., was the son of Matthew Darley, a somewhat eccentric but talented painter, engraver, and etcher of the school of Hogarth, and particularly celebrated as a caricaturist. There is extant a rare portrait of him, painted and engraved by himself, in which the family resemblance can readily be traced. No mention is anywhere made of the artistic abilities of either his son or his grandson, but several sons of the younger John Darley have been artists, the most distinguished of them being the Felix O. C. Darley of to-day—a marked instance of the transmission of genius.

Caulfield, and this new accession proved the cleverer act-
or of the two. Having also engaged his wife and William
Robertson, we then immediately took the packet for New
Haven, on our way home; and as, under a light breeze, our
little vessel flew along like a sea-bird, it was a complete
contrast to what had been our progress down the Hudson.
Not being pressed for time, we delayed a day at New Haven
in order to pay a visit to Humphreysville, the estate of my
sincere and valuable friend, General Humphreys, which
was situated about twelve miles from that town, and where
he was in the habit of passing most of the summer. As
a soldier, a diplomatist, and an author, the general has acquired three distinct reputations, any one of which alone
would have handed his name down to posterity; but he
had rendered so many important services to his country
that his claims as a patriot were perhaps greatest of all.
He was the original importer of the Merino sheep into
America, for which he received a medal from the Agricultural Society, and he had established on his estate several
manufactories, paper-mills, etc., upon improved systems
of machinery and labor, which had their beneficial effect
upon similar works in general. Meeting with a cordial
reception, we passed the day with him, had the pleasure
of inspecting his grounds, and returned in the evening to
New Haven. As, however, the next day was Sunday, and,
according to the laws of Connecticut, it was criminal to
violate Sabbath rest by putting one's self in motion, we
were constrained to abide there until the Monday morning.
Our host at the inn was a very communicative and humorous kind of man, not at all of a piece with the inhabitants
in general, and, though obliged to submit to the laws of
the place in which he lived, by no means backward in expressing his opinion of them to his customers. From this
oracle I gathered some further information as to the working of the famous Blue Laws. As is well known, they

MR. DARLEY AS PERFORMING IN THE ORCHESTRA AT VAUXHALL.

entirely forbade trade or travelling upon the Sabbath; so that by the letter of the law all goods bought or sold upon that day were forfeited to the state, while not, on the most urgent plea of necessity, might an animal be permitted to clink his profane hoof upon the Sabbatical stones of New Haven. From the growing spirit of commerce in the country at large, and the unlucky situation of Connecticut, which rendered it the thoroughfare for business, it was found, however, to be every day—or rather every seventh day—a more difficult task to carry these regulations into effect. Accordingly a multitude of peace-officers under the various titles of beadles, constables, and street-keepers, were posted all day in the streets and avenues, to enforce strict maintenance of that quietude which the statutes enjoined. It was their business to take care that no person appeared without-doors during "meeting time," and on the entry of a traveller into the town, immediately to stop him, lead his horse to a stable and himself to the "meeting."

Thus a sense of duty induced them to violate the law themselves in order to compel its observance by others. The deathlike dulness and absolute privation of sound which prevailed throughout the day can hardly be imagined. The labor of eating dinners, prepared on the previous Saturday, seemed to be looked on as a lamentable necessity, and though such noises as coughing and sneezing were excused if quite spontaneous, it was directly forbidden to induce them by taking snuff, or carelessly letting your liquor go the wrong way. I know not whether the chattering of a man's teeth in an ague fit would have been considered reprehensible, but in the case of your hands becoming dirty I am persuaded that it would have been held more correct to let them remain so than to resort to the labor of using soap, water, and towel. Under the influence of this mournful contrast to the pleasurable tran-

quillity or the light-hearted, innocent gayety of a European Sunday I really conceived myself abstracted from
the world, or, rather, like the personage in one of the
Arabian Tales who wandered into a petrified city and in
the midst of human habitations beheld no sign of life.
But while every noise was totally suppressed in-doors,
what does my reader suppose he would hear or observe
were he to take his seat with me at one of the inn windows and survey the streets? For the most part he would
hear nothing, for when the inhabitants were allowed to
issue from their doors they stole about the highways like
so many sprites or like the mysterious heroes in Mrs. Rad-
cliff's romances, so light were their movements and their
steps so inaudible. The principal object in sight would
be those guardians of the peace already mentioned, looking like a detachment of Cromwell's body-guard as they
march to and fro with the utmost precision and solemnity,
arrayed in the square-cut garments which betokened their
office. Perhaps, at last, some luckless pig would waddle
forth from an avenue upon a muddy research. Alas, his
first grunt of triumph, as he lighted upon some spoil, would
serve as a signal to his enemies, one of whom would secure
him on the instant, drive him ignominiously home to his
sty, and there execute retributive justice for his pagan disregard of sacred ordinances by forthwith despatching him.
Or should some caitiff dog, or even thoughtless puppy, in
profligate contempt of the law, begin frolicking and bark-
ing in the road, he would be summarily shot upon the
spot. Or perhaps some gentleman cat, amorously disposed, would be so unfortunate as to commence an ill-
timed feline serenade under the gutter of his adored
tabby; the vigilant street-keepers, attracted by the sound,
would rush to the place, and at the moment, perhaps,
when a tender response was awakening in the bosom and
the throat of Grimalkin, and the passionate duetto of the

hapless pair rising to a climax, both would be assailed with a battery of staff and stones, to the interruption of their loves and great peril of their lives. The plea was manifest that "love's labor" could no more be permitted than any other worker's. On the inhabitants proceeding to and from meeting these careful conservators of the public tranquillity had to take cognizance of young and old, and prevent any stoppages or chatterings on the way, a nod on such occasions being considered indecorous, and a shake of the hand a tangible impropriety.

In latter years, when beginning to find it impossible to restrain altogether the current of intercourse which flowed through their state, these puritanical worthies resolved to convert the restriction into a source of pecuniary profit, and accordingly permitted a man to pursue his journey on payment of a fine, proportioned, I believe, either to the number of his horses or of his family. A sharp-witted Yankee, returning home through Connecticut, was stopped, therefore, at a little village, and requested to pay the fine, which he consented to do if he were taken before the magistrate who was to receive it, and who was a man of great property and extensive mercantile connections. The Yankee, tearing a leaf from his pocket-book, wrote thereon a few words, and presenting it to the magistrate with the money, requested him to sign a receipt for the few shillings, in order that he might not be called on to pay the fine twice over, should he be stopped again before the morrow. So reasonable a request being unhesitatingly complied with, the traveller put the paper in his pocket and departed, apparently in no worse humor for the interruption he had encountered. About ten days afterwards, business calling the magistrate to Boston, he took occasion to step into his banker's to look over his account, when they informed him that they had duly honored his last week's draft for one hundred dollars. He stared in surprise. They produced it for him, and he immediately recognized the handwriting of the Yankee, with his signature plainly attached.

I arrived in Boston, re-established in health, and not out of pocket, by one of the pleasantest excursions I had hitherto undertaken in the States. The company being assembled, we opened the season with Mrs. Woodham as Frank Heartall and the Widow Cheerly to a very brilliant audience, presaging, I thought, some success, though falsely, as it proved, since this season, in villainous imitation of its predecessors, did not even pay its expenses. Our hopes had been buoyed up in one way or another till its close, when, the unmistakable deficit staring us in the face, we had no other consolation than that of reflecting that, if we were so many hundred dollars in debt, it was not owing to any want of exertion on our part. Mills and Mrs. Woodham had succeeded very well, while Caulfield had nevertheless kept his ground in public favor, owing to the numerous acquaintances he had made; and I now wrote to Mrs. Stanley, in hopes of engaging her on rather lower terms than she had demanded. Green had not joined us, but continued with Mrs. West; Usher, whom I had taken from among the supernumeraries at Philadelphia and advanced to a situation in Boston, had returned from Quebec to engage some of our company, but only applied to those we could well dismiss. From his father, in Kentucky, I received another letter, pressing me to undertake a speculation in that quarter, and pointing out the particular towns which would form a profitable circuit. I had, however, two seasons yet to sustain in Boston, and the great distance to the back countries suggested a hundred difficulties, which I did not like to encounter. Barrett was out of employment at New York; Cooper starring at Philadelphia; Mrs. Warren still attractive; poor Bates, a restless, visionary fellow, engaged to

us for a few nights and a benefit. A Mr. Morse made his
début with us in Osmond, and was tolerably successful;
and that sad speculator, Fennell, who had not got over
his saltworks embarrassments, wanted to perform for a
few nights, in order that by paying his deluded creditors
a trifle he might keep them from putting his honorable
person in " durance vile." Since that speculation he had
attempted another—an academy near Boston upon a very
magnificent scale. Having fixed upon a suitable house
and grounds, he proceeded to make designs for reading-
rooms, lecture-rooms, class-rooms, etc., without having a
shilling in his pocket to carry out such schemes; but no
sooner was the pleasant work of planning over than he
immediately wearied of the whole affair. Such was the
state of theatricals, as connected with ourselves, at the
close of the year 1808.

Our musical parties were in as great vogue as ever this
season, though we had no new members, and, as usual, I
had a multiplicity of invitations to dinners, etc., but, fearing for my health, continued to reside at "The Lodge"
until winter set in, when I removed with my family into
town. The road out to Dorchester, over the "Neck," as
it is called, was at this time even dangerously bad, and in
my daily drives into town I had to practise a difficult kind
of land navigation in steering the gig clear of an immense
bank of stones and mud on one side, while with hair-
breadth exactness I skirted the brink of an unfathomable
gully on the other. These rides acquainted me with a
laughable incident connected with the state of the neighborhood.

A gentleman residing on the " Neck " had a slough before his door of such depth and dimensions as to render
his house all but inaccessible. A " select committee "
having been appointed for the repair of this highway, he
had applied repeatedly to have the slough in question

filled up; but their only answer, from week to week, was:
"By and by, dear sir. But we really cannot stir in the
matter at present." One morning, after a heavy rainfall,
the slough overflowed, and pretty well completed the im-
prisonment of the gentleman in his own house. There
was, however, solace in store for his captivity. It happened the same day that some business called two of the
"selectmen" from town, and their route lay over the
"Neck." Driving by in a gig at a furious rate, and with
some heedlessness, their wheel slid into the gully as they
were passing it, and in an instant the gig was upset, and
both of them precipitated into the filth up to their mid-
dles. The gentleman at the adjacent house, happening to
be at his window, was a witness of this retributive accident, and throwing up his sash as they were attempting
to scramble out of the pool, called out to them laughing-
ly: "Thank you, gentlemen; thank you. I see you are
really 'stirring in the matter' at last!"

The season proceeded with little spirit, and we lost an
excellent friend to the theatre by the death of Governor
Sullivan. Shortly after, however, I brought forward a
play in three acts, entitled "The Pilgrims, or the Landing
of our Forefathers," which locality alone would have rendered a success, as many of the descendants of the first
settlers were still residing in Boston, but, supported by a
strong company, the little merit it possessed was favorably
recommended to the public. It proved, as I had anticipated, "a good card," and, when everything else failed,
drew tolerable houses to the close of the season. At
Christmas I received an invitation to visit New York
during our month's recess at home, but declined it from
apprehensions with regard to health. Mrs. Stanley arrived
in Boston from a country circuit she had been taking;
but as we could not agree upon terms, she quitted us for
a lucrative and agreeable situation in the Canadas, to per-

form there in private with the military amateurs. By the letters I received I learned that theatricals were in a most lamentable state all over the continent. New York and Philadelphia were not paying their expenses, Charleston even worse, and Mrs. West's circuit in Virginia was done up altogether. Thus we had abundance of that negative consolation which some people pretend to derive from the reflection that there are others as badly or worse off than themselves. At last the season came to a close, nothing particular having distinguished it except the *début* of Master Payne, the "American Roscius," in April, 1809, which created some sensation in the theatrical world.*

As the spring advanced I removed my wife to "The Lodge," and, as she was unable to travel, passed the summer in visiting the towns within a hundred miles of Boston, returning home at the end of every two or three weeks, and thus passing my time both profitably and pleasantly. The only incident I remember now of those rambles is the following: Among other places I paid a visit to Newport, with letters of recommendation to Mr. Baring, of London, from whose family I had received attentions in my early days. I had a very brilliant attendance at night, and among my auditors a very infirm old gentleman, who was more or less lame, blind, and deaf. When I began my favorite recitation of "The Three Warnings," this gentleman seemed to pay particular attention, but when I came to the lines

---

* JOHN HOWARD PAYNE, remembered as the author of "one immortal song," was also the author of many plays which are now almost forgotten, and as the Boy Actor, the first of a long line of infant phenomena in America, he met with marvellous success throughout the United States. He made his first appearance as Young Norval, in "Douglas," at the Park Theatre, New York, in 1809, and played the part in Boston in the same year. He appeared in London, still as Young Norval, in 1813, but as he grew in years he declined in grace as an actor, and soon retired from the stage.

" The unwelcome messenger of Death
Once more before him stood,"

he fell back in his chair, uttered a slight shriek, and faint-
ed. He was carried out immediately, and soon restored
to his senses, but did not return to the entertainment.
This circumstance unavoidably threw a gloom over the
company, which, for some time, not all my humorous
efforts could remove, till at last another incident as much
befriended as the other had distressed me. Among my
comic recitations was Cowper's "John Gilpin," and no
sooner had I commenced this than a loud and general
shout of laughter ran round the room, which kept increasing as I proceeded. At length I discovered the cause.
Mr. John Gilpin, a merchant and resident in the town,
occupied a front seat, and having a wife who was rather
fond of him, the story suggested to the minds of the
assembly sundry humorous coincidences. The object of
this merriment bore it with the best humor imaginable,
laughing himself at all the points, and thus quite disarm-
ing any who might have been satirically disposed.

The season of 1809–10 commenced with very inauspicious prospects, and verified our worst apprehensions as it
proceeded. Various novelties prepared during the recess
were brought forward at much expense and with able performers, but comparatively failed; and the opera, upon
which, from the musical disposition of the town, we had
placed great dependence, though supported by Webster,
John Darley, Mrs. Mills, Mrs. Claude Dickinson, and myself, never did more than draw the expenses. This was
the more grievous since New York, Philadelphia, and
Charleston had all by this time recovered from their depression, and were now playing to $1000 nightly. From
the losses I had hitherto sustained, and the gloomy prospects before me, I began now bitterly to reproach myself
for having meddled with management, and wasted five of

JOHN HOWARD PAYNE AS YOUNG NORVAL.

From a painting by Leslie.

the most valuable years of my life in merely getting my livelihood, when I ought to have been realizing an independence. But this cannot interest my reader.

We expected Cooper and Master Payne to join us soon, and in the interim we produced with great *éclat* a comedy, by Mr. White, of Boston, the author inducing us to engage Fennell, who was then in town, to perform one of the characters. Robert Treat Paine wrote a prologue for it in his usual inimitable manner, which I agreed to speak; but, from Paine's negligent habit, I only received it on Saturday, and, finding it one hundred and eighty lines in length, I sent it back to him with an assurance that I could not get perfect in it so as to do it justice by the Monday evening when the comedy was to be produced. Fennell happening to be with him when this message arrived, promptly offered to recite it himself, a proposal which Paine caught at with pleasure. Fennell took the prologue home with him to study, but when the evening came did not know a syllable of it, and, coming forward to the audience, craved their permission to *read* it. After some hesitation this was granted, and Fennell delivered the lines, sparkling as they were with wit and humor, with so much of the correctness of the scholar and the stateliness of the tragedian as to throw a gloom over the audience which it took all the first act of the comedy to efface.

One day I was called out from rehearsal to speak to a gentleman in a coach, and, opening the door, discovered poor Barrett* in a sad, emaciated state. Stretching out his shrivelled hand to me, he exclaimed: "Ah, Johnny, I am come to die with you!" though, but for his appearance, the tone in which he spoke would have induced me to

---

* Giles L. Barrett, the father of the well-known "Gentleman George" Barrett, was a popular leading actor in more than one English provincial theatre. He arrived in America in 1796, but was past his prime, and never achieved greatness on the American stage.

think he was jesting. I had him removed to some lodgings, where his death did indeed take place a few days
after, and we interred the once famous actor in a now
forgotten grave.

Being invited to a party this winter, at the house of
General Humphreys, beneath whose social and hospitable
roof some of my happiest hours were passed, the conversation in the course of the evening turned upon Yankee
characteristics, and several gentlemen present afforded
humorous illustrations of the one by which they are chiefly
distinguished—viz., ingenuity—relating various anecdotes,
two only of which I remember.

A Yankee, performing a journey through the back countries on foot, saw two horses in a field as he passed along,
one of which he determined to borrow for a few miles, as
he was feeling very weary. Accordingly, writing in pencil on a slip of paper that he would leave the beast at the
next town on the road, he tied the note to one horse's fet-
lock, and, mounting the other, with merely a halter for a
bridle, rode off with him. This transaction happening to
be observed, an alarm was given to the owner of the
animals, who, saddling the remaining one, without paying
any attention to the note attached to its leg, rode away
after the unknown borrower, or, as he considered him,
perhaps, thief. Unluckily for the Yankee, he was mounted
on a slow traveler compared with the steed he had left behind, and he soon descried with some consternation a rider
behind urging a powerful beast along the road at full
speed, evidently in pursuit of him. Having neither whip
nor spur, he found it a difficult matter to impel the horse
he rode beyond its usual pace, and his pursuer, therefore,
had every chance of coming up with him directly. At
this moment he perceived a cottage by the roadside at no
great distance, towards which, by blows and kicks, he
urged his steed somewhat faster, the farmer gaining on

him nevertheless at every step. Reaching the door, he dismounted, and went in. The farmer, riding up immediately after in a tremendous passion, threw himself off his horse, leaving it by the side of its fellow, and ran into the cottage to seize and secure the thief. The Yankee, however, was prepared for him. Having slipped up-stairs, he opened the front window, which looked out upon the road, and as the farmer ran into the house let himself down outside, mounted the saddled horse, seized the other by the halter, and rode off securely with both. The hero of the second story was at least as ingenious. A new liquor warehouse opening at Boston on a ready-money and low-price system, Jonathan walked in one day with a two-gallon keg on his shoulder, and asked for a gallon of the best brandy. The liquor having been poured through a funnel into his keg the money was demanded. Pretending ignorance of their mode of doing business, the Yankee said that he would pay the next time he came into town. The shopman demurred, saying that he did not intend to give any credit. "But," asked the Yankee in mock surprise, "do you intend to take back the brandy?"

"To be sure," replied the other, "if you don't pay for it."

"Then," said he, "you must bring your measure, for I had some liquor of my own in the keg."

This was done, a gallon of the contents measured back, and the fellow marched off with another gallon of fine grog, having half filled his keg beforehand with *water*.

Master Payne and other "stars" now visited us, and shed a temporary glimmer over the dulness of our theatrical hemisphere; but we had little relief on the whole, as the darkness only seemed greater after their departure. At length, after great trouble and expense in getting up, we produced the fairy romance of "The Forty Thieves," which proved one of the most successful hits within my knowledge, and by the crowded audiences it drew to the end of the season in some measure compensated us for preceding losses, enabling me to pay in cash, though not in gratitude, the generous friend who had helped me.

At a musical party I was introduced to a Major Henry, just arrived from Canada, who urged me strongly to visit that country, and try to establish a circuit. Albany, I was aware, I could procure at any time, and on this consideration made a proposal to Powell to throw up my share in the Boston concern for $1200 and a benefit. As, however, Dickinson intended proceeding to England for reinforcements, and I meant to visit Canada, I resolved to form my final determination according to the success of the ensuing season.

Visit to Canada.—Anticipations.—A Retired Actress.—Vermont Travelling.—Wit and Humor.—Mixed Society.—Whitehall Table Fray.—Democrat's Estimate of Titles.—Steamboat Pleasures and Terrors.—A Canadian Vehicle.—Swamp Stories.—Driver's Test of Danger.—View of Montreal.—The Theatre.—Actors' Rivalries.—An Indian Settlement.—Off to Quebec.—A Canadian Cottager.—General Sheaf.—Universal Music.—A Forger's School.—A Bateau Party.—A Lone House and its Mistress; Unexpected Company and Unwelcome Revelry.—Reception at Quebec.—New Theatres Proposed.—Amateurs *vs.* Professionals.—Last Season at Boston.—Native Dramatists.—Tom Moore's Sister-in-law.—"*Femme Propose.*"—George Frederick Cooke.—Heroes and Villians.—Mossop.—Macklin and Cooke compared.—Macklin and his Scotch Schoolmaster.—Cooke's Generosity and Eccentricity.—Kemble's Portrait.—An Intrusive Fiddler and his Punishment.

OBTAINING letters from my best friends at Boston, I prepared for my first visit to Canada this summer in tolerable spirits. I had let my country-house for a year, heard a favorable account of my property in Portland, and had a new field open before me. I anticipated, therefore, that by a few years' exertion I should yet weather the storm of difficulties in which I was at present laboring, and escaping both the quicksands of extravagance and the rocks of despondency, the bark of the dramatic mariner might yet outlive all dangers and attain, towards the close of its voyage, a fair and tranquil haven.

At Grotton we made our first halt in order to pay a visit of a few hours to Mrs. Moore (late Mrs. Woodham*), who,

* Mr. and Mrs. WOODHAM were brought to Philadelphia from England, by Wm. Warren, in 1805. The lady was very beautiful and very popular. She played such parts as Volante and the Widow Chervley at the Chestnut

with her new husband, a solicitor, had retired from all the cares and allurements of the world to this secluded village. Pleased as I was to see her happiness, I confess that it surprised me, considering that a few months before all her pleasure had seemed to centre in her profession. When once a woman makes her *début* on "the Boards," from that moment her talents are somehow considered as public property, in which every individual who frequents the theatre conceives he has a share, and therefore some right of controlling her disposal of them. Thus the gallants of Boston felt themselves aggrieved when this lady quitted the stage, and considering their amusement paramount to her happiness, thought she acted improperly in gratifying one man at the expense of a thousand. I believe this to be a very general feeling in such cases.

Brought by the Burlington stage to Rutland, we there engaged a man to drive us in his wagon to Whitehall, to catch the steamer which started thence next day, and this conclusion of our journey was more diabolical and temper-trying than all I had ever encountered before. The road ran either through swamps, or over high, stony, almost perpendicular hills, which we had to walk up in order to lighten the vehicle as much as possible, and which we preferred to walk down, because our driver, saying he wanted to "make up for los' time," whenever he gained the top of an ascent would give his horses the whip and gallop them headlong to the bottom, to the imminent peril of every neck concerned. The swamp roads, however, were still worse, being simply made by throwing cut-down trees of immense circumference across the track at equal intervals, with nothing between, so that our wagon, like a boat on a rough sea, had always one end up and one down. The said wagon was a mere oblong, unpainted box, with three

Street house, with great success. She was in New York in 1805, and, as Mrs. Moore, first appeared in Boston as Lady Teazle in 1816.

seats nailed across, and without springs or cushions, a little grease on the wheels supplying the place of the former, and a scanty sprinkling of straw the place of the latter luxury, while the horses drew us along at a villainous jog-trot, too slow for a hackney coach and too fast for a funeral. Our driver was an odd compound of Yankee, Vermonter, and Hollander; he had the small, gray, twinkling eye, and the twang and humor of the first; the "do-as-I-please" physiognomy, and much of the honest principle of the second; while his clumsy, rotund, ungenteel figure and quiet, dilatory, methodical manners were decidedly Dutch. He united these threefold characteristics not less distinctly in his discourse; for from the abundance of his guesses, calculations, and reckonings, he was as supposititious and indecisive as any New-Englander; in his opinions as stubborn as a mule, and therefore a Vermonter; while in the style of his delivery he savored of the sluggish Scheldt, his words coming from him as slowly and sparingly as though his tongue furnished them by contract and was not sure of being paid. I would that I could amuse my reader by repeating some of his many comical remarks, but as they were humorisms rather than witticisms, which were suggested by circumstances of the time and place, without such settings their value would be lost. Wit, consisting of ideas, may be considered the sterling coin of literature, of intrinsic worth and exchangeable in all civilized countries; while humor, lying rather in words, may be termed the paper money of conversation, and of only relative and local value. If during our communications our driver had offered me any of the precious metal, I might have offered it again to my reader with satisfaction; but as we exchanged nothing but some humorous notes, things of accommodation to facilitate intercourse, in another place and at the present day they would be of little worth. We certainly had time to become acquainted, for though we had started at four o'clock in the morning, we did not finish the twenty-five miles of our journey until nearly eleven, just an hour after the steamer had taken its departure. We had, therefore, to wait a week at the hotel at Whitehall, till the boat should start again.

When travelling I have always liked to meet with a motley assemblage of people for the sake of its variety, a liking that may be due chiefly to my profession.   In the theatre we have an audience in boxes, pit, and gallery, and though at home and in society the boxes are certainly preferable, yet when abroad and rambling about a proportion of pit and gallery are no less desirable.   Society, if but of one kind, allowing it to be the most elegant and amiable, would have soon become tiresome to me if I could never have contrasted it with what was of a lower but more diversified character.   Even had the inferior grades no attractive features in themselves, still an observation of them would always serve to set off the superior, as the lights of a picture are thrown out by its shadows; but I am inclined to think there is no man of a cheerful and true English temperament, like myself, who does not occasionally, after the comedy of genteel life, covet to laugh a little at the broad farce of lower human nature.

At Whitehall, as is generally the case, we found a very odd assemblage of "folks" waiting the arrival of the steamboat to proceed to Canada and elsewhere.   Farmers going to purchase on the lake, tradesmen to try settling in some new town, merchants with speculating purposes, and people of fortune bent merely on pleasure; and all these, owing to the enviable system of things in this part of the world, mingling together with little or no distinction. The *table d'hôte* was furnished excellently, owing to the great abundance of fowl and fish in the neighborhood, and a "vast concourse of people" sat down to it, most of the company showing, in their attentions to the viands and their non-attention to anything else, what it was that they regarded as the only legitimate purpose in coming to table, and giving such an answer to the call of nature as I had previously had no conception of. The landlord and landlady took their places at the two ends of a board large enough to have dined a regiment of infantry, in order to assist such of the guests as happened to be within a certain distance of them, but those unfortunately situated beyond these limits were left to their own resources. The poets, when about to describe a battle or the storming of a town, usually give us some previous information as to the appearance of the troops, and Shakespeare, in the tent-scene of Richard, very beautifully throws the sound as it were into our ears with the description of "armorers closing rivets up" and giving "a dreadful note of preparation." Now it being the custom here, as in many parts of the States, to sit down at the table before the dinner is placed upon it, the few minutes' interim before the edible attack was to begin was passed at first in silence and expectation. I looked down the long rows, and, as far as I could perceive, every individual had a sharp, lanky, resolute expression of countenance, indicative, at least just then, of a "tendency to consumption." Then suddenly arose the glitter and the clash of steel, every man seizing his knife and fork as determinedly as he might a sword and spear, and, thus armed, giving "a note of preparation" by sharpening the former, then drawing it over the ball of the thumb to ascertain its precise edge, then holding it up in a variety of positions as if practising some particular mode of assault, and finally exclaiming with satisfaction, "it's plaguy good stuff!" But a noise is heard in the passage, and every eye turns to the door. It opens, and in marches the fat landlady, with a score of blacks after her, bearing the consumables. No sooner were they on the table than the onslaught commenced in all quarters, and a more terrific

thing of the sort I never witnessed. Such hacking and
hewing, cutting and thrusting, breaking, joint-dividing,
winging and legging of geese and turkeys, such slicing
and sawing of beef and mutton, such harpooning of fish
and spiking of vegetables, could hardly be imagined, much
less described. And this amid a general evacuation and
upset of salt-cellars and cruet-stands, the splashing of
oceans of gravy, and streaming of rivers of melted butter.
To the munching and crunching, the clatter of plates and
clash of table weapons, succeeded sucking of thumbs and
smacking of lips, and then each, taking a potent draught
of exhilarating cider, fell to again as resolutely as Macbeth,
and with as little disposition apparently to cry, "Hold—
enough!" Though intending to be a participator, I was
near becoming a mere spectator of this novel scene, for
the noise and confusion at first almost overcame me.
Luckily I regained my presence of mind time enough to
take part in the fray. Attacking a pullet which lay as yet
untouched before me, I was just carefully dividing the
breast bone from the back, after having helped Mrs. Bernard, when a north-country farmer stuck his fork into its
neck and made a violent effort to draw all that was left of
the bird over to himself; but thus compelled to do battle
for my dinner, I aimed a precise blow with my knife, severed the fowl cleverly just below his thrust, and conveyed
it *en masse* on to my plate, leaving my discomfited adversary to take the rest home to his if he chose. In about
two hours the appetites of the company seemed to be
tolerably satisfied, and the ladies left the table, while the
men called for liquor and made themselves comfortable.

Throughout the evenings the public room was filled with
guests, and a great deal of political, agricultural, and commercial, besides barometrical and thermometrical conversation was carried on, usually either too profound to be
understood or too shallow to be worth attending to. One

evening, however, a spirited dispute took place between two rough-looking men of opposite opinions in politics, which, from the ignorant vehemence of both, became very amusing. One of them was very severe upon all aristocratical institutions, ridiculing, in particular, the titles of distinction which prevail throughout Europe. "Aha!" he exclaimed, "in them 'ere places I reckon they'll call a chap 'highness' who a'n't not above five feet in his shoes; and then again another mister 'excellency' who keeps a gal, perhaps, and never goes to meetin'."

At length the packet arrived, and, embarking for the first time in our lives in a steamboat, I certainly thought it the most delightful kind of conveyance I had ever tried, although I was exceedingly annoyed by an old lady on board, who was continually at my elbow, inquiring if I thought "all was safe," or knew "how hot they kept the furnace." After enumerating with painful minuteness how many cases had occurred during the past year of boilers bursting, and how many lives were lost on each occasion, she always concluded with an assurance that were the engine to give way in the present instance we must all infallibly perish, our only choice being whether we would die by hot water on deck or cold water below.

Arrived at St. John's, we took places for La Prairie on the St. Lawrence in a vehicle which, though bearing the honorable designation of a coach, was really an unnatural cross between a *diligence* and a wagon. The rugged Galli-Canadian who drove it was also a singular combination of the savage and the Frenchman, the former, however, so predominating that nothing was discernible of the latter but the dialect. The road had been noted ever since its formation for a series of ditches and gullies which it required some courage as well as experience to ford, as may be judged by a legend concerning it related to us by a fellow-passenger. He told us how a wedding - party, contained in two calashes, were proceeding by it to the parish church, to have the marriage ceremony performed, when the foremost vehicle, driving into one of these gullies, was completely embedded, forming, however, a secure path for that which followed, bearing the bride, who was thus carried quite unconsciously over the burial-place of her hapless lover. I was able, however, to cap this romance of the mud with a still better anecdote of the same kind which I had heard related of a Kentucky traveller, whose head a farmer descried approaching at a very swift pace just above the surface of a swamp. "Hallo, squire!" cried the rustic, "what hast done with your legs?" "Got 'em under me, friend," replied the traveller. "And how's the walking, may I ask?" "I ain't walking; I'm riding." "What, got a horse?" "Yes, sartinly." "And how's travelling, then?" "Oh, capital, capital, I assure you; excellent footing for him *now*, but about ten miles back we travelled a good piece without footing at all!"

On coming to one of these sloughs of a size which seemed quite capable of accommodating us *en masse*, as our driver was urging his cattle towards it, two or three of the passengers began to murmur, and the females absolutely to scream, at what they considered his temerity. The Canadian, obliged by this clamor to pull up, rose and looked into the coach in some anger. "Why, Diable!" he exclaimed, "what is de matter? why was you 'fraid, eh! of dat littel pool! I've been in dat littel pool von hundred times, and I vas no scare. You tink dere is daansher? *eh bien*, dere vas no daansher even if de coash overturn, or de vater rone into de coash. Vas not dem littel hos to pool you out? Vhy vas I have de hos but to pool you out, when I drive you into de deesh? *En verité*, I tell you, so long I can see de tail of de littel hos I never tink dere is no daansher at all!" This information, however, so far from having the intended effect of quieting the passengers' fears, only augmented them, and every one was loud in protesting that it was shameful that a man who was so careless of his own life should have anything to do with the guardianship of other people's. The ditch, however, had to be passed, and as it stretched nearly the whole width of the road, no little confusion ensued, the water running into the coach, the horses kicking and plunging, the gentlemen grumbling, the ladies shrieking, and the Canadian alternately muttering at his unreasonable passengers, calling on the saints, and belaboring his cattle. Many an exclamation of thankfulness was vented when at last we were driven into La Prairie, where we put up at a French inn with a landlord who wore a queue nearly as long as himself, and "booed and booed" as much as any Parisian. Crossing the St. Lawrence the next day, we saw Montreal in the distance, its spires and house-tops, all sheeted with tin, sparkling in the sunlight like a blaze of fire, and innumerable bateaux gliding in all directions between the verdant, romantic banks of the river, the songs of their navigators swelling in faint response to the lusty staves of our own four Herculean boatmen, in their white cotton night-caps, open shirt-collars, and canvas trousers tucked up to the thigh. It was no slight testimony to the picturesque beauty of the scene that I admitted it to be a full recompense for even all the joltings of Vermont and the mud-gulfs of La Prairie.

I found a company playing at Montreal on a sharing scheme, but as deficient in talent as in numbers. Johnson, their acting manager, I had myself brought on the stage and laid under some obligations; Mills * and

---

* Mr. MILLS came to America in 1805, and made his first appearance in Baltimore as " Bob Tyke," October 4. He first appeared in Philadelphia December 3, in the same part. He was a good comedian, well known in Boston, Philadelphia, and New York. His wife was a fair walking lady, with an excellent voice.

Usher,* the only actors of merit, were both from my own company and had left Boston, the former a month, the latter a year ago, and with the same object, that of anticipating me in securing the Canadian circuit, having learned from my own lips that I intended to apply for it on the expiration of the lease of the Boston Theatre. Usher had so far succeeded as to obtain the Quebec house, in the name of his wife, for five years, but Mills had done nothing here, as the public were crying out for a new theatre, and he had neither the money to erect one nor friends to do so for him. Having many letters to the first families in the town, I at once delivered them, and, returning home highly gratified with the reception I had met with, I addressed a note to the theatre, expressing my wish to perform for a few nights, but received no answer. In consequence of this neglect, at which, however, I was not surprised after the attempt that had been made to forestall me, I gave out my bills for an evening's entertainment, and, the news of my arrival soon spreading, was waited on a few hours later by several gentlemen of the town to know why I did not perform. I referred them to the management, to whom, therefore, a note was immediately forwarded, acquainting them that there would be no attendance at the theatre unless I was engaged. A low fellow, a scene painter, was accordingly sent to me to treat for terms, who actually offered me the whole concern for £300; but, not inclined to talk of this, I told him ˙I would engage with them on my usual terms, viz., to perform six nights for a clear benefit, which was agreed to. As, from their slight pretensions to support, the company

---

* LUKE USHER first appeared upon the stage in Washington, D. C., in the year 1800. In 1814 he made his first appearance in New York, playing "Richard III." at the Anthony Street Theatre. He was for many years a successful and popular manager in the West, opening, in 1808, at Lexington, the first theatre in the state of Kentucky.

had hitherto met with but little success, they resolved to take benefits during my six nights, as their only remaining chance of indemnification. The houses proved all good, and my own an overflow, an assurance to me what Montreal could do for a manager when any proper inducement was offered to it.

During my stay Mr. Sewell, the counsellor, called for me one morning to take me in his carriage to an Indian settlement, a few miles from Montreal, called Cognawagha, of which place he was lord of the manor. As it offered one of the most curious scenes I had witnessed during my wanderings in America, perhaps I may be allowed to devote a few words to it. The settlement is inhabited by a large body of Christian Indians under the control, both civilly and spiritually, of a Roman Catholic priest. They have a church, handsomely furnished and endowed by her late majesty Queen Charlotte; a justice hall in the parsonage house, a public seminary, and one tavern. The habitations of the people, each with its cultivated plot of ground behind, have a uniform appearance of great comfort, though also of great simplicity. They themselves resembled the Canadians in their dress, and, like many of them, spoke a mixture of broken French and English. It was no less pleasing than curious thus to see the savage, under the influence of order and instruction, rising up towards the level of the white, and improving equally in externals and in intellect. One circumstance particularly struck me. In the course of our walk round the town our guide pointed out to us a field in which all the horses belonging to the settlement were running loose, and told us it was the practice whenever a man wanted one for him to take the first that came to hand, whether it was his own or not, to make use of it, and then return it at his convenience to this general repository. This may be a very good practice, thought I, in Cognawagha, but I doubt how it would be found to work in any other part of the world.

Mr. Mills had declined my services on the night of his benefit, but, being much in debt, had not found its profits to relieve him, and therefore made interest with some friends in the town to get a second. They told him it would be of little use unless I stayed to play for him, which was not more a compliment to my talents than a proof of the wretched condition of the company. Much against his inclination, therefore, he was obliged to come to me with a stooping neck to ask the favor. Though I felt that I might justly have retaliated, I chose rather to appeal to the man's better feelings, so agreed to play for him, with the result that he cleared more money than had been in the house altogether on the previous evening.

We set sail for Quebec in a Newcastle brig on her way back to England, and with a favorable breeze made sixty miles by midnight, when unluckily the vessel grounded, and, notwithstanding every exertion, it was found impossible to get her off without relieving her of some portion of the cargo. As this would occasion both delay and inconvenience I proposed going on shore and proceeding to Quebec as best I could, leaving our luggage to be brought by the vessel. Accordingly my wife and I, with our infant, our servant, and a solitary portmanteau, were landed in the boat (the captain accompanying us), at a little farm-house on the river bank. Here we found but one inhabitant at home, a snuffy, superannuated Frenchwoman, who could do nothing but sing out some shrill sentences and then shrug up her shoulders. As we could not make her understand a syllable of English, I was in some perplexity how we should procure any conveyance, when the captain hit on an ingenious plan to make known to her our wishes. Leading her to a kind of wheelbarrow standing near, he sat her down on it, then, catching up the handles suddenly, ran her about the house at full speed; then, pointing to my family, cried "*Cum sa?*" Extraordinary as this method of explanation may seem, the old lady appeared to comprehend it, for, giving a slight chuckle, she nodded her head and beckoned me to follow her up to the roof of the cottage. Here, pointing to some smoke wreathing upward from a chimney at some distance, just perceptible amid a clump of trees, she exclaimed, "*Voilà!*" Much in doubt whether I understood the old woman or she understood me, I descended to the parlor, and was telling what had passed, when a laboring man coming in, she bade him put my portmanteau on his shoulder and gave him some directions, to which he replied by sundry words and gesticulations to us equally unintelligible. The captain, however, was satisfied that they knew very well what we wanted, so, shaking my hand, he jumped into his boat and pushed off. The rustic, shouldering our portmanteau, walked away, and we accordingly followed him towards the house of which I had caught a glimpse, and which was a mile and a half distant. Our guide took his way through wood and meadow without saying a word, merely resting for a minute or turning round when he had a stile or a brook to cross, and I certainly indulged some strange conjectures as to how our adventure might end, when, much to our satisfaction, we emerged into a road and terminated our walk at a kind of post-house. Here a little Frenchman, a perfect image of Bagatelle in the farce, promised us a conveyance that afternoon; so, dismissing our guide with a piece of silver, we begged the post-master to ask him to convey, in as polite language as he was master of, our thanks to the old cottager.

From a pane of glass in this post-master's parlor I transcribed some lines which seemed to me to convey a happy idea:

"Life's like a journey, and it seems to me
Fortune's our vehicle, our luggage Care,
Hope our conductor—but Necessity
That which *draws* most men everywhere."

The Frenchman kept his word, and by dusk we reached Three Rivers, where, calling on the commandant, General Sheaf, to whom I had been introduced at Boston, I found he was intending next day to send off a bateau to Quebec, on which he very obligingly offered us a passage. From the scarcity of inns and all but impracticability of the roads, this was far preferable to making the journey by land, and I gratefully accepted the offer. In the evening I joined a musical party at the general's; he and his lady played delightfully on the flute and piano, some officers sang very well, and some members of the band were excellent musicians, so that the time passed very agreeably. If music is a less rational entertainment than some others, it has certainly the advantage of being held in almost universal estimation; for, wander wherever I would, in England, Ireland, or America, I have found everywhere a taste for music, even in the most humble village, while great differences of opinion existed upon all other kinds of amusement.

Among the residents in this little town, who were principally French, I encountered a Mr. Burroughs, who had once known something of me in the States—a very ingenious man, who had forged to a greater or less amount on every bank in the Union, and, being imprisoned in consequence in several state prisons, had invariably effected his escape. These circumstances conjointly had procured him a reputation in the general opinion of the Americans little inferior to that of a certain sable practitioner who is supposed to confine his personal operations to regions below. Indeed, some people went so far as to believe that this infernal personage had actually established an agency on earth, and that Mr. Burroughs acted for him upon a liberal commission. But whatever profits might thus have accrued to him, they had evidently been evanescent, for he was now living here in poor circumstances and maintaining himself by *keeping a school!* How far he was qualified for such an employment might be open to question, for though his proficiency in penmanship and figures was undoubted, he would have been quite likely, from sheer force of habit, to teach his pupils to sign any other name rather than their own. But perhaps this was only another branch of the aforesaid agency.

The next morning, accompanied by a Dr. Davidson, of Three Rivers, my family and I embarked in the bateau, which was manned by twenty soldiers under the command of an officer. Having put on board the best store of liquor and cold provisions the little town could supply, we ran in to shore about midday to discuss them under some shady elms, and the day's sail proved altogether very pleasant, except when occasionally we came in contact with the rapids, when the soldiers did not prove themselves quite so expert as the Canadian boatmen. In the evening we landed again at a spot recommended by Dr. Davidson, who had some knowledge of the owner of a large solitary house which stood in view a little way from the bank, and where he expected we could obtain accommodation for the night. He accordingly went there at once and soon returned with the information that his friend, a French gentleman, was from home, but that madame, his wife, had expressed great willingness to receive us. This news was warmly welcomed by us all, but particularly by the soldiers, who, it struck me, took the invitation in a more liberal sense than was intended. Leaving one man only in charge of the bateau, who was to be relieved in a couple of hours, we all proceeded over a field to the house in question—rather a formidable body to take up a night's lodging anywhere. The mansion, as we approached it, appeared to be very large, ancient, and dilapidated, displaying windows without panes, shutters hanging on one hinge, and gates all lopsided, while the garden around bore an equal appearance of decay and neglect, its fences broken down, and a profuse variety of ill-weeds keeping the proverb in countenance by " shooting apace " in it. Our summons at the door was answered by madame herself, a tall, gaunt, strait-laced figure with a face so wrinkled and frightful as to be almost as petrifying to the beholder as the fabled Medusa's. She was dressed in the French fashion of the old *régime*—a ceiling-sweeping cap, square-toed shoes, pink-striped gown, and a feminine corselet, designated " stays," which I think our officer must have envied, for to all appearance they would have been impenetrable to any bayonet thrust. Moreover, her petticoats were of sufficient brevity to display a pair of ankles that must have frightened gallantry out of even a Peregrine Pickle, and which were supported by appropriately colossal appendages. She had merely one female domestic with her in the house, a fat, squab, ugly little thing, but she was herself altogether so formidable a being that she need have had no delicate scruples as to admitting even a whole regiment of men beneath her roof. Catching a glimpse of her countenance as I entered, I felt sure, from its expression of mingled surprise and displeasure, that my apprehension had been correct, and that the invitation was by no means intended to embrace so numerous a company. The old lady somehow brought to mind the Thane of Fife, as she stood muttering, and gazing on forms more substantial than he saw, and yet more unwelcome — " a fourth—a fifth—a sixth !"—as we streamed, one after another, into the hall, while she held the lock of the door in an irresolute grasp, as though half inclined to close it violently and sweep some half dozen of the soldiers into the yard. They had apparently an instinctive apprehension of her purpose, and trod after each other in quick time and close order, till the whole nineteen were in, and the hall pretty well filled. Then, shutting the door with a slam, the storm burst, and she gave forth a long roll of vituperative thunder, which I believe none of us understood; or, if any did, at least they took no notice of it. I must, however, speak well of her treatment, though it was due to no generous motive. The servant showed my wife up into a comfortable bedroom, where refreshment and a cheerful fire had been provided. The officer, Dr. Davidson, and myself were ushered by madame into a spacious oaken parlor, and likewise taken care of, while the soldiers, finding their way in a body down into the kitchen, investigated the cupboards, threw logs of pine wood upon the iron dogs, and made themselves at home without any solicitation. I learned from the doctor that this family were supposed to be rich though penurious people, who had formerly been in business, but now lived in miserly seclusion, holding little or no communication with the world. Everything about the house, and the old lady herself, bore marks of attestation that this was the case, and as I have always looked on avarice and inhospitality as two most detestable vices, I did not so much regret the punishment of our visit, nor that our hostess had been betrayed into an act of generosity which she had not contemplated. As it was our intention to resume our voyage at four in the morning, Mrs. Bernard retired to rest early, but we three gentlemen, inspirited by our brandy-and-water, a cheerful fire, and that most convivial of all times—midnight, kept up and awake, indulging in songs and stories and humorous recollections; while the soldiers, imitating our example, began to carouse more deeply below, and raise up a bacchanal strain that made the wide, empty rooms and hollow wainscotings of the house ring again. The old lady's patience here deserted her, and, finding that neither did we mean to go to bed, nor the soldiers to return to the bateau, she flew into a terrific passion. For a solitary and decayed house like this, in which the stillness of desolation seemed to have reigned undisturbed for years, to be converted of a sudden into a scene of mirth and revelry was singular enough; still more singular to us seemed the hollow echoings of our laughter through the gloom; but more singular than all, though at the same time sufficiently laughable, was the conduct of our hostess, who kept running up and down stairs, from parlor to kitchen, like some discontented spirit haunting the mansion and scared from its repose by our merriment. But though, for a couple of hours at least, she kept alternately commanding those below, and haughtily requesting those above to comply with her wishes, she could neither frighten the soldiery from their pleasures nor entice us from ours until, punctually at four o'clock, our sentinel from the bateau came to summon us on board. When the men were called up we found not above five out of twenty able to maintain a military uprightness on their legs, which five were consequently obliged to carry all the rest to the boat. Calling up Mrs. Bernard and our servant, I then tendered my thanks to madame for our entertainment, when I was given to understand that the best proof we could afford of our sense of gratitude was to make our exit as expeditiously as possible. On regaining the bateau the morning air had some sobering effect upon the soldiers, but we did not get into Quebec quite so early as we had expected, though none of us were disposed to quarrel with the men as to the cause of the delay.

Colonel Pye, the head of the Amateur Association in Quebec, on hearing of my arrival, politely called on me to take me to his house; another amateur did me the favor of presenting my bill for lectures to the governor, Sir James

Craig; and I also received many kindnesses from Judge Sewell, whom I had slightly known nearly twenty-eight years before at Bristol, where he was studying the law, and on one occasion, I remember, played "The Gamester" for a charity night. My entertainment was greatly attended, and the company, perceiving this, thought it advisable to offer terms, when I agreed to perform six nights for a clear benefit, my characters to be Vapid, Sheva, Gregory Gubbins, Sir Robert Bramble, Ollapod, and Dashwood; with Lord Ogleby and "The Liar" for my own night. These all proving attractive, both public and company were well satisfied. In a paltry little room of a very paltry public-house, that neither in shape nor capacity merited the name of theatre, my benefit receipted £95, besides ten guineas which Governor Craig sent me for his ticket. My first visit to Canada being thus encouraging, I now explained to some friends my motives in coming. It being evident that if a scheme were to be carried out with any advantage a new theatre was indispensable, Colonel Pye offered me a piece of ground behind his own house to build on, provided I would admit Mrs. Usher, the present manageress, to partnership; but as this lady had no other claim to such a privilege than her simple merits as an actress, I declined the proposal. As Judge Sewell recommended my waiting on Governor Craig to solicit the honor of his patronage and choice of situation, I did so, when he very politely assured me he would not only give his name, but liberally subscribe to the erection. Mrs. Usher, however, took Mills in as a partner for the remainder of her lease, and it was the opinion of my friends that for the present a new theatre would sink under the influence of the amateurs, who supported Mrs. Usher *in toto*. As these gentlemen evidently performed more for their own amusement than the public's, and as under the present system they played most of the characters themselves, I saw how I should be opposed in bringing a company which would only diminish their pleasure. At Montreal the case was different; there were no amateurs, and the public were decidedly fond of theatricals, while, furthermore, the important families in that city had even been the first to speak with me upon the subject of a new theatre, towards which they proposed a handsome subscription. After this view of affairs I quitted Canada, having received a letter from Powell announcing Dickinson's return from England with some fresh engagements, and that the season would commence directly. I therefore returned to Boston with as little delay as possible.

The season of 1810–11, the fifth and last of my Boston management, opened with some prospect of success, but terminated, as before, disappointingly, while Charleston, Philadelphia, and Baltimore were about as prosperous as ourselves, though New York was doing much better, owing to Cooke's* arrival with Cooper from England. Among our new importations Dickinson had brought us a Miss Poole, an actress of very versatile talent; Mr. Drake,† Mrs. Doidge, and others of more or less ability, but not calling for particular notice. Dwyer,‡ the comedian, also

---

* GEORGE FREDERICK COOKE was the first great actor who came to America, the legitimate successor of Garrick, the rival of Kemble, and the precursor of Kean. A man of great possibilities but very uneven performance. After a brilliant and erratic career in England, he made his first appearance in the United States November 21, 1810. He died in New York, September 20, 1812, from the effects of intemperance, and at last found rest in the yard of St. Paul's Church there. He was born in Westminster in 1756.

† SAMUEL DRAKE was born in London in 1772. He appeared with his wife at the Federal Street Theatre, Boston, in the season of 1810–11. He subsequently became a manager in the West; one of the earliest actors to penetrate that then little known region. He was the progenitor of a number of actors and actresses, the most famous perhaps being his granddaughter, Julia Dean.

‡ Mr. DWYER was an Irishman, who made his first appearance in Dublin

paid us a visit for a few nights, and was tolerably successful. He had lately come out to America, rather too late
in the day to answer his purpose, having, he told me, been
driven by the embarrassment of his private affairs from his
metropolitan engagements. In my opinion this was a
great pity, as he was the only "genteel comedian," in my
knowledge, who could have supplied the place of Lewis at
all to the satisfaction of a London public.

We had some novelties this season of native production, Mr. White, whom I mentioned before, giving us a
comedy entitled "The Poor Lodger," taken from Miss
Burney's novel "Evelina," to which Paine wrote an epi-
logue, characterized by a wit and elegance rarely to be
met with in these dramatic appendages. The comedy itself was written with some spirit and humor, but failed in
its general effect. Mrs. Rowson,* who had formerly been
an actress, but was now superintending a seminary, favored
us with another—"Hearts of Oak"—a piece inferior to the
other, but which nevertheless displayed merits worthy of
more praise than it received. The fame of the authoress
rests chiefly on her novel "Charlotte Temple," which has
justly met with very general admiration.

We had fresh accessions to the company in the persons
of Mr. and Mrs. Duff.† The lady, who was the sister of

---

at the age of seventeen. In 1802, at Drury Lane, he made a hit as Belcour in the "West Indian." He came to America in 1810, and made his
début at the Park Theatre, New York, in the same part. He was very
handsome, and in light, dashing comedy was considered almost without a
rival in his day. He was rash and improvident, and died neglected and
forgotten about 1840.

* Wm. Rowson was leader of a regimental band in England. He and
his wife came to America with Wignell, in 1793. He was eclipsed by Mrs.
Rowson, the author of "Charlotte Temple, a Tale of Truth," of a comedy
called "Americans in England," and other works, and an actress of average ability.

† Mr. and Mrs. Duff. John R. Duff and his wife made their American

Mrs. Thomas Moore, was possessed of great personal attractions, and in Romeo and Juliet—which she and her husband played together—I thought them the handsomest couple I had ever seen on the stage. They were young at this time, and improved very much in their acting afterwards. A Mr. Entwistle,* a low comedian, likewise joined us, and displayed much originality in eccentric characters. But we had also some secessions from the company, a party of whom, of no great ability, under the management of Mrs. Shaw and another, engaged the cabin of a brig and went off to Demerara. At parting the manageress said to me, in a very decided tone, "I am resolved, Mr. Bernard, upon getting either a *coach* or a *coffin.*" But mortals may not choose their fate. After playing at one island they proceeded to St. Thomas's. On the passage she died and was lowered overboard. Thus she obtained neither.

Most fortunately we succeeded in engaging Cooke for nine nights, and this great tragedian made his *début* in Boston on the 3d of January, 1811, to an overflowing house, in the character of Richard the Third. Upon the merits of one "whose like we shall not look upon again," I may be permitted to make a few observations, and especially to put him in comparison with his great predecessor,

---

début in Boston in the winter of 1810. Mr. Duff was a native of Ireland (1787), and an excellent actor in the leading tragedy rôles. He died in 1831. Mrs. Duff (Mary Dyke) was the chief actress in America for many years. The founder of *The New York Tribune*, late in life, pronounced her the finest actress he had ever seen. She played throughout the United States with great success, and died, after years of retirement, in 1857, in the sixty-third year of her age. Her "Life," by Mr. Joseph N. Ireland, appeared in *The American Actor Series*, published in 1882.

* Mr. ENTWISTLE was a great favorite in Boston for a number of years. He appeared in New York in 1814, went afterwards to Philadelphia, where he became one of the husbands of the celebrated Mrs. Mason (Mrs. Crooke). His habits were bad, and he died in New Orleans by his own hand.

Macklin. Cooke's best performance, in my opinion, was his Sir Pertinax Mac Sycophant, which in all respects I consider was one of the greatest masterpieces the British stage has produced. Next came his Richard, then Iago and Stukeley, then Shylock and Sir Giles Overreach; his Zanga and Pierre were but inferior performances. In estimating his powers I would premise that in the *dramatis personæ* of tragedy two contrasting characters generally occupy the foreground—the hero and the villain—characters requiring distinct qualifications in the performer, both as regards person and genius. We may take, as instances of the hero, Othello, Alexander, and Brutus; of the villain, Richard, Shylock, and Iago. For the performance of the first it is immediately obvious that a tragedian should have such personal requisites as a commanding figure, a fine-toned voice, and a dignified action, not less from the poetical sublimity of the characters than their general declamatory cast, so often calling all the qualities of the orator into play. For the second, I do not know that in person anything can be insisted upon beyond a strongly marked and flexible set of features; for the peculiarity of this character lies greatly in soliloquy, through the medium of which the villain conveys to the audience, in a series of opinions, reasonings, and resolutions, his own character and his connection with the fable. To perform either well, it is necessary for the tragedian to have a peculiar genius, such as has been instanced, reckoning from the Revolution downwards, in Betterton, Booth, Barry, and John Kemble as heroes, and in Macklin, Mossop, and George Frederick Cooke as villains. These were all tragedians possessing peculiar and opposite kinds of histrionic genius. I omit Quin, who is said to have played both casts of character, and the three English actors, Garrick, Henderson, and Hodgkinson, whom, from personal observation, I know to have done so. Their genius, being twofold, gives them an honorable exclusion from a list of specialties. The villains of the drama may again be divided into two classes: the majestic or heroic, such as the tyrants Barbarossa, Dionysius, Zanga or Pierre, and the specious and designing, such as Richard, Iago, and Stukeley. In the majestic villain our stage has produced a solitary example of a surpassing tragedian, viz., Mossop, whose pre-eminence I must believe, if I can at all rely on those who saw and told me of him, or on the envy of him felt by Garrick, which, of the two, I take to be the stronger evidence. From a similarity of personal requisites rather than from an adaptation to their capacity, actors of heroic tragedy have often assumed these characters. In the insinuating villain we have had but two distinguished tragedians, Macklin and Cooke, whom I will now compare. Of the two Cooke had the larger range of character, though not the superior tragedian; for though Macklin was great, and in some parts of his acting even sublimely powerful (as, for example, in Shylock and Bajazet) his peculiar characteristic—which was power or force, or rather I might almost say *ferocity*—unfitted him for the representation of villains in general, where the opposite quality of a specious softness is wanted. Neither could Macklin assume the majestic villain, for he had neither elevation nor dignity, and I know not, therefore, but that he should be classed alone for a description of acting as original as it was excellent, and thus occupy with Mossop and Cooke a distinct stand in the estimation of posterity according to this classification—which will sufficiently mark the difference in their style—Mossop for his *majesty*, Macklin for his *force* and passion, Cooke for his *speciousness*.

In my boyhood, nearly forty years previous to this period, I had seen Cooke act at Chichester when his powers were, perhaps, as far from maturity as was my judgment. When we were now thrown together at Boston, it might have been supposed that in proportion as I had become more capable of judging he had become less capable of performing, since Cooke, at this time, must have been sixty-five years of age, a period of life when, in the common course of things, the mental as well as physical powers of a man are supposed to have become somewhat enfeebled. When, besides this, we consider the effect which a long addiction to the bottle must have had upon him in every respect, no one can believe that his acting in America could possibly have equalled what it had been in England. On the other hand I had by this time seen Garrick, Henderson, Macklin, Reddish, Smith, Bensley, Palmer, and Kemble in one or the other of Cooke's characters, and consequently not only had a high standard whereby to test him, but was in some degree prejudiced against the possibility of his competing successfully with such rivals. After this, when I say that however, in particular scenes and passages, some of the above performers had exceeded him, or however his own ability was inadequate to fill up with consistent force throughout the brilliant design he had formed, yet that as regards the general conception of his characters he certainly surpassed anything I had ever witnessed, it really amounts to ranking him, in his own peculiar specialty, above the level of even the greatest I have named. And when, perceiving what his conception was, I considered what his ability might have been, when unimpaired by age or bad habits, I could not but come to the conclusion that he must have been one of the most original and highly endowed tragedians the world has ever produced.

The great characteristic of "The Man of the World" being that quality in the representation of which Cooke particularly excelled, viz., speciousness, affords the reason why he so much surpassed Macklin in its performance,

the latter confusing the light and shade of the character
by an invariable roughness, and often attempting to produce effect by a grimacing and bullying altogether inappropriate. But Cooke also excelled Macklin in his dialect,
having caught it while strolling through Scotland, while
Macklin only obtained his (as he himself informed me)
from his Scotch schoolmaster in Dublin.   While still under the sway of his ferule the young "McLaughlin" used
to entertain the other boys by imitating the tone and
manner of this worthy pedagogue, whenever he made a
short exit from the schoolroom.   A little story is connected with this fact.   The master, who was a strict dis-
ciplinarian, had a favorite expression whenever the boys
pressed upon him too urgently with their lessons or copies,
being accustomed to restrain their impatience with, "Bide
a beet, bide a beet; I'm nae prepared," a phrase which
he drawled out in a tone peculiar to himself.   One day,
having quitted the school to seek something in his bedroom, just overhead, Macklin stole to his seat, threw the
morning-gown he had left there over his own shoulders,
put on his spectacles, and, opening a book, began to mimic
his manner of hearing a lesson.   This exhibition all the
scholars enjoyed heartily, and Macklin, imagining he
should be sure to hear the master leave his room up-stairs,
went on in perfect security.   The cunning *magister*, however, was too sapient for him, for, suspecting something
of the sort, he quitted his apartment softly, and stole
down-stairs where, the schoolroom door being ajar, he
could, undiscovered, watch Macklin in the height of his
performance and hear all the pupils manifesting their
admiration of it.   Unluckily, he was provided with a pair
of very long legs, and all at once, making two rapid strides
into the room and up to his desk, he seized the budding
actor by the shoulder with the grip of a vise, and, grasping a ruler in his other hand, brandished it aloft, exclaim-

ing, " Ye daumned scoondrel, shall I brak ev'ry boone in
your boody ?" Without shrinking in the least, or changing his position, Macklin coolly looked up into his face
and replied, " Bide a beet, mon, bide a beet, I'm nae prepared." His extreme composure enhanced the humor of
the mimicry so completely as to overpower the dominie's
wrath. With a shake of the head and an ill-suppressed
smile his arm dropped powerless by his side, and Macklin
was suffered to disrobe himself and go back to his seat
with no further punishment for his impertinence than a
kick from behind as he retreated.

But to return to Cooke: at our first interview his manner was perfectly unconstrained ; " Mr. John Bernard,"
he exclaimed, " or Honest Jack Bernard, as they call you
on the other side of the water, how do you do? I've
known you these thirty years, though we have never met
before. You've heard of George Cooke, too, I dare say.
I wonder who didn't know me. Black Jack [Kemble]
used to say that I was as well known wherever I went as
the town crier or the parish beadle." Put thus at once
upon familiar terms, I took him home with me to dinner,
and, during his stay, catered for his amusement as much
as lay in my power.

That he did not always show himself so genial, we soon
had a proof. He had put up at the Exchange Coffee-
house, in Boston, and here a Mr. Rennie, a Scotch ventriloquist, was also staying for a few days. It had happened,
many years before, that in some country town in England
where Cooke was performing, this Rennie had been thrown
into prison for debt, under very distressing circumstances.
His situation was spoken of all over the town, and particularly in the green-room. Cooke, whose benefit was just
at hand, inquired the amount of the debt, and learned
that it was £40. The benefit yielding him just the sum
required, he went without hesitation to Rennie's lodgings,

threw the whole into the lap of his weeping wife, and told her to go and get her husband liberated; then, with a bundle on his back, and only a few shillings in his pocket, he set off on foot for the company's next town, a distance of thirty miles. One act like this might indeed atone for years of imprudences! But there was a sequel to the story and a curious one. Rennie, of course, never forgot such generosity, and now they were once more thrown together, when his circumstances had undergone a great change; he resolved to express his sense of it in a manner which he thought would be no less agreeable to his bene-factor than satisfactory to his own feelings. Hearing that Cooke was to have a large party to dine with him, he learned from the waiter where the entertainment was to take place, and resolved to enter the room unceremo-niously, relate to the assembled company the whole affair, and then, in their presence, return the £40 to Cooke with his thanks for the loan of it. Unfortunately, on carrying his design into effect, the eccentricity of the actor showed itself in a manner more astonishing than had been even his benevolence. He shook his head frowningly, dis-claimed all knowledge of the circumstances, refused to touch the money, and telling the company that Rennie was an impostor, finally, in rather harsh terms, ordered him to quit the room, since he had entered it without an introduction.

The eccentricity of character which throughout life distinguished him led on many occasions to very amus-ing scenes. I remember going with him to Mr. F. C. Amory's to meet a large party. The portrait of John Kemble, in Rolla, hung over the mantelpiece, and, being pointed out to him, with the inquiry whether he thought it a good likeness—"Yes," replied he, "it is a *great* like-ness, sir, of a very great man; but, great as he was" (here he rose from his seat with an affectation of dignity, and

paused)—"great as he was" (then clinched his fist and
shook it at the picture as, with a smile, he broke into this
comical apostrophe)—"You rascal! I made you shake in
your shoes many a time!" A roar of laughter burst from
every one present as Cooke, with burlesque importance,
resumed his chair. Another evening, at Graupner's (the
musician and music-seller), a little, talkative man, who
was our musical leader at the theatre, had contrived to
squeeze into the party, and annoyed George exceedingly,
not only by the infinity of nothings to which he gave
vent, but by their being exclusively addressed to himself.
At first he was inattentive, then turned his back on the
musician, then moved from his chair; but the fiddler's
good-humor was as indefatigable as his tongue, and he
followed the actor up all round the room until he actually
penned him into a corner, whence he could not escape.
Cooke had been in the best of humors during the first
part of the evening, but his complacency was beginning
to ooze away more and more at the fiddler's pertinacious
advances. Instead, however, of expressing his dissatisfaction at once, he let it go on fermenting in his own
breast, while he meditated some mode of punishing his
persecutor. The latter, having now completely secured
his victim, seized what he thought this favorable opportunity to gain Cooke's attention by playing his last and
most effective card. "Mr. Cooke, Mr. Cooke," said he,
"do you know, Mr. Cooke, that it is a fact, which I dare
say you do not know, that your first wife, Mr. Cooke,
was my pupil?" "Your pupil!" "My pupil, indeed.
It's a fact, Mr. Cooke, upon my honor." "Oh, then,"
rejoined the wag (as he eyed the elated musician with
peculiar significance), "then, for the first time, you have
given me the reason why that poor creature was such an
infernal ninny!" This produced a loud laugh from the
company, while the musician looked as much mortified

as surprised. "And now, sir," added Cooke, in a very stern tone—"and now, sir, will you let me come out?" "Come out, Mr. Cooke?" "Yes, sir, come out. Don't you see that you have cribbed me up in this hole for the last half-hour, till I'm as flat as your own fiddle-case. The musician rose in some consternation. "Hark ye, sir," continued Cooke, with increasing severity in his tone and sternness in the expression of his eye, "I have done you a favor in listening so long to your fiddle-de-dee, and suffering a wretched strummer of catgut to converse with a tragedian of the stamp of George Frederick Cooke; now, sir, will you do me a favor in return?" "Anything in my power, Mr. Cooke," was the trembling reply. "Well, sir, you have chased me all round the room in your chair, now be kind enough to turn round and let me chase you." "Sir?" "In this way, do you see?" said the actor, and, turning round in his chair, he threw his leg across it and galloped it towards the fiddler as though he had been on horseback.

The laughter that now rang through the room was convulsive. The poor little fiddler started up in the greatest fright, ran to a side-table for his hat, and precipitately rushed from the room and down-stairs out of the house, Cooke galloping his chair after him right across the floor, and putting his head out into the passage to listen to his retreat. When he heard the street door close, he turned round with a roguish chuckle, exclaiming, "I've expelled him! Richard's himself again!" This was altogether one of the funniest scenes I ever witnessed.

INDEX.

Abercrombie, Sir Ralph, 97.

Abington, Mrs., 285–6.

Adams, John, 31, 97, 99, 123, 233, 240, 242–3.

Adams, Samuel, 31.

Albemarle, Lord, 110.

Alexander, Hon. William (Lord Sterling), 112–13.

Allen, A., 296.

Allen, Dr., 328–9.

Allen, Ethan, 114–15.

Allyn, Mr. (actor), 270.

Amory, F. C., 312, 372.

André, Major, 106.

Anne, Queen, 161.

Arnold, Benedict, 60, 95, 105–7, 236.

Arnold, Elizabeth; see Mrs. Poe.

Arnott, Mr. (manager), 176.

Ashbury, Mrs. (Eliza Placide, Mrs. Mann), 202 note.

Baltimore, Lord, 2, 138–9.

Bannister, John, 116, 268, 286.

Barrett, George H., 341 note.

Barrett, Giles L., 264–5, 336; biographical sketch, 341 note.

Barrett, Mrs. Giles L., 264.

Barry, Spranger, 268, 367.

Bartley, George, 275.

Bates, William, 121–2, 336–7.

Benezet, Anthony, 64, 66.

Bensley, William, 369.

Bentley, Richard, vi.

Berkeley, Sir William, 163–4.

Bernard, John, iii–vii.

Bernard, Mrs. John (Miss Cooper), iii, iv.

Bernard, Mrs. John (Miss Fisher), iv, 117, 168.

Bernard, Mrs. John (Miss Wright), iv,
v, 33, 276, 282–3, 302, 307, 311, 313, 327, 356, 361–2.

Bernard, Sir Francis, iii, v.

Bernard, William Bayle, vi, vii, 308 note.

Bernard, Mrs. William Bayle, vii.

Betterton, Thomas, 367.

Blake, Mrs. William Rufus (Caroline Placide, Mrs. Waring), 202 note.

Blisset, Francis, 116, 264, 268.

Boker, Miss (Mrs. Robert Treat Paine, Jr.), 300 note.

Bolingbroke, St. John, 238.

Bonaparte, Mme. Patterson, 123.

Booth, Barton, 367.

Bowles, Robert, 277–82.

Brett, Mrs., 264.

Broadhurst, Miss, 264.

Brown, Charles Brockden, 190, 350–5.

Brown, Nicholas, 225.

Bruce, James, 18.

Brunton (Mrs. Wignell, Mrs. Warren); see Mrs. Merry.

Buchan, Dr. William, 325.

Buckingham, Duke of, 74.

Buffon, George le Clerc, 224.

Burgoyne, Gen., 59, 60, 105.

Burke, Edmund, 7, 99.

Burleigh, Lord, 122.

Burney, Frances (Mme. d'Arblay), 365.

Burroughs, Mrs., 358–9.

Butler, Mrs. P. (Frances Ann Kemble), 191 note.

Byrne, Oscar, 123, 228–31.

Byrne, Mrs. Oscar, 229.

Cæsar, Julius, 89.

Canning, Mrs., 142–3.

Carlton, Sir Guy, 115.

Carroll, Charles (of Carrollton), v, 85, 86, 190.

Carter & Hendee, vi.
Cartwright, Mr. (actor), 277, 281–2.
Catherine of England, 121.
Catherine of Russia, 281.
Caton, Miss (Marchioness of Wellesley), 123.
Caulfield, Mr. (manager and actor), 282, 285; biographical sketch, 286 note, 293–6, 300, 302, 305–7, 308, 309, 332, 336.
Caulfield, Mrs. (Mrs. Skin), 296.
Cervantes, 75.
Chalmers, Mr. [–1806], 264, 268.
Charles I., 7, 30, 72, 99–100, 138.
Charles II., 2, 5, 7.
Charlotte, Queen, 355.
Chastelluz, Marquis, 96.
Cherry, Andrew, 276, 277.
Chesterfield, Lord, 20.
Cicero, 74, 75.
Cipriani, Mr. (clown), 276, 282.
Clay, Henry, 189.
Clay, Mr. (manager), 176, 181.
Clinton, Sir Henry, 99, 106–7.
Colburn, Henry, vi.
Coleman, William, 315.
Condé, Prince of, 79–80.
Cooke, George Frederick, 162, 268, 317 note; biographical sketch, 364 note; 366–74.
Cooper, Miss (Mrs. John Bernard), iii, iv.
Cooper, Priscilla (Mrs. Tyler), 164 note.
Cooper, Thomas Abthorpe, 116; biographical sketch, 164 note; 164–8, 171–2, 174, 191, 264, 267–8, 293, 313, 315, 336, 341, 364.
Cornwallis, Gen., 104, 127.
Cowper, William, 340.
Craig, Sir James, 362–3.
Crawford, Gov., 314, 329.
Cromwell, Mr. (actor), 308–10, 312.
Cromwell, Oliver, 7, 72.
Crooke, Mrs. (Miss Elizabeth, Mrs. Mason); see Mrs. Entwistle.
Cumberland, Richard, 262.

D'Alembert, John Le R., 82.
D'Arblay, Mme. (Frances Burney), 365.
D'Artois, Count, 236.
Darley, Felix O. C., 331 note.
Darley, John (Sr.), biographical sketch, 331 note, 340.
Darley, John (Jr.), 331 note.

Darley, Mrs. John, Jr. (Ellen Westray), 314, 331 note.
Darley, Matthew, 331 note.
Davidson, Dr., 359–62.
Davidson, Gen. William, 85.
Dawson, Hon. Mr., 165.
Dean, Julia, 364 note.
De Glaubeck, Baron, 96.
D'Holbach, Paul Theri, 82.
Dickinson, Mr. (Powell & Dickinson), 264, 266, 272; biographical sketch, 317 note; 318, 326, 343, 364.
Dickinson, Mrs. (Miss Harrison), 317 note.
Digges, Sir Dudley, 7.
Dillon, Count, 215.
Douglas, David, 270.
Dowton, W., 268.
Drake, Samuel, biographical sketch, 364 note.
Dryden, John, 167.
Duff, John, 317 note; biographical sketch, 365–6 note.
Duff, Mrs. John (Mary Ann Dyke), 317 note; biographical sketch, 365–6 note.
Dunlap, William, 62 note, 259.
Dunmore, Lord, 127.
Dwyer, Mr., biographical sketch, 364–5 note.

Edwin, John, 265.
Edwin, Mrs., 275.
Elizabeth, Queen, 79, 269.
Emery, John, 276.
Entwistle, Mr., biographical sketch, 366 note.
Entwistle, Mrs. (Miss Elizabeth, Mrs. Mason, Mrs. Crooke), 366 note.
Essex, Earl of, 7.

Faba, Jerome, 79.
Fabius, 93.
Fantoccini, 129.
Farquhar, George, 262.
Farren, Elizabeth (Countess of Derby), 285–6.
Fenelon, 72.
Fennell, James, 73–7; biographical sketch, 73 note; 196–7, 264, 267, 292–3, 296–8, 300, 312, 337, 341.
Fisher, Mr. (manager), 281.
Fisher, Miss (Mrs. John Bernard), iv.
Fontenelle, Miss (Mrs. J. B. Williamson), 256, 264, 265.

Foote, Samuel, 27.
Fox, Charles James, iv, v, 104.
Fox, George, 173.
Fox, Mr. (actor), 116, 121-2.
Francis I., 79.
Francis, William, 116, 122, 264, 268.
Franklin, Benjamin, 77-83, 90, 92, 99, 112, 140, 162, 234.
Frederick the Great, 109, 113, 234.

Gannett, Deborah ("Robert Shurtliff"), 244.
Garrick, David, 32 note, 256, 265, 268, 318, 364 note, 367, 368, 369.
Gates, Gen. Horatio, 59 94, 95, 105.
George III., 23, 92.
George, Miss (Mrs. Oldmixon), 116.
Gifford, William, 49 note.
Gillingham, Mr., 116, 118-22.
Gillingham, Mrs., 116, 118-22.
Gilpin, John, 340.
Girdlestone, Thomas, 99.
Glaubeck, Baron de, 215.
Godwin, William, 164 note, 250, 267.
Goldsmith, Oliver, 262, 325.
Graupner, Mr., 373.
Graupner, Mrs. (Miss Heelyer), 318.
Greene, Gen. Nathaniel, 64, 66, 95, 98, 103-5, 107, 111, 213, 215, 245.
Greene, Mr. [-1816], 315, 336.
Greene, Mrs. (Miss Willems), 264.
Grimm, Frederick Melchoir, 82.

Hackett, James H., vi.
Hallam, Isabella (Mrs. Mattocks), 116, 268.
Hallam, Lewis (eldest), 258, 259.
Hallam, Lewis [1740-1808], 264, 265-6, 269-71.
Hallam, Mrs. Lewis, Jr. (Mrs. Douglas), 264, 271.
Hancock, John, 31.
Hanger, Major, 211-15.
Harcourt, Col. William, 95, 98.
Hardinge, Mr., 264.
Hardinge, Mrs., 264.
Harper, Mr. [-1813], 264, 265.
Harper, Mrs., 264.
Harris, Mr. (manager), 74, 75, 142, 275, 312.
Harwood, John E., 116, 264, 268, 286, 314, 315.
Hatton, John, 221, 282, 311.
Hawley, Sir John, 7.

Heckewelder, Rev. John, 37.
Henderson, John, iv, 256, 268, 367.
Henry, John, 258, 259, 265.
Herbert, Mr. (actor), 135-7.
Hill, G. H. ("Yankee Hill"), vi.
Hodgkinson, John, 26; biographical sketch, 26 note; 27, 28, 29, 256, 257-8, 259, 263, 264, 265, 266, 267, 367.
Hodgkinson, Mrs. John (Mrs. Brett), 266.
Hodgson, Mr., 117.
Hogarth, William, 57.
Holcroft, Thomas, 164 note.
Holland, John Joseph, 261.
Homer, 76.
Howard, Chancellor, 85.
Howard, John, 66.
Howe, Gen., 58, 59, 60, 106, 112, 113.
Hume, David, 99.
Humphreys, Col. David, 93, 103, 286-7, 342.

Incledon, Benjamin Charles, 276, 331 note.
Ireland, Joseph N., 61, 366 note.
Irving, Washington, 315.

James I., 3, 4.
Jefferson, Joseph [1774-1832], 71, 264, 266.
Jefferson, Thomas, v, 92, 93, 123, 176-7, 187, 190, 232-43, 325.
Johnson, Dr. Samuel, 74, 181, 253.
Johnson, H., 275-6.
Johnson, Mrs. H., 275-6.
Johnson, John [1759-1819], 264, 266.
Johnson, Mrs. John [-1830], 264, 266.
Johnston, Henry, 287.
Jones, Mr. [-1806], 264, 265.
Jones, Mrs. (Miss Granger), 264, 292.
Jordan, Mrs. Dora, 256, 268, 292.

Kean, Edmund, 364 note.
Kelly, Judge, 64, 85, 329.
Kemble, Elizabeth; see Mrs. White-lock.
Kemble, Frances Ann (Mrs. P. Butler), 191 note.
Kemble, John Philip, iv, 267, 268, 277, 286, 364 note, 367, 369, 371, 372.
Kent, Duke of, 296.
Kosciusko, 96, 115.

Lafalle, Mrs.; see Mrs. Alexander Placide.
Lafayette, Marquis of, 96, 97, 107–9.
Lauzun, Duke of, 233.
Lee, Gen. Charles, 59, 94, 95, 96–103, 105, 109, 172–3.
Lestrange, Mrs., 264.
Lewis, Monk, 277.
Lewis, William, 265.
Lincoln, Gen. Benjamin, 61, 96, 115.
Linnæus, Carl, 158, 174.
Locke, John, 78.
Loring, Mrs., 60.
Louis XVI., 102.
Loutherbourg, Philippe Jacques, 69.
Lowell, James Russell, v.
Lyman, Gen. Phineas, 110.

Mackenzie, D., 264.
Macklin, Charles, 367, 368, 369, 370–1.
Macready, William, 276.
Madog, Prince, 118.
Mallet, Mons., 301, 318–19.
Mann, Mrs. Sheridan (Mrs. Ashbury); see Eliza Placide.
Marius, 76.
Marshall, G., 116, 121–2, 264.
Marshall, Mrs. G. (Miss Hardinge, Mrs. Clarke), 264, 268.
Martin, John, 264, 266.
Mason, Mrs. (Miss Elizabeth, Mrs. Crooke); see Mrs. Entwistle.
Mather, Cotton, 4.
Mattocks, Mrs. (Isabella Hallam), 116, 268.
McKnight, Capt., 117, 118–20.
Melmoth, Courtney (Samuel Jackson Pratt), 266.
Melmoth, Mrs. Courtney (Mrs. Pratt), 264, 266.
Merry, Robert, 49–50; biographical sketch, 49 note; 57, 61, 71, 72, 72 note, 124, 138, 141–5, 256.
Merry, Mrs. Robert (Miss Brunton, Mrs. Wignell, Mrs. William Warren), 32 note, 49 note; biographical sketch, 72 note; 142–3, 145, 264, 268–9, 312, 336.
Milbourne, Mr. (artist), 261.
Mills, Mr. (actor), 331–2, 336; biographical sketch, 353 note; 356, 363.
Mills, Mrs. Eliza, 332, 340, 353 note, 354.
Mirabeau, 75, 233, 235, 236.

Montgomery, Gen. Richard, 94, 95, 96, 115.
Moore, Mr. (actor), 318.
Moore, Mrs.; see Mrs. Woodham.
Moore, Mrs. Thomas (Miss Dyke), 366.
Morris, Owen, 61–2; biographical sketch, 61–2 note; 135, 219, 269–71.
Morris, Mrs. Owen, 62, 271.
Morse, Mr. [1784–   ], 337.
Morton, Mr. (actor), 264, 268.
Morton, Mrs. (Sarah Wentworth Apthorp), 296.
Mossop, Henry, 367, 368.
Mottle, Col., 200.
Murray, Lindley, 325.

Nash, Gen. Francis, 115.
Necker, Jacques, 233, 235.
Neith, Mr., 172.
North, Lord, 100.

O'Donnell, Mr., 138–40.
Oldmixon, Mrs. (Miss George), 116, 264, 268.
Oldmixon, Sir John, 69, 116.
O'Keefe, John, 256, 262.
O'Neill, Eliza, iv.
Otis, James, 31.
Oxford, Earl of, 7.

Paine, Robert Treat, 300 note.
Paine, Robert Treat, Jr., 292; biographical sketch, 300–1 note, 341, 365.
Paine, Mrs. Robert Treat, Jr. (Miss Boker), 300 note.
Paine, Thomas, 97, 301 note.
Palmer, John, 74, 369.
Patterson, Miss (Mrs. Jerome Bonaparte), 123.
Payne, John Howard, biographical sketch, 339 note, 341, 343.
Penn, William, 63, 64, 65, 66.
Perrot, Sir John, 7.
Pinkney, Hon. Mr., 329.
Pitt, William, 75.
Placide, Alexander, biographical sketch, 202 note; 264, 310.
Placide, Mrs. Alexander (Mrs. Lafalle), 264.
Placide, Caroline (Mrs. Waring, Mrs. Blake), 202 note.
Placide, Eliza (Mrs. Ashbury, Mrs. Mann), 202 note.

Placide, Henry, 202 note.
Placide, Jane, 202 note.
Placide, Thomas, 202 note.
Pocahontas, 159-62.
Poe, David, Jr., biographical sketch, 296 note.
Poe, Mrs. David, Jr. (Elizabeth Arnold), biographical sketch, 296 note.
Poe, Edgar Allen, 296 note.
Poole, Miss (actress), 364.
Pope, Alexander, 238.
Powell, Charles Stuart, 264.
Powell, Mrs. Charles Stuart, 264, 266, 272, 291, 296.
Powell, Snelling, 309; biographical sketch, 317 note; 317-19, 326, 364.
Powell, Mrs. Snelling (Elizabeth Harrison), 264, 266, 317 note, 318.
Powhatan, 162.
Pratt, Samuel Jackson (Courtney Melmoth), 266.
Pratt, Mrs. (Mrs. Courtney Melmoth), 264, 266.
Prideaux, Dr. Humphrey, 63.
Priestley, Dr. Joseph, 238.
Prigmore, Mr. (actor), 264.
Pulaski, Count, 96.
Putnam, Gen. Israel, 96, 110-15.
Pye, Col., 362, 363.

Qualch, Mr. (actor), 271.
Quick, John, 276-7.
Quincy, Josiah, 31.
Quinn, James, 27, 71, 265, 367.

Rae, Mr. (manager), 275.
Raleigh, Sir Walter, 2-3.
Ramsay, David, 181.
Raphael, 78.
Rawdon, Lord, 104, 211, 214.
Raynal, Abbé, 91.
Reddish, Samuel, 369.
Reinagle, Mr. (manager), 259.
Rennie, Mr. (ventriloquist), 371-2.
Rich, Richard, 7.
Richards, J., 261.
Robertson, Dr. William, 185.
Robertson, William (actor), 332.
Rogers, Francis, 278-81.
Rolfe, Thomas, 161.
Rousseau, J. J., 253.
Rowson, William, biographical sketch, 365 note.
Rowson, Mrs. William, 365 note.

Rush, Benjamin, 239.
Rutledge, Edward, 97.

Sandys, Sir Edwin, 7.
Savigny, Mme., 79.
Schuyler, Gen. Philip, 96.
Selden, John, 7.
Selwyn, George, iv.
Sewell, Judge, 355, 363.
Shakespeare, 27, 55, 72, 74, 77, 78, 163, 167, 238, 257, 262, 263, 265, 268.
Shaw, Mr. (actor), 298.
Shaw, Mrs., 298.
Sheaf, Gen., 296, 301, 312, 358.
Sheridan, Richard Brinsley, iv, v, 74, 262.
Siddons, Sarah, 190-1, 256, 269, 317 note.
Sieyès, Abbé, 233.
Silsbee, Joshua S., vi.
Smith, Capt. John, 159-60.
Smith, William, 369.
Smollet, Tobias, 71.
Solée, Mr. (manager), 264.
Southampton, Earl of, 7.
Stanley, Mrs. (Mrs. Twisleton), 276, 282; biographical sketch, 284 note; 284-6, 293, 294, 295, 302, 336, 338-9.
Sterling, Lord (Hon. William Alexander), 112-3.
Sterne, Lawrence, 263.
Stone, Gov. John H., 85.
Sullivan, Gen. John, 96, 112.
Sullivan, Gov. James, 338.
Swift, Dean, 238.

Talbot, Montague, 275.
Tarleton, Col., 104-5, 211-15.
Teach ("Blackbeard"), 175.
"Three-Fingered Jack," 135-7.
Tomolomo, 162.
Tompkins, Col., 124-5.
Trajan, 89.
Tubbs, Mr. (actor), 191-4.
Turnbull, Mr. (actor), 216.
Twaits, William, 312, 314.
Twisleton, Mrs.; see Mrs. Stanley.
Tyler, Pres. John, 164 note.
Tyler, Joseph, 264, 266.
Tyler, Mrs. Joseph, 264.
Tyler, Robert, 164 note.
Tyler, Mrs. Robert; see Priscilla Cooper.

Usher, Luke, 292, 336; biographical sketch, 354 note.
Usher, Mrs. Luke, 292, 363.

Vanhorn, Col., 60–1.
Vestris, Armand, 68.
Vigers, Mr. (actor), 282.
Vining, Mr. (vocalist), 282, 286.
Voltaire, 290.
Von Hagen, Mr. (musician), 301.
Von Kalb, Baron, 96.
Von Steuben, Baron, 94, 96, 109–10.

Walpole, Sir Robert, 162.
Walstein, Miss, 275.
Waring, Mrs. Leigh (Mrs. William R. Blake); see Caroline Placide.
Warrell, Mr. (actor), 264.
Warren, Dr. Joseph, 31.
Warren, William [1767–1832], vi, 72 note, 116, 144 note, 264, 268, 313, 345.
Warren, Mrs. William (Miss Brunton, Mrs. Wignell); see Mrs. Merry.
Washington, George, vi, 59, 60, 85–95, 98, 99, 105, 107, 108, 110, 120, 122, 141, 232, 236.
Washington, Mrs. George, 88.
Wayne, Gen. Anthony, 115.
Webster, Mr. (vocalist), 312, 340.
Wellesley, Marchioness of (Miss Caton), 123.
West, Mrs., 336, 339.
Westray, Ellen (Mrs. Darley), 331 note.

Westray, Juliana (Mrs. W. B. Wood), 144 note.
White, William Charles, 341, 365.
Whitelock, Mr., 264.
Whitelock, Mrs. (Elizabeth Kemble), 190–1; biographical sketch, 190–1 note; 256, 264.
Wignell, Thomas, iv, 32; biographical sketch, 32–3 note; 61, 72, 72 note, 84, 116, 144 note, 164, 258–9, 261, 264, 331 note.
Wignell, Mrs. Thomas (Miss Brunton, Mrs. Warren); see Mrs. Merry.
Williams, Matthew, 231.
Williamson, J. Brown, 256, 264.
Williamson, Mrs. J. Brown (Miss Fontenelle), 256, 264, 265.
Witherspoon, Mr., 124–5.
Wolfe, Gen. James, 234.
Wolsey, Cardinal, 121.
Wood, William B., 33 note, 62 note, 144; biographical sketch, 144 note.
Wood, Mrs. W. B. (Juliana Westray), 144 note.
Woodham, Mr., biographical sketch, 345–6 note.
Woodham, Mrs., 331, 336; biographical sketch, 345–6 note.
Wools, Stephen, 182–3.
Wright, Miss (Mrs. John Bernard), iv, v, 33, 276, 282–3, 302, 307, 313, 327, 356, 361–2.
Wroughton, Mr. (actor), 312.

THE END.